What readers, just like you, are saying about
The Ascension Papers

"With each chapter I read there is a weight lifting. I feel less nervous, less fearful. I am astounded that I actually feel my perspective expanding and opening right up. I feel my attachments to particular ideologies falling way. I just feel open and excited to continue on my journey." -- Niki

"Every word and explanation from 8 is like the truth of life 101 being told to me. The answers I have been without for 42 years. A relief and such excitement to hear them. Such a warmth in my heart and knowing. Thank you both!!" -- Jilly

"Thank you, for bringing Spirit into our hearts, when we most needed it." --Gertrud

"Wow, that was epic. So well worth the read. Resonates very highly with me. Thank you Zingdad." -- Syme

"Zingdad, I want to thank you profusely for everything you are doing here. There are not many places out there where these topics are discussed freely, and I feel like applauding J-D and 8 for putting all of it so eloquently." -- M. Powers

"This is exactly what I have been looking for and what I need right now Thank you". -- Cherrylee

"As always, your understanding resonates with and mirrors my own. Your eloquence in putting it into words, however, exquisite heart-song!" --Mathew

"I feel warmth and joy reading this, the feeling spreads from my heart and into every little particle in my body, what a great feeling." --Ann

"THE INFORMATION HERE IS PROFOUND. Thanks Zingdad for sharing and helping us to wake up." --Boost06

"My mind has been so irreversibly opened by these writings. I am so thankful for the wider perspective. "If you can't see the perfection you are standing to close to the picture." Plays in my mind every time I see or hear anything that displeases me or leads me to habitually label someone or something as evil. This is really powerful." --Oneness411

"When I read The Ascension Papers *for the first time, my heart and soul said yes, yes ,yes..."* --wolfke74

"What amazing material. Rings so true for me." --macelderry

"You have developed an amazing gift and now you share that with others who are willing to listen and I personally thank you for that, as it has helped me to see why things in my life have happened the way it has." --jldy

"It is the first channelled material that I read, and I read a lot... that says something that I feel very deep inside of me but never found reflected before..." --Daco

* * * * *

Visit the author's website at *http://www.zingdad.com* for additional material such on-going writings, the author's blog, recordings of guided meditations, fractal artwork, music and more.

* * * * *

The Ascension Papers

BY

Zingdad
...AND FRIENDS

* * * * *

Me 'n My Dog
Publishers

ME 'N MY DOG PUBLISHERS

Published by
Me 'n My Dog Publishers
Suite 303, Private Bag X31, Knysna, 6570, South Africa

First Published as an e-book by Zingdad.com 2010
First Published in soft cover by Me 'n My Dog Publishers 2011

Printed by Lightning Source, Inc.

* * * * *

ISBN: 978-0-620-49771-8

* * * * *

Contents

To Lisa

For everything

I could not have asked for a better journey-mate
Nor a better journey
…and it's only just begun.

Thank you for living this dream with me.

About *The Ascension Papers*
A note from the author

Dear Reader

When I first sat down to write this work I had no idea whatsoever that the end result would be a book. I had done a few short "channellings" which I had posted on a variety of Internet forums and had decided that it was time to try, for my own growth and learning, to record a few conversations with members of my spirit family. It was meant to be a simple discovery of who they are and what they are about.

What followed was the most amazing journey into consciousness imaginable. Chapter followed chapter, each one building on what had gone before, gradually constructing an unbelievably detailed, coherent picture of the way life works and why things are the way they are. But more than bringing simple understanding, the truths uncovered brought me profound peace, joy and release from the fear and pain that had gnawed at my soul my whole life long. Fear was alchemically transmuted into Love. As a result I came to understand myself and the world I live in, in a whole new way. A way which liberates me to be the very best that I can be. A way that allows me to awaken to the magnificence that lies within. Writing this book has sparked the most profound growth and transformation in my being. It has been, quite simply, the best, most important, thing that I have ever done by far.

What YOU can expect to gain from reading THE ASCENSION PAPERS, depends entirely upon you. This is not a work that demands of you that you should believe what is espoused and does not promise to rescue you from your life. But it is my firm conviction that the content of this book can help you, if you are willing to take the journey, to discover your own magnificence…to discover that you are perfect as you are… that you are, and always have been, the creator of your own reality… that you are a being of pure, radiant Love.

This book is my journey to self-discovery. With the greatest love and joy I share it with you. It might just be what you need on YOUR journey to self-discovery too.

Some of the topics covered in this book include:

- Why are we actually here? Why did we incarnate as humans and what is the meaning of life?

- What can we know of our Creator? Are we all truly one with God? And if we are, what does that really mean for us?

- What is the nature of the "Higher-Self" and what is our relationship with our "Higher-Selves"?

- What is a "Spirit-Guide"?

- What is Truth, what is Love and what is Joy?

- If the Creator, God, is good and loving then why does evil exist? And why is there fear and pain?

- And why is the world in the state it is in and how did it come to be like this?

- Are there shadowy figures running the world from behind the scenes – and what does that mean to me in my life?

- What about 2012 and the apocalypse and the Mayan calendar and all that?

- What about religion… prophets, saviours, angels, demons, devils, heaven and hell?

- And does science have anything of value to say to us as beings that are on a spiritual path?

- Can we find our way to feeling truly at one with ourselves: whole, healed, peaceful and joyful?

…and this is just a smattering of the many interesting topics that will be addressed in, I'm sure you will agree, quite a refreshing new way. But all of the many and varied topics will ultimately serve one grand purpose. And that is to set before you an invitation, an invitation to a whole new life in a whole new world in a grand, golden age of humanity! I, as the incarnated aspect of a much greater being, have the wonderful privilege of bringing this invitation to you here in this life on planet Earth. If you accept the invitation then you will be able to join me and a host of other beings in what appears to me to be the most wondrous future reality imaginable. But I won't go into the details of that now. It will all unfold as you read this work. The point I wish to make is that I DO NOT insist that you must agree with me, believe what I say or subjugate your truth to mine. That is the opposite of what I want. I simply invite you to read what I have written with your own discernment and truth firmly in place. If you find resonance with what is presented, then your heart is telling you that the ideas presented here are "right for you".

You will notice that this work is presented in the form of a series of conversations between myself and a variety of spirit beings. You might wonder how I come to be able to create these dialogues with beings that are not, in the normal sense of the word, present on this Earth. I have spent many years and a great deal of dedicated effort in teaching myself how to do this. I will in due course, as a part of a follow-up work, explain exactly how I do what I do and offer some thoughts as to how you too may develop such a facility should you so desire. I don't like to call what I do "channelling" as I don't give over my faculties to another being to speak though me. I prefer to call it "intuitive conversation". I simply ask the questions and then allow the truth in my heart to provide me with an answer… and then I type what I receive. But it is not really important HOW I derive these words. I do not want to claim any authority for these words as a result of the fact that they ostensibly come from some great beings from the far-beyond. I would very much hope that you will decide for yourself to what degree these words are true for you based upon your own resonance with the words themselves.

Finally: you might notice that the earlier chapters are less fluid and possibly more naïve than the later chapters. In updating this work for publication I considered revising the first chapters to bring them up to the standard of the later chapters. I decided against this course however as this is exactly how the book unfolded for me and for those that were reading it chapter-by-chapter on my website when I was writing it. What you see is the progression of my own soul as a result of being exposed to the ideas presented herein. Certainly the latter chapters are my best but equally they were only possible as a result of the groundwork laid in the early chapters. So I let it stand as is.

And now, without further ado, I present to you my offering of love to the world, a gift which I freely give to you with a joyful and open heart. Here is:
THE ASCENSION PAPERS, by Zingdad …and friends.

Zingdad
Knysna, South Africa
12 September 2010

* * * * *

Chapter 1. An Introduction to Zingdad

When I was young I was taught that it is polite to introduce yourself when making a new acquaintance. And as I always tend to the excessive, so I shall introduce myself to you excessively! This chapter is an introduction to me, to all I have come to understand about who I really am and why I am here including my past-life experiences. One you have read this you will have some context for this work and my motivations for producing it.

I have spent a lot of energy in this lifetime in trying to find true inner-peace, self-love and self-trust. Early on, I realised that I would struggle to heal my inner-pain if I did not know what had caused it in the first place. So, an important part of my journey has included a deep foray into that which occurred prior to this life and the discovery, for myself, of who I REALLY am. I derived this information from conversations like those that will follow in this book, through meditation, hypnosis, auto-hypnosis and also from a couple of conversations with my lady-love's "Higher-Self" whilst she was in a trance state. I furthermore went for an intensive series of amazingly healing hypnotic regressions with a gifted healer who is also a psychologist. And while my story is subject to change as I discover more about myself, for now, here is a brief introduction to who I am:

Origins

I will start my story with a council meeting of the group of Light-Beings that created this reality. They were discussing how this reality we inhabit would be brought to a close so that a new reality could take its place. A bit like one game coming to an end so that another can be played. The way these games are played is that each Light-Being will be responsible for a particular role in each new game. The current game in question, our whole reality, is quite an interesting one. It is a game where some of these Bright Ones had created many manifestations (also called incarnations) that had been able to experience "individuality". In order to make this game work something pretty radical had to be achieved. The aspects of the Bright Ones that were to play inside the game had to actually forget that they are all One... they had to forget their own eternal, immortal nature. Nowhere in All That Is had such a thing been done before.

In order to give the game direction, the concept of "duality" had been set into place. In the absence of the knowledge of their own divine purpose, players needed something else to give them a spur to growth and progression. Previous games had floundered as a result of insufficient impetus. And so it was decided that there would be two main "camps", which would result in rivalry, competition and conflict. The two camps were defined by who the player would serve. On the one side would be those that serve others and on the other side would be those that serve themselves. And so the game is being played out with fragments of the Bright Ones having incarnations in the system through which they have been experiencing the ecstasies and the miseries of life in the system. In so doing they have been discovering who they really are from a position of absolute forgetfulness. It is a marvellous, amazing, grand experiment in consciousness and the rewards are truly phenomenal. But now, as the time approaches to bring the game to a close, the Council gathers to see what must be done. It is perceived that there will be some considerable difficulty in ending the game successfully without causing harm and trauma to the players; those aspects of the Bright Ones that are deeply engaged in the game as incarnated souls.

Can you see the problem?

In order for the game to work, all the players had to forget that they were just players and engage very deeply with the game as if it were their only reality. As they played the game of duality they would come to feel powerful emotions, such as hatred and anger towards some and kindness and need towards others. The duality of fear and love would compel them to bury themselves very deeply in the game. And so it was that players would find themselves unable to even begin to conceive of it that the game was not completely real and completely serious. Which was fine for so long as the game was to continue, but a problem occurred when the Bright Ones wanted to end the game. Beings as totally engrossed in the game as the players are will not simply stop playing and return to full remembrance when it is time to stop! And their Free Will cannot simply be breached and the game forcibly ended, as this would cause the players profound trauma and teach them that they are NOT the creators of their own reality. This would undo the whole point of the game which is growth and learning, and especially learning about creation.

So, ending the game would have to be done carefully and with some delicacy. The only way to do it would be for each and every manifestation to awaken to the fact that they are in fact immortal beings of light simply experiencing an illusory, transient reality. They would each have to choose to leave the game voluntarily. And so it was decided that each player would be awoken at an appointed time. Each of the Light Beings then put their plans in place to bring the game to a successful close.

It is not mine to know what all of the Light Beings decided. I know only a little of what one of those Light Beings did. And now I will draw your attention to this one particular Light Being. Though names are of no use to such beings, they are of some use to us, so we shall call this being Joy-Divine or J-D for short. J-D was invited to come and play this game specifically to assist with the ending. In order to do what he came to do, J-D saw that he would need to re-order the whole game just a little. For these beings, you see, there is no such thing as time. There is consequently no problem in redoing the game from the beginning in order to end it differently. And you can keep re-doing until you get the desired outcome and then THAT is the version of events you go with. So J-D came to hold one of the roles in the game. But J-D did not create the endlessly recursive self-fragmentations that many of the other Bright Ones did. This was not originally his game, you see, and so he did not seek to populate it with many billions or even trillions of aspects of himself as some of the others did. But he DID seek to understand the game in great depth. And it is really so that the deepest, hermeneutic understanding of a thing can only come from experiencing it yourself. J-D knew that he needed this kind of understanding in order to offer the assistance that was required of him. And so it was that he decided to introduce a manifestation into the game. From within his own being he created a being which may be called "Delight". Delight would be that which carried the light of Joy-Divine into the densest depths of the game. Delight would in fact be the incarnating portion of Joy-Divine...

And that, perhaps you have realised, is ME.

A Beginning...

In the very earliest memory of my individual existence that I have been able to find, I was slowly, dreamily, driftingly becoming conscious of "selfness". I was being lovingly cradled within the very being of Joy-Divine. I knew only Oneness and belonging. Infinite love was my sustenance. The deepest bliss was my every experience. Slowly, my consciousness arose from this slumbering joy and I began to formulate my first thoughts. As I became aware of my own beingness I conceived the thought: *"Here am I."* And then the question, *"What am I?"*

And with infinite love and gentleness, J-D began to answer me. In some ways, this lifetime and those that went before it are a part of the infinite, unending answering of that question. For by living and BEing I am discovering myself, who I am and what I am. You see Bright Ones don't communicate in thoughts and words as we do. Their communications are in whole creations! Our entire universe is really just a part of an unfolding conversation between the Bright Ones. And as I am here discovering who I really am… it is also Joy-Divine engaged in the act of telling Delight the answer to the question *"what am I?"* played out in dramatic form through all the occurrences in my various incarnations. It's an amazing thing, really. And maybe it is thus for you too? Maybe you too are that which is busy answering the question *"what am I?"* for yourself. I think this is so, don't you?

But now to the question of why Delight is here and therefore why I, Zingdad, am here. For beings to move forward they must conceive of a purpose for themselves. Delight has the purpose of being "an Interventionist". What exactly "an Interventionist" is, is a long story that I shall tell on another occasion - for now kindly accept that it is a being that travels around the spiritual realms assisting others when they become stuck in the creations of their own reality. And so Delight would help here in the work of the ending of this reality in a... well... a delightful way, really. But you know; you can't help a friend with their pain if you don't understand what they are going through. So before Delight could help, he had to immerse himself in this reality completely. He had to incarnate a few times and completely lose himself in this reality. And then, right on time during his final incarnation at the end of the game, he had to find himself and awaken and ascend back out of the system. Only then would he have sufficient understanding to really help and do what he had come to do. And, of course, this is what I am right now endeavouring to do.

I remember beginning my descent into this system. I left the warm embrace of Joy-Divine and began to enter via the higher dimensions of this reality for the very first time. And then, with a shock, I began to fall. I fell and fell. As I plummeted though the densities of creation I began to realise that I was losing my connection with the Oneness. I began to feel the terrible pang of a completely new experience – and I was lost in the coldness of desperate aloneness. My vision began to shrink – I could no longer see what the results of my actions would be! I no longer knew that everything was perfection. There was so much I suddenly couldn't and didn't know. As I conceived of the fact that I didn't KNOW what would happen, an entirely new experience gripped my heart – FEAR! If I didn't know what would come next, how could I know I would be okay? I couldn't! I felt the black robes of the Veil of Unknowing close around me and it felt like icy fingers squeezing my heart. This was agony! And still I fell and fell. And then came the oblivion of forgetting both the pain of the falling and the bliss of what had come before that. The anguish faded. Memory faded. Consciousness became dim. Everything turned slowly to blackness. And then I began to look through blurred eyes upon a strange and incomprehensible new world.

I didn't know it then but my first incarnation had begun…

My Life in Lyra

My first lifetime was on a planet in the star system of Lyra, so-called after the Lyre (a type of harp), which is also a useful analogy for the way in which life was created there. Many beings had their first incarnation in Lyra, which were much less dense than here on Earth. Bodies were far more subtle than these that we inhabit now. A tonal vibration in the Light was what caused bodies to manifest – hence the "harp" analogy. Life on this planet in Lyra was good. It was a place of love and gentleness where they used joy as a vehicle for teaching. Each person was encouraged to follow their greatest bliss, to find their unique and special gift and then to express that which they most loved doing. There was no competition and no punishment. Each being was valued for who they were and the contribution they made. And everyone gave their best at all times.

Physically, the beings were fair of skin and hair and had blue eyes. I still bear those features now out of a sense of identification with them. They were a graceful and vital people who knew that their bodies were a divine gift to be loved and cherished and understood how to treat their bodies respectfully. And this is one of the reasons that they lived to incredibly great ages. But there was another, more important reason: in the societies of this place were teachers who passed on to others the teachings of physical ascension. As a result of learning this, the Lyrans did not age as we typically do here on earth. As young ones grew up and matured into adults they would, at some point, begin to show an interest in learning the ways of the Spirit. They would request to be taught. The process of learning about this was slow and gentle, with the process itself being valued far more than the outcome. As their training advanced so these beings would become wiser and more powerful in the ways of spirit. Eventually they would begin to gain a brightness, as their aura would begin to glow and beings of great age could immediately be identified by the radiance of their aura. But their bodies, strangely enough, did not age. To look into such a being's eyes was to feel blessed and loved. As their training and spiritual growth continued, these beings would become more Light and less matter. And then, when they had done what they had come for, they would finally and completely transform their physical bodies into light bodies and leave that world for subtler realms of spirit. A wonderful thing to see.

The Lyrans lived in absolute harmony with the land. They did not think of plants, animals and their planet as something to use and consume but rather knew that they were One with these. The land was respected as their own mother. If a plant or animal was required to sacrifice its body for something that was needed for the people then it was respectfully asked for that sacrifice. If permission was given then the ending of the life was done with great reverence, respect and appreciation. Life there was truly a great, harmonious partnership and each worked always for the greater good of the All.

My clearest memory of my own life in Lyra is of me standing looking over a moon-lit ocean with a being called Adamu. Though not my father, he had been the one that had raised me and had taught me the ways of the people. He was a wise and respected elder. A powerfully built, leonine man with a flowing beard, sapphire eyes and the brightest auric glow.

My memory starts with him standing opposite me engaging me in a serious conversation. He was explaining to me that I was not to remain with them... not to eventually return to the Light in the way they did. He was pointing to the stars and telling me that my destiny lay "*out there*". He skipped a stone across the still, moonlit ocean as a metaphor for how I must hop across a few other lives in other places in my coming progression: not stay in one place with them. I was sobbing. The fact that my leaving meant that I would have to physically die did not bother either of us. Everyone in that world knew that death was nothing more than a transition to another state. So that was not the source of my grief. I simply did not want to leave there. I had found a great love for those people and Adamu with his gentle, loving guidance of me in particular. I didn't want to go and Adamu of course didn't want me to go either, as he loved me. But this was my destiny.

Adamu said to me, "*Soon enough you will be on your way and you'll have forgotten us*".

"*Never!*" I said, "*I'll never forget you. And I'll remember this moment forever*".

And I have.

I will always love the people of Lyra. They gave me my first life and my grounding in this whole new reality. I knew such unconditional love and true belonging amongst them. I had a place "to come from" and even though I would always be a wanderer, I would always have had a HOME.

And I would remember Adamu. This current incarnation of mine has been infused with a sense of missing someone, an older, fatherly figure who I knew should be there in my life, but was not. As I began to remember Adamu and find him in my meditations and hypnotic regressions that gap in my life came to be filled. I came to remember the depth of my love and connection with this most amazing being. And this is how this memory survived the deep forgetfulness that comes from reincarnating into this world. I said I would remember… and I did. And as I re-connected with Adamu in this life-time and was learning to have intuitive conversations, I also realised that he was a font of deep wisdom and profound truth which always came cloaked in compassion. So I started to make his words available for others to read on various forums on the Internet. It was thanks to Adamu that I could develop this skill at all. He has again come to be a wonderful source of guidance and advice to me. And friendship too.

Isn't that strange? I appear to be a grown-up, adult man with an imaginary friend!

But back to the story. As I have mentioned, most beings left life in Lyra by means of a bodily ascension into the Light. But this was not my path. I was to go the way of those that did not leave into the Light. I walked into the ocean in the Bay of Leaving until I was chest deep in the moonlit water and then, just as I had been taught to do, I lifted my spirit-body out of my physical body and severed the connection between the two. My lifeless body fell back into the waters, the waves closed over it. And then I was gone.

The oceans would, in due course, take care of the cleansing and nothing would be left of me but memories and stories.

A Soldier's Life

Life number 2 was my life as a soldier.

The civilisation into which I was born was engaged in an inter-planetary war with another civilisation. I have no memory of the specifics and so I can't tell you if there were great galactic alliances at war or just two opposing planets battling it out. These things I don't remember at all. What I do know is that I had been born into the life of a soldier garrisoning a mining colony on a little planet far from our home-world. The planet itself was not quite solid. I can't say for sure what it was composed of but the effect was that one could pilot a vehicle into the planet without too much difficulty. Perhaps it was a bit like Jupiter or Saturn and was essentially condensed gasses? Certainly, the planet was utterly inhospitable to life, as we had to be inside protective vehicles or structures at all times. But whatever the case, in this life I was one of a group of soldiers who had been assigned the role of protecting the mining operations on this semi-solid little planet.

The life I lived there was quite different from any here on earth. For one thing, it seems we soldiers were genetically modified to fulfil our function. One of the results of this was that none of us was able to reproduce, as this would have been counter-productive to the optimal fulfilment of our role. It seems our bodies were designed to remain sexually immature our whole lives and so the distinction between the genders was definitely not as pronounced as it is here on earth. I am confused about this but there might even have been more that just two genders! What I am sure of is that the soldiers were not exclusively male. But as I say, gender wasn't the same issue as it is here on earth. I believe we were however somewhat sexual with each other but it was more of a playful, loving, bonding thing than anything else. But, be that as it may, the group of soldiers with me on that planet were my everything. They were the only family I had ever known; they were my friends, my lovers and my reason for being. If I think back on it now, my situation in that life seems very peculiar to my current sensibilities but it felt completely natural and right to me then. We were happy in our own way and there was certainly a greater sense of belonging and group identity than I have ever felt in my current lifetime.

As a soldier, my designated role was to pilot a particular military vehicle. It was something between a very small space-ship and an armoured car. This one-man vehicle could not only travel on the surface of the planet but could also push down into the planet itself and manoeuvre under the surface. It sustained life-support for me under all the varied and extreme conditions on that planet. I'm sure this was a scout craft and if it had any armaments at all, these would have been quite light. I think my role was really just to guard and patrol. In the memories that I have it seems I didn't take my responsibilities too seriously at all. Like a big kid with a toy, I really enjoyed driving my little craft around and pushing it down into the depths of the planet only to pull back up and come bursting up onto the surface. I got quite a thrill out of that craft but I certainly did not behave like a soldier engaged in the life-and-death responsibility of defending a strategic asset in times of war!

On a day, it was my turn to man the control room in a satellite high above the planet. While I was on duty I was looking through a window at the planet below and something completely beyond my comprehension happened. All I can say is that the little planet, with all its inhabitants, was stomped out of existence before my very eyes! Everything was, quite simply, wiped out of existence by some inexplicable phenomenon. A HUGE grey "thing" passed though that reality and utterly obliterated the whole planet! I had no way of making sense of what I had just observed. This didn't relate to anything I had ever even heard of. I was thoroughly traumatized and left in a deep state of shock. Everyone I loved – all my friends, my family, my lovers, my home, my reason for living – EVERYTHING that had meant anything to me was wiped out in one unfathomable instant. I was left utterly alone in a small satellite that was now no longer tethered to a planet. I don't know what I did next. That little satellite would not have sustained my life for very long. I know I drifted for a while, lost in abject grief. Maybe I died of a lack of air, food or water. Maybe I terminated myself. That is not in my memory. All I find there is a muggy fog of loss and grief... and then nothing.

Lost in My Own Dream World

In life 3, I had some kind of mental incapacity. I am almost completely certain it was Autism. What I know is that my thoughts did not have the same structure as they do now. It was as if I thought in comic-book pictures and icons rather than in words or complex ideas. I was unable to speak and instead made gibberish sounds. This life played out in what was quite possibly 16th century Europe (or some reality quite a lot like that) and life there was hard, mean and cruel. People with challenges such as I suffered were considered a useless burden.

This life was dichotomously desperately unhappy and yet also blissfully joyful. You see I was not treated very well by my fellow human beings. For example, as soon as I was old enough to go out amongst the other children they noticed my strangeness and began to taunt me mercilessly. They threw stones at me and chased me with sticks like a wild animal sometimes. The only one who really loved me and was eternally kind to me was my older sister. She was pure gentleness and goodness.

Then there was an uncle who was horribly abusive of me. He sexually abused me whenever he could because, you see, I was powerless to ever tell anyone about this. My only protection was to stick to my sister's side whenever he was around and then he'd leave me alone. But if he ever found me without her… well, it got pretty awful. An uncomprehendingly painful, wrong, strange experience that hurt and hurt and I had no way of processing it or even of defending myself.

But that life was far from being all bad. Sometimes I would able to slip into an altered state of consciousness in which everything was beautiful. I remember seeing angels of light and fairies and sprites. I saw the golden auras in the life around me. I saw the pulsations of energy in the plants. I saw the zip-zap of energy communications between the stars and the flows and spirals of energy in the planets etheric body. I saw wondrous things in those times. This brought me deep joy and healed my pain. So that was okay. But I think my family were disturbed by the fact that I'd sit on my own, staring into space, cooing and giggling to myself with pleasure.

And then, things being what they were in those days, my sister was no more than 15 or 16 when she was married off to some veritable stranger in the next town and she had to leave to go and live with him. I know now that she tried very hard to make this okay for me. I remember lying with my head in her lap while she cried bitterly. You see she knew she was going away but could not explain this to me. All I knew was that she was unhappy and then she was gone. A horse-drawn carriage came to fetch her. I remember it driving down the lane into the bleak snow-laden forest.

Soon after that, the abusive uncle came around again. When I saw him I knew what was coming and in my desperation I ran away to find my sister. I ran down the road along which the carriage had gone. I ran and ran. I ran until my lungs ached, I ran until I fell down exhausted. Night began to fall and I huddled against a tree for some shelter from the cold. I was very, very scared - every forest sound and shadow caused monster images to flash in my head.

I died of exposure in the forest that night.

A Meta-reality

Life 4 is the most difficult to explain because it occurred in a reality very unlike this one and things just don't translate well. I guess it might actually have been in a kind of etheric realm because in this place ideas and thoughts really were tangible things. I somehow had an ability with the crafting of ideas that could… I don't know… the analogy I get is that I had a "sword of words". I could somehow do great harm with the constructs of my mind and the others around me seemed to be quite defenceless against me. I had great anger and rage towards them. I think these were the same beings as in the life before because my sister was there again and this time she was the only one I loved. All others I struck out at and hurt very badly. They had no way of defending themselves and I just went around doing harm – exercising my rage, I guess. This lifetime ended quite strangely too. The others captured me and confined me. And then they brought my sister and killed her before me. In so doing I saw that she and they were actually One greater being. I saw that the good and the evil, the positive and the negative, were all from within the same being. That which I loved the most and that which I despised the most was all the same one being – just different manifestations of it. I was shaken to my core. They then killed me too. This somehow was a favour to me. It somehow absolved me of my karma. They actually did this as an act of love. None of this makes much sense to me now from the perspective of my current life but that is how it was.

Also, I later came to understand that what I had done to them was somehow a service to them. Much worse was to come and I assisted in some way to prepare them for this. It was as a result of me that they would later survive.

I don't really understand much about this lifetime and I hope to puzzle it all out some day.

The Wizard

The story of Life 5 is uncomfortable for me to tell. The setting was quite possibly medieval Europe. I was born to some local lord. We lived in a castle on a mountain overlooking a valley in which there was a village. Our village was quite isolated and transport through the mountain was by slow horse-drawn cart, so we lived quite an insular life. Most of the villagers would live their whole life without ever venturing out of the valley. Very few ever saw even the next village. Transport was difficult and slow and communications almost non-existent.

For this lifetime I had been given a spiritual gift: a connection to a special form of spiritual "energy" that is mine for the work that I am to do. I was to use this energy to show the people how to do healing and other such spiritual work.

I think my mother was quite sickly and she had struggled for many years to fall pregnant. Being the wife of the local lord, it was important that she give my father an heir. News of her pregnancy was therefore greeted with great joy. When I was born a perfectly healthy baby boy, the village was overjoyed and a great celebration was given. I was the village's "golden child" and was much loved and celebrated. I soon began to display my gift in doing small magical things. The people saw this and wondered at it.

Somewhere in my teens, events conspired to take me in a dark direction: firstly my mother never properly recovered from giving birth to me. She was bed-ridden for a few years and then just faded away and died while I was still a child. My father was pre-occupied with his grief and his responsibilities as the lord of his lands. When my magical abilities became obvious, the village witch asked to be allowed to teach me – to "mould" my abilities. Despite the fact that she had shown herself to be capable of quite a mean streak, she was allowed to take me into her care. As I say, my mother was gone and my father's concerns were elsewhere.

The witch did indeed teach me quite well. I had some impressive innate skill with manipulating matter and energy and she taught me how to channel and focus it. In time I became quite proficient at this. I was able, for example, to do weather working to bring rains for the crops when needed and so forth. I was also able to do healing work. I think there were some other skills but I can't quite remember them now. But all through the process of teaching me what she knew, the witch was also engaged in manipulating me to suit her own agenda. She wanted power for herself and, I am now sure, decided that she would turn me into her puppet. She attempted this by playing to my ego. She told me I was special beyond all other people. She led me to believe all others should serve me and be as slaves to my will. She taught me to believe I was some kind of a demi-god. I came to believe that my magical abilities were not to be placed in service of the people but instead were proof that the people should serve me. So that wasn't exactly healthy.

Then there was the way the peasantry treated me. You must understand that the social dynamic of feudal society is nothing like the life we live now. A feudal lord has absolute power over his lands and vassals. They scrape and bow around him, never speaking unless spoken to and never looking their lord in the eyes. They will almost always run and hide if they see him coming so that they do not have to engage with him and risk causing offence. It's almost as if these are two different species: the ruler and the ruled. The point of all this is that I certainly did not feel belonging and community amongst the village people. If I left the castle and went down to the village I was not welcomed with singing and dancing… Oh no. Many scurried away and all fell silent. I felt like an outcast. It felt as if my presence was resented. And then, as soon as I left their company, the villagers' conversation would once again pick up behind my back with nervous laughter breaking out. I thought they hated me. And maybe they did!

To complicate matters my father had, while I was still a boy, refused to send some of our peasants to be soldiers in a crusade (or something very like that). As a result of this we were considered pariahs and no self-respecting noble family would consider me a suitable marriage candidate for their daughter. So, upon coming of the age where I would have gone to the royal court to meet young ladies of my station, it was made clear that I would not be welcome.

So I was alone.

My only companion was the witch who was busily implementing her ego manipulations on me for her own ends. As it transpired, this eventually backfired on her. In time I came to believe her lies and felt I was too powerful to have to put up with her and her constant meanness. So I simply sent her away. Somewhere around that time my father died too and I became the lord of the lands. Not only did I have all the power of being a feudal lord but I also had the power of magic. To the peasants of the village I was something quite separate, other and strange. And there really was no one else in my life. No friends, no family, no lovers, no confidantes. Just me and the village peasantry to whom I was an utterly alien thing. This was to be a life of deep isolation.

But I was still a human being with human needs and desires. I guess what I wanted most was to be loved and accepted. To belong. To feel needed and wanted. And so, of course, I noticed some of the more attractive village girls. I wished I could have one of them be with me and love me. On a few occasions I would approach one and try to strike up a conversation. But the gap between us was just far too wide to be breached. In my presence they were uncomfortable and wary. As I approached they would be all apologetic and cowed – probably assuming I wanted to berate them for having done something wrong (why else would the lord of the land speak to a peasant girl?). They would not look at me and would only answer my direct questions in as few words as possible.

Eventually I demanded that one of the girls come back to castle with me on some pretext or another. I knew nothing of love and tenderness and even if I had, she would not have responded. I am ashamed to admit that instead, I forced myself upon her and took what I wanted. In so doing I ruined her chances of ever finding a husband. But I cared little of that. This abysmal behaviour brought me some kind of a feeling of power and, I guess, it was better than being completely alone. And so it became a bit of a habit for me. I repeated it a few times with the same girl and then moved onto others. My appetites changed and grew more dark. It soon became quite abusive. I prefer not to go into details. This is not easy for me to write about. All I will say is that I got quite darkly inventive about my abuses.

Obviously, at some point, the villagers decided they needed to do something about this. They needed to tell me to stop. So a meeting was called in the clearing in the middle of the village. I got to hear about this. I rushed out of the castle and went and stood on a cliff overlooking the village to see if it was true. And, sure enough, the people had gathered below and someone was standing up talking to them. I was enraged! I have a picture of myself standing on the cliff overlooking the village with the castle behind me. My emotions boiled and stewed. I was going to show them all! They would never again try such insolence! I began to raise the storm to end all storms. I pulled the wind in towards me – pulling and pulling, I drew in great storm clouds until, roaring and raging, they towered above me. The sky darkened to black and lightning raced. I was connected with these profound forces and I felt the lighting in my own body. It exhilarated me. I felt so large… so powerful… so alive. I revelled in it and in the punishment I would bring. I felt like a god. A very dark and powerful god. I drew in more energy. The wind whipped against my body almost pushing me right off the cliff-face. I saw the villagers below scattering and rushing to secure their homes, the fire in the marketplace around which they had gathered blowing up cinders onto the thatched roofs of their houses. I was gleeful at their fear. They would pay! The storm developed and developed – the forces straining to break and smash themselves against the village below. And then... nothing. My body collapsed lifeless on that cliff. I had over-done it. I had pushed too much energy through a vessel that was not capable of containing it.

Overloaded, my body simply ceased functioning and then, there I was, a spirit-being looking down on a lifeless form.

That was my last lifetime before this one.

A Life Between Lives

I spent a LOT of time between that incarnation and my current one. As a spirit-being I reviewed the life I had just left – I looked at the pain and devastation I had caused and I was aghast. I felt such remorse and anguish. I began to try to terminate my own existence. I'll spare you all the details but I spent a lot of effort simply trying to destroy my own beingness. I tried everything I could but I simply could not end myself. Whatever I did... I just continued to exist! I seem to have spent some time obliterating my connection to everything – in other words I tried to cease being by ceasing to DO and by losing my memory of all things. Eventually I found myself in a kind of stasis. I was nowhere, did nothing and knew nothing. But that didn't help because as soon as I wondered how I came to be there, it all came flooding back. I realised there was no escape, no cessation. I had to deal with what I had done. And as soon as I decided THAT, I found myself in the company of a group of spirit beings. They brought me before an ancient, wise and beautiful one. I assumed this "head-wizard" was to be my judge. I assumed he was going to sentence me for my grave wrong-doings. I immediately began to declare my guilt to him. I was like a limp, wet rag – all tears (metaphorically) and abject apologies. I alternated between earnestly swearing to do better next time, dedicating myself to endless service to repair the wrongs that I had done and begging to be punished or destroyed. On and on I went and the wise one just listened. When eventually I ran out of steam he asked, "*Are you quite done?*

Because I have someone you should meet."

And then I was introduced to a very special being. A being of pure, unblemished truth. I shall call him "8". I came to see him as the sharp blade-edge of TRUTH. He was hard – but ultimately and completely fair. He took one look at the snivelling damp rag that I was and simply said, "*You need to grow some back-bone*".

He took me in hand and worked with me. We were not inside of time so there is no way for me to say for how long he worked with me but I would say it was the equivalent of very many lifetimes. I learned a great deal from him. First he pretended to give me work as "punishment" until I discovered that the work was not punishment but simply an opportunity to express love as a gift of service. Then, when I finally realised that I no longer desired to be punished, he began to help me to see my own beauty. He helped me to see my worth and what I have to offer. Slowly a deep and amazing bond forged between us. He was my guide and teacher but I also knew that he was respected (even revered) by some of the most wondrous beings of this reality. I was blessed beyond my ability to tell of it that he had come to my assistance.

A Returning to Incarnated Life

Then came the time when 8 said to me that it was time to finish what was started: I needed to have one final incarnation so that I could let go of the incarnational cycle and rise up to find what I really am. I was filled with trepidation and self-doubt. I really did not want to go into density again. I feared that I would do damage again and did not want this.

"*Come with me,*" 8 said, "*I have someone I want you to meet.*"

"*Who?*" I asked.

"*Someone who is to be your partner in your journey in the next incarnation. You won't be alone.*" And then, before us was the most incredible sight: a being of the most radiant blue light. I had never seen so much light compressed into such a small space. I was awestruck.

"*What does this being want with me?*" I whispered to 8.

"*This one will take a challenge to planet earth: she will struggle with the lesson of self-love. You are to love her.*"

"*Well of course,*" I replied, "*how else can I respond to such a being?*"

"*You are to love her consistently and ceaselessly until she finds her own self-love and in return she will be your truth until you find your own inner-truth.*" And in that simple sentence the partnership was sealed. With such a being at my side how could I fail? And so it came to pass. I was born into this life and was just a very young man when my lady-love and I met. It was love at first sight and we have remained pretty much in love for all of the time since. We have a partnership that amazes even us. A miracle of love. And I HAVE loved her until she loved herself and she WAS my truth until I discovered my own truth within myself.

At the time of writing, it has been 18 years that we have been together in this, my Life 6. We have completed our contract, agreed to there in spirit form with 8 as our witness. And now, here on earth, as we find ourselves, we discover a partnership too special and wondrous to simply end. And so we create a new agreement based not upon a hurt and a need that the other must fill but upon pure love and a desire to give to the other that which we each are.

And that, more-or-less, brings me to the present moment.

So here I am now. Awakening. Discovering myself. And along the way I discover a few other things:

Firstly, 8 is my guide while I am incarnated but the reality that I hid from myself is that he and I are actually partners, that is to say, we are a team. He has looked after me through my journey (though I mostly did not know it) so that I can come out the other end and then we can do our work together. My unending gratitude to him for his help is mirrored by him to me. He tells me he is unendingly grateful to ME because I was the one who took the tough job of descending into this reality for us. So we are in balance, he and I. My job here is really just to find myself and awaken from within the system so that, with an hermeneutic understanding of the system, I can begin to do the work 8 and I came to do.

Secondly, I realise that the "head-wizard" was not some wise old judge but was actually just ME… my own Inner-Self. You see, only we can judge ourselves – no one else can or will. And anyway he did not come to judge at all. He simply came to be a part of assisting me in finding my way back home. I guess you could say the judge was a face of Joy-Divine. But equally you could say that I too am a face of Joy-Divine. So… it's all just me…

Thirdly, I discover that I really love myself. And like myself. And trust myself. I realise that my journey was a path that we all travel when we come here. We go via Forgetting to a place called Not-Self. When there, we do all kinds of interesting things like fear, pain, hatred and abuse. Then, slowly, we begin to discover that this doesn't make us happy and so we begin to replace it with love, joy, kindness and healing. And <u>this</u> makes us happier. Along the way we leave Not-

Self and find ourselves well on the road back to Self. And Self is not a being that has forgotten so, inevitably, as we become more Self so we ascend out of this duality-reality.

Fourth, to my utter surprise, I realise that I really love what is here in this reality. I love this planet with a love that sometimes aches in my heart. I love all that is upon the planet too. The people? I also love all of them. Although I do not always love all that they do! Some of them do some very hurtful things to self and to other/self. But that is only because they are lost and confused. If you look in my story you will see I also did some very hurtful things in my confusion. So I cannot judge another. And now I discover something interesting: our darkest, most dismal secrets are actually our most glorious jewels. You see, when you are in your greatest pain, you give someone else the gift of being able to express love to you by allowing them to help you to heal. Then, when you do heal, you come away with great compassion for all others that have pain. Then these "others" give you the gift of allowing you to help them with their pain. This thing – this helping of each other – this flows from compassion. If we each see the darkness within ourselves with clear and open eyes then we find compassion for the darkness in an other/self. And compassion is the route to Oneness. It is the healing of that which is fragmented.

And this is what I wanted to share with you… the very briefest summation of my story. Along the way, I have seen that all that has happened to me was perfect. It was exactly what was needed to allow me to become who I am. And I love who I am, so I have no regrets.

In love and laughter,
Zingdad-that-is-Delight

Oh yeah, P.S.

I forgot to include this other thing that I discovered. It's a loopy one: I discover that, outside of time, I am already that which has ascended and always was ascended. In fact I am a being that has already expressed itself eternally in an infinite number of realities because I am already an infinite, immortal creator being, and always was. And so my beginning, as laid out above in this story, is not really my beginning - it's just a convenient place to start a story. I am myself, I am my Higher-Self and I am One with God. And so are you. So you and I are One. So I am you and you are me and we are All That Is. And that's just the freakiest, happiest truth ever! And so I greet you:

"Hello God!"

P.P.S.

People often ask me where the name "Zingdad" comes from. And why I don't just use my "real name". So here is the story: Firstly, what exactly is a REAL name? My name is one chosen for me by my mother before I was born. My surname is one that comes to me from some point in distant history via my father's line. Now I AM quite fond of these two names but, to me, they signify me in my personal life. It is who I am when I am at home with my friends. That which I present to the world, as an author and musician, well that is a different "me" needing a different name. I wanted to publish on the web and engage on forums with a new name, a name that would suggest my light-hearted nature. A name that would be unique and easy to remember. Given the potentially "heavy" nature of some of the spiritual matters I was writing about, I really wanted to let people know that I am not in the business of taking myself too seriously. So I set myself the goal of coming up with such a name but it was my lady-love who eventually came up with the winning choice. She suggested Zingdad. The name derives from the fact that I have a little Dachshund with whom I have a really deep bond.

His name is "Zing" (which is short for amaZING). And I am his "dad", sort-of. So "Zingdad". But really I just liked the light-hearted, fun sound of the name. I liked that it was totally unique (go ahead... google "Zingdad"... every single result pertains to me! Cool, huh?). I liked that it is neither an existing name nor a word that that means anything and will therefore not trigger any preconceived notions. I just liked it! So I took it for my name. And that's all there is to it really!

And that's it for the introduction.

See you in Chapter 2!

* * * * *

Chapter 2. What is the Higher-Self?
A Conversation with Joy-Divine

Here begins the first intuitive conversation of this work. I will be typing a record of a conversation with my own Higher-Self.

Zingdad: I wish to speak to my own Higher-Self. To the being that has previously identified itself to me as Joy-Divine.

Joy-Divine: Hello. I am here with you, as always.

Z: Hello. I will want to discuss a number of issues with you and then record the conversation to share with others. I feel it is a good idea to first introduce you to my readers so that they might have a context from which to understand your words.

J-D: Yes, this is good. I am happy to do an introduction but I would suggest that we can hit more than one bird with this same stone, so to speak. We can have a series of chats that introduce me and, at the same time, introduce a number of spiritual concepts.

Z: Okay, excellent! What sorts of spiritual concepts?

J-D: Well, for example: if I were to introduce myself to your readers saying something as simple as "*I am Zingdad's Higher-Self*" then we will immediately find ourselves having to take a detour to explain what a Higher-Self is so that we can be sure we are all on the same page. But in order to explain this concept I am going to introduce other concepts and they too will be in need of clarification. And very soon, in simply trying to introduce myself, I will have opened a whole gamut of topics that will need to be addressed. This is a conversation which might never end. Indeed it is so that the simple question, "*Who are you?*" is an invitation to a life-long association if the two of you are serious in your endeavour to explore the answer to that question. But in answer to your question, a few points that will come up for discussion quite soon will include, "what is Oneness?", "what is ascension?", "why am I called Joy-Divine" and "what is truth?".

Z: Sounds exciting!

J-D: ...and potentially confusing if we don't handle this carefully. You will still come to be quite surprised at how much beauty, truth and wisdom will come from this simple beginning.

But for now what I am going to ask you to do is to make this a multi-part series of conversations. I will open today with a discussion with you which you may title "What is the Higher-Self?" And then, in this discussion, we will come up with new topics for conversation which we shall address in follow-up sessions with either myself or some of the other members of our spirit family. Okay?

Z: Yes, of course! Well then, best I start the ball rolling and ask the question... ta da da dum... What, pray tell, IS a Higher-Self?

J-D: I am SO glad you asked (he smiles).

Firstly, let me say that, while the most commonly used term is "Higher-Self", I actually prefer "Inner-Self" or in a certain context, "God-Self". How this all works can be very, very simple to explain or terribly complex. The simplest explanation that I can offer is this:

> *"There is only one being experiencing the illusion of being many."*

I like that statement so much that I am going to repeat it in a slightly different way:

> *"The One is engaged in an experience of Itself as being many."*

This statement is true on many levels. If you really get that concept, then you get the essential thesis of what I would present as the spiritual cosmology of All That Is. This understanding serves you irrespective of the size of the spiritual concept you are trying to understand. Let's start big… from the top and work down:

We are all ONE. But the ONE – which you may call God, or Source or Creator or whatever term you like – has created for itself some very powerful thoughts about itself such that there are Many. To illustrate this I shall use the example of an author who is writing a story. The author creates the characters of the story in his mind. As the characters gain greater and greater validity in the author's mind they begin to take on distinct personalities. Often the author will find that it seems like the characters have a mind of their own! They feel, to the author, as if they are autonomous beings and he is just chronicling their behaviour. Can you see how this could be for that author? That he can create many personae in his mind? And give them each their own nature and personality? And in the telling of their stories the characters seem to be quite oblivious to the fact that they only exist in the author's mind? That the world they live in, though large and complex, is also only in the story-teller's mind?

Z: Oh wow, yes. The author analogy is awesome.

J-D: Now I tell you it is not only authors that do this… that create characters in their minds. In point of fact all sentient beings do this, to one degree or another. Everyone creates fictitious conversations and interactions in their own minds. Everyone has day-dreams and fantasies and imaginary discussions. And everyone dreams whilst sleeping. These, and similar processes, are all story-telling with character creation.

Can you see how each of you then, already have the beginnings of the experience of creating "another" inside your own minds?

Z: Yes, I can see that.

J-D: Now imagine you have an infinity of time to perfect the art of powerfully imagining these characters. Imagine you have infinite creative resources. That you are greater than the greatest creative genius that has ever walked the planet. Now possibly you might have the first glimmering of what this might be like; how the ONE can create within Its mind, so to speak, various characters and personalities.

Z: So that is how we here on earth come into being?

J-D: No, not quite. I am endeavouring to give you a simplified understanding of what might otherwise be an impossibly complex subject. And I am going to need to keep oversimplifying things a lot for the sake of being able to express these ideas at all. If you want to understand how beings on earth come to be here, then you should rather imagine a hierarchy of creator-beings. Imagine that the beings that appear in the mind of the ONE should create in their minds more beings. And they, in turn, do the same thing. And this happens over and over and over again. Then, at some point, you would get to the soul-fragments that incarnate on planet earth.

You have heard that this world is deep in the densities or, as others express it, of a low dimension. Well, this is essentially the notion: each lower density requires an additional level of creation. You would have a "Higher-Self" on every one of the levels or densities or dimensions above you; right the way "up" to the ONE. Which is why you call such beings "Higher-Self". But I tell you, it is not "up", it is "inside". A better understanding is that these levels are within you. You go inside your heart to find your "Inner-Self". And the further inwards you travel, the greater the version of your Inner-Self you will find.

Z: Right the way to God?

J-D: Yes. Have you not heard it said that God is inside each and every persons heart? Or that the kingdom of heaven is in your heart?

Z: Ah, yes. So to sum up: there is The One, which is God. And God has created us all within Its mind. But indirectly. There is a structure and we are the creations of the creations of the creations…

J-D: …and so on, yes.

But do not suffer the impression that you are not therefore very powerful! All parts of The One are imbued with the essential nature of The One. It is said that you are made in God's image. Well, that doesn't mean that God has a body like yours. It means YOU are made in God's image. The you that is still you when you are no longer in a human body. It means all spirit is God-like. All spirit is creative and self-creative.

Two concepts that you personally have been encouraged by me to understand are fractals and holograms. For a very good reason. I can strongly encourage everyone to at least read a little about these two phenomena. They provide a wonderful way to understand creation. A hologram is an object which provides a three-dimensional picture. If you break that hologram into numerous smaller pieces, then each of those pieces will once again contain the whole three dimensional image. And you are like this. Every being contains the whole.

And the thing with fractals to understand is that you can find a point that interests you and from there you can zoom deeper and deeper into the fractal. You will never get to the end of it. It is endlessly recursive in any direction you wish to travel. And you are like this too. If you look within yourself you can go on looking forever and ever. There is always more to discover in any direction you wish to search.

So I tell you this: It seems to you as if the universe lies outside of you. It does not. In fact it lies INSIDE you. Each of you contains the whole and one can "zoom into" each of you infinitely. All parts are connected to all other parts.

Z: You're kidding, right, about the part about the whole universe being INSIDE me?

J-D: No, I am being completely serious. It is a point you shall come to understand as we proceed with these conversations. But we must shelve that for a moment so that we can finish THIS conversation.

Z: Ah. Got it. So we were talking about you being my Inner-Self and that there are levels of Inner-Self-ness.

J-D: Yes. Essentially all I am trying to say is that, depending on how you look at it, there might be only one ultimate Inner-Self or an infinite number of levels of Inner-Selves.

Z: Wow. Er… the one ultimate Inner-Self would be…?

J-D: The Source of all that is, of course. God. We are all One, as I have mentioned. So ultimately we are all joined by the fact that our ultimate greatest version of Self is God.

Z: That's a big thought. I struggle with it a bit.

J-D: That's fine. If you already knew this to be true beyond a shadow of a doubt then you would probably not have a need to be incarnated anymore. So it is natural that this should be a difficult concept for you and anyone else reading this. But don't stress about it. You can, if you choose, simplify matters and understand that within the creation of The One are many great spirit beings. You can call them Demi-Gods or Arch-Angels if you like. They are your God-Self. They are both aware of themselves as unique and separate individuals AND at the same time, are absolutely aware of their Oneness. They have created (together or separately) lower levels of self. Each succeeding level is more separate and less ONE.

Z: But how can someone be both One AND separate?

J-D: I shall address this in one of the conversations about the Oneness. I shall call it "the rainbow metaphor".

Z: Sounds colourful - I look forward to that. Okay then, back to this discussion. So there is a continuum from a feeling of oneness at the top right down to a feeling of separateness at the bottom?

J-D: Yes, exactly. And at each and every level the being is creating other characters and personae in its mind. All are always in a process of the co-creation of Self. As you get down to this reality you currently inhabit you get to a feeling of profound separateness such that you can actually totally forget that you are One and that you are a creator being. In fact, that is what your whole plane of reality was created for: to experience separateness. Which is also called individuality. "Not-Oneness" is a wonderful way for you to experience a great degree of free will.

Z: Why is that?

J-D: Briefly, it is because when you know yourself as an individual... as truly separate from All That Is and from your own spiritual hierarchy, then you can decide things about yourself without the baggage of knowing what has gone before. You are in a state of not-Self. And only from that state can you truly discover anew who you really are. This can be quite a complex thing to understand. Let's give it proper attention on another day, shall we? We'll talk about this again when we discuss "Free Will".

Z: Okay. So then to come back to this discussion, we were saying that there is the Oneness at the top, which is God. And then God creates the many and in the minds of the many are many more and so on and so on all the way down to us here on earth who are a great many and who have the freedom to believe that we are not One. We can believe that we are separate and individual. And we did this to ourselves on purpose so that we could discover something about ourselves and re-create ourselves. Right?

J-D: Good. Yes, that's the first half of the story. You now have a rough sketch of how the structure works from the top down. But until you see it the other way round, from the bottom up, you won't really get it. So let's tell that other half of the story.

The thing to understand is that each of you on Planet Earth are playing out the roles you have chosen for yourselves. You play massive long-running games that span many lifetimes so that you can experience yourself as an individual. As separate from each other. As "not-One". And that is what life on earth is like. But every game must come to an end at some point. Eventually you will say to yourself, "*I have pretty much seen everything I want to see in this game*" and you will want to take your self-knowledge and go and play some other game. Maybe you'll want to play a game with less constrictive rules next time, for example. Anyway, the point at which you decide you have seen what you want to see here is the point at which you usually choose to begin your ascension process. Even though I don't really like the word "ascension" I will use it as it is the commonly accepted term.

Z: What a minute. Sorry to interrupt. But why don't you like that word?

J-D: Ascension? For the same reason I don't like "Higher-Self". The word "ascension" implies an upwards movement and you don't go "up". You don't actually go anywhere at all. You heal, you re-integrate all aspects of yourself, you become more whole and at one with yourself and then you begin to remember who you really are. Once you have done this, you are free to take your consciousness "inwards" to other densities or sideways to other time-lines or wherever else you like. You see, essentially what you are doing in the ascension process is pulling yourself inward towards yourself. You need to do this if you are going to remove yourself from this system of reality so that you can go and play in other realities.

Right now there are quite a number of people on Planet Earth who are engaged with their ascension paths. They are finishing off with the game and its rules at this level of reality and they are preparing to become a greater version of themselves. You are doing this yourself and probably everyone reading this work is doing this too. Those who are not on an ascension path will resonate very poorly with what is written here. They will probably feel this is all nonsense. So I can state with some confidence that you and your readers are all busy "ascending".

Z: And what then? What happens when we have ascended?

J-D: It is not a single-step process, of course. As you "ascend", so you awaken to greater and greater realizations of self. You begin to see through the illusions of this world that keep people trapped in the game. You begin to find true love and compassion for yourself and for all others. You begin to release the fear and pain that you have created inside yourself across your many lifetimes. You cease thinking of yourself as a victim to your experiences and then understand with greater and greater clarity that you are the creator of your own experiences. And as this becomes true for you, so your experiences will corroborate your beliefs. In short, you become a creator-being and cease being a lonely, lost victim.

Z: Ah. But what about the whole Oneness thing?

J-D: Good question. You see, as long as your view of yourself resides primarily in your ego – this is the aspect of Self that sees itself as "separate" and as that which must do all the doing - then you are not co-creating with the rest of All That Is. You are not in alignment with the greatest forces in all creation. When you begin to create from your heart and in Love then you move towards Oneness. Then All That Is co-creates with you. It is a profound difference. You, on your own, against everyone else compared with you, in harmony with all of creation. In the latter state you will find your life awash with miracles and magic. In the former state you get the kind of reality espoused by Murphy's Law: you get to be a person on your own slogging it out against all the odds and then indeed, anything that can go wrong usually will. So the choice is yours. You can remain attached to being separate and alone and keep playing the games of density or you can release this; you can decide to see all others as another aspect of self. You can choose Oneness and love and then you will begin to "ascend".

Z: What is the ascension process like?

J-D: In short it is a process in which you become more and more the creator of your own reality. What that means is that each person will create their own path and their own experiences of it. Each will walk a unique path. So it will be impossible to describe in detail what everyone will choose. But we certainly can speak to some of the more general experiences and these understandings will unfold for you from many different perspectives throughout the conversations that follow. For now, all I really want you to understand is that you and others like you are now experiencing your own ascension. It is not incorrect to say that you are becoming your own Higher-Self.

Z: Oh wow. I am sort of moving up a level.

J-D: Yes. There aren't really strictly defined "levels" like floors in a tall building but it is less complex if you think of it like that for now. As you contemplate this, can you see that it is so that God created your God-Self who, essentially, created your Inner-Self, who created you and your other incarnations. But, by living the life you are living, by making the choices you are making and holding the beliefs you are holding, you are re-creating yourself as you go. And when you re-create yourself, you re-create a part of your Inner-Self. You and your Inner-Self are engaged in a process of self creation. So it could be said that you are your Inner-Self engaged in the experience of your life. So… if you follow all this… can you see that your Inner-Self creates you and then you create your Inner-Self? That we are one being in a constant process of self-creation?

Z: Okay, WOW! That is awesome! But uhh… why does it mostly not feel like this. I mean, I think of you as being quite powerful and amazing and stuff and I am often quite confused or in pain or filled with feelings of being lonely and lost.

J-D: It comes down to the fact that you didn't come to live on earth only to immediately ascend. You came here to BE here. To experience yourself as being a separate individual. So, in that state, you DO often feel these lonely, lost and disempowered sensations. It is, unfortunately, a part of the turf, it seems. It is only when you are essentially done with the game that you begin to remember that you are actually a powerful creator being. Then, as you begin to remember this, so you begin to release some of the separateness and then you truly begin to create yourself AS your Inner-Self.

Z: So, at every level we are one being creating our Self through the experience of many.

J-D: Yes! As above, so below. And as below, so above. So you co-create yourself. In so doing you co-create your Inner-Self. Who is, essentially, engaged in the process of co-creation of your God-Self. And the God-Selves are all essentially in the process of the co-creation of God. You see? Extend this far enough and you understand that we are all One. There ultimately is just One of us creating the many so as to experience Itself in a myriad new ways and to re-create Itself. The many create many more and so on and so on, without end, for all infinity. And the very smallest and youngest of the many creates itself and in so doing re-creates the All. Like a fractal that you can eternally zoom into or out of in all directions. Like a hologram of which the very smallest particle includes the whole image.

Z: That's so beautiful!

J-D: I'm glad you like it. It is my perspective and my truth. There are many other perspectives. And there will be perspectives that do not agree with mine at all but that are equally valid.

Z: Uh. Waitaminit. How can your truth and someone else's truth both be true and yet not agree?

J-D: Easily. All truths are true and no two truths are identical. But I can see how this might seem odd to you. In due course, when the time is right, I will ask you to speak to our soul-partner (and your Spirit-Guide),8, on this subject. You can call that chat, "What is truth?" Ask him about it okay?

Z: Okay.

J-D: So now. If we can move along… I will say to you that I am YOUR personal God-Self. I hold within myself all the other versions of Self that you are, and will be. You are my creation and… as explained… I am yours. You are a part of a much, much greater Being and we together are intensely involved in the process of constant Self creation. From my perspective I will say that this is true for everyone on planet earth.

Z: I am an incarnation of you?

J-D: Yes, if you wish to see it like that. Or you could also say I am experiencing one of my creations of myself AS you.

Z: And, besides me, how many other incarnations of Joy-Divine are there on planet earth right now?

J-D: This is a far more complex question than you have intended it to be. I will have to deal with it by saying that, from the perspective that you are asking this question, there is only one human incarnation of Joy-Divine on planet earth in this space/time nexus within which you exist. There is only you. It is not congruent with our soul-purpose to have a great many incarnations, as some of the other Bright Ones have had.

Z: Cool. But now you have totally blown my mind with all this and I don't know what else to ask.

J-D: (He laughs) That is good. I think we should anyway end this session now so that you can rest your poor blown mind. But you now already have the beginnings of a structure for where we are going to go from here. You can pick it up next time with me when we begin to talk about the nature of Oneness.

Z: Awesome. I just want to say: isn't it weird that actually this conversation is really just me talking to myself?

J-D: Yes. But if you understand it correctly, then the whole universe is just one small side-conversation that God is having with Itself. So… not so strange really.

Z: A SMALL SIDE CONVERSATION! Isn't the universe All That Is?

J-D: Hardly. I know it looks pretty big to you, but it is just a small part of one reality construct. There are an infinite number of other such constructs. And all the realities together make up just one way for God to express Itself. There are an infinite number of others.

Z: Wowzer. Now you really are blowing my mind. I can see that there is A LOT still to talk about. Thank you so much for talking to me today. I feel such love and gratitude.

J-D: Good feelings those. I feel the same. But, as the song goes, "*You ain't seen nothing yet!*" We're still going to have lots of fun with this. We'll talk again soon.

* * * * *

Chapter 3. The Veil of Unknowing
A Conversation with Joy-Divine

Zingdad: J-D, you said in our last chat that we should talk about Oneness.

Joy-Divine: Hello. Yes. I want to more-or-less prove to you that All is One and then, when we've established that, I want to talk about what that means for you.

Z: Great. Why "*more-or-less*" prove it?

J-D: Well, let me first tell you about the reality you inhabit and then I shall get to my main arguments. Primarily your reality was created for the purpose of experiencing individuality. In order for this to be possible, a consciousness-construct was set in place to sort-of "filter" the information that might be available to you. This has often been called "the veil" or more specifically "the Veil of Unknowing" and I am happy to keep using that term. What the Veil essentially does is to guarantee that you cannot prove that you are One. Anything that approaches true, irrefutable proof will always come with enough cause for doubt that each individual will simply have to make up their own mind.

Z: Okay. Doesn't the veil also hide other knowing and info from us though?

J-D: No. All it does is hide from you your essential Oneness with All That Is. But you need to think about this for a moment. If All is truly ONE... if the most essential truth about everything is its inherent Oneness... and if the Veil hides the Oneness from you, then I'm sure you can logically see that the Veil will hide the most essential nature of EVERYTHING from you. It will mean that you cannot know the deepest truth about anything at all. Because, as you approach the deepest truth of anything you'd approach proof that All is ONE. And the Veil forbids this. Do you see the circular nature of the problem? The essential nature of EVERYTHING is that it is all One with everything else. But this is hidden from you.

Z: So you mean we can't know the true nature of anything?

J-D: It's a fact. What is remarkable to me is how few people on earth are concerned about the fact that nothing is known down to its root. Nowhere can you look and say, "*We really understand this or that thing and can therefore build upon a solid foundation of knowledge*". You can know about the surface, about the characteristics or the effect, but you cannot know about the true cause.

Z: Uh. I'm not sure that I know this to be true. Our science has surely gotten to the root of SOMETHING?

J-D: Alright. I'll go there with you. What is your world, and all the animals and plants and so forth, made of?

Z: Matter.

J-D: What is matter made of?

Z: Um. Molecules. And they are made of atoms. And they are made of sub-atomic particles.

J-D: Good. Carry on. What are sub-atomic particles made of?

Z: Energy, I think?

J-D: And what is the nature of that energy?

Z: Uhh...

J-D: What is this energy made of? Where does it come from? Was it created? If so, when and how? And if it wasn't created, how does it come to be?

Z: I don't know. I don't know any of those answers.

J-D: Well don't feel bad. Neither do your scientists. They have a few postulates and theories but other than simple observations about energies, your planet's science knows next to nothing about the nature of this energy that they say all things are created of. And if EVERYTHING you can observe and engage with, including your own body, is made of this energy about which you know nothing then, it can be seen that you really know nothing about everything!

All but the most enlightened of scientists generally make the mistake of saying that there is nothing, but that which can be observed... there is nothing but the material world. But the problem is that the material world does not exist! It is a function of this ephemeral world of rapidly shifting energy. And this energy is an impenetrable mystery to those self-same scientists. They do not know what it is, where it comes from or really anything about it other than a few observations of how it might behave under particular circumstances – and even there they have mystifying incongruities. So they fail utterly to comprehend or explain the very root of that which they say is real.

It is my contention that you will never truly begin to comprehend the fundamental energy of the universe without first understanding the nature of consciousness and, specifically, that all energy and matter that springs forth from consciousness is one single thing.

Z: All matter is the same thing?

J-D: As above, so below, and as below, so above. Everything is ONE. This is mirrored everywhere you look if you only know how to see. But the problem for you is that you are restricted from being able to prove this by the Veil.

Z: Okay, that's pretty interesting to me and I want to discuss this with you but before I do, could you perhaps give me another example or two of things that we only know the surface of? Other than energy and matter, I mean.

J-D: Sure. I could give you countless examples. I could use the example of anything you could name to prove it to you. But some examples are more time-consuming than others. So I shall choose a simple one: light. You know next to nothing about it. And yet it is actually the most fundamental constituent of your reality. You know how fast it goes, but not why. You know it has some highly curious properties – for example that it seems to be have both a particulate and a wave-like nature . And so on. But you don't understand much about it beyond that. And why, for example, is the speed of light the speed limit for other things? You can, if you try, describe these phenomena, but you have very little clue as to how it comes to be as it is. Until you understand that light (or rather all electromagnetic radiation) is really just a function of the particular dimension in which you reside, you will remain baffled by it. But you need to be willing to concede that your whole reality is just one little piece of the picture. Your whole universe is like a single key on one piano keyboard in an orchestra of an infinite number of musical instruments. And all those instruments together are playing the same ONE symphony.

And here's another example of something which your scientists don't really understand, another fundamental force of your reality: gravity. It is a constant force upon your body. Not a waking second goes by that you are not affected by it. But you haven't a clue about how it works.

Z: Wait a minute? Isn't it due to the warp in space time caused by mass or some such?

J-D: No. I didn't say there were no THEORIES about this. There are plenty of those. But they all have some flaws in them and remain unproven. Go read about it, if you like. Your science does not know where gravity comes from, why it is there or how it propagates. The theory that comes closest is a new one that presupposes the existence of other dimensions. But they will need to greatly expand their view of what those other dimensions might be before it will all begin to come together.

I'll give you another example. More philosophical than scientific, maybe. It is this: what TRULY are YOU?

Z: Let's see… I am a human?

J-D: And if you had another incarnation as something other than that which you would currently define as a human? Would you cease to be you?

Z: No. Then I'd be a Zorg from the planet Zug. Or whatever (laughs). Okay I get your point. What am I REALLY? I mean I know I HAVE a body. But I am not my body. How about I use Descartes famous quote: "*I think, therefore I am*". And then I will say that I am my thoughts. How about that?

J-D: That's cute. But wrong. What happens if you stop thinking? Do you stop existing? For example – one of the goals of meditation is to cease all thought. What happens if you attain that goal? Do you pop out of existence?

Z: Hmm. No. I know that it is true for me and others that such moments bring with them the most amazing expansion of consciousness.

J-D: Ahh. That IS interesting then. We must explore this further some other time… the less you DO and TRY and THINK, the more your consciousness expands. This is because DOing and BEing are opposite states. And the nature of your BEing is… consciousness.

Z: Ah. So then the answer to your question is… I am consciousness?

J-D: Yes. But then, what is consciousness? I mean every single human being is this (or at the least HAS it), but can you explain it? Can you tell me where to find it?

Z: I'm not sure. Could it not be argued that consciousness is produced by the brain?

J-D: Not very convincingly. Some have tried but there are always holes in the theory. For example: what happens when someone is declared "brain dead" and then, by some miracle, later they are resuscitated? How do you explain the fact that they sometimes recall events occurring in their consciousness at a time when the brain had ceased to function? And, even more amazingly, those who have experienced this often tell of events that didn't even occur in the proximity of the body housing the apparently dead brain. And what of the fact that in various neurosurgical operations on various people, pretty much every part of the brain has been removed. This one loses eye-sight. That one certain emotional responses. And so on. But everyone retains their consciousness. Unless the body dies, in which case they STILL have consciousness but, of course, you can usually no longer engage with them to determine this.

So, no, there are too many anomalies for consciousness to arise from the brain. The point is this: your most essential and fundamental attribute, your very consciousness, is something that you know nothing about at all. Why? My contention is that this is because your consciousness is the very stuff of the Oneness. But people just accept that they know nothing about themselves and go about paying the mortgage, watching sport and news on the television and arguing vociferously about religion and politics. Or whatever else keeps them entertained enough so that they don't have to confront the fact that NOTHING is truly known. The miracle of the mystery should overwhelm you constantly. But it doesn't. You declare life to be boring and mundane. "*No miracles or mysteries in MY life*", you all say. But this is only because you mesmerise yourselves into not looking at ANYTHING deeply enough to see the unending mystery of EVERYTHING.

Now, I could go on and on with this because, literally in every direction you look, you run into an edge which is unexplained and undefined. Essentially what I am saying is that the simple directive of the Veil of Unknowing, that it should shield you from knowing the Oneness of All, has profound implications. It means you really know nothing about anything at all. And of course this effect doesn't only extend to that which is physically around you. It means that you cannot, beyond all doubt, prove the existence of God. Which is quite an amazing thought. The Prime Creator, which is in everything, contains everything, created everything and of which you are an inseparable part, cannot be proven to even exist! I'll tell you something: spirit beings that have not experienced this reality directly find it nearly impossible to believe that this effect has been achieved over here. Often they come and have a look, just to marvel. The deepest, most essential and most undeniable truth of all has been hidden in plain sight! What a wonder and a miracle!

Z: Are you sure it isn't possible to prove God's existence? I vaguely recall reading some philosophical treatise, which presented a set of proofs. Are none of them valid?

J-D: Let me answer it like this. If just one of those proofs were infallible then there would not be any clear-thinking atheists or agnostics on the planet. You'd show them the proof, they'd fail to find the inconsistency and they'd have to concede that there IS a God after all. And you can say what you like about atheists but amongst their number are some very clear, rational and logical thinkers. So my point stands. Despite some concerted effort by some very lucid spiritual philosophers over the ages of your history, not one person has ever been able to prove the existence of God beyond all doubt. Or even the existence of spirit. Which is bizarre. Every single one of you IS spirit and yet it is quite a reasonable and defensible position to claim that there is no spirit! In every direction you look, you will find a few steps of understanding based upon tried and tested hypotheses, followed by the fuzziness and darkness of ignorance. Nothing is known to its core. And if you don't know about the fundamentals you cannot REALLY claim to understand their effects. And THAT is all because you cannot know that you and everything else is all ONE.

Z: Phew! That's wild. So why would we do this to ourselves? Why would we choose to come here and be stupid for a number of lifetimes?

J-D: Oh no, not stupid. Just forgetful. This is a very large subject on its own and there are many ways this question can be answered. Time will not now permit me to do this justice. It will have to suffice for me to say that each and every spirit being that decided to manifest an incarnation here had a reason to do so. There is profound value to be found in this experience. But your perspective is, perforce, very limited. You can only see things from where you stand INSIDE of your reality. But I shall state, in my truth, that for the beings that are your "Inner-Selves", this experience is one of the most valuable that can possibly be had. It is possible to gain great understanding of the Self and to find profound healing if one manifests a set of incarnations here.

The very forgetting ITSELF is a wonderfully useful tool for self-discovery and healing.

Z: I know you don't want to dwell on this point now but could you please give me just the briefest explanation why?

J-D: Alright. Let me try a little story:

The Parable of The King and the Potion of Forgetfulness

Once there was a rich and powerful king of a vast kingdom. He was known to be quite wise and knowledgeable. One of his duties was to be the final judge and jury for all legal disputes in his land. But this was not something he enjoyed because he just didn't understand what it was like to be a poor, destitute, starving peasant. He could not understand some of the peasant's motivations and actions and felt, therefore, ill-equipped to pass judgement on them. But how would he come to truly understand the life of the peasant? His wizard had a suggestion. He would cast a spell on the king such that the king would forget absolutely everything he knew. Then they would dress the king in the clothes of a peasant and leave him somewhere with just a few coins in his purse. In a year's time the spell would lift itself and the king would remember who he was. Then, for a year, the king would have lived as a peasant so he would know what that life was like. The king agreed to this plan and so it was. He was dressed as a poor man and left under the influence of the spell at an inn. When he awoke he did not know who he was. Some locals took pity on him and helped him out for a day or two. But he didn't seem to have any practical skills with which to repay them. And he had a haughty attitude they did not like. So soon he was out on his own. Hungry and miserable. In his desperation he turned to theft. But he was caught and flung into jail.

Or was he?

Maybe instead he saw the kindness of the people to a stranger and decided to try to return their good favour? Maybe he found within himself the resourcefulness of a natural leader which, combined with a well-tuned and educated mind, allowed to him be valued and appreciated by all that he encountered. Maybe he became a celebrated leader anyway.

How will we ever know what happened to him? The only way, of course, is for the story to be played out and observed. And that is exactly the point. The king wanted to know about the experience of poverty but, by going though this experience of forgetfulness, the king would actually find out far more about who he really was. Not who he was set up to be by his circumstances, but rather his true, essential nature.

If we extend this metaphor and allow the king as many lifetimes of forgetfulness as he would like before he awakens HIMSELF to who he really is through a process of profound self-discovery, then this would be similar to what is happening to you on earth.

You have placed yourself under your own forgetfulness spell and you journey in the world of forgetting until you are ready to remember. And in this twilight world of forgetting, you discover the most amazing things about yourself and life and All That Is. And you remain there until you yourself discover and create your path out of there. And the path, really, is the discovery that All is One. That is what the Veil is hiding, so, logically, knowing that to be the truth is the path out. Not just knowing it intellectually of course; knowing it in your every thought, word and deed. Knowing it to the core of your being.

But we will have a good many opportunities for you to gain a far deeper understanding of this concept. For now, even though this is a very simplistic and somewhat flawed illustration, I'm sure you can see that there is value to be had from the Veil?

And something else to consider is that there is protection inherent in ignorance.

Z: There is?

J-D: Sure! The further up the dimensional ladder you move, the more powerfully you can create. The more powerful a creator-being you are, it stands to reason, the more powerfully you could potentially do harm. Let us hypothesise a very powerful creator being that has yet to deeply plumb its own nature. It has yet to discover what it is capable of and how it would react to various circumstances. But it has great power at its disposal. That would be like putting a child in charge of the world's munitions. So this does not happen. There are various ways in which this situation is resolved in various realities. But certainly one very powerful way is to allow such a being to go and test all its limits as an incarnated being in your reality behind the Veil. You see, if you do not know of your true power then you cannot express it! It is locked away from you. And that is a lovely fail-safe. Those abilities always derive from the Oneness. In other words, discovering that you are One with All is exactly the same thing as discovering your true, greatest, most magnificent nature. And, if you know that you are One with every other being, you will not desire to harm any other. Then it is the same thing as harming yourself.

Now, these are just two little illustrative sketches. Please understand that this doesn't even begin to represent all the perspectives of the value that can be obtained from going into this reality as you have. It is an amazing, wondrous system and to experience it is something beyond comparison. And the heart of this system is the Veil of Unknowing. In fact, this might come as a surprise, but another way to look at the Veil is that it is an agent of the Law of Free Will, or, as our esteemed colleagues of the Ra Material called it, the Law of Confusion.

Z: How is that?

J-D: To answer this fully we would have to get into other topics, such as your own creator nature, which we are not quite ready to address yet. But the gist is this: if you do not, and cannot, know What Is, then you have free choice as to what you might choose to believe. I mean seriously… you that dwell on earth have so many different religions, each one claiming for themselves absolute truth and damning all the others as out-right liars. And then each religion has so many schisms and sub-sects within it that one can never keep up with who really believes what. And that is just the organised religions. What of all the variations of agnostics and atheists? And then there are more and more people all the time that regard themselves as deeply spiritual but not religious. They look for their own truth in their heart. But each heart is different. So there are just more and more different "truths" all the time. And Every view slightly different! And if you take a minute to think about it – either everyone but those that agree precisely with you is cracked – or there really is a valid reason to believe almost anything under the sun.

And there is. It is this: if you combine the Veil with the fact that you create your own reality, then we get to the understanding that, firstly, you do not know that you create your reality. And secondly, as you believe, so you shall conceive. Which is just a pretty way of saying that you will always find more and more evidence for the stuff you believe to be true. And because YOU find evidence, you get re-affirmed in your belief. But because of the Veil you cannot prove that belief to anyone else. And since they too are just seeing more and more evidence for their beliefs… well… it becomes a recipe for disaster for the dogmatic. Anyone can see that there will be plenty of opportunity for conflict for anyone who wants to experience that! But that's not the point I wish to really make here. The point I wish to make is that you have the free will option to believe whatever you want about your reality. And, as you believe it, so you'll get evidence to prove yourself right to yourself. And, no matter what anyone else says, they will not be able to prove you wrong unless you are open to seeing things their way. It is nothing less than free will to believe anything you want. And to pretty much DO anything you want too. I mean there are human laws and societal norms which try to govern your activities but there are precious few God-made laws that stop you from doing whatever you want.

Z: Whoa! What about… like holy scriptures and so on. What about, "*Thou shalt not kill*"?

J-D: No. No disrespect to those rules. But they are man-made. If God made the law "*Thou shalt not kill*" then you would not be able to kill. Period. Either you would not be able to formulate the thought to kill someone else, or it would be physically impossible, as it is in higher dimensional realms. Where I am, it is totally and utterly impossible for a being to "cease to be". There is no death. From certain perspectives you could say we have a great deal less free will than you do.

Z: That's amazing. But can't you can create more powerfully than we can?

J-D: Yes. But we are constrained. I mean I can create very powerfully but I cannot create with the belief that I am not a part of the Oneness. Not unless I send a part of my consciousness to beyond the Veil. Which is exactly what I have done, of course.

Z: You have?

J-D: Yes. (smiles) You are it, remember.

Z: Oh right! (laughs)

So you are saying we have a lot of free will over here. And that means we have very few God-made laws.

J-D: Yes.

Z: What about the law of gravity, for example? Or the law of the speed of light?

J-D: Those are not laws. They are suggestions. You can beat gravity with a rocket. You can beat the speed of light with other, slightly more advanced, technology. If you believe in UFOs coming from other solar systems then you pretty much have to concede a belief in faster-than-light travel. I am saying, believe it or not, that this is not just possible but, technologically, not that far off. The speed limit set by light can be beaten and it is done so all the time by races only a little more advanced than your own. These are not God's laws. They are simply constructs of the mechanics of your reality.

Z: So do we have any great spiritual laws then?

J-D: Yes. How do you like this one: *"Thou shalt do as thou pleaseth but thou shalt get the the consequences-eth of thine choices-eth"*.

Z: (laughs) No, seriously?

J-D: (laughs) Imitation-archaic phrasing aside, I actually am serious. That is my humorous way of stating the law of free will.

You know in some places in the universe there is a curse that some beings fling at each other when they feel the other is doing wrong. They say, "May you get exactly what you are creating!"

This is interesting because there are other parts of the universe where beings offer each other a great benediction when they feel the other is doing great things. They then say, "May you get exactly what you are creating!"

Isn't that strange? Especially since there is really no point in wishing such a thing on anyone else because, of course, everyone ALWAYS gets exactly what they are creating. That's the point of Free-Will. You can create whatever you like. And you do so by making choices. The outcome is your life.

So you can do whatever you want, think whatever you want and believe whatever you want. These are your choices. But your choices will always create results and you will get precisely the results of your choices. That way you can see if you like what you are doing, thinking, believing and choosing. If you do, then you can continue to make more of the same choices and if you don't, then you can change your mind and make new choices. That's the law of free-will. There are other realities in which it is enacted much less than it is for you. But if you really want to know about the great laws that govern creation then you'll have to wait for another future conversation for that to be handled conclusively.

Z: Okay. But before we go on, please just remind me why the Law of Free Will is also called the Law of Confusion?

J-D: Ah. That will lead us nicely back to the main subject. The Law of Confusion was introduced to you by a channelled work called *The Law of One*, also known as *The Ra Material*, right?

Z: Right.

J-D: So let's see how the Veil, or the Law of Free Will, pertains to channelled messages. Firstly, anyone reading any channelled words CAN doubt that there is a spirit being speaking through the channeller, can they not? I mean there is nothing in such channelled words that cannot be dreamed up by a sufficiently creative imagination with a little thinking and a little effort, right?

Z: Yeah, I guess. I mean, for years after I first started to have intuitive conversations like this one, even I doubted what I was experiencing. I thought maybe I was engaged in some grand self-delusion. But I now have enough evidence that I am sure it is what it seems to be.

J-D: Is it not possible for you to doubt?

Z: Oh, of course it's possible. I mean I have masses of circumstantial evidence and synchronicities and what-not. But not one of those is incontrovertible proof.

J-D: Right. But if I am who I say I am, and if I am really speaking with you, do you not think it would be the simplest thing for me to give you absolute proof? For example: what if you and a friend got together and he wrote down a long string of random numbers on a piece of paper and then hid it in a box. I can very easily know what those numbers are and then simply pass them to you. Repeat this exercise on international television and that would be the end of all doubt. Right?

Z: Yes, right!

But we can't do that, can we?

J-D: Not without violating the Veil of Unknowing. And not without taking away from everyone on the planet their free-will right to doubt, and more importantly, their free-will right to create their own reality as they see fit. I mean, if you can prove that you are having and intuitive conversation with me and I can prove I have all kinds of amazing knowledge, then people would be silly not to stop searching for, and creating, their own truth. They'd just come to you and I for the truth. And that would negate the entire point of this whole reality you are living in.

Z: That's a really good explanation. I never thought of it like that. Thank you. But you still didn't explain the Law of Confusion.

J-D: I'm glad you are paying attention. I was just getting there. I am saying that the various spirit beings that might speak to earth people cannot take liberties with the Veil. We cannot give you direct information about anything which would conflict with the Veil and the law of Free Will. But you folks are desperate for both proof of these psychic phenomena and all kinds of personal advice and guidance which, were it given, would be in contravention of the Veil. So the spirit being that is being conversed with has some options. I take the approach of simply not discussing topics that would breach the Veil. You will notice that, in the past, when people have asked you to do personal "readings" or to get into facts and details of their own stories, beings like Adamu and I have chosen to rather talk about the "spiritual concept" or the underlying philosophy rather than go into those personal details. It is sometimes possible to talk about very personal and specific issues where the individual has already done the work but, as a rule, it is preferable to avoid these.

There are other beings that take a different approach. For reasons of their own, sometimes the spirit being and the channeller might decide they want to get into as much detail as possible. Such cases unfortunately often occur with channellers who desire to use this facility for personal gain or ego enhancement and, as such, become eager to prove that they are the "real deal". You are advised to use your utmost discretion when dealing with such ones. Their approach will be one of, "*Only I know the truth, not you and not anyone else.*" This is a potentially harmful stance to all concerned. It creates dependencies. Unfortunately that is often what such beings desire. They have not understood how this is harmful to their audience AND to themselves. But, be that as it may, in order to gain the credibility which they desire to support their contention that they are the only source of truth, they will often seek to make claims about the accuracy of their predictions and so forth. They will seek to gain information via phenomena like channelling which, due to the Veil, is simply not possible. If you were to do the research and see exactly what their track record really is (as opposed to what they claim it to be) you will find they often have a hit-rate which is no better than average probability. In other words they could have done equally well with random educated guesses. You see the Veil WILL SIMPLY NOT be breached. Certainly not like this in the name of pure self interest.

The same effect, unfortunately, also applies to channellers who are genuinely and earnestly trying to work out their doubts. First they begin to channel and it seems good to them. But then fear creeps in and they doubt. They wonder if maybe the whole thing is a huge self-deception.

Z: That's exactly where I was until quite recently.

J-D: Right. And what happened to you is what will happen to everyone in these circumstances. In an attempt to put your doubts to rest you demand proof. Solid, verifiable, incontrovertible PROOF. In such instances you risk finding more reason to doubt. You might invite interaction with a spirit being of relatively low vibration. Such a being may lead you on a merry dance but you will not get proof. If, on the other hand, you remain fixed on the idea of speaking to a being of higher vibration, then you will gently be coached to release your demand for proof and to rather learn to create the outcome you desire. The other option is that your own psyche might, as a result of your desire for proof, insert distortions into the material you are receiving.

Z: Why?

J-D: Because demanding proof of the truth from an agency outside of yourself is actually a kind of spiritual neurosis. There IS NO proof outside of yourself. Because your truth is within you. If you encounter "the truth", it is only "the truth" because your own inner knowingness approves of it. Otherwise it is just another story. As long as you are demanding that another being must create your truth for you, you are distorting your lens. And as long as you are full of fear and self-doubt, such that you do not trust yourself to formulate your own truth and find your own path and create your own reality, then your lens is dirty and your perceptions will be clouded.

So a rather interesting irony is set up:

Those who seek provable, verifiable facts from channellings will often end up getting messages which are, for one reason or another, quite obviously doubtable or outright wrong.

Those who seek to show that they are the legitimate source of all truth will often end up creating evidence showing that they are frauds.

Those who come from a position of doubt will find more reason to doubt.

And all this is a wonderful illustration of how the Law of Confusion applies to channelled messages. And it gives you some insight into how it might apply more generally. Essentially, if Free Will is to be observed, then your right to doubt cannot be taken away. Your right to see it another way cannot be taken away. Your right to create it differently cannot be taken away. Your right to make another choice cannot be taken away. There must always be a space for a little chaos and a little confusion.

If you look at it correctly then this is a wonderful and beautiful thing. This means that you always have options. You always have freedom. You can always express your will. Creativity can come into play in every situation. Miracles can happen. Magic can happen. Wonderment and delight can happen. You can get something other than the expected.

And this is essential. If everything were fixed and ordered and contained then there would be no point in trying to do anything: the outcome would be assured and there would be no challenge, no learning and no growth. Progression and life would cease.

So I would encourage you to embrace the mystery rather than despise it. It is a wondrous thing that nothing is ever absolutely certain and fixed and ordered and dead. Everything is always alive and changing and in flux and brimming with surprise and mystery.

But to come back to the point I was making… perhaps now you can see that endeavouring to concretise things, endeavouring to find proof for our words and demanding that they must be eternally TRUE, is counterproductive.

Z: Wow. Yes. So I guess I should finally give up on seeking proof, huh?

J-D: I would say anyone that wants to find proof is, by their desire, actually affirming that they doubt. That they believe it NOT to be the case. If, as I contend, you are the creator of your reality, then each sponsoring thought will result in evidence cropping up that is congruent with that thought. So not only does this illustrate the Law of Confusion, it also illustrates that you are the creator of your reality (which is another law). But, more about that later. We have progressed quite far on this topic already.

If I may return the train of thought to its tracks, then I have made the contention that there is a consciousness construct called the Veil of Unknowing, which is very much in evidence in your experiences (but of course it works so well that you can indeed doubt that it too exists, if you wish). The implications of this Veil are that the one most fundamental truth of all creation, that All is One, cannot now be proven beyond a doubt.

Z: But that means that all this stuff you have told me is simply one possible perspective just like any other? That all perspectives are equally valid?

J-D: Yes. Exactly. Never stand in judgement of another's beliefs or perspectives. Never assume yours are more valid than theirs. But what you can AND SHOULD do, is strive to refine or adjust your own perspectives and beliefs so that they optimally serve you. In my conversations with you I am going to provide you with my own understandings and perspectives. They are delivered with the sole intention that they should assist you to empower yourself, find yourself and remember who you REALLY are. And so, while I very much hope what you read here will be of use to you, you should enact your own truth in choosing to adopt or discard what is offered. If it resonates with you then you are finding truth here for yourself - you are actually creating your truth out of the information presented to you. If it does not resonate then you are not "wrong"; your truth is simply taking you in a different direction to mine.

There are many truth sets available to you and each will lead you on a different path and all are equally valid. Some will serve you for a while and then no longer be of value, as you and your circumstances change. Some will cause you pain and will eventually force you to release them. Others will serve you for an eternity of time as they bring you ever greater self-love and inner peace on your homeward journey to blissful union with the Oneness of All. My invitation to you and your readers is to have a good look at the perspectives offered to you in these conversations. I propose that they are of the latter type. They are a part of my service to this reality and are my contribution to the ascension process that is now occurring. But mostly I urge you to follow your heart and trust to your own truth and intuition above any words you would find anywhere… including these here.

Z: Got it. Thanks. But now I am confused. You said you were going to prove Oneness. But then all you did was to tell me that it can't be done because of the Veil. What gives?

J-D: I actually said "more-or-less prove", remember? And you asked me why "more-or-less". And that was my answer.

Z: Ah. Correct. So are we still getting our more-or-less proof?

J-D: Yes, you are. But this is a good spot for us to take a break. Please call this conversation, "The Veil of Unknowing". It is the first part of the topic, "What is Oneness". We'll continue from here in the next session.

Z: Okay awesome. So in the next session…?

J-D: In the next session we can move on from the understanding that there is a Veil in place which makes direct proof impossible. I will however make some good arguments to show that "All is One". Readers can each decide for themselves how close this comes to constituting proof. As usual I will not attempt to transgress the Veil.

Z: Okay, great See you in the next chapter!

* * * * *

Chapter 4. Scientific Proof of Oneness
A Conversation with Joy-Divine

Zingdad: J-D, can we pick it up in this session with the question: "Is there proof of Oneness"?

Joy-Divine: Hello my dear Zingdad. The point of the "Veil of Unknowing" discussion was really to say that, no, we will not be able to prove that All is One. Not in the sense that we will be able to make a statement that cannot be argued or refuted. But we will be able to make some very powerful arguments which will either resonate with the reader or not. Some will call these arguments "proof" in that it provides them with solid reason for what they already know to be true, others may decide to pick holes in my arguments and refute them and say they are NOT proof. Both of these will be valid positions and neither will exclude the other. Each reader will decide for themselves where their truth lies.

Z: Just a moment please. I'm not sure if I am happy with all this "your truth" and "my truth" and "all truths are valid" stuff. Doesn't the word TRUTH imply that it is TRUE? I mean true for everyone?

J-D: It might imply that to you. If it does, you are going to get very stuck very fast and you are going to find yourself in non-stop conflict with yourself, your life and others that you engage with.

I see you are struggling with this. We have already touched on this, but I will address it again.

Insisting that there is only one truth which must be valid for all perspectives is an insistence that you and everyone everywhere must all have the same perspective. Which clearly will not happen. And worse than that, insisting that there is only one truth means that there is no room for growth and change. You are, in effect, insisting that everyone and everything in the whole universe must all have exactly the same experience of life as you. And it's worse than that; you have found, have you not, that some things you believed very strongly to be true when you were younger have, given a little time and a little life's experience, become less true for you. Other things which were not true for you now are. This is growth. It happens to everyone. Now, if you are insisting that everyone everywhere must share the same one truth-set with you then you are actually insisting that everyone, including you, must cease all development and growth so that their perspective remains fixed exactly as it is! Clearly this cannot and will not happen. But those who are determined that is should be so, that they are right and all others must agree with them, find themselves getting very angry with the world around them for its "wrongness". They often feel they must fight with the whole world to "fix it" and make it "right" so that it will conform to their expectations. Which it never, ever will. Such beings create a world of pain and conflict for themselves which doesn't end until they themselves begin to loosen up and allow all others to express their own unique, individual truth.

You see, what you believe to be true is based upon your experiences and inputs and your thoughts about these. If you experience something then you believe that experience to be true. So, logically, if someone experiences something else then they will have a different belief. Now if two beings get together and talk discuss their beliefs about life with each other you will find some less mature soul will, as just outlined, want to fight with each other to attempt to force an agreement. More mature souls, on the other hand, will accept that there is a difference of truths. But it is the master that will understand that another perspective is a gift being offered to them. Ask yourself, "under what circumstances could BOTH of these things be true?" and you begin to think like a master. Then you begin to reach for transcendent truths that allow you a greater perspective than that which you have obtained from your own experiences. Then you obtain growth from not only your experiences but others too!

For example: the sky above you is blue. If I told you it was purple then how should you respond? Like an immature soul and tell me I am mad, deluded and wrong? Like a mature soul who might understand that I see things differently? Or like a master that might reach for a greater truth, that some skies are blue and some skies are purple, that maybe the sky is the colour it is as a result of its gaseous make-up and that I come from another planet with a different atmosphere. Logically then there must be all kinds of OTHER colours of sky. "How marvellous, how exciting!" the master will conclude. How much better than having an argument!

I very much do suggest, therefore, that coming to understand that which you believe to be true as "your truth". It is that which is true for you, for now. Nothing more. Be willing for your truth to change. Be open to the fact that other's truths are as true for them as yours is for you. You will find this to be quite a healthy psycho-spiritual position to take. It will allow you to be flexible when dealing with others who hold different perspectives from your own. And it will allow you to be flexible with yourself as you grow and inevitably discover that what you have held to be true no longer serves you. In this way you will enable growth with a minimum of pain. It will bring you greater peace and harmony if you take this position. And it will allow you to being to think like a master.

You will gain a far deeper insight into the whole subject of truth in due course when you introduce your readers to our beloved associate, the being called 8. He is very well suited indeed to such a conversation. But until then, for the sake of continuing this discussion, please accept that it is MY truth that each and every person has a different perspective; each holds a different set of things to be true.

Z: Okay. You have made a very persuasive case. So you are saying no-one's truth is better than anyone else's?

J-D: "Better"? That is a rather pointless value judgement. What I am saying is that anyone's truth is as valid as any other's if it serves them on the path they are travelling. What you need to consider is that your truth is the scaffolding upon which you build your reality. Some people's truths cause them much pain. Some other people's truths bring them a great sense of joy and a love for life. The reason I am here now having these conversations with you is this: I wish to impart a new truth set to you. It is a truth set which may be of great value to anyone who desires to ascend their consciousness, anyone who wishes to find self-love, love for All and inner-peace. I am here now in these conversations with you to offer my truth set as that which leads to unity consciousness, to wholeness, to love, to peace and ultimately to the greatest possible JOY. I think you will find that it offers you the "truth scaffolding" upon which you can build a reality which is very joyous indeed. You will come to discover in yourself a magnificent, beautiful, wondrous Self that is in a state of oneness and bliss with All That Is. A powerful creator being that is totally in harmony with the IS-ness… with God. I offer my truth as a gift to any who might read this. The deal is: you can take the gift or leave it as it suits you. You can even take the bits you like and leave the rest. Or you can take it, try it on for a while, see if you like it and discard it if you don't. Whatever you want to do with this gift of my truth is up to you and is fine by me. I contend, from my own vast, multi-dimensional experience, that the view I offer will promote an ascension path.

Yes, you can find your way to ascension via other paths. But what I offer IS the path of JOY. It is most certainly a happy path.

Z: Okay, thanks for that explanation. But before we pre-amble this to death perhaps we can get into the topic itself?

J-D: Exactly right. Let's do that. I said I was going to sort-of prove that God is One with All That Is, right?

Z: Right.

J-D: Well, to make an argument, it is often easiest to have a position to debate against. If I want to make the statement, "*God is One with All That Is*", then probably the most radically opposed position would be that of the atheist. As atheists deny the very existence of God, they therefore would not accept anything one might say about God. Right?

Z: Right. It can be quite hard to argue with an atheist.

J-D: That's right because, usually, atheists pride themselves on being very logical and rational. They don't go in for airy-fairy nonsense that can't be proven empirically. They claim that the universe can be explained without the need for a God and since there is no direct evidence for God, what the heck is everyone doing with all this religion nonsense? And their position, due to the Veil, is of course quite a reasonable one. If you insist that there is nothing beyond that which can be directly perceived by the senses then it certainly can seem as if spiritual beliefs are just superstitious nonsense.

Z: So you can't prove the Oneness of All to them, right?

J-D: Hold on. Not so fast. I have a lot of love and respect for rational people of the mind. The scientific method is a wonderful thing and has deepened the human experience immeasurably. I wouldn't want us to start a whole new level of the game only to desert all our atheist friends here in this level. So there is a little surprise in store for them. You see the Veil is, and has for a while now, been thinning.

Z: What does that mean – the Veil is thinning?

J-D: It means that it gradually becomes easier and easier to penetrate the mystery. It is slowly becoming more possible to discover that there IS in fact a God of which everyone and everything everywhere is an indivisible part.

Z: WHOA THERE! So what was all the stuff about the value of the Veil and how important it is? If it's such a hot idea why is it going away?

J-D: Good! Here's the answer: No matter how much you like a game and no matter how important a science experiment is, the process always comes to an end. At some point those engaged with it will say, "*We have got what we wanted from this, let's do something else*", right? Well that is a very, very rough paraphrase of the greater situation here. This game (or experiment) that is your reality is about to come to an end. But the high-order spirit beings that are involved with its creation and planning are very loving beings. They love you and, in fact they know that they ARE you. So, while it is ordained that the game must very shortly end, they desire to give you every opportunity to leave the game in the most joyful way possible. So they are encouraging everyone in the system to begin to wake up. So, as fantastically valuable a construct as the Veil is, it is also so that it is necessary for it to slowly become more transparent now. Over time it will just get thinner and thinner until you can see right through it.

Z: Hmm. I had noticed that it is getting progressively easier and easier for me to advance my own spiritual process. My own ascension. Does this mean that everyone is experiencing this?

J-D: No. Not everyone approaches things as you do. All perspectives are valid, remember. And so, there is of course nothing essentially WRONG with being an atheist. It is a perfectly reasonable, logical response to this reality. And an atheist, by definition, does not perceive himself to be engaged in some "spiritual path" or another. But the atheist will not be punished for taking a completely reasonable stand! Everyone MUST have the option to be able to choose to see the Oneness and so ascend to a higher level of reality. So, how do we offer this possibility to the atheist? Well, certainly, to those that base their atheism on the scientific method and empiricism, we have an answer. And what I was getting to was that this answer now becomes available as a result of the thinning of the Veil. You see there are no co-incidences. With the thinning of the Veil the awareness of the Oneness MUST now begin to penetrate into all those previously inexplicable areas. It means that those that ARE searching to understand the nature of matter, gravity and light (to name but three) will begin to find God and Oneness there.

Z: Really? How?

J-D: Well the first glimmerings have been there for a little while now. Physicists engaged in Quantum Mechanics are endeavouring to understand your reality by understanding the nature of matter and energy. I heartily recommend that you find a good book on Quantum Mechanics. Find something that will explain all this in lay-man's terms. Or research it on this wonderful tool called the Internet. You will find yourself stunned at the discoveries and their implications. I will give you one example: these physicists, in trying to explain why minute sub-atomic particles behave as they do, have come up with a theory which suggests that no quantum reaction can occur without there being a consciousness to observe it. In other words, consciousness precedes all matter. If you take the view that the first quantum reaction in your universe occurred at the very beginning of the "Big Bang", then essentially they are saying there must have been "someone" there before the Big Bang to observe that first reaction. If that isn't God then it must be something very like it, right?

Z: Interesting!

J-D: Very. And here is another one I want to tell you about. It is something called the zero-point energy field. This was proposed by Einstein and is now pretty generally accepted in scientific circles. Essentially this is a description of the "base state" of your universe. There is a field which is everywhere, all the time. It is a field of infinite energy. But you can't normally detect it because, well, it is everywhere all the time. You can therefore only detect this field by becoming aware of the variations in it.

Z: I don't understand?

J-D: Okay, how's this analogy: if the air around is dead still and at body temperature, are you likely to be aware of it?

Z: I guess not.

J-D: But if there is a breeze or if the air changes temperature then you will begin to sense it, won't you? You see? It is very hard indeed for you to detect something which has no variation because there is nothing to actually measure. Another example is if you were to sit blindfolded in a luxury motor car which moved quietly at constant speed. You would not be able to detect the motion of the vehicle until it accelerated, slowed down, changed direction or went over bumps in the road. Things that are constant cannot easily be perceived.

Z: Okay. I get that. Thanks.

J-D: So the zero-point energy field is a field of infinite energy that is everywhere all the time. It is there in equal quantity where there is the densest matter at the heart of a collapsed star as it is in the near-vacuum of deep space. It is everywhere and it is always infinite.

Z: But if this is infinite energy and it is everywhere then why can't we use this to power our cars and homes. Like instead of fossil fuels or whatever?

J-D: That is certainly possible. There is a small problem and a big problem that hinders you. The small problem is to discover an appropriate technology that will allow this and the much bigger problem is bringing this technology to the fore without having certain vested interests stopping you from doing so. But this is a big kettle of very contentious fish and I don't really want to spend a whole lot of time on it now. I am actually just wanting you to understand the concept so that I can make my point.

Z: Okay. So then you were saying there is this infinite energy field and it is everywhere all the time…

J-D: Right. Remember in our previous chat we discovered that all matter is actually just energy?

Z: I do.

J-D: Well what I want to say is that it will come to be proven that this energy, which makes up all the matter in your universe, comes from the infinite energy of the zero-point energy field. It is fluctuations (like waves or ripples) in this field that form the most basic building blocks of matter: sub-atomic particles.

The problem with this is that waves are not static. They move around. And they interfere with each other and cancel each other out.

Z: Why is that a problem?

J-D: Because it would happen so fast and so repetitively that no matter would come into being. Sub-atomic particles would appear then disappear. There wouldn't even be a single atom in the universe. All the matter that now already DOES exist in the form of your body, your planet and your universe would simply dissipate into chaos and revert to the energy of the zero-point field quite quickly.

Z: Why?

J-D: Because if matter is ultimately composed of waves of energy, then what is keeping those waves from dissipating? Can you see it? If the sub-atomic particles which together make up your body are made of waves, why do those waves not simply ripple away as waves do? Or why do the peaks and the troughs not simply cancel each other out and cause the matter of your body to dissipate out of existence? Instead of this happening, why does the matter of your body appear to remain constant?

What I am saying is that your scientists will come to understand the zero-point energy field such that it will be clear that all matter is essentially composed of complex inter-relations between fluctuations in that field. But they will be unable to understand why these fluctuations remain stable. *"If it is all just energy fluctuations, why do they not fall into chaos?"* will be the question. And it is apparent that they don't. Your physical body is one such energy system. And it is apparent to you that you maintain a degree of physical integrity. Your body continues to exist in the expected form from moment to moment without falling into chaos. So this might seem incongruous and confusing. But the beauty of this is in the solution: as I have said before, your theoretical physicists have already begun to talk in terms of consciousness. Well, consciousness is once again going to have to be invoked here. The one hypothesis that will resolve the problem and continue to make sense will be one which understands that the matter of your physical universe doesn't fly apart because there are blueprints for everything in your reality in a higher dimension. Quite literally this will suggest that there must be a "someone" who is creating (or imagining) every single element of your reality and holding this image (or blueprint) in their creative mind.

Z: So you are suggesting that this blue-print that exists in a higher dimension acts as a mould into which you can pour these sub-atomic particles?

J-D: No, that would not be the best analogy. It will need some more explaining before I can get to a good analogy. The first thing you need to understand is that these waves don't stand still. They flow endlessly onwards. So rather think of these blueprints as an impediment in a stream which causes an eddy in that stream. For example if you open a tap and watch the stream of water, and then put your finger in that stream, you can notice what happens to the stream after your finger. If you hold your finger still, there will be a "shape" to the flow of the water after your finger and that "shape" will remain fairly stable and constant. This is despite the fact that the material (the water) making up the shape is in constant flow. Do you follow this?

Z: Yes. That makes sense.

J-D: Well then let me apply that analogy. There are ripples in the zero-point energy field. These ripples cause sub-atomic particles to pop into your reality. At the most basic level a few simple blue-prints are created which cause these sub-atomic particles to move in such a way as to become entwined in a dance. Once bonded in such a way they form together particles such as electrons and protons that compose the atom. Certain sub-atomic particles, when entwined in one way, may cause an electron to form. Others, when entwined another way may cause a proton to form. It all has to do with the way these subatomic particles are caused to interrelate.

Z: That is quite difficult for me to visualise.

J-D: Yes. I am explaining things for which you have almost no frame of reference. If this REALLY interests you then you should first go and make a study of what your scientists are saying so that we have a grounding upon which we can build. I am simply using this to illustrate a philosophical point.

Z: Okay. Carry on please.

J-D: Thank you. The point is that, even at this most basic level of reality there is an interaction between two God-like things. The one is the infinite energy field which has been called the Zero-point energy field. The other is consciousness, which creates the moulds that cause the energy to form stable patterns which creates the illusion of the matter of your universe.

Z: Ah. So you are saying that, over time, for those who are avidly watching scientific developments, there will be evidence of God?

J-D: Certainly it will make them ask some very interesting questions! It will become ever more difficult not to conclude that consciousness exists independent of human brains.

Z: Okay, but now I am curious. What happens to the atoms so that they eventually become people and planets and stars and stuff?

J-D: Ah. This is a very long and complex story to get through. Seeing as it is not necessary to THIS discussion, as my point is already made, I will simply say that there are ever more complex blue-prints. So the first blue-prints make atomic particles. The next set uses the previous set to make atoms. Then molecules. Then more complex forms. Essentially I am saying that there are blue-prints, within blue-prints within blue-prints. The more basic a blue-print is, the more often it is re-used in other more complex blue-prints. Your body is a mind-boggling interplay of an astoundingly large number of blue-prints of all kinds of levels of complexity. The final, highest level of the blue-print is held by your body-spirit. But that too is another conversation for another day.

Z: Okay. I'll make a note to get to that. But for now I do see that you have made your point that an in-depth understanding of the matter which makes up our bodies and our reality is, as you say, an interaction between consciousness and an infinite energy field. Excellent! What's next?

J-D: Not so fast. I'm not quite done with this topic. There is another God-like understanding to be had out of all this.

Z: Okay, shoot.

J-D: Let's go back to the analogy of the stream of water. Remember I said that the stream flows past the "blue-print" and that makes a pattern?

Z: Yes.

J-D: Well that means that the pattern is static but the material that MAKES the pattern is not.

Z: Yes. The water flows on.

J-D: Right. So what does it mean to you if I say that the "stream" of the zero-point energy field passes through you. It does not reside within you. The stream of ripples flows constantly into and out of your body. The only reason there is a body there at all, is because your body is the place where there is a confluence of all the blue-prints. The blue prints are steady, the energy itself is not.

Z: Okay that is an odd thought. But respectfully... so what?

J-D: Ha! So what? I'll tell you "so what"! It means that there is no separation between your body and anything else in the universe. Your body and every other person and thing in your whole universe are all THE SAME THING.

Z: Wow!

J-D: Yes! Let's go back to the water analogy. If you held two different forms in the water stream, one below the other, and saw two different "shapes" of eddy in the water. You would see that the shapes are different but you would not think of them as different "things", would you?

Z: No. It's all just water, isn't it?

J-D: Right. And so there is the third God-like thing that will cause the scientifically-minded a spot of wonder: it will transpire that all things are one. Nothing that you can observe is separated from anything else. It's all just different patterns in the same one thing. And that same one thing flows endlessly and continuously through everything.

Z: Wow. That's actually quite beautiful.

J-D: As above, so below and as below, so above. You see, Zingdad? If you are willing to truly look you will see God in everything. But the Veil has made this quite difficult. And now the Veil is thinning and it becomes ever easier to truly see. I am saying it is now already possible to discern, but in very short order there are going to be headlines coming from the scientific community which are going to point these sorts of things out:

All is ONE.

Everything is completely and absolutely interconnected.

The Oneness is infinite and unending.

It is of infinite energy.

EVERYTHING is of consciousness.

Consciousness pervades all things everywhere.

Consciousness is greater than, and pre-exists, matter.

Z: Wow! Those are some pretty God-like statements. Pretty mystical stuff.

J-D: Yes. And this is what is already starting to come from Science. I am saying this will increase dramatically soon.

Z: Okay so… just for clarity. Are you saying the Zero-point energy field is God?

J-D: I am saying it is an indivisible PART of God. And, as with all indivisible parts, it cannot but fail to have many of the attributes of God. That is why, if you study it and understand it, you will begin to discern those attributes.

Z: Ah. And who creates all the blue-prints you talked about?

J-D: Various creator beings working at various levels of creation. You and everyone with you here on earth are engaged in holding many combined blue-prints. You just don't yet know it yet. But again, you and the creator beings of this reality are also indivisible parts of God.

Z: …and as with all indivisible parts we cannot fail to have some of the attributes of God, right?

J-D: Spot on! Is it not said that you are made in the image of God? What does that mean? That God has two arms and two legs and so on? No. That is to view the thing the wrong way round. It means that what God is can be seen reflected in what you are. You are consciousness. You are creators. You are infinite and immortal. You are ONE with everything else that is. And so on and so on.

Z: Sheesh! And this will come from Science?

J-D: No. Science will make it possible to see things this way, if you so choose. It will always also be possible to doubt and to try to see things another way.

Z: Okay. But would it not be better if we could just get to firm and incontrovertible PROOF that no-one can argue with?

J-D: Alright, you want to go there again. Let's go back to what I was saying earlier about there not being "one truth". I will touch on it again. It is something you MUST get used to if you wish to ascend your consciousness. There is no "one truth" about anything that will ever silence all other perspectives. Everything is created and, as such, is subject to re-creation or being created differently. So, as you go, you can see things in your reality that very much support a particular view – you can take this as evidence. And you can claim that view for yourself. You can say, "*It is so*". And then it is so… FOR YOU. You may say, "*It is my truth*". But someone else can be busy with something else and hold a different view. Neither of you are more right than the other. I have said that the truth you hold is the scaffolding upon which you build your reality. And in fact your "reality" is really just a reflection you hold of how you REALLY view yourself. So I will state it like this: Your truth is that which you use to create yourself. I will repeat that because I think you should remember it:

"Your truth is the tool you use to create yourself."

So, for example, if you are working on a truth that each person is separate from every other and everywhere is separation and division and it's a dog-eat-dog world… then that "truth" will cause you to create your reality in a particular way. You'll get lots of opportunity for conflict over resources and so on. And, because your reality is really just a mirror you hold up to show yourself what is going on inside you, it is all actually just inner-conflict that rages inside you.

Which is fine, if that is what you choose for yourself. Everyone on earth has done this and it is a very instructive and valuable process.

HOWEVER, I am telling you this: if you wish to ascend then you must be willing to see others who hold very different truths from your own as "another self". Another being that is doing what they should be doing in their own way. Because, as you ascend, you will eventually come to hold the truth that "all is One". But this is like saying, if you wish to be a human then you must come to hold the truth that you are a human. The ascension process IS the unification process.

Z: I didn't know that. You are saying it is impossible to ascend my consciousness without attaining unity consciousness?

J-D: If I have to be specific then I must admit that it is possible for you to ascend your consciousness a little bit from where you are without recognising that all is One. But only a little bit. And doing it that way is the long and difficult route. I am Joy-Divine, I would not recommend such a route to you. And if you do it that way you will quite soon come to a boundary where you will not be able to ascend any further until you are ready to accept that All is One. So why not choose the path of joy from the beginning? I am offering a path to you for your consideration. I am here offering you the invitation to evaluate the truths I am presenting. If you like them and find they serve you, then you will find a way to ascend your consciousness and it will occur with maximum joy and minimum pain.

The truths you hold take you in a particular direction. I am saying IN MY TRUTH, the most beautiful, joyous and loving path I can conceive of for you is the ascension path. And the most beautiful, joyous and loving way to travel that path is via the understanding that "all is One". This is a theme that will keep developing as we talk. I will go into it in greater depth when we talk about ascension. Right now I simply want to try to grasp the prickly nettle which is to get to the understanding that there never will be proof of anything such that it absolutely cannot be doubted or denied. It MUST be possible for new thoughts to be had. This is how beings create for themselves whatever variation of a reality they wish to explore. So, to come full-circle, I am saying that your scientists will find themselves presented with all kinds of interesting data about your physical universe. There will be many possible theoretical hypotheses to explain this data. I am saying a model which includes consciousness and the Oneness of All will not only be possible but will provide a highly satisfying hypothesis. It will make sense and the data will fit the model in a way that is simple and elegant. I am also saying that it will be possible to doubt that and to keep looking for other hypotheses. Some of these others will hold promise but, in order to make them work, the hypothesis will just keep requiring ever greater levels of complexity. Which is fine if you like complexity.

The bottom line here is this: for those who are of a highly analytical mind, those who are rigorously logical, rational and scientific by nature, those who have chosen to say they are atheists because there is no evidence for God - . I am saying now, for THOSE, there will be the opportunity to see God in the evidence. They will be able to follow the mathematical models and actually find evidence for a God which is One with All That Is.

Z: That's fantastic. When will this happen?

J-D: It is busy happening. It is busy unfolding as we speak in the minds and laboratories of the scientists of your planet. Some of this has already been reported on in scientific circles. More will come. But please listen carefully: the point is that everyone will be able to CHOOSE. If you choose to be open to it you will find more and more evidence of a unifying God. But if you are wishing to play another round of the same old duality game you may reject this and choose not to see it as proof. Everyone has free will. And if someone desires to keep their consciousness in duality they have every right to do so. If they will not see the light that is offered, then it will not touch them. And that is okay.

Z: Are they then lost?

J-D: NO! No one and nothing is ever lost! I will talk more about this when we talk about ascension. Right now I will just say that All is already ONE. It always was, always has been and always will be. You, in duality, are aspects of The One that have chosen to forget this. This was not "wrong" of you; it was what you were meant to do. And now that many of you are choosing to remember that you are One it does not make the rest that are NOT choosing to remember "wrong" either. You were never lost in duality even if it felt like that to you. People who do not take advantage of the opportunity to remember now will also not be lost. They will just remember at some other time when they are ready.

Z: Okay. So, I think I get it. A truth will be made available via science that there is a God who is One with All That Is. Then, as now, each individual will be able to choose to accept it or not. And there is no judgement either way. The difference is that holding this perspective will take you towards ascension while taking another perspective with allow you to remain in duality.

J-D: Yes. That is a good enough summary.

Z: But what about the non-scientific types? I mean there are very many people on earth who will not be touched by the rather rarefied theoretical constructs of Quantum Mechanics, right?

J-D: Correct. Way back in the beginning of this topic I said I was going to use the scientific/ rational/ atheist position as a vehicle to make my case. Next I am going to use the religious position. But that is enough for now. We'll take a break here and pick it up again in our next conversation which we shall call "Religious Proof of Oneness".

Z: I look forward to it...

* * * * *

Chapter 5. Religious Proof of Oneness
A Conversation with Joy-Divine

Zingdad: J-D, I take it we are not going to "prove" the Oneness of all beyond all doubt from the religious perspective, either?

Joy-Divine: No, you are right. It doesn't matter how one addresses this, people will always have the right and the ability to doubt or to choose other. This is very much NOT about silencing other views. This is about presenting a view which you and your readers can choose to accept if it resonates with your heart. I previously addressed it from the atheist/ scientific perspective, not because I in any way wish to attack or persuade such people. Not at all. Simply because one needs a starting point from which to make a cogent argument. And now I am going to do this again. I am going to stand in another place and make the same argument from this other perspective. This new perspective is that of organised religion. For my purposes, I will divide religions into two groups: those that see God as separate from the Self and those that see the Self as One with God. The latter group are already in agreement with the point I am making here so we can, for the purposes of this discourse, just let them be. So I will use the former belief as a starting position: the view that there IS a God but that God is separate from, or outside of, God's creation.

I would like to offer certain observations: if someone already believes in an omnipotent Supreme Creator being then I would make the following contention. Being omnipotent, the Supreme Creator can do whatever It likes, right?

Z: Umm. Just a minute please. I'm sure if I'm really happy with the "It" label for God.

J-D: Yes. I know. I am sorry. You have cultural associations that "It" is somehow inferior to Him or Her. Well I am afraid I am not going to pander to those associations. The Supreme Creator does not have a gender. It is way, WAY beyond such petty issues. It is both and neither and very much beyond gender. So, until there is a better word in the English language which signifies "*Him, Her and It and every other gender that could possibly be in all creation and all of these and none of them*", then I am going to be stuck with using "It". This is very much the opposite of being derogatory. Restricting God to one gender is far more derogatory in my view. So bear with me and please forgive me if it offends. Okay?

Z: Okay with me. But seeing as I have already interrupted and am busy nit-picking: what of the label "God". I mean, does that not imply one religious perspective? Should we not maybe say "Source" or… something less restrictive?

J-D: Ooooookay. Let's quickly deal with that. No name or label you might choose to come up with will ever suffice. A label is, by its very nature, reductive. It excludes everything that is not that. No label is ever going to do the job of describing God because God is everything and yet more than that. God is beyond complete comprehension and description. So we should probably just choose to be silent on the subject of God altogether because everything that you might say about God is a reduction of the truth. No names and no descriptions and no attempts to understand. But that would be silly. Surely we should at least TRY with what we have to comprehend God. Make a start and keep improving our comprehension as our abilities to comprehend increase? And since you on planet earth use language to communicate and develop your thoughts, we must find SOME label for God. If we disallow a label then we cannot speak of It. And if we come up with a descriptive term then that is even worse, as it is even more restrictive. So, in the interests of just allowing the conversation to happen, I simply choose the name that has the greatest resonance in the culture you currently inhabit. If I spoke of The Mighty Zeelagzog (or whatever invented name), you'd say "who?" So rather, if I start out by speaking of God, then you know of Whom I speak, even if I thereafter have to clarify what my view is of God. Which is EXACTLY what I am doing right now. If your view of God is that It is separate from the rest of us, then I am here telling you what my view of God is: which is that It is One with us and All That Is. So I will use the name "God" and over time you will come to understand what I mean by that name. If your reader prefers another term, then I humbly beg their latitude in this regard.

Z: Okay, got it. Thank you for the clarification and my apologies for the interruption. Can we please pick it up again where we left off?

J-D: Yes, certainly. I was making the observation that, if God is omnipotent, then God can do whatever It wills, right?

Z: Right.

J-D: So if such a being wanted to experience the world from your perspective, It could. In fact It could, if It wanted to, experience the world from the perspective of every single living being AT THE SAME TIME, could It not?

Z: Yes. I guess the word "omnipotence" pretty much means that you are not restricted. You can do anything. Including, I am sure, seeing everything from every perspective.

J-D: So then the only question would be IF God would desire this. Would God desire to see things exactly as you (and everyone else) does or would God desire to view Creation from "above" or from a "separate" position? I will answer this question like this: what is the very most loving perspective for God to take? What perspective would God hold that would give God the most love and compassion for you? Clearly, in order for God to REALLY understand you, God would need to be willing to experience life AS you. Otherwise God would stand outside of you and look at all your little foibles and fumbles and just see you as flawed and broken. But if God experiences the world through you, AS you, then certainly God can have nothing but compassion and love for you. So I present you with a choice: do you believe God is a loving Being or not? I would most strongly assert that God IS Love. And I present to you the simple truth that the most loving choice for God is that God does not see Itself as separate from you. But if God only chose to see things through your eyes, but still KNOW that It is God, then that would NOT be your perspective. Your perspective is EXACTLY the way it looks for you. I am saying that the most loving thing for God to do is to hold EXACTLY your perspective too. God therefore experiences the world through you, AS you! Even when you don't know about God's existence or believe in God or whatever. God is still in you. And in every other possible perspective. So God does not enter only into certain pious and "godly" perspectives when they are well behaved! No. That is conditional love. And I am saying God IS unconditional love.

Z: You are saying this. But can you prove it... that God loves us unconditionally.

J-D: Again I can only make a strong argument. You will believe what you want. But if you believe that God is omnipresent and omniscient then you are by definition agreeing with me.

Z: Huh? How?

J-D: Omnipresent means present at every point. There is nowhere where God is not. Including, obviously where you are. Now if you broaden your understanding of location you will understand that you are not just geographically at your present location, you are also spiritually at that location. You are spiritually where you are as a result of the beliefs and ideas you have about yourself, life and God. Well, God is omnipresent. This means God is ALSO at that exact location with you and everywhere else at every other location with every other being and thing in All That Is.

Z: Hmm. Good point.

J-D: And omniscient means "all knowing". Do you know what it is like to be a dog?

Z: No… not really.

J-D: But you have dogs living in your home with you. You love them like children. You observe everything they do and often study their interactions and processes with great interest. Why do you not know what it is like to be a dog?

Z: Because I am a human! I have no knowledge of ever having been a dog!

J-D: Ah ha! In order to TRULY know what it is like to be someone, you actually have to BE that someone. Otherwise you only know something ABOUT that being. Now it is the same with God. If God is truly omniscient, then God cannot only know about you. If God observes you from outside then God will never really know what it is like to BE you. So instead God does that: God IS you.

Z: But… isn't that a ridiculously egotistical position to take - that I am God? I mean God is so great and...

J-D: No. It can't be egotistical to claim for yourself what you are claiming for everyone else. In fact I am claiming this same thing for every animal, plant, insect, stone, molecule, atom… you get the picture. From this perspective, I am saying you are as great as the sun and you are as great as an ant. How does that sound like egotism? It doesn't make you either greater or lesser. But it does make God MUCH greater.

Z: How's that?

J-D: Obviously a God of infinite perspectives who is everywhere and knows everything and is of infinite power and ability is greater than a God who only hold some perspectives and can only live outside of you until you do certain "good and holy" things.

Z: Hmm. Another good argument.

J-D: So I present you with a conundrum. If God is omnipotent AND if God is love, then it would seem God MUST be One with you. And, omniscience and omnipresence make the case that that indeed this is so. So, do you want to give up on these? Do you want to say that God is not omnipotent, is not love, is not omniscient and is not omnipresent? Or do you want to accept that God is One with All… including you yourself and each of your readers, of course?

Z: I'm sure there must be other arguments to be made.

J-D: You're right! There are always other arguments because there is always room to doubt or to create another view. That is your free-will choice coming into play. And if that is the direction your heart is leading you then you must, of course, follow your own truth. I am not here to tell you what you your truth must be I am here to tell you what my truth is. I make my case and I support it. Then you can decide.

Z: No, wait a minute. What I want to get at is that you have made quite a strong case that God holds all perspectives. I can agree that this might mean that God is able to know exactly what it is like to be me and have experienced things exactly as I did and all that stuff. But that is not the same thing as saying that God is One with me?

J-D: How is it not?

Z: Well, umm… what if god sort-of piggy backed with me in my mind… you know?

J-D: No. Either God IS you experiencing your life exactly as you are experiencing it or God's experience of your life is different from yours. You can't have it both ways. No matter how small the difference ANY separation at all would break the rules of omniscience and omnipresence. But, as I say, we can keep riding this pony round and round finding little points to debate if we want to.

Z: No, I can see that. I accept what you say. It DOES resonate in my heart too. But there is something that I can't quite figure out: Why is God doing this? This seems like an awfully elaborate thing to do… to create this whole universe and fill it with who knows how many trillions of particles of Yourself who, none of them, know that they are You. Why go to all that effort? What is it all for?

J-D: Remember the parable in Chapter 3? The one about the king who drank the potion of forgetfulness? Well, it's a bit like that. God is engaged with an endless process of self-creation and self-discovery.

"How would it be if I was like THIS?" is the question which creates a new being… or a whole new universe. The journey into forgetting which happens here in this reality is one possible means of self-discovery.

"How would it be if I did not know who or what I really was?" leads to any number of realities. This is one of them. The reality is the question. You, each of you, are one possible answer.

"I am what happens to God under THESE conditions," is the answer that you are busy returning.

Z: Okay… so I am One with God and we all are. And we are engaged in a journey of self-discovery. By engaging in my own personal journey of self-discovery I bring more self-knowledge to the All.

J-D: Good! Yes! If you would like to discover God then the best place to begin is by discovering yourself.

Z: Hmm. I follow the logic but… That seems awfully… I mean… won't some people find that a bit blasphemous?

J-D: Oh, assuredly! But then there are those that will find the very notion of this conversation blasphemous. Look hard enough and you'll find someone who will label just being happy as blasphemous. So I cannot concern myself with what others will choose to think or believe. For myself, I find the whole concept of blasphemy to be without meaning. It is ridiculous to think that you are capable of offending God or hurting God's feelings. You most certainly CAN hold beliefs and opinions that can hurt YOU though. And holding hateful thoughts about God, for example, will do that. But, given enough time and a little loving guidance, all beings eventually come to decide that they don't like hurting themselves and then they stop doing this and choose something more constructive instead. Something that brings them peace, love and joy. And loving God will certainly do THAT. God knows this. God sees you as you truly are. You cannot do or say some momentary little thing that could offend God. God is bigger than that.

Z: So what then is blasphemy? If God cannot be offended why do we even have this word?

J-D: The notion of blasphemy is a fiction used by some to control others via fear. It dates back to the most ancient times when shamans and witch-doctors would tell the tribe that they had to behave in certain ways or the gods would be unhappy and then there would be a poor harvest…

or some similar notion. This is exactly the same idea that is presented to you in your society by religious authorities who demand that you think, believe and act a certain way and only say certain approved things. If you step outside of the bounds they set for you then, they tell you, you will displease God who will then make your life hard or even smite you with pestilence and cause you to die. And then, of course, will make you to be tormented with agony for an eternity. It is the same story of manipulation and control all over again. The only difference is that the newer religions are maybe a little more cruel and violent in their imagined punishment for those that don't do as they demand. But no matter. It is all equally erroneous. God does not create narrow rules for you to follow. God gives you free will instead. God is not a petulant child to throw a tantrum when you take up the offer of free will. God is not a vindictive, cruel sadist to hurt you for making very human, very normal errors in judgement. You hurt yourself over these errors and will, absolutely guaranteed without fail come to make better decisions. So what would be the point of punishing you? Punishment does not teach you anything. Letting you get EXACTLY what you have created is what teaches you. God is certainly not unobservant, ignorant or unintelligent. God will not do what does not work.

The entire notion of blasphemy and divine punishment is utterly without merit.

God is One with you and God is beyond the desire to hate or punish Itself.

Z: Alright. I am ready to accept that. So then clearly it isn't a blasphemous thought to think that the best place to discover God is to look inside my own heart.

J-D: It certainly isn't! I'll remind you of one of my old favourites again: is it not said that you are made in the image of God? Is this not another way of saying, "*If you want to see an image of God… then look at yourself!*"

Z: Ah. Yes. I suppose that is so.

J-D: Again. I don't mean just your physical body. I mean that which you really ARE. Your truest, deepest essence. And if this is so then it follows that striving to truly, deeply comprehend your own deepest essence IS striving to know God.

Z: Ah! That makes sense. But we are all God. I mean everything is. So why can I not begin discovering God by looking around me at another person or at nature or something.

J-D: You could try that. And it would work to the degree that observing what is around you helped you to find greater comprehension of yourself. You see you cannot understand something in another if you have not seen it in yourself first - it will just puzzle you.

"How can they be that way?" you might ask yourself as you walk away shaking your head. If, however, you have seen this thing in yourself then you will be able to empathise with this other. You will give them a gift of your comprehension that may even help them to understand themselves too. So self-discovery is the key. And self-love is the door opening. And this is the journey for which you were created. You see, not only is God looking out at the world through your eyes but… by looking inwards from your perspective, God is looking at Itself. And so it is that you gift God with a new perspective of Itself whenever you discover a little more about yourself.

Z: Hey, that's pretty cool! It means God is in a constant process of Self-creation and Self-discovery as a result of all these processes all of us are engaged with.

J-D: Yes! We are God discovering Itself.

Z: All of us altogether are engaged in the same great work then?

J-D: Yes. Even the aspects of God that are doing that which seems to be the worst, darkest things. Even they are creating an opportunity for Self-discovery. They do this directly through their own experiences as they grow and discover themselves and also indirectly because they offer light-oriented ones the opportunity to define themselves and discover themselves in opposition to the darkness. If there were no great and powerful enemy, you would never have the opportunity to discover that you are courageous, that you will stand up and do the right thing despite the odds. If there were no one doing wrong how would you decide to do right? And so on. The dark ones are just as valuable to the greater process as the light ones. And if you are playing a dark game then the joy to be had out of changing course and returning to the light is sublime. And of course there really is no such thing as "dark ones" or "light ones". Not really. You all hold both of those states within yourselves. You have all, at some point in your incarnational story and even at some point in this life, done some very unloving things and been to a "dark" place. And everyone, no matter how "dark", will at some point turn around and return to the light. If not in this lifetime then at some future point. I tell you ALL IS ONE. And we are all engaged, each in our own way, in the process of the discovery of who we really are. And in so doing we are in a process of constant creation. And this is our service to God

Z: That is pleasing to me to think. Thank you for that awesome perspective. But there remains one last obstacle to me accepting your premise that All is One. It is a belief that would seem to me to mean that there is no good and evil, no right and no wrong. That we can just do whatever we want, however we want to whoever we want and that all things will just be acceptable to God. And that doesn't sit right with me. This "All Is One" thing seems to lead to a rather amoral stance.

J-D: Only because you have misunderstood it. I want to take a break here. I feel I have addressed the question in that I have made a case for God being One with All when viewed from the religious perspective. You are now asking the perfect question to lead me directly to the next topic, "The Implications of the Oneness". You have hit on an important issue which is the question of morality and rules for living. You have made an incorrect assumption, though, which I would like to correct. But all this is in the next chapter...

* * * * *

Chapter 6. Implications of the Oneness
A Conversation with Joy-Divine

Zingdad: Hi J-D, I know we said that we were going to talk about the moral implications of the Oneness but there are a few questions that I'd like to ask first.

For starters: you have explained how we might come to see that "all is One" from the two perspectives of science and religion. But are there not a few other perspectives from which we could look at this?

Joy-Divine: Hello Zingdad. Yes. There certainly are a number of different and equally valid perspectives from which this might be addressed. I think, for the people living on your planet right now, there are very nearly 7 billion different valid perspectives.

Z: What? But that is as many people as there are! Oh. Right. I get it. Each person has their own unique perspective and each person's perspective is valid.

J-D: That's right. But you see we don't need to debate this from all 7 billion different perspectives because we are not trying to argue with people. We are not trying to convince anyone of anything. The only reason I used the two perspectives I did is that they are relatively prevalent and understood positions in the society you now live in. I simply used them as a framework from which to make my case.

Z: Okay. I understand. But I'm afraid that brings me to another question. If you aren't trying to convince anybody of anything, then what ARE you trying to do? I mean why are you having these conversations with me?

J-D: Ha! Let me first ask you what YOU are trying to do? Why are YOU having these conversations with ME?

Z: Well... I don't know really. It all started a few years ago when I was trying to find some answers to the questions that bothered me. There was so much about this world and this reality that really made no sense to me. I had so much inner pain and conflict and stuff that I was in a bit of a mess. And then, somehow, in my confusion and pain, I managed to find a way to talk to 8. I started to get some answers. And then I started to talk to Adamu and other beings and the stuff I received was just unbelievably helpful. As I worked with it, it brought me a great deal of inner-peace and facilitated healing and growth. I learned to trust and love the process. And it just keeps getting better. It seems the more I grow the more I am able to receive. So... I guess the answer to your question is that I am just trying to heal myself, trying to love myself, trying to discover who I really am and who God really is and trying to find and fulfil my soul purpose... that kind of thing. That's my answer. What is yours?

J-D: Ditto.

Z: No, no, no, no, no. You can't do that to me! How is your answer the same as mine?

J-D: Two reasons. The first is very easy. I am you, and you are me, remember? I am your Inner-Self. When you are aspiring to your Highest Good, then you are aligning yourself with me. Then we are in simpatico. So your goals and motivations are mine. You and I are answering the questions we have together. That's the first answer and the easiest to explain. The second answer comes with a small shift of perspective. You see "I" am a gestalt being that absolutely knows, as a fact of my existence, that I am One with God. It is a fundamental truth of my being that I am One with everyone and everything everywhere and together we are all One with God. So, obviously, FOR ME this means that I know I am One with every single inhabitant of Planet

Earth, right?

Z: Whoa! Does that mean you are everyone on earth's "Inner-self"?

J-D: No. In a previous conversation I said to you that you are the only one incarnated in your "here and now" on Planet Earth who has THAT relationship with me. What I am saying is that everyone on Earth is One with God. And, whether they know it or not, I know it. And I also know that I am One with God. So it is true for me that I am, by obvious extension, One with everyone on Earth. Okay?

Z: Oh! Okay. You are saying from your perspective you see us ALL as One!

J-D: Yes. Logically that is the case. But let me explain something. I am like you in some ways and unlike you in others. My perception of my reality is very different from yours. I won't be able to describe this to you in a way that you will fully comprehend but I can give you an inkling.

One example is that I am not limited to a single perspective as you are. You perceive your world as one single being who can only stand in one place at a time and can only feel or think one thing about your life at a time. Even if you have conflicting thoughts you leap from the one perspective to the other. One at a time. That is how you are created to be. You are a single-perspective being. I, on the other hand, am actually a multiplicity. I should correctly refer to myself in the plural as "We" but that would make for a confusing conversation. You see I have an infinite number of points of view. That is like saying I am an infinite number of people all at once.

Z: Whoa. Infinite? Doesn't that mean you are God?

J-D: No. I am One with God. But I am very, very far from being ALL of God! Compared to ALL of God I am... minuscule. A very, very small babe of a being.

Z: And yet you have infinite perspectives?

J-D: Understand that I am outside of the construct called the Space/Time Continuum. So I am able to see, at one glance, all the interactions my beingness might have in every single moment. Each moment is a perspective. Every interaction is NOW for me. And since Space/Time is infinite, I have infinite perspectives.

Z: Okay that is a bit mind-boggling for me.

J-D: Yes. And I am only referring to this one sliver of a reality in which you now exist, which you call "the universe". To me this is one sub-set of one reality where I am interacting with Life. There are, for me, an infinite number of other realities where I know myself to be.

Z: An infinite number of other universes?

J-D: You could see it like that. But that is already far too restrictive a conceptualisation. In later conversations I will try to convey to you the magnitude and vastness of the unending realities that I am aware of. And there is much more that I have yet to discover and place within my awareness. Much, much more. Now I don't say this to make you think I am something wondrous and special. I mean I AM wondrous and special, of course (he smiles). But so is every other being that exists. Everyone on earth has within themselves a God-self that has this God-like awareness. So what I tell you is both amazing AND a bit of a "so-what?" all at the same time. The reason I tell you this is to find a way to begin to explain to you that my perceptions of myself and my reality are somewhat different from yours in some pretty fundamental ways. And so, when I say that, for me it is true that All is One, I do not mean this in some abstract, philosophical way. I do not mean this as a derived theoretical understanding. No. I mean it is my absolutely perceived reality from a very broad set of experiences.

Z: What does "*absolute perceived reality*" mean?

J-D: Alright. How about I ask you this: are you alive? And if you are alive can you prove this to me?

Z: Of course I am alive. Can I prove it? Well, I can try. I am a living, breathing biological being. And I am conscious. I think and I feel and…

J-D: Good, good, good. I don't really need proof and we don't really need to have this debate. I merely wanted to show you something. You KNOW you are alive. It isn't just an idea you have or some theoretical construct. It is YOUR "*absolute perceived reality*". It is unarguable to you. Now, if I ask you to prove that you are alive, you CAN go digging around in your mind for thoughts that would explain this or attempt to prove it. You can do so as an intellectual exercise. But it is completely irrelevant and redundant TO YOU because you know it to be true, with everything you are, without even thinking about it. It is the most self-evident thing possible. Well in just such a way it is true for me that All is One. And I am saying this with all the authority of the rather extensive experience of my whole being.

Z: Ah. I begin to get it. Thanks. But that hasn't answered the bigger question about your purpose in having these conversations with me.

J-D: No. But I didn't explain this for nothing either. I was laying the groundwork for my argument. What I need you to understand is that I really, truly, completely perceive every being on earth as being One with me and All That Is. And since I very much love and care for myself, by extension I love and care for every "other" that exists. And so, when I hear a cry of pain it is my desire to see if I may assist in turning that pain into Joy. That, in fact, is my purpose here. I have come into this system of reality because there was a cry of pain. And the reason I heard that cry is because I was meant to answer it. So I am here. And I am engaged in answering that call.

Now let me go back to your question. Understanding that I can hold the perspective that every person on this planet is just "another me" let me read back to you what you said YOUR purpose with all this was. You said: "*I'm trying to heal myself, trying to love myself, trying to discover who I really am, who God really is and trying to find and fulfil my soul purpose.*" Can you see how it is that I am doing exactly the same? If, for me, the Self can be pretty much any person on the planet, then this is what I am trying to do. In fact this is what I am doing, have always been doing, will always be doing and have ever done.

Z: Huh?

J-D: I am outside of time. It is only from your perspective that this is really a work in progress. My perspective on that is quite different. This work is both perfect and complete AND still a work in progress… and everything else it could possibly be. That is how it is from outside of time.

Z: Oh. Okay. But please don't tell me these conversations of ours are meant to make SUCH a big impact on humanity! I mean I just can't see them reaching far enough to…

J-D: Please. Silence your fears and your doubts. These conversations will undoubtedly have great value. More than you can now imagine. But this is not THE WORK! You will, as we proceed with these conversations, come to understand what the work we are doing really is. These conversations simply act as a sort of an invitation to others to come and co-create with us. As the conversations unfold, you will slowly get a better and better idea of what their value is. So, while it is true that these conversations will have profound value for many and will go far further than you now have any ability to imagine, I have to say that this is certainly not "it" for me. The "work" I do is accomplished in ways you have not yet understood. I don't actually have to "DO" anything. I simply am here. I accomplish everything I need to accomplish by simply BEING that which I am. I bring my energy to bear and make it available and that shifts things in the desired way.

Z: How? How can you change stuff by just "being there"? Surely you have to actually DO something?

J-D: Hard to explain the power of BEing to earth humans. You only think in terms of the power of DOing. You think you are more powerful and effective when you DO something. The opposite is true. DOing only steps down your true power. But you won't understand that. Let me rather tell you about this in the form of a parable.

Z: Excellent! A story...

J-D: Yes, here we go:

The Story of the Darklanders

Once upon a time there was a race of people called the Darklanders. They lived in a vast, dark cavern deep underground. Not one of the whole race of Darklanders had ever been outside the cavern, but their myths and legends told of an ancient time – a time before time – when their gods had come down from the great Brightlands above and created the Darklanders here in the dark cavern and then left and returned to the Brightlands. It was said that the gods would one day return and bring the light down to the Darklanders. The Darklanders tried to imagine what the Brightlands above must be like but could not, as no one had ever seen so much as a single light. Then some of the Darklanders began to feel constrained by their dark world. They longed to experience the mythical world above. The legends told of amazing vistas and wide open spaces and wondrous experiences and these sounded very desirable to some of the Darklanders. In their hearts these few Darklanders felt they KNEW it existed and cried out for it. Other Darklanders of course said this was all "superstitious nonsense". They said people should be practical and just get on with life as it was without hankering after nonsense. And so we see how types emerged: the Dreamers who longed for the life beyond, and the Realists who were interested only in the mundane. The Realists, instead of wasting time with myths, legends and dreams, explored the cavern and tried to understand all that they could perceive so that they could make the best of the life they had. They came up with practical solutions to their problems instead of wasting their time with what was out of their reach. But still the Dreamers continued to dream and pray. And then, on a day, when the time was right, their prayers began to be answered in an unexpected way. The gods sent a very tiny, very dim Light to the Darklanders.

Z: A tiny, dim light? How did that help?

J-D: It didn't. But it also didn't hurt. You see the tiny, dim Light of this parable was different from the light you know of. It was given to each of the Darklanders ... placed inside each of them. But it was so tiny and so dim that only the most observant noticed anything different at all. In fact it was so tiny and so dim that, even if they noticed it, the Darklanders were able to think they were just imagining it. They could choose to tell themselves there was "something" or they could put it down to their imagination playing tricks on them and say it was "nothing". If a Darklander accepted the Light then it increased. You see the very desire to look and SEE, the desire ITSELF, caused the Light to slowly increase. And so, over time, those that desired it, meditated upon it and worked with it, got brighter and brighter.

Z: Surely you mean they saw more brightly?

J-D: No, I mean they themselves became brighter. They themselves shone with the Light. I'll say it again: This Light was different from the light you know. It was placed INSIDE each of the Darklanders. By accepting it, paying attention to it, respecting it, nurturing it and loving it, so it grew within them. It became their own Light which shone from within them and by which each of them might see. And as they became brighter and brighter so they could see further and further.

Z: And how did THAT help?

J-D: It didn't. The Light did not help at all. It didn't move them out of the cavern. It didn't bring them tools or maps or instructions or new information or tell them that their legends were true or anything like that. The Light did nothing whatsoever except BE. It simply was what it was. It did what all light does… it shone. It shone in its own special way: a beautiful soft, shimmering, golden Light. But it came to them in such a gentle way, only increasing when it was actively desired, so that for quite some time no one spoke about it at all. You see, at first, those who noticed the Light and worked to increase it were the greatest Dreamers. They were the ones that were most open and available to this gift. But being such great Dreamers they were very used to being told that they were crazy, lazy and bad. They were used to others no listening to them. They were used to having no power in the Darklands. So they didn't try too hard to share their discovery of the Light with others. Most of them thought they were the only one to have this strange but wonderful new experience. But they did not mind too much because, though they felt no-one else would understand, for the first time, as a result of the Light, they did not feel so alone.

Z: So the Light didn't help. It just was… the Light. So how did that answer the Darklanders' prayers?

J-D: Well you see not EVERYONE prayed for the Light or for a return to the Brightlands. Only some did. So if the Darklanders were just moved out of the cavern up into the Brightlands then that would have given many of them what they DIDN'T want. So the Light did nothing but gently shine and then only for those that chose it and who, by their actions and decisions, created the Light for themselves from within themselves. And here is the thing… you see, for the most avid Lookers, the Light eventually got bright enough that they began to see some interesting things. Like the beautiful crystals hanging from the cavern ceiling. And this is where things came to a head. You see a few of the Lookers noticed each other staring up at the crystals on the ceiling… and then, for the first time, they knew they were not alone! They began to talk to each other about this. They got Lookers Groups together to share their experiences and help each other with tips and strategies to increase the Light. Some non-Lookers came to listen to what they were saying. Some became interested enough to practised what they heard and became Lookers too. Word spread and for a while it was quite the most exciting thing that had happened in the cavern. Which would have been fine except that those who chose the Light were most likely to be Dreamers and those who didn't were most likely to be Realists. And you see, the Realists were the ones who were running things. They had the power. They had the resources. They made the rules. And since they hadn't chosen to See and since they hadn't created the Light inside themselves they simply denied that it existed. Which wasn't strange because - see it from their perspective - if they looked around they saw no light! So it was all a lie as far as the Realists were concerned. And not only was it a lie but a dangerous one too! These Lookers were, they said, becoming a social nuisance. They were refusing to obey the edicts and instructions of their superiors! They were not being proper productive members of society! All this "Looking" nonsense was disrupting the very fabric of society!

Now, those in power couldn't very well outlaw the Light or Looking because they were claiming it was all just a fabrication anyway. So they used their influence and power to ridicule anyone who was talking about it. They publicised authoritative claims that it was only mad people who tried to see the Light. That it was all a lie. They let it be known that no good, healthy, sane Darklander should try to see the Light.

"If you want to know what is out there," said those in power, "we have experts that can tell you." They were the authorities, after all.

"Experimenting with attempting to See is socially disruptive and needless nonsense. It is un-Darklander!" they declared.

But of course they failed to stamp Looking out. In fact Looking slowly grew in popularity. And then it happened that a group of the most avid Lookers discovered something new. They discovered that, by joining their Lights together as one, they could co-create a much, much brighter Light. They discovered that they could see quite far and quite clearly. And so they got together each day and searched the roof of the cavern. It was but a matter of time before they would see the distinct fissure in the roof which was exactly as was described in the ancient myths as the gateway to the Brightlands above!

This was all the impetus they needed! The Lookers began to work together with a fervour none of them had ever known before. They gathered together materials and began to build scaffolding so that they might ascend to the fissure and see if that was the way out. Their work was occasionally hampered by the authorities but not badly so. You see the authorities did not have the Light and could therefore not see what the Lookers were doing. They therefore did not understand their plans and as they could not even admit to the fact of the seeing of the fissure or its existence they could not do much to stop the construction. So the Lookers carried on and built their scaffolding.

Our story comes to an end here as the Lookers' scaffolding was reaching up to the fissure. They were hopeful and excited. The rest of the Darklanders below mostly knew nothing of what they were up to. Some heard about it and were intrigued. Some insisted it was all foolish nonsense. What happened next? Well… unfortunately this is where the parable ends.

Z: Oh no! Why?

J-D: Well you asked a question. You asked how by simply BEing, rather than DOing, I could accomplish the work for which I have come here. Is that now what you asked?

Z: Yes, that IS what I asked.

J-D: Well let's see how the parable fared: can you see how, in the parable, the Light managed to come into the Darklands and how it could, without DOING anything - by just BEING - bring options, choices and change? Though it was very much there, it was still up to the Darklanders to choose to see it or not. And if they DID choose to see it they could choose for themselves what they were going to do with that Seeing. So the Light itself did nothing and yet the whole social structure and dynamic of the population changed. Without doing anything the Light offered those who wanted, it a way to find their way out. But, you see, it didn't DO anything for them actually. No. Something much better happened: It allowed them to create their own way to help themselves to see their own path out IF THEY SO CHOSE. Only those who wished for the Light really got it. Those who denied the Light did not. No one was forced to do anything they didn't want to do. Everyone got to create the reality they desired. And yet, everything was changed by the existence, by the simple BEing, of the Light. So, I think the parable did quite a good job of expressing to you not only how BEing can change everything but also brought in a number of parallels as to how things have played out in your reality.

Z: I agree it is a pretty cool parable. Thanks. I think I get the power of BEing now. But now we have spent a whole lot of time on tangential issues. I feel quite bad. We were supposed to be talking about the implications of the Oneness. And instead I have taken you on a wild goose-chase answering all these question that just cropped up in my mind and we haven't even started to talk about the topic at hand!

J-D: Have a little faith. Do you not know that "*everything is always perfect*"?

Z: Umm. No. I mean I have heard it said. It's one of those "fully spiritual" things that enlightened souls sometimes say. But it isn't REALLY always perfect, is it?

J-D: Only because your perspective is too close. Here is something to remember:

> "*If you cannot see the perfection then you are standing too close to the picture.*"

Z: Again, that sounds way deep and stuff but, practically, how is that so?

J-D: Would you like an example?

Z: That would be nice.

J-D: Good. I shall give you one: it is… this very conversation! We are still busy with it and so you look at the incomplete product and see the mistakes you have made by asking the wrong questions. You see the mistakes I have made by long-windedly answering them. And this is all a big mistake because this is not what you had in mind for the way this topic should flow. But here is the twist: I am telling you now it is only imperfect because it is still incomplete.

Z: Okay? So what must I do with that information?

J-D: Thinking would be a start! Think. What have I said?

Z: That it is only imperfect because it is incomplete?

J-D: Yes. So what strikes you as incomplete?

Z: Uh…

J-D: Another word for incomplete is "unfinished"…

Z: The story! The story! You didn't finish the parable. I mean… you finished it in so much as it perfectly answered my question. But I have to admit I was disappointed because you just left the actual story hanging.

J-D: RIGHT! So? What do you want me to do?

Z: Well, umm. Could you please tell me how the parable ends?

J-D: Why, yes, I'd be Delighted to do that!

Z: Thanks. Because I can see how that parable actually relates to us here on earth. And I can see the cute "ascend the scaffolding" thing you have done to allude to the ascension process. So I am pretty keen to hear how it ends. I think that might give me some sort of insight into what is going to happen in the future to us here on earth.

J-D: Yes, the parable DOES allude to life on earth. But not as you might think. There is quite a twist in the tail. But you'll see when we get there. Let me continue the parable.

The Story of the Darklanders, Part 2

I could end the whole story by simply saying, "*Everyone got exactly what they created for themselves*". That would be true of this story and true of every other true story in all of reality. But it would be unsatisfying. Because even though, still people want to know details of the stories. So let's see how that rule of always getting what you create applied to the Darklanders.

Remember most of the Darklanders chose not to see the Light. Most of them stayed behind in the Darklands, right?

Z: Right.

J-D: Okay. So clearly their belief was that they could not see the Light and that they had to remain in the Darklands and that things would continue more or less as they had before. That is what they believed and that is therefore what they experienced. Their new story starts pretty much exactly where the old story left off. The Darklanders are still in the Darklands and they still have no Light. BUT there is now a difference. They now know about their friends and family members that WERE there with them in the Darklands that simply disappeared. They also know that the ones who disappeared were Lookers. They know that the Lookers were talking about going up into the Brightlands. And then they were gone. So they are confused and many of them are now asking questions.

"What happened to the Lookers?" they ask.

"The gods came back for them!" claimed some.

"They were punished for their evil ways and taken away!" others postulated. And so it continued. No one knew for sure what had happened but what they DID know was that their neat, tiny, closed, little world would never be the same again. Something inexplicable had happened. And in their confusion many of them remembered the gods of old and began to pray. And that is where we shall leave them for now. Next we'll pick up the story with the other group - the ones who went up the scaffolding.

Z: The Lookers. They obviously found the Brightlands!

J-D: They certainly did. They began their new story at a new level of existence. They emerged from the land below to discover that the reason for the Brightlands being so bright was not because there was some bright light source there… no… these were the Brightlands because everyone there was THEMSELVES a bright source of Light.

Z: Oh wow! Everyone shone!

J-D: Yes. And what it meant was that everyone clearly saw the reality around them as THEY themselves were. Do you understand? In the Darklands people thought they perceived the world as IT was. In the Brightlands they realised they saw it as THEY were.

Z: Um. Slow moment over here. I don't get it.

J-D: Well, the truth is that you each create your own reality. When you see clearly, then you see that your reality is the way it is because of what you most deeply believe – which is what you are perceiving from your heart. So those who ascended to the next level immediately realised that the reality they saw around themselves was a direct result of their own beliefs and choices. This means that they knew that they created their own reality. This is something we'll have to talk about more in following conversations because this is going to be difficult for you to understand. You are still very much living in your own "Darkland". You still believe you see things as they are. And because you believe it to be so, so it is! There is much more for us to discuss about this soon. For now, please accept that those who have ascended to the next level will have a different experience to what you do.

Z: Okay, I guess that's obvious – it stands to reason that a different level of existence will be quite different from this one.

J-D: And the difference will be difficult for you to comprehend precisely because you don't have any experience of it.

Z: Okay. Agreed.

J-D: Well I am saying the next level of reality for you is the level of self-mastery. You have heard of "ascended masters"? Well what precisely did you think they were masters of? I am telling you they are masters of themselves. True self-mastery means they are ready to believe, know and experience that they create their own reality completely. They are ready to see the world as they each believe it is. They are ready to create their world as THEY are. And that is what I am talking about with this Light. They shine their Light and it shows them the world as they each believe it to be.

Z: Wow. So I guess the next level of reality is a pretty amazing place.

J-D: It can be. Unfortunately it is possible to attain self-mastery without attaining universal love.

Z: It is? What happens then?

J-D: Well let me get back to the parable. This conversation is going to be a long one. There is quite a bit still to tell. But stay with me okay?

Z: I'm not going anywhere. I'm fascinated to see how this all turns out!

J-D: Good. I think you'll find your patience quite well rewarded. So, back to the parable. For the purposes of the story we shall divide the ones who ascended to the Brightlands into three main groups. First there were those who were of a Service To Self (STS) mentality. These STS beings thought that the fact that they had made it out of the Darklands proved that they were more special than the Darklanders who had remained below. They decided that they must be very powerful and wise compared to the Darklanders who were still in the cavern. Now you can hear from what I am saying that, even though they had escaped the Darklands into the Brightlands, still they were framing themselves in terms of the Darklands. So they would therefore begin their new story back in the Darklands.

Z: Er... no, I don't really get that. They have just escaped the Darklands. Why would they go back?

J-D: Okay. Follow me on this one... You get what you create, right? And when you have the Light then you get it immediately. Whatever you focus your INTENTION and ATTENTION on is what you get. Now this group of beings, even though they found themselves in the Brightlands, were still thinking in terms of the Darklands below. They were thinking, "*We are the best and the brightest of the Darklanders*". That is where their thoughts were. So that is what they got... to be the "*best and the brightest of the Darklanders*"! And of course there was something else motivating them too. Now that they had this new-found power, what do you think they wanted to do with it?

Z: Uh...

J-D: Let me give you a hint. Don't you think these STS beings might have a modicum of revenge on their minds?

Z: Revenge? Oh right! Like a "revenge of the nerds" sort of thing.

J-D: Explain that phrase?

Z: Revenge of the nerds? Well in the Darklands these guys were considered outcasts, remember? In the Darklands they were the Dreamers and were considered undesirable elements of society by the Realists and especially by those in power. They were the weirdos and the nutcases who were disrespected. And so now, when their ways have paid off, perhaps they think it's payback time. The underdogs strike back. Revenge of the nerds.

J-D: That's quite a good analysis. And so NOW can you see that, even though they found the Light and the Brightlands, STILL they never actually escaped the Darklands. They were trapped by their negative emotions.

Z: Yeah. That makes sense. I can see how that could work.

J-D: If you find your intrinsic power, but you do not find healing and love first, then you again trap yourself… only you do so at a higher level. But anyway, back to the story: what happened next is that the STS beings brought the Light with them back down into the Darklands. So we shall henceforth call them "the Lightbringers". They were the "seeing eye" in the land of the blind, you see. And this would, of course, mean that the STS beings were much more powerful than the regular Darklanders.

Z: And what did these Lightbringers do back in the Darklands?

J-D: Well, do you remember where we left the Darklanders? They were thrown into a state of disarray and confusion by the leaving of the Lookers. Try to put yourself in their position for a moment. Suddenly they were in a profound state of doubt about everything that they had before taken to be true. Many of them began praying to the gods to save them. But can you see the problem with praying like this?

Z: Not really. How can there be a problem with praying?

J-D: Not with praying *per se*. But with praying for a rescuer to come and fix all your confusion and troubles.

Z: Why is that a problem?

J-D: The problem is you will get what you ask for. Or rather, what you are REALLY asking for. Let me help you to understand this: if you are saying that you are weak, confused, powerless and lost, that you don't know what you want or even what you SHOULD want. And that you want someone to come and tell you what to want, what to do and how to choose. That you want this great Rescuer to come in to your world and take from you your choices and creations and give you, instead, what they want to create for you and that you will serve them and worship them for doing so and do whatever they say… Well, then you are creating a world of pain for yourself. You are creating an opening for someone else in your life to fill a particular role. You are creating yourself as the perfect Victim and, while you are saying you want a Rescuer, what you are actually asking the Universe to provide you with is a Perpetrator.

Z: I'm not really following that.

J-D: Alright then, this is a good moment for me to tell you about the Victim/ Perpetrator/ Rescuer triangle.

The Victim Perpetrator Rescuer Triangle

If something appears to be going wrong in your life and you believe yourself to be a victim then you will choose to believe that someone else is "doing this" to you. Someone else is the Perpetrator who is responsible for all your misery. And, as you are a powerless victim, you must therefore find someone to help you out of this situation, someone that will be responsible for Rescuing you and making everything better. And so the three relationships are set up: Victim, Perpetrator and Rescuer ALWAYS go together. Where there is one, the other two are there also. So the Darklanders were very clearly declaring their status as Victims. And while it is true that they told themselves they wanted to be rescued, what they first invited was a Perpetrator. They made themselves available to it. They created that opening.

Z: I don't get it. Surely it doesn't follow. They wanted someone GOOD to come to help them. Why would that invite someone bad?

J-D: Because they are creating with fear and with doubt. This is an idea I will go into detail with you when I talk to you about creation tools. But the point is quite simply this: your tools of creation are your emotions. If you create with Love then you get what you really want. If you create with Fear then get what you don't want. If you create with Doubt then you get a mixed bag or nothing at all. Now the Darklanders were in Fear AND Doubt. So the first thing they got was what they DIDN'T want. And you MUST get what you create. How else will you learn to create properly if you don't?

Z: Wow, this is tough for me to understand. But okay, let's go on with the story. I will want to come back some other time and talk about this… about how to create what I DO want.

J-D: It's a promise. We'll talk about it soon. But for now perhaps you can accept that the Darklanders were not creating a clear, unambiguous outcome for themselves with Love and positivity. So an opening was created. And if we bring this together with what the Lightbringers were creating we have quite a good match. The Lightbringers were quite happy to be received as the "returning gods" by the Darklanders. They were quite willing to be served and worshipped and have their egos buffed and polished. A lot of humble bowing and scraping served them just fine, thank you very much. Not only were they willing to be gods but they were also quite willing to teach the people of the Darklands how they should be worshipped. They taught them songs of praise to sing. They taught them to bring offerings of the very finest of the foods of the land prepared by the most skilled of chefs. They promoted the Darklanders that served them best to positions of power, thereby creating a priest class so that only these most loyal servants ever came near them. And the rest of the people were nothing more than slaves. Slaves to the priests and to their prideful gods. They were forced to work and work and work for all of their waking hours. They were forced to built great palaces to appease their egotistical gods. And then they built temples to appease the burgeoning egos of their gods' priestly pets.

And then something interesting happened. The gods began to get jealous of each other. They began to compete with each other. Each wanted to have more power and control of the people than the next one. Each wanted a better palace than the other. They each started to instruct their priests to gather worshippers to them, to tell the Darklanders that they must worship only this god or that one and forsake all others. This continued for a while as egos clashed and tempers simmered, and then war broke out. Worshippers of some of the gods began to get instructions to kill the worshippers of the other gods. Retaliations quickly escalated to all-out war. And then the gods used their powers to smite each other's worshippers too. The Darklands were rent apart! After some time a certain degree of stalemate was achieved. Each of the gods, with their surviving minions, were living in a different area, removed from one another by some distance. There they established their cities. And though they continued to war on each other, there were also intermittent times of peace for the poor Darklanders. But their lives were hard. Now, not only did they have to labour to build and serve but they intermittently had to turn their agricultural implements into weapons of war and go off to be killed and maimed. All in service of the Lightbringers' egos.

But through all this something new had begun to dawn in the hearts of the Darklanders. You see, they were no longer the haughty Realists of before. They had come through some very tough times. And they had come through together. They had survived thus far by finding compassion for one another. Brother helping brother, they had pulled through. Their travails had opened their hearts to each other. And now their hearts began again to cry for rescue. But this time they began to call with hope in their hearts. Hope, because they had seen love and compassion in each other's eyes. They began to hope for love and compassion from the gods. And again they got what they created. As it always was and always will be. Because remember…

Z: "*You always get EXACTLY what you create for yourself*"

J-D: Spot on! And so, who do you think came to answer their prayers this time?

Z: I'm not sure. If I recall then you said that the Lookers who ascended into the Brightlands were to be divided into three groups. The first group was the STS-ers who we are now calling the Lightbringers. So I'm guessing you are now going to tell us about a second group of Brightlanders. I'm guessing they were somehow a more loving response to the calls of the Darklanders.

J-D: That would be a very good guess. So let's look at that second group. They were of a Service To Other (STO) mentality. When these particular ones first made it up into the Brightlands they felt it was a wonder, a blessing and a privilege. They desired to use this privilege to dedicate themselves to being of service to others. They felt love and compassion for their friends and family members whom they had left behind in the Darklands and so they decided to go back and help those remaining Darklanders in whatever way they could. And so it was that they heard the agonised cries for loving help from the Darklands below. They heard the call and they responded. And when they arrived in the Darklands the STO beings were horrified to discover what the Lightbringers had gotten up to. The misery and death that they had brought to the lives of the Darklanders was too terrible for them to contemplate.

Z: Wait a minute, please. I don't understand. It seems to me you are saying that the STS guys arrived first. And that they spent quite a long time down in the Darklands building empires and then making wars and what-not and only THEN after, like, hundreds of years or something, did the STO guys come down. Is that right?

J-D: A great deal longer than just hundreds of years, but yes, that is what I am saying. You see time is not the same in the different realms. You do not move between dimensions and still stay on the same time-line. They operate on entirely different systems of sequentiality. So, when you pass from the Brightlands to the Darklands, for example, you arrive at the time which is resonant with your arrival. You arrive when the Darklands are ready for you to arrive. You arrive when it is time for you to play your role. A stage-play is a good analogy. Imagine a stage-play in which all the actors walked on together right at the opening curtain and then all of them at the same time spouted all their lines in one long, non-stop monologue. It would be a chaotic babble and would make no sense to anyone. So instead, each enters at the right moment and each plays their part in perfect response to the other.

Z: I see. But that creates another question: Who decides to bring them on at "*the right time*"?

J-D: They do. They create this with their desires. Let's look at the sponsoring thought behind the wishes of the STO beings. They desired to be of service. They desired to HELP someone. They wanted to save the Darklanders from their lot. But they wanted to do it out of a loving, kind motivation. It is a generosity of spirit that wished to express itself. So you see? The STO beings get to go to the Darklands at exactly the moment when the Darklanders are most powerfully creating an opening for what the STO beings are offering. And that perfect moment was not back at the beginning of this part of the story when the Lightbringers arrived. No. The Darklanders first needed to meet the Lightbringers and see how the Lightbringers responded to their call. Only then, when they had walked that path together a while, would the Darklanders be ready to make a new choice. You see, a Victim needs a Perpetrator before he needs a Rescuer.

Let me explain something else here. Remember, back in the first part of their story, the Darklanders had been haughty and had victimised the Lookers. That is how they were and that is what they knew. To the Darklanders, therefore, beings in a position of authority were ego-centric and imperious. That is how they treated each other. That is what they knew and so that is what they were able to imagine as a response to their call.

Z: Because if you can't imagine something then you can't create it?

J-D: That is a profoundly true thing you have just said. Sometime soon, when we talk about the tools of creation, you will come to understand what a very powerful thing this is that you call "imagination". And yes, if you can't imagine it then you can't create it. But now, in this part of the story what had happened to the Darklanders was that they had been put through a long series of very traumatic experiences. And it's a funny thing about such events. When people go through such difficulties it very often brings out the best in them. And so it was that the Darklanders responded to their harsh treatment at the hands of the Lightbringers by expressing support, compassion, love and kindness to each other. Friend helping friend, strangers offering unexpected assistance to each other… so those dark times ignited a spark in the hearts of the Darklanders. A new and different Light was fostered in their hearts. The Light of compassion began to softly shine. And so it was that the Darklanders were ready to meet the STO Brightlanders. If I may summarise it like this: the Darklanders would first have to have a new thought about themselves before they would be able to have a new thought about their world. They needed to find love and compassion in their hearts before they could frame their need in terms of a loving, compassionate response.

Z: And how did the STO guys come down and rescue the Darklanders from the Lightbringers? I don't imagine they came in like cavalry on white horses with guns blazing.

J-D: Well there are a number of different ways they could have entered the story. And later when you understand the complexities of alternate time-lines then you'll understand when I say that all of the possible ways actually happened. In some of them they DID come in all wrathful and angry: angelic hosts with flaming swords of righteous vengeance. In these realities there was a great battle between the STO and the STS. But that didn't work out very well for anyone. Everyone just got hurt and no one was helped. That is a game that, once started, has no end. War causes fear and pain. Fear and pain breeds loathing. Loathing causes war. Round and round you go. And seeing as the STO beings wanted to help the Darklanders, not hurt them, this didn't serve their best interests at all. There is second set of time-lines in which the STO beings came into this reality as good, kind and benevolent demi-gods. They didn't fight with the STS beings. They caused no harm and waged no war. What they did was to be in their power and do all they could to help the Darklanders. Great, kind, benevolent gods who taught and helped and healed and did endless services of goodness.

Z: Ah! A better approach!

J-D: Maybe. But, in the final analysis, not much more successful than just waging war.

Z: No way! How come?

J-D: Well this way round the Darklanders just stopped doing for themselves. They saw that it was pointless for them to even try to do anything. There were the good gods and the bad gods. If you managed to appeal to the good gods, you had good things happen to you. If you angered the bad gods then bad things happened to you. In this way the Darklanders decided that they had no power whatsoever and simply ceased trying. And so the STO beings failed to help them to ascend into the Brightlands. The Darklanders just said, "*We are not like you. You are gods. We are powerless. We will serve you and you can do these things for us.*" And no matter how much the STO beings professed that they were all actually the same and that the Darklanders could do all the things they had done, still the Darklanders could not believe them. Why should they? It was completely apparent that these gods were capable of great magic and miracles and they were not. So that too was a failure. Then there is a third set of time-lines. In these time-lines the STO beings saw the folly of being "above" the people. Instead they now chose to be a part of the Darklanders. So they entered the game by being born as babes to Darklander parents. In these time-lines most of them would manage, in one way or another, as they grew up, to begin to remember the Brightlands. They would remember the Light. And then they would, as a Darklander themselves, begin to help and to teach the others.

Z: And THIS worked out better?

J-D: To some considerable degree. What happened with this is that the Lightbringers quickly saw what was going on. As these STO teachers and healers went about doing their thing, so the Lightbringers began to lose their grip on the people. So they made laws against the teaching of the Light. They took the Light teachings and changed them and corrupted them so that they would again serve the purpose of the Lightbringers in keeping the people trapped, in keeping them servile, in keeping them serving the interests of the Lightbringers. What they succeeded in doing is driving the teachings of the Light underground. Secret groups were gathered. There, in these little secret schools, the mysteries of WHAT IS, were taught. And so the word was spread. Sometimes a teacher would rise up and become a bit noisier. Sometimes he'd gather enough followers to disturb the *status quo*. Always he and his rebellion would be put down by the Lightbringers, with force and violence. But by then his message would have gotten out to more than just his immediate followers and a growing group of people would have become conscientised. And so it was that this way of being did some good. But it wasn't ultimately successful either. Still most people believed that only the gods were able to create their reality. Only the gods could take you up to the Brightlands or deny you admission. STILL most of them failed to understand the truth that each goes to the Brightlands because THEY are ready to do so… because they have gained self-mastery. They ascend to become masters because they are willing and able to create this for themselves. Only a minuscule percentage got this and only a minuscule percentage were able to ascend. And that is where the second part to the Story of the Darklanders ends.

It ends with a cycle that just goes round and round and round. And round. This time line is actually not a line, it is a circle. So the end is the beginning is the end is the beginning is the end… There is an endless, complex interaction between those who have chosen Service To Self, those who had chosen Service To Other and those who remained Undecided. There is a point at which the cycle seems to end and that is where there is a harvest of all the Undecided who have eventually reached a decision point. They stop being Undecided and then ascend to the next level where they become either STO or STS or, very rarely, the third type of Brightlander.

Z: Oh yes! I'd forgotten that there was still a third type. What do THEY do?

J-D: It isn't QUITE time to introduce them to the story yet. I first need to finish completely with

Part Two of the Darklander story. I was saying there is an event at the end of each cycle. It is called the harvest. This is when those who have made a choice cease to be Undecided and ascend to the Brightlands. Usually this is quite a small percentage of the Darklanders.

Z: So, over time, there are less and less Undecided.

J-D: There would be. Except of course this is not a closed system and the time line doesn't truly end. Beings from elsewhere might decide this is a good place to come to learn about themselves, to come and experience life here in the Darklands. From a certain perspective it can be seen that this is a very beautiful and elegant game. You can enter at the bottom as a newcomer to the game who is Undecided. You can remain Undecided for as long as you like and then, when you have given it a good look, you can decide which you want to be: STO or STS or the third type (still getting to that!) and then you move up to that. And if you choose STO or STS you can play that role for as long as you like and when you are done with that, you can ALSO still choose the third type. And what is unique about the third type is that this is the only type who can choose to leave the game altogether or continue to play. But before we finally get into what exactly the third type is, let's take a moment to admire the beauty of this system. Can you see how it is something that can go round and round forever? The Undecided Darklanders, the STO Lightbringers and the STS Rescuers together get themselves locked into a dance. They form a triangle: the Darklanders playing the role of victim, Lightbringers playing the role of perpetrator and STO beings playing the role of rescuer. And once that pattern is set up it can go round and round forever. It is an internally conflicted game that just goes on and on for all eternity. Individual souls can enter the game at the beginning; move up through the game into STS or STO (and very often one and then the other) and then eventually the third type. And then, if they like, they can leave the game from the third type.

Z: Okay, I simply CANNOT wait any more. Please tell me what in goodness name IS the third type?

J-D: I was wondering how long before your curiosity overcame you. Alright, I shall tell you and then you can see if it all makes sense. The third type of Brightlander is what I am going to call the Unifiers. They are the ones that KNOW that All is One. They know that they are, each of them, STO and STS and Undecided. All of that, none of that, and at the same time so much more than that. They know that when they look at another being there can be no judgement because they see that being as another self. They know therefore that all is perfect. They have really and truly seen the Light. Not the first bit of Light seen by the others in the Brightlands, no, the depths of Light that shines from the heart of every being, which is that being's connection to Prime Source. When such a being looks at you they do not see your temporary situation: your foibles, your self-limiting illusions, your fears... no, they look into your heart and they see God there! As they do when they look at themselves, of course. God is everywhere when you look with the eyes of a Unifier. And they can also, of course, see that they have been, in this game, the Undecided, they have been STO and they have been STS. They will therefore not stand in judgement of any of these. And it is with these, the Unifiers, that we start the next level of the story of the Darklanders...

Z: Whew! This is turning into a long and complex story!

J-D: You have no idea how complex it actually is. I have taken HUGE liberties compressing things and lumping things together so that this story can be told.

Z: So, this story is true?

J-D: All stories are true. All stories are fiction. Both of these statements can be true depending on your perspective. This story is just a story - a fairy-tale, if you like. But it represents aspects of that which has occurred, and continues to occur, in your world in an interesting way. In a way which will, I hope, lead you to think about things. Lead you to ask new questions, come to new conclusions. It is about suggesting to you a way to understand the situation without tugging on the fear and anger strings. Without dragging you through the misery of doom and gloom. Because those things do not serve my agenda. They serve the agenda of those that will keep you here playing the game in their service.

But onwards now…

The Story of the Darklanders, Part 3

The thing to understand about the third group, the Unifiers, is that they do not frame themselves in terms of who they serve. They don't necessarily serve themselves OR the "other". They know the "other" and the "self" are, ultimately, the same being. They know that what you do to the "other" you automatically and directly do to the Self. So while they are good and loving and kind as a rule (because that is what they would want done to themselves) such beings would not automatically swing into a mode of either serving themselves OR serving others. The whole notion of "service" is not of great importance to them at all. Instead what usually drives such a being is pure expression of the Self. The understanding for a Unifier is that each and every particle of the Oneness is absolutely and completely unique. And if each one were to find that which is their greatest bliss and simply express THAT, then all would be well. Because, you see, no two beings anywhere are ever the same. So no two beings' greatest bliss would ever be exactly the same thing. Each one would be loved and cherished for that unique thing that IT has to offer. And what IT has to offer would be the perfectly needed thing, SOMEWHERE.

For the Unifiers there is no scarcity and no competition. There is balance and perfection. And instead of springing into action, these beings would choose instead to simply BE. To explore and SEE. To journey into the heart of God and find that which calls to them to do their unique Greatest Gift. And then they'd express themselves in pure love and joy.

Z: That sounds beautiful. But there is something I really don't understand. How can you KNOW yourself to be ONE with everyone and everything else without losing yourself. I mean I understand the Oneness conceptually, but if it is literally true as a fact of your being that there is no separation between you and any other being… then how can you still be YOU?

J-D: Your question is about individuality. About losing your identity. Let me take a moment out of the Darklanders story for a quick diversion. Can you remember in our first conversation, in chapter 2 of this work, I promised to tell you about "The Rainbow Metaphor"?

Z: Oh yes. Now that you mention it, that does rings a bell.

J-D: Well here it is…

The Rainbow Metaphor

Imagine there is a rainbow and you are one of the colours.

You and all your brother and sister colours might SEEM to be individual and separate up there in the sky. But are you?

Z: Oh, I see. No. The colours are continuous aren't they?

J-D: Yes, what you are seeing is actually an even, unbroken, undivided spread of light frequencies. It is the observer that decides, in it's mind to lump a selection of these frequencies together and to identify this area as a band of yellow and that area as a band of green, for example. But there is in reality no place where one colour stops and another starts. There isn't in any real sense a "band" of any colour whatsoever except that you might choose to imagine it to be so.

Z: So you are saying that all the colours are really one. They just seem like separate colours up there in the sky. And from that, we can understand how a being might perceive itself as having a different or unique nature, but at the same time know that it is actually also a part of the ONE bright white light.

J-D: I like how you've put that. Yes. But we can wring another pleasant little observation out of the rainbow analogy. How about the fact that, of course, there IS NO RAINBOW there. It is all an illusion. There is light and there is moisture. The interplay between these two things results in you believing that you are seeing these colours in the sky. But what are you REALLY seeing? Are you seeing raindrops? Or are you seeing sunbeams?

Z: Both, I guess.

J-D: But then why would a different person standing somewhere else see the rainbow at a different location to what you do? It is because two observers standing a few meters apart are actually seeing the light play off different raindrops. What I am suggesting is that there is a third component. The light, the moisture and... YOU, the observer. Your absolutely unique perspective is the third component. To every observer the rainbow will look a little different. It will, for one obvious thing, be in a different location depending on where the observer is standing.

Z: And the great spiritual truth we get from this is...

J-D: Seems I must do all the work. Okay. Let's go back to you and all your brother and sister colours. You do not exist in a vacuum. You have your own experiences but each and every observer, every being you interact with, sees you slightly differently. You are created again in the mind of every other that you will ever have an interaction with. And THIS is actually something that should be deeply pondered. I want you to think about this because it is a very important notion that will crop up again in our dialogue as it unfolds.

Z: Wait a minute. But then... if I am me; let's say I'm the colour yellow in this rainbow. And a hundred people see me and they each see me slightly differently then... which version of me is me?

J-D: That's one interesting point. Another is: do they see you as YOU are? Or do they see you as THEY are?

Z: Oh, right! We've come back round to THAT.

J-D: Yes we have. But I hope you can see from the Rainbow Metaphor that it is very possible to have your own unique and individual identity with its own characteristics and nature and yet to still be absolutely aware of your Oneness with all the other colours AND even to be aware of your Oneness with all observers AND your Oneness with all other phenomena that make up your existence.

Z: Wow, yes. That's very cool, thank you.

J-D: And now we need to get back to our parable, don't we.

Z: Sheesh! Yes. This is turning into an epic conversation! So, okay, we were saying that there were these Unifiers who believed that all was One. And so they didn't rush off to be of service to anyone particularly. They just observed stuff and hung around.

J-D: They were engaged in BEing and in observing What Is. Yes.

Z: Didn't they get bored?

J-D: Very, very far from it. Quite the opposite, in fact. The less you DO and the more you simply BE, the closer you are to God. By that I mean that your experience of yourself elevates and you are able to be a greater and greater version of yourself. You are able to expand your consciousness. The most magnificent, transcendent and blissful experiences that people ever have in deep meditation come from being truly still. From not even thinking a single thought. From just Being.

Z: So okay then. In practical terms. What did these Unifiers experience?

J-D: One can't lump all their experiences together. What they would experience would depend on what they were creating. But let's make it a bit easier. Let's pick one of them and see what he experienced, shall we?

Z: Okay. Do we have a name for him?

J-D: Alright. Let's call him… Happy.

Z: Happy? Like one of the seven dwarves?

J-D: If you like. Or maybe Happy, as in Joy, or maybe even, Joy-Divine.

Z: Oh right! Is this story about you then?

J-D: It is a parable. A story which illustrates something about life. It is about all of us.

Z: Okay. Please continue. What did Happy experience?

J-D: Well, you see, Happy was the kind of being who loved life. Loved experiences. Loved seeing and knowing about things. He found joy in all these experiences. Which is why we are calling him "Happy". That is what he was and happiness is what he pursued. So when he first ascended the scaffolding and arrived in the Brightlands he looked around himself and was astounded at the beauty he saw. He allowed himself to be really still and with great reverence in his heart to deeply appreciate the wonder of it all. He found, after some time, that doing exactly this allowed him to get even brighter. He began to see more and the world showed him ever more magnificence and splendour. He began to find that by closing his eyes, releasing his intent, and simply reverently and joyfully experiencing all that was brought to him he could go on some truly wondrous journeys within his own consciousness. And then, one day, he had a breakthrough. He discovered another new level of existence.

Z: You mean above the Brightlands?

J-D: In a manner of speaking. He came to the realisation that the Brightlands are bright, not because of the PLACE but because the inhabitants have a certain level of awareness. This meant to him that, obviously, it wasn't the Darklands that were dark or the Brightlands that were bright. What was different was the beings choosing to experience them; their level of consciousness and the truths they held about themselves. And so he desired an even greater truth. He realised it didn't lie above, beyond, or outside of himself. He realised the change would come from within, just as it actually had when he and the others ascended to the Brightlands. So he sat still and looked within. He stilled his mind and waited on the Light. It took him some time to get the discipline right but he eventually did arrive at a new level of awareness. Inside of himself he found whole new realities. He found a new level of being. He found a place where he was not so much a being with some inner-light, as a being actually made of pure light! And there, inside himself, he could interact with other beings of light. He and they all played and loved and created together. They were One, and yet still individual.

Z: Like the rainbow.

J-D: Exactly. At last, at this level, he really was experiencing himself as a colour of the rainbow that is one with all the other colours… yet still conscious of Self.

Z: And what happened then?

J-D: Well, we could now say, "*He lived happily ever after*", and that would be true. We could also say, "*He got EXACTLY what he created*" because that is ALWAYS true. But then the story would be a bit unfinished. You see, at this level of reality that he had now attained, at this light-body level, he was also aware of countless other realities. He and the other light beings created an infinite number of them and played in these creations. And he was also aware of yet other realities that he wasn't a part of creating, but was able to explore and see what others had created. And then, also, he was aware of HIMSELF as a being who lived in many, many realities. Realities beyond number hosted him in one way or another. And all of these were RIGHT NOW for him.

Z: How can that be?

J-D: Well, you know the thing you call "remembering"? For him it wasn't an attempt to try to bring something to mind. No. For him it was to be right there in the moment he desired to remember. Like if you were trying to remember your childhood and then suddenly you WERE THERE. Suddenly you were a three year old boy in your mother's garden playing on the swing. It was like that for him. Except of course he had access to, literally, an infinite number of "lives" in an infinite number of realities.

Z: Like many, many incarnations?

J-D: Yes. Sort of. I put "lives" in quotes because most of them were experiences completely different from what you understand as a lifetime. Other realities entirely.

Z: Hard to explain then?

J-D: Very. Maybe we can try for that some other time. The point here is that Happy was able to shift himself at will from a state of BEing, in which he was in the seat of his own inner bliss and perfect KNOWING, into any one of an infinite number of states of DOing and experiencing at will. And this he did. And it was wondrous and beautiful. And of course he became aware of himself as something much larger than that too. But that is another story. To come back to THIS story I will simply say this… Happy held within his consciousness a memory. He remembered the Darklands. He remembered being there. In so doing he came to be in the presence of other light beings who were also remembering this. They remembered the pain of calling out for help. They remembered and they were there together. In their truest light bodies they were there.

Z: In the Darklands?

J-D: Yes.

Z: What did they do?

J-D: You haven't been paying attention, have you? They did NOTHING remember? All they did was BE there.

Z: Oh wow! That's so cool! They went back to themselves and rescued themselves!

J-D: Rescued? I don't think they quite "rescued" themselves. They loved themselves. They went to be there with the memory of Self and this time round they saw there were not just a few time-lines and a few parts to this story. This time they were able to see with sufficient clarity to see that there were an infinite number of versions of the story, each with an infinite number of time-lines. And they saw that, in one of the versions of the story, ALL the beings - the Darklanders, the STO beings, the STS beings, the Unifiers - all of them, found a way back to the Oneness. They each did so in their own way. In one version of the story or another they all found their way home. And yet… there is also always sufficient intersection of stories in which sufficient of them DO NOT find the Oneness that the story can still play out.

Z: Uh… sorry… I don't quite get that.

J-D: You are inside of time and so you are constrained to think in terms of linear time. But let me explain. Outside of time, a being can be in as many places as it likes. It can be in the Darklands reality and also Home with the Oneness. Such a being can then play many roles. It can be a hard-hearted Realist and at the same time a starry-eyed Dreamer and at the same time a Brightlander and at the same time a Light Being. And many, many other things besides. And if this is so, then there is no contradiction. It is merely a matter of perspective. And so it is for you too. Right now you hold the rather interesting perspective of being just one human being on planet earth. But you are many other things besides, including being me, Joy-Divine. And at some level each and every person on earth is also a Light Being who knows the Oneness of All. And at some level each and every person on earth actually IS God.

Z: Wow. Big concept that.

J-D: It is, and it's going to take a little work for you to really get this properly. But there is no rush - we will keep conversing and keep addressing this in new and different ways until it works for you.

Z: Thank you. But… um… this chapter was supposed to be about the "Implications of the Oneness". I get that we have been talking about that… that all is perfect and so on. But…

J-D: But you want me to actually talk about that which is promised in the heading?

Z: Yes please.

J-D: Good. That was coming next. What I wanted to illustrate is that there are many levels of existence here in this reality you inhabit. There is the deepest level - the one you currently reside in - at which you can absolutely forget that you are One. There is a level or two above this at which it is still possible to proceed whilst hiding the fact of the Oneness of All from yourself, if that is what you choose. But one can only go inwards so far before one is forced to confront and accept this fact… All is really and truly One. If you refuse to look at this and refuse to make it true for yourself then you can continue on for as long as you wish in a state of separation and duality. There are many amazing things you can do and many wondrous experiences you can have, but it is a simple fact that you will never graduate beyond a certain point. When, on the other hand, you accept the Oneness as a fundamental fact of your being, not only can you graduate beyond that point but you also gain access to infinite realms beyond.

Z: So let me understand this… beings who do not believe in the Oneness of All get what they believe. They get separation.

J-D: Yes.

Z: And this limits them.

J-D: Yes. Being One with God obviously makes you infinitely more powerful than being separate. Ironically when you ARE One with God, then those who believe they are not One with God are also one with you.

Z: Huh?

J-D: Hard to understand, I know. But let's take yourself as an example. You are within me. All your experiences are mine too. You can believe that you are separate from me if you want, but I know you are not. I know that you are an aspect of myself that is perfectly fulfilling your role in bringing me the experiences that I desire. You cannot but be serving my agenda. If you don't want to recognise that fact, then you can serve my agenda whilst choosing separation and the pain of being alone. Or you can recognise the truth of the Oneness and harmonise yourself with me and realise that I too am serving YOUR agenda and you can then travel with me in loving unity and joy. So it's an important realisation. EVERYTHING is One with God and within God. Even those who cannot see this for themselves. And those who cannot see this are out of harmony and feel they are fighting an uphill battle to achieve anything. Those who do choose to see this suddenly awaken to a whole infinite, unending reality packed full of beings who wish to work with them and co-create with them. They awaken to their true power and gifts and they find themselves surrounded by others whose true power and gift complement theirs perfectly.

Z: This begins to make sense to me now.

J-D: We'll come back to this until it is perfectly bedded in your consciousness. What I want you to understand is that there is a level of consciousness at which all beings know their essential Oneness. Beings at this level are the Inner-Selves of all who are incarnated with you on Planet Earth who do not know of their Oneness. And while it is so that these Outer-Selves that reside in separation might decide to hurt or even kill one another, the Inner-Selves who know of their Oneness know that this is just a very temporary, illusory experience. They know that the combatants are really just like actors who are pretending to kill each other who, in reality, have nothing but love between them. For the Inner-Selves this is so. They love each other because they are One. At this level of reality they know it is actually impossible to really desire to hurt each other. For them they know that to hurt another is to hurt the Self. Truly. For them there is no difference. Whatever such a being does to another they do instantly to themselves.

Z: Because they are One being?

J-D: Yes, exactly. One that is also many. Many that are truly One.

Z: So at this level you wouldn't find ugliness. I mean no one would attack or hurt another. No one would try to manipulate or take from another, right?

J-D: It could only happen if both parties agreed to it all up front.

Z: Does that ever happen?

J-D: Oh yes! How do you think your world can be as it is? How can it be that within these Light Beings there are manifestations that are doing all these things to each other? It is all agreed to in advance. There is always a contract.

Z: If one person hurts or manipulates another, then their Light Being has agreed to this?

J-D: Yes. That is what I am saying. You on earth are within us. You are our creations and we are yours. We jointly create the whole world you are experiencing. You bring certain experiences towards yourself with your thoughts and beliefs. With your ideas about yourselves. We are a part of that. We do all manner of facilitation so that all proceeds, in a greater sense, exactly according to plan.

Z: Something doesn't rhyme here. What about Free Will?

J-D: Oh you have Free Will alright! We do all this facilitation precisely so that everyone does have Free Will. So that no-one's Free Will is abrogated.

Z: Explain?

J-D: Well what if you, by your thoughts, your choices and your beliefs, were creating for yourself a circumstance in which you wanted to feel what it is like to be a perpetrator? Let us say you wanted to do some crime in which you felt like you gained some power over someone. As a part of your soul-journey you chose that. Then how would we accomplish this? We'd have to find a partner for you; someone who is willing to be the other half of that transaction. There will be someone out there who, for reasons of their own, chooses to see what it is like to be a victim.

Z: You are saying that people who have bad stuff happening to them have chosen this?

J-D: Yes. This is often the point at which people balk. They often walk away from the truth of this because they are unable to accept that they themselves have created the "bad things" that have happened to them. Immediately they will want to fling back at me, "*What about the child who was raped?*" or some such equally horrific experience. They will insist that there is no way that this was chosen by that person.

Z: And you are saying it was?

J-D: Yes. I know it will take a lot for some to accept this. This is why a message such as mine is not for everyone. Not everyone is ready to hear this message. Many still need for there to be an "evil other". They want and need to believe that there are evil beings outside of themselves that create all the bad that happens in the world. They want to remain victims of their circumstances. And this is perfectly okay. If people want to stay at that level of realisation for a while, then there is nothing wrong with that. But if you are willing to move on to a more empowered level of consciousness then I am offering another thought. I am saying something quite simple: YOU are the creator of your own reality. If this is so, then obviously you cannot also be a victim of your reality! "Victim" and "Creator" are two opposite states. I am saying you already ARE the creator of your reality. You have chosen to forget this so that you can play the game you are now playing. You can keep this forgotten if you like. Then you are creating, "*I am not the creator of my reality*". And, if you are creating that, then you are also creating, "*I am the victim of my circumstances*". And if you are creating that, you will experience that, because…

"You always get EXACTLY what you create"

And so you will create for yourself opportunities to experience victimhood. Hence the so-called "bad stuff" that you allow to happen to you. You will keep getting such experiences until you have a new thought about this… until you decide to take back your power and stop being a victim. Until you decide to take responsibility and become a creator. And when you DO, these things will begin to change. The more you believe that you are the creator of your reality, the more you will experience that. The more you will see all things that you experience as being a direct result of your choices.

Z: Like the "Light" in the parable!

J-D: Ah, yes! And now you too are beginning to see the Light!

Z: Ha! I like the word play. So, if we believe we are victims then we will get victim experiences as negotiated by our Inner Selves.

J-D: Right.

Z: Until we are ready to discover that we have created all these experiences and rise above them and begin to create experiences that we like more.

J-D: Correct.

Z: Then we become, ever more powerfully, the creators of our own reality.

J-D: Yes.

Z: But what about the children. I mean, you used the example of a child who is raped. Surely it is unfair to expect a young child to make the choice to transcend its victim status?

J-D: This is an emotionally charged issue and I can easily comprehend why this is difficult for you. But you must understand that a child is no more and no less an expression of a spirit-being than an adult is. You yourself had a pretty horrific experience as a handicapped child in one of your other lives.

Z: Yes. I have shared this with our readers. (Zingdad note: see *"Lost in My Own Dream World"* in Chapter 1)

J-D: Well, when you eventually come to understand your story correctly you will begin to see the symmetry in your choices. You will see how these lives all balance each other out and how these experiences were all brought to you as a result of the choices you took and the decisions you made. You experienced being a sexual predator in one lifetime and you experienced being sexually predated upon in another. Remarkably enough you will even come to understand that your perpetrator and your victims are all from within the same Light Being. In other words, you and this other Light Being exchanged roles so that both of you could really and truly understand what this was about by experiencing it for yourself first hand. In Chapter 5 I told you that if you encountered something in another being but had not encountered this in yourself you would not understand it. It would puzzle you. You will quite likely move to judgement of this other. But if you had experienced this thing in yourself you will be much more likely to move to compassion and in so doing be able to help this other being find healing. It is, in fact, this self-comprehension that allows you to be of service to the other. And so it is for you that your experiences in your other lives can be used, if you are willing to choose this, to feel profound empathy for those who are deep in a victim state because you were there AND you can also find compassion for offenders because you know that you too are capable of being an abuser. That is one result of the choices you have made. The point to remember here is:

> *"If you cannot see the perfection then you are standing too close to the picture."*

Z: Oh, wow, yes! That is most applicable here.

J-D: And it can most poignantly be illustrated by the horror of an innocent, such as a child for example, going through some abusive experience. We look at this and it just seems so very wrong. So very unfair. So unaccountably incongruent with there being a loving God. And how can I tell you that you are wrong if you feel this? I cannot. But I can tell you that there will come a time when you will stand back enough from the picture that you will see the perfection. And I can also tell you that, if I say this to you when it is YOUR child that has been abused, you will say "NEVER!" And you will think me a monster for even suggesting this. That is how these things go. Beings choosing a victim status are, by definition, not able to see that they are doing this. If they were, then they would realise they are creating their own reality and would no longer be victims. It's a bit of a catch-22 situation, really. The only way out is for you to make a choice. To decide to claim responsibility and to decide to be the creator of your own reality and to take the time to allow that to become true for you. But it's not something that everyone will be able to hear, that is for certain.

Z: And what about the perpetrators? Surely they aren't aware that they are the creators of their own reality?

J-D: No. Excellent question though. You recall I said there was a triangle of Victim/ Perpetrator/ Rescuer?

Z: I do.

J-D: Well, that is how things appear to those who are not aware that they are the Creators of their own reality. It appears to them as if they are always in one of these three roles with respect to each other. But this is not how it appears from a higher perspective. From a higher perspective there is only Creator and Victim.

Z: What happens to the Rescuer and the Perpetrator?

J-D: If you look at them hard enough you will see both of these are also just victims. I challenge you to go and find any number of perpetrators. Look at their stories properly. You'll find, I promise you, that they came to act as perpetrators because they believed themselves to be victims. It is as a result of their own belief in their own victimhood that they acted out as they did.

Z: Always?

J-D: Always. The worst criminal offenders in your jails all have the worst childhood circumstances. They are all traumatised in their own psyches. If their psyche was healed and loved then they would not be expressing rage at the world at large. Witness what happens when one such a perpetrator finds healing, self-love and acceptance. He transforms. He becomes an agent for good. So clearly his perpetrator-nature is tied up with his own sense of being a victim.

Z: Hmm… so perpetrators are actually victims. What about rescuers?

J-D: This is also a victim but quite often it is the last step before someone releases themselves from victimhood. It is a way to still engage with the Victim/ Perpetrator game whilst not actively being either of those. You see, before you can leave Victim/ Perpetrator behind you will need to heal yourself of the pain and trauma that you feel was inflicted upon you whilst you were in that game. You can do so by trying to help others in similar circumstances. You can turn your pain around and make something useful of it. You can overcome it by being a beacon of love. For example, a rape victim might establish a counselling and advocacy group. You often find that the people who originate such initiatives were victims who stood up and took back their power. Or sometimes even perpetrators who decided to make amends. Beings who want to be done with Victim/ Perpetrator often go through a cycle of Rescuer before they leave the game behind. There are other reasons for rescuer too. Sometimes the rescuer simply wishes to feel "noble". They wish to earn self-love through doing good deeds. Often this results in a kind of interfering rescuer whom the victim doesn't really appreciate. Another case would be a reformed perpetrator. For example, a husband, who for years committed spousal abuse, might start a "men's group" in which these men support each other in finding ways of dealing with their issues of rage and disempowerment. There are many permutations of this and I cannot elucidate all of them. I simply make the case that Victims, Perpetrators and Rescuers are all still in a state of believing that they are ultimately victims. Creator beings, on the other hand, know that everyone is a creator being. That all is perfect. That there is nothing and no one that needs to be fixed. It is always perfect.

Z: But that sounds uncaring and callous to me.

J-D: Why?

Z: Well, that means, if I see someone in pain, I should ignore them and just say, "*Oh, you created this for yourself*".

J-D: You COULD. But remember, in every moment, in every thought and in every action you are creating yourself and your reality. If you are a creator being then you know this. So if you see someone else's pain then you are actually experiencing it somewhat yourself. You must decide what you are going to do with that. You must choose.

Z: But...

J-D: No stay with me a minute. You, where you are now, living on earth, you do not KNOW the Oneness of all. No matter how advanced your consciousness. By definition, in order for you to be on earth you MUST see others as just that: as other. You are not yet of true unity consciousness. If you were you would be here with me. Not down there on earth. So you might accept the things I say in an intellectual way but you are not yet experiencing it as your reality. Am I right?

Z: Yes. That is so.

J-D: So you are still seeing this other that is in pain as an "other". You still think the pain you are observing is THEIR pain, not your own. And in that moment you are called to decide what to do with what you observe. And your response to that call will define who you are in that moment.

Z: Ugh! Now I am confused. What then must I do? Must I help everyone or must I let them create for themselves?

J-D: Ah. Now we get to the ethics and the morals. Good. Remember this is where it all started? You said you wanted to know what it might mean morally and ethically to understand that All is One?

Z: Ah yes. That feels like a million pages ago!

J-D: Quite. We have been on a bit of a journey since then. In order to answer this question I am going to ask you to think back on the story of the Darklanders. There were beings of many different types of consciousness in that story. There were the Darklanders who remained Undecided about how they wished to create themselves. Then there were the Brightlanders who chose one of three expressions: the duality-conscious STO and STS beings and the unity-conscious Unifiers. Of all of these, it was only the Unifiers who knew the Oneness of all. And so, if you want to understand the morality of unity consciousness then you should read again how the Unifiers behaved.

Unifiers know that you and they are essentially the same being. They therefore look at you with the eyes of love and compassion. They do not see you or your choices as "wrong". They do not judge you and they do not pity you (for that is also judgement!). If you call for help then unifiers will come to your assistance in a way that IN THEIR TRUTH is the best way to do so. That DOES NOT MEAN they will rush in and rescue you. It does not mean they will give you anything and everything you ask for. Because very often the very thing you are begging for is the thing that will keep you in a state of separation and pain. So they will help you as they themselves would wish to be helped, in a way that brings to you the realisation that you are the creator of your own reality and an indivisible part of the Oneness

I'll give you a practical example: If you say to me, "*Please J-D fix my life because it's a mess*" and I rush in and fix it up for you, then what are you and I really saying? We are saying that you are incapable and that you are NOT the creator of your reality. Right? But you see I KNOW that you are me and I am you. So I am therefore saying that I TOO am incapable and not the creator of MY reality. Which then makes it impossible for me to help you. So nothing happens. You see?

Z: That's pretty cute! Okay. So you can only help me in a way that is congruent with your truth.

J-D: Exactly! And my truth is that All is One with God and everyone, whether they know it or not, creates their own reality. I cannot go about doing anything to you or for you in a way that negates that truth. So the help I can and will offer you will be in the form of assistance that helps you to help yourself. That enables you to more powerfully understand that you are the creator of your own reality. That gives you the tools to stand up and take the things you don't like in your life and create them differently until they are the way you DO like.

Z: Ah! And that is why the Light in the parable is the way it is. It doesn't come in and change stuff and make stuff the way IT would want it to be. It is just there to assist those who are ready to see that they can make a different choice and create their life as THEY would want it to be.

J-D: Exactly so. That is exactly the point of the whole parable. You see the light is not there to judge anyone wrong. It is not there because IT thought the Darklanders were bad or wrong or incapable. Remember how it got there? It got there because many of the Darklanders themselves were calling out for help. They called out, and what essentially turns out to be an aspect of themselves, replies because it remembered its own inner-pain. No judgement. Just an answer to a call. And the answer does not come in the form of a Rescuer, nor in the form of a Perpetrator. We can see what happens with such answers - they just keep the cycle going. No, the answer comes in the form of a gently offered gift of Love which each person can accept or refuse. And even if they refuse it, there is no judgement. It remains there for them to accept later. And when they do accept it, there are no demands about what they must do with it. They can always create exactly what they desire and they will always get what they create. So they can even use the Light that is offered to create pain for themselves and others. If that is their choice, then they will continue to get what they create. And this will go on until they are ready to see that this does not bring them love or joy or peace.

To know the Oneness of All is to gain a much broader perspective. It is to see the perfection of all things. And then you cease judging others and begin instead to simply discern what is right, good and true FOR YOU. Then you go where your truth takes you instead of being blown around by judgement of what is going on around you.

Okay. Now we are still very far from being done with talking about the Oneness and what it means. But I feel I have laid some important ground-work. I want to ask you one simple question. Given that which I have laid out in this conversation, do you think a knowing of the Oneness is likely to lead to unethical or immoral behaviour?

Z: No. I want to thank you for this conversation. Because I can really see that beings that are of unitary-consciousness will only ever desire what is best for every other being. It seems to me they will, by definition, be the most loving of beings. And that they will never be able to do something which they know to be harmful to another.

J-D: Okay. Then I have answered the question from the end of Chapter 5, which is what we set out to do in this Chapter. And now that I have done so, I want to conclude by making another little point. Can you remember a few pages back you were in turmoil about how this conversation was all going wrong? About how you had wasted time in this chapter with irrelevant questions?

Z: Yes, I remember.

J-D: Well in your mind at that point the wasted conversation was basically the Darklanders story. You wanted an answer to the moral and ethical implications of knowing the Oneness of all and you felt that we had taken a HUGE tangent that was just a waste of time. But now I want to make the point that not only did the Darklanders story form the basis for a very good understanding of the implications of the Oneness but that we have laid the groundwork for many other future understandings. I am saying that we have not only done what we set out to do but have also achieved many other beautiful things besides. You gained an answer to your question and it brought a richness of understanding way beyond what you expected. Am I right?

Z: Yes. That is most certainly so. This particular conversation has been my favourite thus far. I'm sure I will re-read it many times

J-D: That's a good idea. I suggest you re-read it soon. You will find I have planted understandings in it that will open up for you if you give it another pass or two. And if you come back in a year's time you will gain other new and deeper insights. That is how much richer this chapter is than it would have been had we just got down to brass tacks and I directly answered your question as you thought I should.

Z: Oh wow, I can certainly see the beauty and the perfection in that.

J-D: And that is because,

> *"At the level of Oneness, all things always conspire to the greatest good."*

Which is another way of saying,

> *"Everything is always perfect."*

And, at the risk of flogging this one to death,

> *"If you cannot see the perfection then you are standing too close to the picture."*

Z: That is awesome, J-D! Thanks for bringing this all home so powerfully for me.

But I have to admit… there is STILL something that bothers me about all this.

J-D: And that is…?

Z: That it's all good and well for you to talk about all this Oneness stuff but… well… here I am on Planet Earth doing my best to figure stuff out, doing my best to be a good person, doing all this spiritual questing… but still I am separate from you and God and everything else! I mean I HEAR what you are saying. But for me this stuff is all still just theoretical. It is not my direct personal experience that All is One.

J-D: And is that a problem for you?

Z: GOOD GOD YES!!! I feel in my heart a craving for this. I want to KNOW the Oneness of all. And talking to you has just deepened that desire. But still I don't experience it. I mean I have had some awesome experiences in some meditations but STILL, here I am separate from you and from God and everyone else.

J-D: And so? Do you have a question?

Z: Yes. I want to know how I get to experience this - how do I get to know as a direct fact of my own experience that I am absolutely and completely One with All That Is?

J-D: I am SO glad you asked that question. It is the perfect question. Because the very reason I am here now in this reality at all is tied to the answer to that question. You see there are a great many paths home to the Oneness of All. Some are painful to travel. Some are long and hard. Some are really treacherous and you easily lose your way. Many seem to have nothing but dead ends. But fortunately not all paths are like that. Some are a bit easier. And there is one particular path which is full of Joy and is all about Love and is remarkably easy to find. But you must choose which path you would like. So, I ask you, what kind of path would you like to travel?

Z: You're kidding, right? If I get to choose then I will always choose to travel in as much love and joy as I can. And I have to admit this - I'm not REALLY into all kinds of hard work. I mean I'd rather have it easy than hard, if it's all the same to you?

J-D: That's my boy! And yes, of course I was joking with you. I wouldn't offer you a path that is painful and hard. I love you!

Z: But isn't there value to be had in doing it the "hard way".

J-D: Look: my name is "Joy-Divine". I am not "Work Ethic-Divine", or some such. I am here to inspire joy. That's the first point. The second point is this: every single being who has gone into duality has created loads of hard work for themselves. Lifetime after lifetime of hard work. And pain and loss and suffering and so on. You have done WAY enough of all of that. There is absolutely NO REASON why this last bit of your journey - the path home - needs to be anything other than the greatest joy of your whole existence. That is, in fact, exactly what it is meant to be. Now you can choose to make it miserable and tough if you want to. But you need to know that it needn't be so. It can be easy, love-filled and joyous. All you have to do is choose that.

Z: Okay! I choose that!

J-D: Good. Then I am ready to tell you how to have that. What you have to do is to open a new conversation. Title it, "The Singularity Event" and then commence the conversation by asking me *"What is the Singularity Event?"*

Z: Excellent. I'll do that. But you have me intrigued… what is the Singularity Event?

J-D: In the next chapter, you brat!

Z: Okay (laughs). See you there…

* * * * *

Chapter 7. The Singularity Event
A Conversation with Joy-Divine

Zingdad: So, J-D, here is the BIG QUESTION: what IS the Singularity Event?

Joy-Divine: I am really looking forward to telling you about this, as it is a wonderful, exciting topic. Now, before we start, I want to ask you what 2012 means to you?

Z: 2012? Wow, this is such a big topic right now. It seems to me to be quite an important date. Probably the most important year in all of our history. From all kinds of different perspectives it seems something fundamentally game-changing is going to happening then. The end of time. Or the ascension of this planet. Or the big "Kablooee" – the end of the world. Or something. Depending on who one speaks to, there are all kinds of possible things coming then. And from my own conversations, particularly with Adamu, it would seem to me as if there might be something quite wonderful about to happen. But possibly mixed in with some scary stuff too about earth changes. And then also it seems to me that there might be even be contact with races from other planets and…

J-D: Right, so you have quite a complicated and confused set of ideas running through your mind, all attached to this same date. Essentially this is what we are going to talk about now under this heading, "The Singularity Event".

Z: Ah. But as I say, I have previously received quite a bit of information on the topic of 2012 and, with all due respect to you and Adamu, whilst what I received was great, I am still confused. Why will THIS conversation be any different?

J-D: Fair question. What is different now, is YOU. You need to understand that you are the lens through which you perceive your reality. If the lens is a little dirty or a little warped then you will perceive with some inaccuracies. You are not able to receive information about Self-creation if you are deeply in victim mode. This is why I have waited until now to begin THIS series of discussions with you. You recently completed some pretty intense inner work, as a result of which, you decided to be ready to be the creator of your own reality. You decided to trust yourself. You therefore released a whole lot of that which was warping and obscuring the lens which is you. Please understand that all the conversations you had with spirit beings before beginning THE ASCENSION PAPERS were really sort of "practice sessions". A lot of it was very beautiful and useful, but it was really about you learning how to do this and learning to trust what you had received. It was in preparation for this moment now when you are, for the first time, able and ready to receive this material. Your lens is now, for the first time, sufficiently clear that THE ASCENSION PAPERS may pass through it. And you have the practice and the trust to be able to write it down

Z: Well that is pleasing to know!

J-D: It is a never ending process. You will, for the rest of all of your experiences, be in a process of enlarging your ability to perceive. As will everyone. And as you do so, so you will be able to receive ever greater views of What Is. But I don't want to get into a discussion about that right now. I am simply saying that you and I are now ready to have THIS discussion.

Z: Great. Let's have it then! Please tell me what is the Singularity Event is.

J-D: Here is the story: from a certain perspective, one might say that God is always in a cyclical process of breathing out and then breathing in again. The out-breath could be seen as The One creating diversity and many-ness, extending away from the Self. The in-breath is the returning of that many-ness to Oneness. In your personal experience the out-breath would be the process of "stepping down" from your Inner-most Self through all the various "layers" of Self right down to the incarnation which you now experience yourself to be having. You are actually many incarnations at that 3rd Dimensional level that you now inhabit. You think of these incarnations as "this life" and "past lives" but actually you are all of those incarnations right now. That is the result of the out-breath of your soul. Then the in-breath would be the opposite; it would be the so-called ascension process, which is a process by which all the many fragments down in the deepest density begin to come together in healing. As they begin to find their way home to integrate with their "Inner-self", that is the beginning of the in-breath. The in-breath ends when the whole of this reality, and all that are in it, are returned to a state of Oneness.

Z: And that final ending is the Singularity Event?

J-D: Oh no! The Singularity Event will occur in the moment of perfect stasis when the out-breath is complete, but the in-breath has not yet begun. Between the two. If you were to breathe out, hold, and then breathe in, then that "hold" would be where the Singularity Event would occur. One could say that the Big Bang, which began your universe, is the beginning of the out-breath. Then the out-breath comes to an end, followed by the Singularity Event. Then the in-breath begins. In fact the Singularity Event is a critical part of changing from an out-breath mode to an in-breath mode. It alters the perception and the awareness of the players. It changes the balance of forces from mostly diversification to mostly unification. And then the in-breath may proceed. The in-breath ends when all in this universe is again returned to Oneness. It is, from your perspective, a process of unimaginably large scope.

So you see, what we are talking about here is a reality being rolled out and then, when it has concluded the first part of that for which it was created, it begins to roll up again. On the out-bound side you find the impulse to create great diversity, fragmentation and many different and differentiated opportunities for expression and then, on the in-bound side, we have the impulse to re-integrate all the elements, help them to find their way back to where they belong so that all can be made One again. But the challenge is that, as you get to the end of the roll-out, beings living here in this density have forgotten who they really are. They have become so embroiled in the games they are playing that they have completely forgotten WHY they are playing the games and, more importantly, how to stop playing them. This results in these beings experiencing a great degree of momentum – left to their own devices they will just keep on creating more diversity and more separateness and they will continue on an out-breath trajectory. And this is despite the fact that this is causing them pain. If you ask them, they say they desire peace and love but, due to this "momentum", they continue to create fear, separation and unhappiness for themselves.

But to continue in this fashion is not in harmony with Universal Will and it is not what was decided upon and agreed upon by all aspects of The One that came to play here when this reality was created.

Z: So what about their Free Will?

J-D: Well it's like this: let's say you are the striker in a soccer team. It is your job to get the ball in the net and score points. You are playing a game and the score is currently a tie. Let's say it's 1-1. But right now you have the ball and you are running forward with it. You have a good feeling about this: you are sure you are now going to score. Some defenders come at you but you out-manoeuvre them. You pass to a team-mate and he passes back… and… then the half-time whistle blows. What do you do?

You stop playing and walk off the field, that's what.

Because although you were in the middle of playing at that point and although you are disappointed that you didn't get to score that goal, there is also a greater sense in which you agreed to certain rules before you started playing. For one thing you agreed that the game would change direction after a certain duration and that it would end after a certain duration. Throwing a tantrum and demand of the referee that you must be allowed to play on because, *"What about Free Will?"* will not bring you any reward. You will understand that, as the whistle blows, much as you might have wanted to play on, THAT is where play ends. And so it does and everyone walks off the field for the half-time break.

The timing of the game, when it starts, when it changes direction and when it ends are built right into the very rules of the game. The game is not played at all without these rules. And in just that same way the Singularity Event is built into the fabric of this reality. It is an event that has been created to occur at a specific moment and everyone that is now in this reality has at a deep level agreed to it before they came to play here. It is a necessary cessation of activities at this critical juncture so that all aspects of The One, all beings in this whole reality, can re-align themselves with the in-breath phase. Like the whistle blowing, it pauses the current game so that the direction of play can be changed. But what the Singularity Event itself is, is quite the most wonderful thing. Each being will have a unique experience of it, but essentially it is a moment of ecstatic union with God. A moment of blissful Oneness.

Z: We'll all experience this?

J-D: Yes. A true mystical experience will be had by all.

Z: And then, what will happen after that?

J-D: AFTER THAT? You want to zip on by as if I just told you we'll just be handing out free lollipops. Don't you want to know more about this amazing event?

Z: Oh! I thought that a full mystical experience would be sort of indescribable other than to say that one has this experience of total unity with All and with God?

J-D: Indescribable? Well I don't know about that. I do most certainly agree that no words will do this experience justice but I also think we really should give you at least some idea as to what it is all about. I mean this Singularity Event is really the most important thing to have happened in all of time.

Z: Really?

J-D: Yes. It will be how time itself will end. You'll understand that statement in due course when you come to understand what time itself is. But first I think we should talk more about the event itself.

Z: Well, that's great then. Thank you. Please tell me about that.

J-D: When the Singularity Event occurs you will, each of you, have an experience of being in the heart of God. It will be a state of pure Being-ness. You will BE what you truly are. There will be no doing, no thinking, no action whatsoever. You will be perfect and complete. And you will have perfect knowing. All things will be shown to you in their completion and their perfection. Now these might seem like nice, flowery words to you. And it might seem like something that you should look forward to experiencing, but you have no idea how amazing an experience this will be. And more importantly, you have no idea how powerful this can be, if you let it.

Z: What do you mean, *"if we let it?"*

J-D: Well, you asked a moment ago about Free Will and THIS is where it comes into play. You see, you agreed to the ending of the game in this way, but you have left it up to yourself to decide HOW you will experience that event when you get there. So, for some, the Singularity Event will be a quick thing. They will think that something happened to them that lasted maybe a minute or two. It was a strange and wonderful interlude in their lives... and then they will go on with a life that doesn't seem to them to be very different from what they had before (though, of course, it will be). On the other end of the scale some others might choose to open themselves to the experience as much as they can and it will feel to them as if they are off on a grand voyage through All That Is. It will seem to them as if they spent the equivalent of a million lifetimes in deep experience. They will voyage to the heart of God, passing through as much of All That Is as they are experientially able to touch. And everything that fascinates them, that brings them a feeling of joy or love, will be amplified and brought further into their consciousness until they are sated of it and ready to release that experience and move on. And so they will go. On and on. Deeper and deeper into the Oneness of the All. And since the Oneness is infinite and unending, such beings COULD carry on like this forever. Literally. They could forever, and for always, be tourists of What Is. Sampling and seeing and touching and feeling and, especially, KNOWING as they go through all the realms; all the densities and layers; out into other realities altogether; through all the variations and changes that constitute the unending multifarious magnificence of That-Which-Is.

Z: You could travel like that forever?

J-D: Yes.

Z: So why don't we? That sounds so great!

J-D: It IS great. Which is exactly why many beings DO spend all of eternity in such blissful states of experience. And by being that which simply experiences EVERYTHING with a heart full of unending Love, they become something like the connective tissue of Life which holds all else together. They perform a great service to Life. They are the ones that see, experience and know ALL without interference or involvement. But there is something of a paradox here: Some things can only be known and experienced from a state of limitation, division and separation. And so it is that, paradoxically, in order for these beings of Oneness to know all, they must also experience not-Oneness. The heart of the paradox is that they can, and do experience this separation whilst still being in a state of Oneness. Or they might choose to create degrees of separation within their Oneness.

Does this seem confusing?

Z: Somewhat, yes. I am trying to follow but I don't understand how you can be both One and not-One.

J-D: To help you understand I am going to tell you a little story using the example of water. Water is a substance that is composed of molecules with the chemical formula H_2O. Let us pretend it is possible for you to meet and talk to a single water molecule to get its perspective on life. Let us imagine we randomly choose one such molecule and we find it in a wintry landscape high on a mountain. If we enquired of our new acquaintance what it is doing it might say, "I am sitting quite still, holding tight to all the other water-molecule friends around me. Together we have formed a glacier."

This is what water molecules do when they get cold enough. They slow down and become quite still. As they do, they cosy up with the other molecules around them and bond together into a crystal lattice. This is what ice is. And that is how they remain, relatively still and bonded together, until heat is applied.

Which brings me to the next time we meet our little water molecule: Winter passes and the warming rays of the spring sun heats the glacier. It energises all the the water molecules and they begin to dance. Eventually some of them are moving too vigorously to maintain their bonds and they break free, tricking away into a stream. When we eventually find our new friend and ask him what he is up to he says, "I am rushing down a mountain side in a fast-flowing river!"

Again we allow some time to pass. Summer comes. The stream is caught in a large lake and the hot summer sun bakes down on the water. Water molecules on the surface of the lake are heated up some more. The extra energy makes them dance even more vigorously and they fly free from the water's surface as vapour. Now our friend might report, "I am drifting free, flying away on the breeze!"

In due course, our friend is likely to find a cloud to join and will eventually cool and make water-bonds again and fall to earth. And so it will go around the cycle yet again.

And now that you have gotten to know the water-molecule a little, which you its states is the most like being part of The Oneness? Being still and peaceful and connected with others in the glacier? Being fluid but still connected in the river? Or being free and unencumbered and energised as vapour?

Z: I think the glacier. I think he felt most connected to other water molecules. And he was still and peaceful.

J-D: Its a good guess, but it is not correct. But then I have to admit I cheated; I'm afraid it was a trick question. None of these states of water are much like an experience of Oneness. All three are states of DOing and separation. In all three states, the little molecule is still just a single-perspective being. This is similar to your current experience of life. As with the ice-state, you might find yourself doing things that bring you into closer harmony and connection with others. You might become still and peaceful. You might introspect and meditate. But still you are an individual, experiencing separation. And if you choose to do more highly energetic and individualistic things this will not actually make you any more or any less a single-perspective being.

But now, let us imagine that our water molecule becomes part of a cloud. But this time, instead of talking to an individual molecule, imagine we can talk to the whole cloud. Inside it there are very, very many molecules of water. Many more than the biggest number you know.

Z: More than a trillion?

J-D: By my estimate there might very well be a trillion water molecules in about 5 or 10 raindrops. So, no, a LOT more than a trillion.

Z: Gosh!

J-D: No kidding. So this cloud includes a great number of molecules, each of them having a unique, individual perspective. Let us imagine that the cloud knows, feels, thinks, sees, remembers and experiences everything that all the individual molecules do. The cloud is truly the collective of all the molecules together. But it is more than that. It does not ONLY know what the molecules collectively know... it knows more than that. It knows what it is to be a cloud as well. It knows what it is to know, all at the same time, what this mind-boggling number of little beings know. And here is the thing you might struggle to understand: The cloud is not a being that has other beings inside it. It IS all those little beings. The cloud IS the water molecules and they ARE the cloud. There is no separation. There is no cloud without water molecules. But the cloud is, quite simply, a lot more than the sum of its parts. Imagine how it would be for you if you could, right now, be thinking all the thoughts that every person on earth is thinking. It would enlarge your capacity for perception and self-awareness in an unimaginable way. You would not simply be a human being who is now seven billion times cleverer. You would be an entirely different order of being with an entirely different perspective of what Life is and what Self means.

Do you follow?

Z: Wow, I think so!

J-D: Good. So now, do you think the cloud knows what true Oneness is?

Z: It sounds like it does, yes.

J-D: The cloud certainly knows what it is to have many perspectives, this is true. But that does not mean it knows true Oneness. It doesn't know, for example what it is to be an ocean. But it will have more than just an inkling because all of the water molecules that make up its being will, at some point in their many cycles, have been in the ocean. So the cloud will begin to FEEL the essence of Oneness but it will also very much still be a separate, individuated consciousness, even though it is yet composed of many.

Now, I can take you on a journey of meeting ever greater constructs of water. We could meet a being called Spirit of Cloud who is composed of all the clouds on the whole planet. Then we could step up and meet Spirit of Earth's Water who is a being composed of all the water on the planet in all of its forms. Each of these beings would, as a result of their greater and greater level of consciousness and their ever-increasing number of perspectives, be closer and closer to knowing what true Oneness is. The larger their consciousness grows the more "others" it knows of. Somewhere along the line you get someone like the being that we shall call Spirit of All Water. Let us imagine that all the water that has ever existed anywhere is all a part of this great being. Every single water molecule is just one mote of consciousness in this beings great mind. Now, what do you think? If we were to ask Spirit of All Water what it is doing right now, what do you think it would tell us? Would it talk of icy glaciers? Of raging torrents? Of huge lazy oceans? Would it tell us of towering thunderclouds? Or of rainstorms, snowfalls or hail? Or of the blood that flows in your veins? Or what about whole planets composed entirely of water in one state or another? What do you think?

Z: I can't imagine...

J-D: Well, I think this great being would gently smile and say, "Child, I am beyond the considerations of 'DOing'. What I am is BEing. And in this here-and-now, I am being water."

And here, finally, we would have found a being that knows what Oneness is. Though it still has an identity, and a unique nature, this being is not misidentifying Itself. It does not think it is what it does. It knows it simply IS. It is consciousness. It is Life. And right now it is being water. But it is also very much conscious that it is also One with every other being everywhere in all that is.

And with that we can leave the story of water.

Now, what do you think? Is it so that there is Oneness, on the one hand, and not-Oneness on the other hand and that these are two separate states?

Z: Yes, it seems so. The water molecule knew only its individual perspective whereas Spirit of All Water knew Oneness.

J-D: Okay, good. But then is it not so that there are in fact degrees of Oneness and not-Oneness?

Z: You mean like the cloud? Yes, it seems there are also degrees of Oneness.

J-D: But then is it not so that actually, there is only Oneness. And all else exists as creations and illusions within the Oneness? That all DOing is only an illusion from within BEing?

Z: Whew! Yes, I guess that is also true. That is what it is like for Spirit of All Water. This being knows that all the rushing around and DOing of all the water molecules only takes place inside Its own mind.

But what I don't understand is how can all these contradictory things can be true?

J-D: It is a matter of perspective. Perspective is a very important word. You see, by shifting your perspective you can be either a single little molecule on a grand adventure down a white-water rapid or you can be all of water, or all of Life. Or anything else that exists. Because there is, in reality, no separation between any one being and any other. We are all one great being. We are ONE. But we have chosen to work very hard to see ourselves as separate. And we have accomplished this. And having accomplished this we have seen, known and discovered everything we wanted to about this particularly powerful version of the separation illusion. So now we are ready to bring the illusion to an end. And now we must begin the task of bringing all that is fractured, broken and separated and putting it all back together again. Whole, healed and One.

Z: And so we have the Singularity Event?

J-D: Just so. It is the turning point as we head back towards ultimate reunification of the whole system of reality.

And in the Singularity Event you will have the opportunity to change perspectives and see and know any and every other perspective that you might desire. You will be at one with The Oneness. The troublesome paradox is that this experience will include all the individuated and separated perspectives. You will be able to know those as well. But from a position of Oneness. You will not again have to enter into an incarnation and forget what you have discovered of yourself. Unless you really want to, of course. If, for example, on your journey through the Singularity Event you suddenly understood how you could live this lifetime that you are now living in a way that would please you more, then you could, in the next instant, find yourself right back here in this lifetime with, for example, your hands on your laptop keyboard writing something surprisingly, spectacularly different and inspired. If that is what you desired, then that is what you'd get. Or you could find yourself at a whole other level of this reality, at the 6th Dimensional reality for example, where you perceive your body to be made of pure light and you are aware that the light of you is really everywhere. And you are busy spinning your light with the light of others into whole new galaxies which, at the same time, you know are already created and you know you have already been a part of populating those galaxies with many incarnations. Perhaps even billions of incarnations. Or you could choose to end up in a reality so different from the one you are now in that any attempt to describe it to you now would be nonsensical.

Z: Or I could just stay in the Singularity Event?

J-D: Yes, you could. And, as you reside in that state of oneness, your consciousness keeps expanding and then, eventually, your consciousness will become merged with the afore-mentioned unified-field gestalt-consciousness at 8D. And that is how it will remain until this game is complete. Until the end of the in-breath, when All here is truly One again. And then you will be free to go off and play other games.

But you won't do that.

Z: I won't?

J-D: No. As soon as you begin to gather knowingness in the Singularity Event you will find something that fascinates and excites you. SOMETHING will intrigue you and you will respond by wanting to play again. And then you will. Either you will play a similar game again or you will go and play some game with quite different rules. Possibly a bigger game with a less restrictive rule set. Possibly one in which fear and pain are correctly understood and do not hamper you. I think, for you personally, you will come to realise that you wish to design a whole new game of your own which will be played by rules which will lead to a truly joyous experience for yourself and your co-creative game partners. But you will most certainly enter the game again. And I would be MOST surprised if many of your readers do not likewise re-enter that same game as your co-creators.

Z: How can you be so sure?

J-D: Because I cheat. I see you completely. I know you to a depth that you yourself have not even an inkling of yet. I know what you are about. You and I are one and we are engaged in a game. And PLAY is very much what we are about. And as for everyone else – your readers and others – well, I have seen this kind of thing play out an infinite number of times. Everyone eventually gets hooked back into some aspect of the game until the game is really done.

Z: But I thought if we'd really found inner-peace and healing then we'd be free from getting hooked back. Isn't it only those who have great inner pain that will want to come back like this?

J-D: No. You must understand that I am not really referencing those who have a great deal of inner-pain in these conversations. My audience for this series is those who have at least begun on the path of healing themselves and loving themselves and the world around them.

But let me briefly address the question. Those who are in the greatest amount of pain will only very briefly experience the Singularity Event. It will be like a momentary flash of… something… something strange. Because their inner pain will disallow them to LET GO and BE. These who are deeply in pain are also deeply in anger and hatred. They hate themselves, they hate the world. They are not in any way, shape or form ready to be at peace, to be still and silent. Not for even an instant, because they know that even a moment's stillness will threaten to overwhelm them with all their buried fears and pain. So for them the Singularity Event will be but the very briefest possible moment of strangeness – a flash of bright white light on a cold and lonely night. If they would but let their fear and pain go and release themselves to it they would quite soon find that they have comprehension. They would see how and why they have hurt themselves. They would see that their enemies are really One with them and that healing lies in loving themselves and releasing their pain. All this would be possible for them. But they are most unlikely, in that moment, to just let go. Most unlikely indeed. And they will not be forced. Tragically, their fear, pain and hatred is most likely to ensure that, after their Singularity Event experience, they will immediately desire to be right back where they were battling their demons. And that is cause for sadness within my heart. Because, of course, I see them as aspects of Self even though they would look upon me as a stranger. But they must be allowed to create their own reality and to get what they create. And so, but an instant later, they might find themselves in some alternate time-line where they are surrounded by those they wish to dominate, to control, to hurt, to strike out at. All those still wishing for such dramas of fear, pain and loathing will get to acto out those plot-lines together. The fact that it will not be *quite the same world* as they had inhabited before the Singularity Event will not be apparent to them. When you move realities in this way it is transparent to you. You are in a new world, but because you have moved yourself entirely there you do not perceive it to be so.

Z: I don't understand that, J-D. Wouldn't they have a moment of wondering why the world had changed?

J-D: Try to remember the dreams you have had. When your body is fast asleep and you are dreaming, you experience yourself to be wide awake and fully engaged in another life in the world in your dreams. How often has it happened to you that, in your dreams, you have suddenly thought, *"Hey! This is not my real life. Why am I in the wrong life?"*

Z: I don't think that has ever happened to me.

J-D: Which is exactly my point. It is very rare indeed for any being who is in a reality to become conscious of the illusory nature of that reality such that he questions its validity. It only really happens right at the termination point, as a reality begins to fall away, and then only to the awakening ones. This is why it begins to happen to you who are awakening now in your normal life. You are beginning to question the validity of the dream which IS your normal "waking life". But it won't happen to someone who is buried deep into the illusion of the reality as a result of their profound pain. For these beings, their new reality after the Singularity Event will BE THEIR REALITY. It will be as if they have always been there. They will have a full set of memories in that reality and all will be normal and correct, as far as they are concerned.

Z: But why, J-D? Why all this new-time-line malarkey? Why don't they just come back to the world they were in before the Singularity Event?

J-D: There are two reasons. The first is that the world they were in before will not be available to them - I'll explain this to you in a moment. The second reason is that they don't choose it. They choose to go and work out their inner-pain and conflict. They choose to be in a reality where they can do so, unhindered by other beings and experiences which will take them away from that which they desire to experience. You see, they don't choose to live in a world where they can see how others are ascending and how things are changing. They want to go elsewhere where this doesn't occur and they don't have to see this. Just as you no longer want to create a reality populated with people who want to hurt and destroy and abuse and make war, in the same way they do not want to engage with you as they travel their path. You are no longer appropriate travel-mates for each other. And so there is a separating of the ways. Which is why, after the Singularity Event, they will create for themselves a reality in which they can express all their deep seated inner–pain, as it will be populated with all the things they fear, loathe and despise.

Z: But J-D that doesn't sound right! How can it be that they get such a horrible reality?

J-D: It is painful to contemplate, I know. But each being must be allowed to create as they wish. And until these beings are willing to let go of their fear and pain and hatred and bitterness and anger… until they are ready to release all of that… no one can force another experience on them.

Z: But what if they need help?

J-D: Oh, they WILL get help! They'll get all the help they need just as soon as they are willing to accept it. Always it is so. You yourself have been to some quite dark places at various points in your story – most especially in some of your other lives (Zingdad note: See Chapter 1, *"The Wizard"*). You know this. And when you felt the pain of this and wished to make better choices, help was there. Sometimes it has been 8 who came to your side, but other times it has been other beings who have given you aid – whether directly or through the agency of their incarnated aspects.

You have a truly blessed partnership with your beloved Lisa who has very often been there for you in exactly the perfect way when you have most needed it, just as you have been the perfect response to many of her calls for help. And you have also helped many other human beings who found themselves in spiritual and emotional confusion and pain. Sometimes you have done this consciously with an intentional intervention and sometimes you have been the conduit of healing without being conscious of it. Sometimes you have gone on a spiritual journey in deep meditation and reached out to other Selves who were in pain and offered your help. Occasionally, when you have been asleep, your consciousness has been drawn to where you were called to help, and in the morning you awoke remembering a strange dream, which seemed to be very real, in which you experienced another life that was in a state of pain. What happened was that your presence brought with it the quality of Love and Light that you bear and it assisted with healing that other being's pain. And so it goes.

Now if you, who are incarnated here in 3D and who have forgotten almost all of who you really are, can be doing this work of offering healing and love to other beings and aspects of self, do you not imagine that we of the higher dimensions are able to do the same thing, only much more powerfully, consciously and consistently?

Assistance is ceaselessly offered to all beings who are in any kind of pain, and often you, who are yourselves still deep inside the illusion, take part in delivering that aid. But it is so that the beings who are in pain MUST be willing to accept the help and begin to create a new direction for themselves. They must be willing to receive the Light that is offered to them and use it to see a new path. Loving assistance simply cannot be coerced.

You would do best to understand that these beings who are very deep in their pain are not broken or wrong or in any way "less" for the fact that they are, in this moment now, making different choices from what you are. If you stand in judgement of their choices then you cannot but interfere and involve yourself even when you are not wanted or needed. If you release your judgement of them and find your centre and your truth then you can discern for yourself that their path is not what you choose for yourself, but that it is okay to allow them to follow this path if it is what they choose. Then you free yourself to carry on and create whatever reality you wish to create. You see it is also true that they are only doing this self-harming stuff down here in the lower densities. They are also a part of a grand and beautiful Inner-Self that is elsewhere creating with love. So this too is just a perspective issue.

But before we dwell on this one thing too long, what I want to say to you is this: one of the most powerful ways we can experience ourselves in this reality is through DOing. And the way we come to experience ourselves differently is by choosing to do new and different things. It's as simple as that. And each of you are the creators of your own reality. When you know this, then you will know that you have the power to change any aspect of your reality that you don't like. But if we are to rescue someone who is in pain and take from them the opportunity to discover their own creator nature for themselves, then they will be our victim. They will always need to come to us whenever they need something changed. Then we are saddled with the task of weaning them from ourselves. Now that too might be a valid path, but more often than not it does not serve them nor does it serve us. And so, what seems to you like a lot of pain and difficulty as you live your lives on earth is, I assure you, a very temporary thing. And when you learn the value of your experiences and learn the truth of yourself then you will see what an incredibly useful thing it was to have had these incarnations on earth. You will walk away with profound self-knowledge.

So, to conclude the issue of those who are creating difficulty and pain for themselves, I will say this: they MUST be allowed to do so. And the instant they make a better choice, they will have help to release themselves from it. But THEY must make the choices. They can be helped, but ultimately they must create the situation they desire for themselves. Anything else will only continue their difficulty, I assure you. It has all been tried a great many times in a great many different ways and there is no situation in which it has worked to have one being rescue another from their pain and then remain in that rescuer relationship. All that happens then is that the rescuer discovers he is stuck with the victim and the victim remains a victim. And then they are each the victim of the other! So, in general terms, it is wise to offer guidance and assistance but not to interfere or to remove from a being the results of their choices.

Now I'd like to get back to your question and the first answer that I offered you. You asked why those who are in a deep state of pain don't just come back to the world they were in before the Singularity Event. The first answer I offered was that the world they were in before will not be available to them, remember?

Z: I do.

J-D: Well here is what that means.

The Singularity Event will occur on a cosmic date. It will occur when your heavens are aligned for it to occur. This was understood by the ancient Mayans and their understanding of that cosmic date has been translated to your calendar as being at the very end of 2012. And that is the origin of all the hoopla and excitement around the date of 2012. But what you need to understand is that this is not a earth-human-only phenomena. It is something that will impact everyone and everything in your whole galaxy. Your planet will itself be experiencing this too. Just as you are a spirit being inhabiting a physical body, so is your planet. You are aware of her physical body as the big globe upon which you live. But perhaps you are unaware that this is essentially also just a physical vehicle for a spirit being. Many civilisations that pre-date yours have come to this insight, and one of the more recent ones gave this being the name, Gaia. As this seems to retain a fair amount of resonance in your current culture, that is the name I shall use for her.

Z: You are saying that Planet Earth is someone's body? And her name is Gaia?

J-D: Yes. That is exactly what I am saying.

Let me change tack for a moment to help you to understand the situation: do you know that right now you have an enormous number of bacteria living in your gut?

Z: Eeeew! Thanks for that!

J-D: It's nothing to feel odd about. Everyone has them and pretty much all of these bacteria are useful to you. Very nearly all of them, in one way or another, are actually helping you to stay alive. One group helps you to digest something you otherwise couldn't, another group helps you to fight off invaders and supports your immune function and yet another group actually manufactures certain nutrients that you need to stay alive. In many ways you really should regard them as your microscopic friends. Certainly your body does. Which is why it has a détente with them and doesn't attack them as it would unfriendly invaders. You could say that the human body and these friendly bacteria evolved together. These bacteria and the human body are created to be partners! And here's something you may not know: the cells of your body are actually greatly outnumbered by these bacterial cells in your intestines. There are very many more of "them" than there are of "you" in your own body! So whose body is it really? Are they there to "help you out" or are you really just a convenient servant who carries them around and feeds them?

Z: I'm not sure I like that thought...

J-D: I am really just joking with you. But what I do want you to understand here is that there is a wonderful, mutually beneficial, relationship between you and these micro-organisms that you play host to. As long as these hundreds of species of beneficial bacteria living in your gut are doing their job and are happy, healthy and strong, then they take care of you, protect you and even feed you certain nutrients without which you could not live.

Z: That is amazing to know!

J-D: Yes, and of course you don't just need them; they need you just as much. Essentially you give them a safe place to live, you feed them with the perfect food, provide them with an environment which is to their liking… I mean, for goodness sakes! All you need to still do is give them an education, name them and claim them as tax deductions!

Z: Oh you are too much!

J-D: I know. But seriously: can you see that what you have here is a beautiful symbiotic relationship?

Z: Yes, I do see that.

J-D: Alright. Well then, here is one last thought. If these wonderful little friends in the gut increase and proliferate beyond certain parameters or if they get into places in the body that they shouldn't be, then they can make you very ill indeed or even kill you.

Z: Yowch! What kind of friends ARE they then?

J-D: Interesting question! Let's move on a bit and I'll remind you of that question later.

You see, Gaia also has many li'l critters living on her body. And Gaia has pretty much always been in a wonderful symbiotic relationship with all the many species of small beings, which exist in astoundingly huge numbers on her body. You might even call them her little friends. She needs them and they need her. It's a beautiful thing. But you see, every once in a long while, one of these species might get a bit out of hand. There is a bloom in their number beyond normal healthy parameters. And usually, when that happens, some percentage of these li'l critters become quite virulent in relation to Gaia. Then things might get a little unhealthy for her. If this is left unchecked, they could seriously harm Gaia's health or even kill her body! And so I remind you of your question, but now turn it around. From Gaia's perspective: what kind of friends are you humans really?

Z: Ouch! That is a good question.

J-D: Each person should ask themselves that question. It's an important one. I mean the earth is the true mother of your whole race. It is that which gives you life and sustains you. You can tell a great deal about a person from the way they treat the earth. In large measure you define yourself by the way you treat her. But that's another topic. I have made the first point I wanted to make with my li'l critters story, which is essentially that Gaia is a being who also has free will, just as you do. She also has the right to make choices. And sometimes there are parts of the task she has chosen that can be quite difficult. Like dealing with these cyclical blooms of her li'l critters. You don't know this, but your current human civilisation is only the latest one in a series of such painful events for her. There have been other civilisations before yours which have also caused her some heartache. And so, just like you, she has the right, at the Singularity Event, to decide how she is going to create her new life afterwards. With me so far?

Z: Yep.

J-D: Good. Then I'm going to change gears from li'l critters to cosmology so that I can finally finish answering your question.

Now. You are obviously quite aware that your planet circles around your sun. Each cycle equals a year. What you probably aren't aware of is that your solar system is also moving in very much longer cycles, rotating around the galaxy. There are many other cycles of course, some shorter and others much longer than these two. There is, in fact, a beautiful and complex dance of many cycles-within-cycles going on. Every few billion years a number of these cycles will coincide in quite a dramatic way to bring your solar system and your planet into a particular zone in the galaxy of exponentially increasing energy. This is important, so please pay attention to what I am about to say: your solar system is right now moving deeper into a band of increasingly high energy. And, as your planet moves forward through what you perceive as "time", it makes cyclical movements into areas of ever greater energetic input. Now please understand that the vast majority of this energy is not observable to you or your scientific tools. Firstly, your scientists are not aware that they should be looking for this and, if they were, they would use tools that are able to pick up only the narrowest sliver of that which is now coming in. But certainly, ONE effect of this area of higher energy is that all the planets in your solar system are heating up in ways which would be hard to explain otherwise. But that is the least of what is going on. For example, there is an almost infinite range of other density tonalities at which your planet also exists and at which this energy is also coming in. I am going to call all of this special incoming energy "God Light". It is very special because not only is it like the Light in the story of the Darklanders in that it is conscious, alive and infinitely intelligent Light, but more than that, it is every Light of every type, every frequency and every density. And that is what is coming in now. Cyclically you are now moving into ever higher intensities of this God Light.

Z: Can you explain what you mean when you say that the God Light is of every type, frequency and density?

J-D: The fullness of that concept will not fit into your consciousness, but I will say a few hopelessly inadequate sentences to you about it and that will have to hold you for now until you experience it for yourself in the Singularity Event.

God Light is the light of the creator as it shines from every heart of every being and at every dimension of this whole reality. It is intelligent, creative and wise. It is pure love and it gives everything of itself to you, completely, without asking for anything back and without giving any stipulation about what you may or may not do with that which it gives you. It exists at every density of this reality and every one of the infinite number of tonalities of all the densities. It is the very essence of all the love that has ever been felt by every mote of consciousness anywhere in this reality, ever. It is all the knowing and understanding that has ever been attained. It is all that and so much more than that. I, Joy-Divine, am very aware that I am a part of this God Light. I am within it and One with it. But I am as a single colour compared to all the rest of the God Light. I am one of the Light Beings, but there are many others. And all of us give all of ourselves to a full unification of what we are. And that unified being attains a kind of a consciousness which is infinitely greater than the sum of all its parts. It is alive and conscious and powerful in ways that I simply cannot comprehend. It surpasses my capacity to begin to understand.

Z: And this is God?

J-D: You keep asking that question about beings. No. This is not God. This is a part of God. It is just one very, very small part of God. Bigger than you and I, that I will concede, but minuscule compared to ALL of God. Truly, all of God is unfathomable. So no, this is not all of God. But it is, I suppose, all of God that is here in this reality. And it's a whole lot more of God than you would ever otherwise have been able to experience in a life down here in density on planet earth!

Z: And this being, this wondrous, amazing, God-like being, is going to come shining itself here on us on planet earth? We are going to see this?

J-D: I'm not sure exactly how each of you will experience this. Certainly for each of you the experience will be unique. It will depend very much on yourself how you respond to it. But anyway, I have introduced you to the concept, as I said I would, in a few sentences and now I ask you to believe me when I say these words are some of the most inadequate I have ever uttered because the concept is just that much bigger than words can be made to convey.

Z: Okay, I'll accept that. Thank you. And I really do look forward to the moment when this God Light begins to shine on us!

J-D: Well, you see the thing is it already is shining upon you. It has been for a while now. But only at low intensity. Remember the Darklanders? Remember how their Light started out a very small, very dim little Light so that they could think it wasn't even there? Well this is what happened in your planet. The very moment you moved into the light is not discernible because it was too dim. So an easier way is to look for some discernible peaks and troughs in your recent history. There was a very small peak in the early 1920's for example. It was small but it was just discernible as a rise in optimism and a feeling of unity amongst people. Then there was quite a deep trough in the early 40's when it was possible to sweep half the world into a state of war. Another rise in the 60's when, despite there still being many wars, a spontaneous peace movement sprang up. This was a novelty in your world – a whole counter-culture that was for peace and love and unity. Then, the next peak was in the 80's, when the incoming light sparked all kinds of gatherings for peace and love and consciousness again shifted. The so-called cold-war came to an end, which was something of an improvement. But then you cycled back from the Light a bit and new wars, hatreds and disunities were created. This time religion was used rather than political ideology. And so it goes – in and out. Each time you move into the light you move further in and each time you move out you move less out.

Z: Forgive me for saying this, J-D, but it doesn't really seem that way to me. I can see that there are some high points and some low points but the world seems, in many ways, to be moving in the wrong direction rather than the right direction.

J-D: No, don't apologise, you are right - it DOES seem that way to you. The fact that this impression is a mistaken impression is not your fault at all. I don't want to go too far off on a tangent but I must address this issue quickly. Please understand that you are only able to directly perceive a very limited and local perspective of what goes on in the world. I mean you yourself DIRECTLY can only know of that which occurs in your immediate neighbourhood at home and at work. For the rest you rely on reportage. You rely particularly on the news media to tell you about world events. And what you are told about those world events deeply colours your perceptions. The sad thing that I must relate is that the news media is quite furthest thing from being an unbiased source of understanding. There are a few reasons for this. The first is that news is not a service. It is a business. You do not sell news if the headline is, "*All is going quite well for the Republic of Blissvania this year. No war, the economy is okay and the weather looks fine.*" You see, people need some excitement to encourage them to buy the paper or to be glued to the TV screen. And the kind of excitement that works the very best is naked fear. Give them a bit of a panic and they will go from the morning paper over breakfast to the radio news in the drive to work to the afternoon paper at lunch to the radio news as they drive home to the evening news on TV at home. A good ol' international scare is addictive stuff. So… if news is a business and if the news business is to be successful can you really blame them for engaging in a little scaremongering from time to time?

Z: I must say I often did wonder why you never really see much "good news" on the news.

J-D: Yep. And given the fact that media businesses are some of the most lucrative and powerful businesses on your planet then it is apparent that they know exactly how to play the game. But there are other reasons for mainstream media not being the most reliable brokers of the truth. I'll touch on one of them. It is this: the biggest and most powerful media businesses are the "wholesalers" of the news that is disseminated to almost all the local news outlets on your planet. Ultimate ownership and control of these few huge corporations vests in the hands of a small number of very powerful and wealthy men. And they did not become powerful and wealthy though great acts of loving generosity! They got there with cunning and ruthlessness. And people who operate at these levels do not retain their power and wealth without diversifying their interests and ensuring that other sectors of the global economy also support their continued acquisition of ever greater power and wealth. In simple terms, this means they also own chunks of the other biggest money-spinning businesses. Like the manufacture of weapons, for example. That's extremely lucrative. And pharmaceuticals – also very lucrative.

But does it not strike you as very dangerous indeed to have the same small group of people hold in their hands the means to fan the flames of division and strife while amassing huge fortunes every time there is war? If those that profit most from war have the direct ability to cause war then you are going to live in a very dangerous world. A world that finds itself constantly at war.

Z: I see. And the world we live in is very much, constantly at war.

J-D: You catch on quite quickly. Yes. Did you know that during the Great Depression one of the only business sectors that actually managed to boom was the media? When people are scared or in pain they alternately want to be fed lots of information and then they just want to escape. First news then entertainment. The media booms. So all of this is very good for business. And more than that, the depression allowed these moguls to buy up everything worth buying for peanuts. They were the only ones with money and so they bought pretty much everything. And then, once they had cleaned house, and desired to have their possessions flourishing again, how do you think they got the economy up and running again?

Z: Uhh…

J-D: You're not nearly cynical enough to guess, so I'm going to tell you. They started a big ol' war.

Z: No! Surely war drains the economy?

J-D: It drains the people. It kills and maims and destroys. But, surprisingly, if you do it right, it can be the most amazing tool for wealth generation. Certainly it can get an economy riding high again. And of course there is the huge contributing benefit of getting all the citizenry behaving in the most unbelievably obedient way too. Lining up to die. Willingly suffering hardships and deprivations. Working like slaves to serve the war effort for next to no pay. You name it; the people will give it during time of war. Patriotism flies high.

As I say, the people who operate right at the very rarefied top of the business pyramid are very much not saints. And you have to understand that they are really the ones who call the shots. Governments come and go. Elected officials change guard every few years. But the super powerful remain.

And if one of them should suddenly catch a bad case of conscience then he'd instantly lose his place at the top. It's the nature of the machine that is global business. Gentle and kind does not get to the top of it, ever. And the point of all of this is that global mainstream media is a vital and integral part of that machine. In some ways it runs the machine and in other ways it is the machines' servant. So the media is many things. It is a completely fascinating thing to observe, but it is NOT a source of objective truth of what is going on in your world. Quite the opposite. If you even vaguely give credence to what is presented to you via the mainstream news media then you are being tugged into duality and density. You are being driven away from unity consciousness. From compassion and love. From your own truth that lies in your heart. And dare I say it… from God. The message of the mainstream media is quite the antithesis of my message.

So you may do with THAT news flash what you will… but I do suggest that, if you wish to ascend, you probably should not allow the news media to inform you of what you should hold to be true, valid and important.

Z: But J-D that is awfully doom-and-gloom-ish. I mean, if that is the state of the world… if our planet is being run by these few people and they are willing to behave like that… I mean, this is very worrying indeed!

J-D: Alright. Listen to me. I have chosen to step lightly around these darker scenarios. It is why I have, for example, preferred to tell you about your world with stories like the Darklander story. It permits me to tell you things without getting embroiled in fear. Because focussing on fear will not serve you. But that doesn't mean all is glorious and happy. If everything was wonderful then there would not be a cry for help rising from your planet. It is very blatantly apparent that what occurs here causes a great many players a great deal of pain. Even the ones who are leading nominally happy and comfortable lives experience in themselves a lot of pain. And the ones that sit right up at the top of the pyramid? These most powerful of business moguls? Do you think they are happy and content? I assure you they are not! They are racked with all kinds of inner-pain of their own. So if that is so, if the wealthiest and most powerful are in pain and the poorest and humblest are in pain and no-one seems to be wanting all this pain then you have to ask yourself… why does a whole planetary reality exist where everyone has a great deal of what they DON'T want? Especially if everyone is actually creating their own reality and is therefore able to stop doing this at any time!

It just doesn't make sense, does it?

Z: No. Not when you put it like that, it doesn't.

J-D: And if things are as confused as all that, then clearly it is time for some radically new thinking. You cannot take the kind of toxic thinking that has lead to the perpetuation of this situation and tweak it just a little and hope for a happy and healthy outcome. No, I'm afraid you need a radical shift. You need strong medicine. So the first thing is to take off the blinkers for a moment and look around and ask yourself: is the world as it is okay? Is it alright for things to be as they are? Is it fine that there is crushing poverty? That there is debilitating illness? That there is war? That there is child abuse? That women are raped? That people are murdered and sometimes over nothing more than a crust of bread? That animals are kept alive in barbarous, overpopulated conditions and then killed in the most noxious, inhumane fashion and then you eat their fear- and pain-laden flesh? That your food and water is often a toxic concoction of inedible laboratory compounds? That your health professionals often give you medicines that assist you in one place and damage you in three others? That people are locked into cycles of slavery by such insidious instruments as debt and inflation? That mind-boggling quantities of poisons are pumped into the air that you breathe, the water that you drink and the soil upon which you grow your food?

Is any of this okay?

Z: No. No it really isn't.

J-D: Well then let's take a moment to register that a clear-eyed appraisal of the situation does not come up roses. And observing that and seeing it for what it is, is not doom-and-gloom. It is not fear-mongering. That is not my game. I am not interested in trapping you where you are, I am interested in helping you to achieve what you most desire, which is your self-liberation from the situation which is causing you that pain. This is not best achieved by denying that there is any pain. Nor should we constantly deny that there is a cause for the pain we feel. There is no way to get around it… the world is NOT in great shape! And observing "what is" and then stating the obvious about your observations is not fear-mongering. It is simply the first step in the process of making better decisions, which will lead to better outcomes.

Z: Okay. I get that.

J-D: And the first bit of medicine Dr. Joy-Divine prescribes is that you get your own truth in shape and stop taking on board the mucky sludge of fear, propaganda and half-baked truths that is the news. And while you are at it, give a very good look at what you call entertainment too. Mostly it comes from the same kinds of people who are making the news. Very often it has a similar agenda. If you are pumping your mind full of fear, horror, aggression and pain and calling that entertainment, then you seriously need a re-think. They do not call television shows "programming" for nothing! And you are allowing your psyche to be programmed with poison. So be very careful about television, movies, computer games, music and the like. Be very careful about what you are programming your psyche with. You make it exceptionally difficult for yourself to find healing, love, centredness, unity-consciousness, joy or peace whilst blasting your mind with such fare.

I am not saying you should never read another newspaper or cease watching TV altogether. I am saying be judicious in your consumption of these things and be VERY clear with yourself that they are not offered to you without an agenda. These things are NOT the truth. I'm not saying they are outright lies either. What they are is one set of stories told from one perspective. Told with an agenda. Told to obtain a particular response from you. And even in the weakest case, if that desired response is only to sell more papers and to keep you watching more television, then that is not healthy for you. So be very careful with all this.

Z: Okay, but if I am not to trust the news, then what am I to trust?

J-D: Yourself!

In your own heart is your intuition, and in your own life are your experiences. Trust those!

Let's go back to the main thrust of my argument by way of an illustration. I am saying that there is this God Light and that it has slowly been increasing. I am saying that the increase is accelerating. I am saying that consciousness is therefore moving towards love, joy, unity and greater awareness. The illusion is slipping. The veil is thinning. Consciousness is rising. I am saying that all of these things are just a few of the symptoms of the increased God Light.

Now, if you follow this external source of putative truth called the news media, then you'll certainly not agree with me that things are getting better. But if you forget about the news and look to your heart and to your own experiences, then let us see what happens:

Tell me, have you not noticed that right now, all around you, there are more and more people who are opening their hearts to amazing new truths? That the Internet is full of material written by such people, expressing love-filled ideas? That the book stores are selling more and more books now with concepts that you simply wouldn't have found expressed just a few short decades ago? That it is quite prevalent now to find people speaking magnificent new truths from their heart and channelling works of spiritual upliftment from advanced beings, where before it was almost unheard of? That YouTube, blog sites and Internet forums are full of powerful upliftment, offered from hearts aflood with love for their fellow human beings? That people are, in greater and greater numbers, reporting that they have personally had some wondrous, mystical or divine experiences which have touched and changed their lives? That a concept such as beings from other planets coming here in their space ships to assist humanity is no longer universally silenced with derision but is being taken seriously by some serious people. And are you yourself not able to access understandings and truths in your heart in a way that you never before were able to? And what about the amazing stuff coming from science? Are not such sciences as quantum mechanics and cosmology offering profound and amazing new insights that seem quite mystical in their interpretation?

And here you are, Zingdad, sitting quietly on your own, thinking up the biggest, most important questions that you can and being touched by the Light in such a way that you are getting answers which you find nothing short of astounding… And you KNOW you are not generating these answers in any normal sense because you KNOW you are not able to just sit there and thumb-suck such answers to your questions. You know all this… you experience it directly in your own life… and STILL you doubt whether the Light is increasing! Does that not strike you as preposterous? You are willing to doubt the increase of the Light because of a slew of words in newspapers written by a random collection of unknown strangers whose agenda is not known to you in place of trusting that which is nearest and most known to you: your own intuition, your own truth, your own heart and, most of all, your own experiences!

No, my beloved young one! This will not do at all!

And likewise to our dear readers I will say this: you have been guided to this work and it is speaking to your heart. It is speaking to you there where you KNOW the truth when you see it. You are in a state of resonance with this. For if you were not, you would not have soldiered on thus far, would you?

So let's do a little better. Let's take a moment to check your truth. If I say to you, "*The Light is Rising!*" then how do you feel? Take a moment please. Say it to yourself (you too, dear reader). Hear the words as you repeat them to yourself. Close your eyes and plumb your heart and your feelings. How do you FEEL?

"The Light is Rising!"

Z: (Sits still and feels this) I have done this and I can honestly say I feel "right" about that statement. I feel a flutter of excitement in my belly that runs up to my heart. A smile comes to my lips and I feel joy and love in my heart. I feel hopeful. I feel proud to be a part of this. It feels good. It feels right.

J-D: Then trust your feelings! You have been indoctrinated and lied to by your society. You have been told that you must trust the "experts" because they know best and you know nothing. You have been told that the truth is outside of you. But see where believing THAT crock of lies got you! And see also where it got the Darklanders. It got them to stay in the Darklands. If you want to get to the Brightlands, you must be a Looker. You must trust your own experiences and your own truth. You must see with your own inner-light. I tell you, if you are willing to choose it and live it, then without a doubt you will experience it directly in your life and in your heart that there is an increase in the God Light and that this increase is just accelerating. And if you engage people that you meet, talk to them and REALLY LISTEN to what is important to them, then you will find more and more people around you who similarly are engaged in a path that leads to ascension. They might not call it that, but if it is about unity and compassion and love, then it is leading towards a similar destination. And you should reach out to them. Create communities of the Light. Talk together. Learn together. Teach together. Create your scaffolding to the Brightlands together. Each will have something special to add. Your job is to find your unique gift, and to give it. As each gives their gift, so you shall find that between yourselves, you will be able to ensure that all receive exactly what you need when you need it. You will find you are at your most joyful when you are giving the gift you were made to give.

Z: Thank you, J-D, this is right for me. And I appreciate all the straight-talk. I have needed to hear this. I consume a fair amount of news and other entertainments in my average day and I know I am not nearly as discerning as I could be about how I let that colour my beliefs about the state of the world. I'll be more careful. And I will work to hone my ability to find my own truth on things, as you have just shown me.

J-D: That is well. But now we really need to get back to the main conversation. I was saying that this God Light was cyclically increasing. That each peak is higher than the last and that the peaks are coming closer and closer together. At some point the peaks will run together into one constant peak level and will all be at maximum intensity. That occurs when your planet moves into the fullness of the heart of the God-Light. It is the maximum. Ordinarily the planet would, after that, begin to move out of the Light again and it would go around for another cycle, some billions of years long, before it returned to this point again. But that is not going to happen this time round. You see Gaia is taking in this energy. She is drawing it in as the most wondrous, heavenly nourishment. She is healing herself, feeding herself and energising herself. And this is all in preparation for an amazing event. You see, Gaia is also choosing to ascend. When the God Light is at its absolute peak, Gaia herself is going to undergo a "bodily ascension". She is going to "breathe in" or "roll up" this body, which is your planet at this density. She is going to use the energy that is increasingly streaming in to power this "quantum leap" to the next dimension. And the exact moment she does that will be the moment of maximum God Light, which will occur at the end of 2012.

And after that she will not be present in this 3D reality.

The next lowest density you will find her at will be the 4th density and then only as a home for beings who have shown a commitment to being of Service to Other. But you will also find Gaia manifesting a presence higher up than that. For example, you will find her in many tonalities of the 5th dimension. And while you will also find her at 6D, there your body and hers will both manifest as a light vessel and at that level you are as big and as magnificent as Gaia. You certainly won't need a planet to live upon!

So Gaia is ascending. She has come to the end of this particular contract. She agreed to play the role she is now playing as a host to the diversity that is on planet earth. She knew and accepted that some portion of that experience would result in her having a bit of pain with her "li'l critters" when they turned infectious and made the occasional rash on her otherwise very beautiful skin. But the contract had an expiry date as marked by the moment of maximum God Light. Then it's contract expired, time's up and Gaia is going home! And the "home" Gaia is going to is a place where her "li'l critters" will never again cause her pain and illness. Where, in fact, they will always be the beautiful friends that she loves and needs. There will only ever be a healthy symbiosis between Gaia and all those that live on, or in, her body.

Z: Oh that's awesome. I'm so glad for her. But how will that work? How can we arrange things so that we don't over-populate and so that we don't pollute and stuff like that again.

J-D: These things will be impossible for you to do when you are of an "ascended consciousness". But how about we talk more about that in another conversation?

Z: Okay. They're starting to add up.

J-D: Which is no problem. We'll keep talking for so long as you want or need to. But if we don't stay focussed in THIS conversation, we'll never get through it. Now did you notice that I have already answered your question?

Z: Huh? Which question would that be?

J-D: I know it gets difficult to keep your eye on the ball the way we keep kicking it around.

The question you asked, way back, was about those who have a great deal of inner-pain and are deeply involved with their anger and hatred. You asked why they don't just come back to the world they were in before the Singularity Event.

Z: Oh yes! That's right. And from what you have explained I now understand that this is because there will be no planet to come back to! Earth herself will have ascended.

J-D: Bingo!

Z: Wow, that was a very long answer to a very short question! But I'm deeply grateful that you did it this way, as I now have a much fuller understanding of what is going on.

J-D: Nothing is wasted. I used the opportunity to touch on some quite important points which will be fodder for future understandings, as we continue to broaden our discussions. And these thoughts will inspire different insights for some of your readers too.

Z: Thanks, J-D. So you are saying that December 2012 is the end of the process. But surely we don't just sit around and wait for this to happen to us? Surely it isn't just business as usual and then, WHAM, Singularity Event?

J-D: That's a good question. I mentioned earlier the concept of Unity-Consciousness Moments. These are like mini Singularity Events which each individual might experience, as and when they are ready. They will come as a result of a combination of inner-work and the increase in the Light. These function to align you with the main Singularity Event of 2012.

Perhaps it is time for a story to help you to understand.

The Story of the Little Sailing Boats

Imagine every human on earth today is actually a little sailing boat. You are, all of you, somewhat stuck in shallow water. You cannot move because your hull has run aground. But this fact doesn't bother any of you because, for as long as you can remember, there hasn't even been a whisper of a breeze. Nothing. So, instead of sailing the world, you have learned to make do with being where you are. You've made a community where you are and made the best of being stuck there. And that is how it was until a few years ago, when some of you noticed the first gentlest little breeze stirring. Some of you immediately responded by hoisting your sails. Those that did, noticed that their sails were in a terrible state of disrepair. They were rotten and full of holes and tears. Some set about repairing their sails. Some even checked and repaired their masts.

Observant ones noticed that the breeze has subsequently been steadily increasing; every once in a while getting incrementally stronger. And now, some continue to work on their sails, making them bigger, making them stronger and strengthening their masts too. The most adventurous souls have also begun emptying their cargo holds of all the years' and years' worth of accumulated junk that was weighing down the boat. Some, on the other hand, have done little more than to hoist old perished sails onto rickety rotten masts. And many, it seems, have done nothing at all. It must be that they like it where they are, for certainly they are not taking any steps to try to utilise the ever-increasing wind to shift themselves. So it is, ironically, that these are the ones most likely to complain about their current location. But irrespective of what anyone does, still the wind keeps rising. At some stage soon a tipping-point will be reached. At some point the lightest boats, with the least baggage on board and with the biggest sails, will be pulled free of the sand. If their masts are strong enough, then they will be tugged free and be able to sail a short way out to deeper waters. When this happens some of the stuck ones who are still working to repair their sails and lighten their loads will notice this and will be inspired. They will realise it IS possible to sail free after all and will increase their efforts. But many others will not. You see these others will probably not even notice that a few of their number are sailing away. They are so laden down by their baggage that they can only see events that occur right there where they are.

And still the wind will pick up. Soon a second tipping point will be achieved. And then a third. On each occasion it will be a combination of a big enough sail, having a sufficiently empty cargo-bay and having a strong enough mast that will allow each of the little boats to join one of the flotillas that are making their way out to sea. And then, eventually, a truly phenomenal wind will blow. Those boats that are already out to sea will be sped along, each to their ideal destination. Some boats will go a short distance to a friendly harbour where they will weigh anchor for a bit. Some will go very far to exotic places. And others will sail out into the wild deep seas and have glorious adventures. Each will get what is exactly right for them.

But, sadly, for the boats still stuck in the mud of the harbour, this will be a disastrous situation. The harbour will be destroyed in the storm and many little boats will be damaged or even sunk.

And now I will decode the parable so that it makes sense to you in terms of your own life. You are all, of course, stuck in the mud of duality and deep density. You have forgotten what it is to be mobile, to be able to freely move between states of being, to be able to change perspectives at will. Part of what keeps you mired here is the heavy baggage you carry. This is, of course, what you will understand as your emotional and spiritual "baggage". It is your fear and pain. Your incongruities. The self-defeating lies you have come to believe about yourself. Your unresolved "past-life" pain. The hurts you feel others have done to you. The hurts you have done to yourself. All kinds of stuff that you hold onto and feel you cannot let go of. What I want to tell you about all of this baggage is that it is all actually the result of just one thing: FEAR. And it is possible to release all this fear. But you can only do so with love. That is how you jettison your fear and lighten your load.

Z: Alright, that is very easy to say but some fears run quite deep and are very hard to resolve. Sometimes we have fears that lie so deeply buried in our psyches that they cause us to respond to the world in strange and incomprehensible ways. They make us do things when we ourselves don't even know why we do them. And some fears are completely valid, aren't they? So how do you release a fear when it's a totally valid way to respond to your situation?

J-D: These very conversations that we are now having are in great part about helping you to come to see how you can, and should, release your fears. They are about healing the pain that comes as a result of those fears. They will also show you that there are, in fact, no fears that are really valid. What I mean is that your fears are only valid for so long as YOU give them validity. And it is very possible for you to come to a new decision about these fears so that you can release them. And not only is this possible, but it is also essential that you do so and inevitable that you will.

Z: Really? It is inevitable that I will release all of the fears I hold?

J-D: Yes. Every single being will inevitably do this. It is an integral part of the ascension process that happens to every single being sooner or later. So, if you are on your ascension path now, then you are also busy releasing your fears. Fears about being unworthy, about not trusting yourself, about not being capable, about damage that you might do, about not being loved, about being rejected, your uncertainties and insecurities... on and on... all these self-limiting beliefs that come from a place of fear will be released. You see, you really cannot be creating yourself as the most magnificent and glorious being you can imagine yourself to be whilst still holding on to this kind of nonsense. And believe me; in time you WILL come to see it as nonsense. In just the way you now think back on your experiences as a child, when you were scared there was a monster under the bed, in that same way you will come to look back on the fears you now think are valid.

Z: But what about REAL fears? I mean real things that can happen. Like being robbed, mugged or raped. Or losing my job. Or having my partner leave me or be unfaithful. Or something happening to my kids. Or getting swine flu (right now, as I write this, the swine flu epidemic is starting up in Mexico and everyone seems to be talking about it). And what about AIDS, cancer or a heart attack? Or being maimed in a car crash? These are surely very real fears and not just neuroses of the mind.

J-D: My answer is simple. You are the creator of your own reality. If you choose to create that you are NOT the creator of your own reality, then that is what you will experience. Then things will happen to you and you will feel like a victim. Which is right because you are creating that and...

"You always get EXACTLY what you create."

If, however, you choose to know that you are the creator of your own reality, then you will become the CONSCIOUS creator of your own reality. Then you will be in a position to decide that you won't be mugged. And that your job is actually just a little distraction that you have used to keep yourself busy while you were waiting to discover your TRUE purpose. And that swine flu is a manufactured event that actually has nothing to do with you. And so on. Each of the fears you have listed can be dealt with in a similar way.

The point is, when you are ready to claim for yourself your own creator status, then you cease to be a victim of anyone or anything. And then there is obviously NOTHING to fear. And, working with you until you are ready to understand this, feel this, know this and practice this, is a big part of the objective of this work. Through this work (and also more directly than you are currently able to understand) I am shining my Light upon you and every other being on planet earth. And I am but one of many Bright Ones who are doing so. Now it is up to you. You can choose to see the Light or not. If you choose it, you can choose to use it to see yourself as the creator-being that you really are. If you do, then you may choose to use your creator status to re-create yourself and your reality as you desire.

Now there are many paths which could get you from where you are to that place of being a master of your own reality. And this work, THE ASCENSION PAPERS, is intended to provide you with one such path. But you must choose.

Z: Okay and what do I do if I am ready to choose this?

J-D: You state it to yourself. Repeat after me:

"I am an infinitely powerful, eternal, immortal creator being"

Z: I am an infinitely powerful, eternal, immortal creator being.

J-D: How does that feel.

Z: A little bit like a lie. I mean, I say the words but that doesn't make them true, does it?

J-D: Yes it does. Say the words out loud. Say them as an oath to yourself. Say them a few times every single day. Write them in places where you can read them and every time you see them, say them again. Say them with feeling and conviction. Lie down and daydream how it would be if it was true: what you would do and how you would feel if it was true. And then know that it is just a matter of time before it does become true because now, at least, the goal is set. For the first time you are now using your creator status to create that you ARE a creator. Before now you were using it in the opposite fashion. So know now that you ARE going there. Now you are at least on the journey. Every time you repeat these words, you again adjust yourself to be facing that destination again. This is powerful stuff. You WILL come to see this. You just have to choose this, and KEEP choosing it, as you go. But be patient with yourself. It doesn't have to happen immediately. There is a path to travel. And if you'll bear with me, as these conversations unfold I will come to show you this.

Z: Okay. I have travelled enough of a path with you that I have come to trust you and to take you at your word. If you say you will show me all this, then I accept that. But I am going to hold you to it and come back to this in later conversations if I don't feel this is being shown to be true.

J-D: That is exactly as it should be and I would expect nothing less. I do not say things and expect blind faith. I say things that you might test and query and probe until you have satisfied yourself that what I say works for you. As I am your Inner-Self, you will inevitably find at some point that this will be true for you. And I feel your readers will find satisfaction just as you do. But essentially I am saying that I encourage you to be quite rigorous with me. If I say I will show you something, then you must not let me off the hook if, over time, you are not satisfied that I have done as I said I would.

Z: Thank you J-D. I deeply appreciate that you are the kind of being who is willing to deal with my incomprehension and my doubts by patiently staying with me through it all and not telling me to just "shut up and believe" because you say so.

J-D: You are most welcome. And you know… you are going to find pretty much all spirit beings of higher vibration to be patient and loving in this way. It is really only other humans upon your planet and spirit beings of a very low awareness who might demand blind faith and subservience to dogma. But now I'd like to get back to the story of the little sail-boats, if I may?

Z: Certainly, yes!

J-D: Then the next point I will address is that of the sails. These represent your level of consciousness. Or perhaps I could just say, it is the amount of love you have in your heart. It is what you, in your heart, resonate with. You see you are, each of you, engaged in holding certain things to be true. That determines how much Light you are able to catch. And the wind, of course, is a metaphor for the Light.

Z: There's "Light" with the capital L again. Is this the same Light as in the story of the Darklanders and the same Light as in God Light?

J-D: The very same. Remember how Gaia was using the God Light to power her ascension? Well it can do the same thing for you. Your needs are different from Gaia's needs because your awareness, consciousness and experience is different from hers. So what the Light offers you and what you might take from it will be different from what Gaia does. But the Light is offered to you that you might choose to See – as it was in the Darklanders parable. If you allow the Light in, then you may use it to see things differently. This may cause you to ask new questions and help you to see through the old illusions. This in-streaming from Source is touching you on every level of your being. It feeds your heart, your mind and your soul. Indeed it is so that this beautiful Light will take you and lift you and move you to the reality with which your heart resonates. And so, in the metaphor of the boats, I used sails to show your consciousness level. If your consciousness is still deeply rooted in duality, in "us versus them", in fear, in hate, in money, in power, in control… in any of these kinds of things… then your sails have not been raised. Then you will remain where you are spiritually. Which is okay too. You see it's all perfect; by definition such a person is not done with the duality experience. There is more they need to do there until they too are ready to move on into higher dimensions. So then the choice not to make sail and not to jettison baggage is a fine one. If, on the other hand, you feel in your heart that it is time to move on, then there are various "levels" of moving on. You can go far from where you are now at, or you can go less far, depending on what you, yourself, resonate with.

The final thing I want to talk about is the mast. This represents something which doesn't have an easy equivalent English term. It is a spiritual attribute. It might equate to that which you would call "backbone". Obviously not your body's spine…I mean your spiritual and emotional backbone. It is your will, your resolve. It is about a willingness to declare yourself. To stand in your truth. To be forthright. To be fearless. To stick to your guns. Primarily it is your trust in yourself. That is the idea I am trying to communicate here.

And so these three things: the Baggage, the Sail and the Mast will be dealt with in many ways in the conversations of THE ASCENSION PAPERS. We will talk about releasing your baggage. We will talk about looking to your truth-set and your consciousness. And, as we go, so you will have many opportunities to develop your back-bone. We will also continue to talk about the Light that will shine, which in this parable was represented by the wind. We will talk about all these things and many others besides that will be pertinent to the ascension process and the God-realisation, which is the knowingness that All is truly One.

The goal of all these conversations will be to allow you to further your preparations so that the Light can, and will, lift you when the moment is perfect and you are ready. And when it does, you will find yourself altered. You will find your consciousness expanded. You will be further prepared for the final big moment, the Singularity Event.

Does that help you to understand? Do you see that there is a continual process of inner-work and expanding of consciousness that must be engaged with on an on-going basis between now and the Singularity Event? And do you understand that you can experience more than one of these Unity-Consciousness Moments? That, if you get out with the first wave, you can move a little further out on each additional wave?

Each time you catch the wind, you will have a wonderful mystical experience and then awaken to a greater realization of Self. I can put it like this: the Light will shine on you and cause you to awaken a little from your dream. The dream you will awaken from will be your current 3D life. The first awakening will be to 4D consciousness and then to 5D and finally 6D. If you are open to this, and if you are willing, you will be able to experience these awakenings of your consciousness while you continue to reside physically in this 3D world. Your body can remain 3D while your consciousness can awaken all the way to 6D. You may indeed become ascended masters walking the earth… your own Inner-Self incarnate!

Z: That sounds like a very worthy thing to aspire towards!

But J-D, I'd like to know what will happen to us here on planet earth when Gaia ascends... what then?

J-D: There will be many different experiences according to your own consciousness and choices. It is impossibly complex to get into what each being will experience, as time-lines will diverge. In broad-strokes though I can suggest the following things will be experienced: The systems and social structures upon which your civilisation relies are going to break down. I mean things like financial systems and so on are not very much of the Light. There will be disruption to things such as electrical and communications systems. And, as these things all disintegrate, so it will allow people to untether themselves from the consensus reality you currently share. Some will awaken, as I have described, and become an enlightened version of themselves. Others will experience catastrophic events and will die to physicality. All kinds of variations are possible. And, yes, we do in fact anticipate interaction with civilisations from elsewhere in the galaxy and beyond. Some of you might be uplifted and taken "home" by such space beings. Others of you will be able to interact with them and share learnings with them. All of these things and so much more will be going on as things wind down. And then the Singularity Event will occur and then all will choose the new reality which is resonant with their own consciousness where they many continue to play out their continuing creations of Self.

The general experience is very hard to speak about as each being will bring a somewhat unique experience to itself in this time. One particular group that I can speak about in more detail is the a group called the Earth Partners. Members of this group have a very special, deep love for Planet Earth. They are the ones who give thought to matters such as minimising their own pollution impact on the planet. They are the ones who choose to spend their free time exploring nature. But it is not so much their activities that will distinguish them as Earth Partners as the way they feel inside their own hearts. These are beings that feel a profound connection and bond with the earth. Many of them will have had some transcendent or mystical experience in nature as their heart was opened to the fact of their status as an Earth Partner. But the Earth Partners themselves won't need any external validation. If they read these words then they will know they are a part of this group.

The Earth Partners are special to Gaia. These are ones who have a soul-contract with her. There is an agreement that they will have a kind of a custodial role in a version of higher-dimensional earth. They are the true residents of earth in the golden age that lies beyond. And what is envisaged to happen to these people is that they will have their Singularity Event WITH Gaia. They will not only experience all that I have already discussed but they will also know themselves to be a vital part of the planetary system. They will have a role, a Life Purpose, to fulfil with respect to Gaia after the Singularity Event. And so, while they will return to an ascended version of Gaia, they will return completely and utterly changed by the Singularity Event experience. Their consciousness will be expanded immeasurably. They will KNOW who and what they really are and exactly what their role with respect to Gaia is. But for them there will now be one version of the Self which is a human being resident on Planet Earth and other versions of Self elsewhere doing other things. They will be multi-dimensional personalities. They will know, in their direct experience, that they are AT THE SAME TIME these different life-streams in different realities.

The life-streams of the Earth Partners which are on 3D earth now will ride with Planet Earth through the changes. They will, in fact, go WITH the earth from this current 3D reality into the next world where they shall live on a higher-dimensional earth. Their consciousness will sojourn in the Singularity Event but their body will travel safely and smoothly through the changes. For them there will be no bodily death at the 2012 ascension of the earth. Instead they will simply change state WITH the planet as a part of the planetary state-change so that they may fulfil their

Life Purpose of co-creating one or more of the versions of the new Earth that they will inhabit. Their intense love for the planet is what causes Gaia to want to co-create with them in this way.

Does that answer your question?

Z: That not only answers that question but a number of others that I hadn't even asked. Thank you. But now I'm curious about something else. I notice that you go into a lot of detail about all the happy outcomes, but the unhappy stuff you usually just gloss over. Like, for example, where you tell about the ones who die in the 2012 changes, they only get a sentence or two. The Earth Partners, who have this amazing outcome, on the other hand, get a few paragraphs. Why is this?

J-D: Good observation. Primarily it is because, as I have said before, I am speaking to a particular audience. You, and those who will read this, are of a certain consciousness – your sails are already out. Engaging in spiritual work and reading material such as THE ASCENSION PAPERS is the process of repairing your sails. I assure you as an absolute fact that there is no way anyone who is going to die as a bitter-ender will have read this far. It is impossible. However, it is my intention that as many as possible of the Earth Partners should come across these words. It will come to be that these words will be translated into other languages to further this goal. These words will find wings. They will go to places you cannot now imagine. Those who will have value of them will find them.

Z: Really? How will I get all that done?

J-D: You won't. It will happen. You do your part and the rest will happen. The power and magic of co-creation will still astound you, as you see more and more of it in action. Your co-creators will come to you with their gifts and they will offer them as gladly as you are offering this work now. Everything will be exactly as it must.

But now, before you ask more questions, there is something I want to tell you. I want to tell you a bit about what it is like to be me; what my experiences are like with respect to all this.

Z: Oh! That sounds exciting. I'd love to hear…

J-D: Okay then. The version of Self that I am – that which you call Joy-Divine – I speak to you from the perspective of 6th and 7th Dimensional awareness. I am also aware of myself as something greater than this and aware of myself as a being who resides in other realities altogether, but these to me are a bit like my own "Inner-Self" and my own "other incarnations".

Now, for beings like myself who have attained 6D consciousness or higher (6D is the level of unity consciousness), there is an awareness of ourselves flashing between all states of DOing and the state of BEing at a very high rate of oscillation.

Z: Uh… what exactly does that mean?

J-D: Well I COULD try to go into the technical details. I could try to have you understand the nature of time and space on the level of things that are so small as to have no size or mass. I could talk about how these elements move in a granular, rather than fluid way and that this causes your density (or dimension) to be defined by the resultant flicker-rate. And that the flicker rate creates a very specific speed of light propagation in your reality – which is different for each density tone. And from there I could segue into telling you that we, of 6D-and-above consciousness, are creating all the granular moments of time, then pausing between them for a BLINK of BEing. And then you might be impressed. But the show-off value I'll get out of all this is not worth the difficulty involved in communicating all this. So instead, in this time-line, I am going to try to tell it to you more… poetically… than scientifically. Okay?

Z: What do you mean, "*in this time-line*"?

J-D: There are other time-lines in which I have tried other ways of telling you some of the things in these conversations. Sometimes it didn't work out optimally, so I took a few steps back and began a new time-line. Trying to get you to understand the concepts in a clear-cut, scientific way didn't work very well for us. But because I didn't want to just discard all that hard work, I have, in THIS time-line, just given you an abstract of those concepts in the above paragraph. And now we shall address it in a more poetic way. I have seen this time line and it works out fine.

Z: Well, you are really blowing my mind with all this time-line stuff. But, okay, who am I to argue?

J-D: Good. So FROM MY PERSPECTIVE (and indeed from the perspective of your readers' 6D-and-above Inner-Selves), your whole reality is composed of an incredibly large number of Moments. In this context, if you managed to freeze your whole universe dead still in time such that nothing moved, then that would be a Moment; every photon, lepton and quark standing dead still. That is a Moment. Then we, the creator beings of your reality, choose how we will change things for the next Moment. And once so changed as we desired, then the next Moment is created. Again the universe is created whole and complete and perfect but very, very slightly different. Everything is "moved on" a minuscule amount. Between those two states of doing and creating, way down there in your reality, there is a BLINK. That is when we all are One, and in a state of BEing. You see we come together and BE One so that we can have perfect knowing. Because only from a state of perfect knowing can one create perfectly. Or as perfectly as we desire, anyway. So there is a perspective from which one could say that we flash between DOing and BEing at an incredibly high rate… that we BLINK at a rate too fast for your science to detect.

Z: Wow, so that must be pretty FAST.

J-D: No, it's fssst!

Z: You're funny! So these moments are each whole and complete, but we here in 3D see them passing us by so fast that they seem fluid and continuous?

J-D: Yes, except they do not "pass you by". It isn't a movie (although that could make a useful analogy). It is your life. I mean the very sub-atomic particles that make up your physical bodies are themselves "flickering" like this too. And so, because your sensory apparatus flickers in synch with the universe you are in; you experience that universe. But you also do not experience any other universe or reality other than the one that flickers at exactly the rate you do. If you could alter your flicker rate (and therefore the rate of your perception), then you would suddenly find yourself in a whole different, alternate universe!

Z: That's amazing! How does that work?

J-D: Well yours is certainly not the only version of reality that the creator beings wished to create. So there exist a great number of other realities that overlay your own. Some that are very near to your own flicker rate are only slightly different, others are at a much different flicker rate and are quite vastly different. They exist at slightly different tones of your current density.

So, your universe consists of a series of Moments. Progress though time is therefore granular, like a flickering series of events, not smooth and continuous. And the granularity is a function of all of us creator beings BLINKing at a rate faster than you could possibly comprehend. And while that is true from one perspective, it is equally true from another perspective that we do not BLINK very fast at all… that we are outside of time and so have an infinity of "time" to do all that we desire to do. And to that I can add that it is also true that we do not create only in one direction with respect to time. We can create in any direction in time that we desire. And that is exactly what we do.

Z: Explain?

J-D: Okay, briefly…

Do you know that, from our perspective, you live your lives backwards? We do things exactly the opposite to what you do. We start with that which we wish to create. We start with the outcome. When that is firmly fixed and created then we move back from it towards the beginning point. In this way we can be sure that no matter what we find on the journey we always get the outcome we desire!

Z: That's a bit mind-boggling. But it does sort of make sense too.

J-D: Don't struggle with it too much. When you are ready to work this way it will be very apparent to you how to do it. Let me carry on and give you another example of the variable directionality of time from my perspective: if I came to see that you were going to get stuck in this reality that you are now living in, in a way that I did not desire, then I could, for example, go back to before you began this incarnation. And we could arrange a contract with another soul such that they would appear in your life and impart some teaching that you would need. And we'd agree with them that they receive some reciprocal value from you that they needed. When the negotiation is complete, it will be so that, as you approach the sticking point, there you will find some friend who has exactly the help you need to be able to navigate your life so that you don't get stuck. From your perspective you might think this was a random event that just magically worked out perfectly. A co-incidence. A synchronicity. From my perspective there are really two separate time-lines that you have travelled. Both are equally real, true and valid. The one has a dead-end, the other does not. And we can, and do, arrange such interactions many, many times resulting in many, many life-streams for each of you. But YOU will only hold in your consciousness the experience of one of them: the one that got you to the place you find yourself now. That is just one example of the non-linearity of time from the 6D perspective. We can create backwards or forwards. And we can create cross-wise between lifetimes and alternate lifetimes and possible and probable lifetimes too.

Z: What are those?

J-D: This is a phenomenally huge topic. Let me again give you one brief example. There are mezzanine realities. One can create a bubble reality in which certain situations can be played out, but without there being the need for a whole lifetime. You can sometimes experience these as dream-lives. Sometimes when you dream you can return to a certain "alternate dream world" many times. And each time there are new events and experiences. Well, this could be one such mezzanine reality. A "possible" life. But, as I say, this is an enormous topic and the variations in which souls can express themselves in their desire to discover Self and create Self are truly astonishing. But I don't want to get bogged down in describing all this now as all this will be covered in the forthcoming conversation called "Densities and Dimensions". All I want to say now is that every single person incarnated on earth has an Inner-Self of 6D consciousness who is aware of all of this. Who sees all the moments of all of that person's many probable and possible lifetimes as RIGHT NOW. And that is how such a being can create itself. It does so by constantly involving itself in one Moment or another. It realises that all of these Moments are intimately interwoven. It knows that, as you change one Moment, so the others around it are also altered. And between all the work on all the infinite numbers of Moments at all the various levels of reality and all the densities - between working on any and every Moment - there is a BLINK. There is a period of rest, of Oneness and truly… of LOVE. That is what the BLINK is. It is LOVE in a very pure form.

Z: Wow. I am in awe. That is an amazing story! Thank you so much for sharing that perspective with me.

J-D: You are most welcome. But I didn't do it to provide you with an entertaining interlude. I did it because there is something very important I want you to understand. You see, I want to bring this conversation to a close now. I know you have more questions about the Singularity Event and I am happy to address them in follow-up conversations. But I really do want to wrap-up now. AND SO! The point of all this is…

Are you paying attention?

Z: Sir! Yes, sir!

J-D: Good. Because here comes the good bit. The point of all of the above that I want you to understand is this: the Singularity Event will be the first BLINK that you will experience with me, that each of your readers will experience with their Inner-Self and indeed that we will all experience with each other.

For the very first time in all your experience of all your many lifetimes; for the first time since you were created from within me; for YOUR very first time ever; you will be experiencing the BLINK with me. You and I will be one being. We will have exactly the same experience. We will, in fact, be the same BEING.

Of course I have always known that you and I are one but this will be the first time that you will experience this too. For the first time you will be me. For a moment there will be no difference between my experience and yours. Just as I have always known everything you know, for the first time you will also know everything I know.

Z: That IS amazing. I am totally blown away!

J-D: I'm very pleased you feel that way. You see for me there are many, many BLINKS all the time. You, however, are about to become conscious of having your very first one and you are going to have it with me. THAT is the true meaning and significance of the Singularity Event. You will have it with me and each of your readers will have it with their Inner-Selves and we will all have it with every other being in this entire reality. We are then, all of us, truly ONE.

Z: Uh, wait a minute. Sorry, J-D but I've just had a funny thought. I'm suddenly not so sure about this.

J-D: Why?

Z: Well… I love you very much and all and I think you're really amazing and stuff… and I'm sure it will be wonderful to be a part of you… but I really don't want to cease to be me. You know what I mean? I like being me. I don't want to…

J-D: You are concerned that this unification will end your individuality, your essential uniqueness?

Z: Yes. That's it.

J-D: Okay, well let me allay your fears. You only feel this way because you don't realise you are ALREADY an indivisible part of me. Just as we are all already an indivisible part of the Oneness. You see, the thing is, it is possible for us to procure as much illusion of separation and individuality as we desire. The more of that we desire, the lower down into the densities we go. But you know, even for me, even though I am absolutely and completely a part of the Oneness and know this as a fact of my very existence… yet still it is so that there is an essence of ME that is unique and that conscious of Self-hood in a way that has eternal validity. Remember the rainbow metaphor? Well it will be so for you too. You will know the Oneness of All and yet you will ALWAYS be YOU. No matter what. You cannot cease to "be". And you cannot cease to have consciousness. Certainly your experience of life CAN change. Your ideas about yourself can change. Pretty much anything and everything can change except this: you ARE. Your soul is infinite, eternal and immortal. And the Singularity Event will not make this less so. Quite to the contrary, it will make this more so. You will discover more and more of what you really are. You will realise that you can create far greater versions of Self. If that is what you wish, of course. You could also choose to remain at exactly this level of creation if you like.

Z: Ah. I see. That really has helped me a lot.

Alright then, I am willing to move towards having this experience. But I have one more question: How do I go about choosing my next reality? I mean the reality I will land up in next, after the Singularity Event.

J-D: I'm glad you asked that. Because that is going to be a very important topic of conversation soon. It is very important that we address the issue of how you create your reality now before the Singularity Event, after the Singularity Event and in the future that will follow that. So I promise we'll come back to that too, but now I feel it is time to wrap up this long conversation. I know you have a lot more questions to ask about the Singularity Event but, for now, I feel I have given you a pretty good introduction to the subject. You'll recall that we ended chapter 6 with you asking me how you can remember that you are an indivisible part of the Oneness?

Z: Yes that's right.

J-D: And then you'll also remember that I said there are a few paths. And you chose the one that is about love and joy and is easy?

Z: Yep, that's what I chose.

J-D: Okay. Then do you agree that the Singularity Event and the Unity-Conscious Moments are pretty easy? All you have to do is to follow your heart and be true to yourself. Live your greatest bliss. Release your fears. Good stuff like that. The heavy lifting, which is the in-streaming Light, will be taken care of for you. Pretty easy, huh?

Z: Yes, true. You don't get much easier than that!

J-D: And can you agree that, if you have understood this correctly, that you can now choose to experience it as really joyful and loving?

Z: Again, yes, for sure. While I am loving my life and really looking forward to doing all kinds of stuff in this world as it is, I must say I am also REALLY looking forward to this Singularity Event thing. It sounds like the epitome of a Joyful and Loving experience to me.

J-D: You're right. That is exactly what it will be for you… and for everyone else who also creates that possibility in their lives. Okay then. It seems to me that I can tick this one off as "mission accomplished". I have in this chapter achieved what I set out to do.

Z: Thanks J-D.

So what are we going to talk about next?

J-D: What I want to do next is to help you to gain some clarity on the direction we will be taking and then also to help you de-program a little bit.

Z: De-program? What does that mean?

J-D: Well, you see, in order to stay in the density you currently inhabit, you need to think a certain way, believe certain things, and hold certain things to be right, true and important. Essentially you need to hold a "duality & third density truth-set". If you didn't, you wouldn't be able to remain in that reality. But now you want to change your perspective and ascend your consciousness out of that reality into a greater awareness of the Oneness of All. So we need to do two things:

1. Help you to shake loose the old truth-set that anchors you there, and;

2. Offer you a different truth-set that supports you in the move to the new reality you have chosen for yourself.

We've started on that journey as we have done the ground-work for this chapter. And now that this chapter is done - now that you understand a bit more of the beauty and the wonder of the Singularity Event - now we can get down to the real work. And the first step of that would be to help you to understand the situation, as it is, so that you can finally let it go. And for that I would very much like you to open Chapter 8 and call it, "Truth according to 8".

Z: Fantastic! I was wondering when I'd start talking to 8. And here we are doing it in chapter 8! That's perfect.

J-D: Nothing by chance, beloved one.

Z: Okay. Thank you so much J-D. It has been simply AWESOME talking to you. These last 7 Chapters have been some of the most amazing conversations of my life. I love you SO MUCH! Thank you!

J-D: Perfect. You are most welcome.

Z: And now I'll go talk to 8…

* * * * *

Chapter 8. What is Truth?
An Introduction to 8

Remember when you were a young child and you first went to school? How you'd be dropped off in the morning and, even though you really missed your family, you knew it was actually okay because they'd be there when you got home? Well, in quite a similar way I always had a "dropped off at school" feeling about living my life here on earth. It felt hard for me to be here. And really quite lonely. But what made it okay for me was my "spirit friend". As a little kid I'd do this thing where I'd sit and stare into nothingness and fall away into another world. And in this other world I had an amazing friend. He was as real to me as anything else in this world; the only difference was that I had to sit very quietly to go and visit him. But he really loved me and helped me with all the difficulty and pain that the "real world" caused me. When I tried to tell people about him, it was considered "cute". As in, "*How cute! He has an imaginary friend!*"

I got pats on the head and smiles and giggles but I certainly didn't get taken seriously. So I quickly realised that people weren't really "getting it". I stopped talking about this and just let it be something that only I knew. Eventually I even stopped visiting him.

Somewhere in my mid teens an older friend mentioned to me that he believed we each had a "Spirit-Guide". Something about that concept leapt out at me. I deeply felt this to be true. It was the first big "resonance" that I remember receiving in my life. I asked him about it but he didn't seem to have much more to say… just that he believed in this. It was a thought that stayed with me. I kept thinking about it. I knew I had a Spirit-Guide and I knew he was with me. I felt his presence. I felt his very attentive and loving guardianship of me. So, at about age 16, I decided it was time to take matters in hand. I decided to find a way to contact this being. Which is funny if you understand the context of my life at the time. You see, I grew up in a pretty conservative Christian society. I had never even heard of Ouija boards (nor the attendant horror stories of treating spirituality like a parlour game). I hadn't heard of pendulums or dowsing. I hadn't even heard of tarot. And, I can categorically assure you, if I had heard of such things it would have been in the context of a stern warning not to dabble in the occult because "*It is all devil worship!*" Such was the *zeitgeist* of my upbringing. So, when I DID decide to contact my Spirit-Guide, I knew I was going to do this entirely on my own. There was no-one I could talk to about this. No-one from whom to seek advice. No one to share the journey with. No-one to tell how it was going. No-one. Not for any part of it. I am convinced, beyond a shadow of a doubt, that were it to have emerged that I was planning to "contact spirits", someone from the church would have been called in to counsel me and to help save my soul. There would have been endless praying and anguish until I eventually promised to stop. Or something along those lines. But the issue for me was that I KNEW I was reaching out to someone who loved me and protected me. Someone who was ANYWAY there with me all the time. So I avoided the inevitable pain and just kept all of this very private.

There was one particular occasion when matters took a step forward for me. I was sitting quietly in the garden one evening thinking about the problem of how to make contact with my Spirit-Guide. As I was contemplating this I was fiddling with a pebble. Deep in thought I was balancing the pebble on two outstretched fingers and then watching to see which way it would fall. The pebble was well balanced and seemed to randomly fall either left or right. Inspiration dawned. I rebalanced the pebble on my fingers and quietened my mind. I sat there for a few moments and then sent out this thought:

"*I know you are here with me. If you are willing to talk to me, please unbalance the pebble*".

And the pebble instantly fell from my outstretched hand.

"*That side is now 'yes' and the other is now 'no'*," I said. "*Do you love me unconditionally?*" I asked.

YES

I don't know what made me ask that as my first real question. I guess it was more inspiration. It's a really good place to start with spirit beings. At first, speak to those who love you only. But, you know, I FELT his presence and I knew it was love. In my heart I KNEW this was okay. And so I carried on. I asked a few more questions like that with my mind in a curiously dichotomous state: on the one hand I was elated because I knew I had finally hit on a means of speaking with my guide, and on the other hand I also had the strongest feeling that this was all just nonsense and I was managing to play games with myself, tipping the stone in the desired direction in response to my own questions. Both of these things were true for me. I decided to carry on and see where it would lead. At some point, I told myself, proof would arrive. At some point, if I just stayed with it, I would find rock solid proof either that this was true or that I was deluding myself.

That was about 25 years ago and it still hasn't happened.

It's true! I graduated from balancing stones on my hand to having some pretty fluent intuitive conversations, but no matter what process I tried, I could never find a way to make these conversations prove themselves conclusively to be either true or false. It just resolutely stayed there in the middle ground of "could be". Not only did it stay "doubtable but possible", but as I got more sophisticated in my methods it came to be explained to me how and why this was so… that this would ALWAYS be where it would be at. And now that you have read the preceding seven chapters you also understand some of that. Essentially I come to realise that conclusive proof would take from me my free-will right to doubt and would also violate the Veil of Unknowing. But I can tell you that the first few years were quite frustrating. Especially when trying to get answers to complex philosophical questions with "yes/no" answers from a pebble balanced on my hand!

But back to those early conversations… One of the first things I wanted from this being was a name. So I took a piece of paper and wrote all the alphanumeric characters on it. I divided them up into quadrants. Thus prepared, I called to him and asked, "*Will you spell your name out to me?*"

NO, was the answer. I was nonplussed. I will spare you the excruciating process that I had to go through to eventually gain an understanding and simply tell you what it was: it turns out this being simply did not have a name. As he had never incarnated in a human form he had never needed a name. And, when asked, he was quite adamant that, NO, he didn't actually want one either. And NO, he also was not willing to have me just invent one for him. To the whole question around him and a name, he simply said NO.

But then I appealed to him. I explained that I really needed a name for him. I needed something to call him when I called for his presence and I needed something to call him in our conversations. I practically begged. And then I felt a shift… a relenting… and then I actually felt what I can only describe as a loving, gentle laugh. I asked again: "*Will you give me a name I can call you?*"

And this time the answer was YES. With great excitement I fetched the alphanumeric sheet and by process of elimination ("*Is the first letter in THIS quadrant? How about THIS one?*"), I got to the first letter. But with some confusion I noticed that the first letter was a digit: The number "8". Somewhat confused I asked, "*Is there more?*"

NO

And so it was. My Spirit-Guide's name was 8.

Latterly I have gained a bit more insight. Had he chosen a name that had any meaning at all, I would have analysed it for its meaning and made all kinds of assumptions about who he is and what his character is. I would have drawn (inevitably wrong) conclusions about him from this name. Choosing a digit kept me flexible about all that. But the digit itself is not randomly chosen – it has many meanings on many levels. It is like a multi-layered puzzle that 8 has set for me to tease me and entertain me as I proceed. Even now that I can have free-flowing conversations with my beloved friend 8, still he laughs at me when I ask him about the meaning of his name. He tells me that there is much for me to discover and that I will enjoy the joke SO much more if I figure it out without him telling me. So I have a few bits of the puzzle but there is more to unravel.

The bits I have include:

If you turn an 8 on its side you get: ∞, the symbol for infinity. 8, in music, is the number of tones in a complete octave. 8, in this reality, is the number of densities in the complete reality. In the same way we really have 8 main chakras (the first is in the earth and the other 7 are in the body). So there are all these 8's which all seem to point in the same direction. To completion and perfection in infinity. How does that relate to my Spirit-Guide? And what ELSE does the number 8 mean? I don't know. At some point I'll figure it all out, I'm sure.

Then also, although rhyming words can mean nothing, I have understood that things that are significant about 8 are the rhyming words "fate" and "gate". But I still lack specifics here.

But the interesting thing is that, through all this, 8 succeeded in keeping me playing and guessing instead of forming a narrow, fixed idea of who he is and what he is like. Instead I learned to know 8 by his "feel" - his energetic print - whenever I spoke to him. And I learned even more about him from what he said and the truths I gained from him. And finally I learned to know about him from all the things he has done for me. I won't go into details because I have no desire to tell long rambling personal accounts of the somewhat far-fetched-sounding tales of times that I had been protected and looked after and other supernatural events that I have witnessed which have, I know, been 8's handiwork. These are my experiences and cataloguing them will add nothing to the narrative here. Instead I will say this: in my experience and in my truth, 8 is simply amazing. He is TRUSTWORTHY. That word seems too weak to express this. I trust 8 completely. I would, without a moment's hesitation, put my whole universe in his hands. He is steadfast, loyal and sure. 8 is a being of truth. In fact he told me once he is made of the very energy of truth itself. So don't go to 8 if you want pretty words dressed up nicely! He has a habit of putting things rather bluntly that, if you will listen to them, will move you forward. Always in a good direction, but not always in the gentlest fashion possible. And as 8 is a being of pure truth, he is the best spiritual protection I could ask for and I am endlessly grateful that he is journeying with me.

And this is what I would say to you about what is coming next: I am going to talk to 8 and I am going to share these conversations with you. This is a bit odd for me because it's a bit like having a private phone conversation with your very best friend and then broadcasting it to the world. But it's also pretty cool because this is the very first time 8 is permitting this. He wasn't willing to have me channel him for public consumption until now: "*Not while you still have your trainer wheels on*" was how he put it. But quite recently he said, "*It's time. You may now channel me in your new series. You'll be told when.*" And seeing as J-D just told me to do so… I guess I'm finally here.

Now before I begin. A quick word about 8's style. If you need all that fluffy "dearest beloved ones" stuff in your spiritual messages, then this is not going to tickle your fancy. 8 doesn't do that stuff. He says what needs saying. He answers question without first stroking your ego or soothing your nerves. You see 8 is unconcerned with what you do with his words. You can take them, you can leave them, you can roll them up and smoke them. He speaks his truth as it is, without trying to sell it to you. Now, if it sounds as if I am apologizing for him, I am not. Of all the beings in All That Is, 8 is the being that, in my opinion, is the least in need of apologies. He is awesome. And I love him completely, exactly as he is.

So, without further ado, I give you my Spirit-Guide, my partner, my dearest friend… 8.

Zingdad: Hi 8. I want to do an introduction to you, but I'm not sure where to start.

8: Start with answering this: do you know what you are doing here?

Z: Where? In this conversation?

8: This conversation. The conversations that went before. The conversations that will follow. Your whole life. Everything. Do you know what you are doing?

Z: Uhh… sort of. I think these conversations are about me searching for answers. I'm asking questions of beings whom I love and trust, and getting answers.

8: That might be one perspective. But it's a very small and limited perspective. Shall I offer you a broader perspective?

Z: Please.

8: You are engaged in a game called "reality creation".

Z: How so, 8?

8: Let me answer that by telling you about this series that you are writing. When you sat down to write this work you didn't actually have a clue where it would lead. You thought you were just going to ask some questions and get some answers and bumble your way through to getting some info that might be a bit useful. Right?

Z: Yeah. I guess that is the unflattering way of putting it.

8: Flattery is not my strong suite. Essentially you didn't know what the greater picture was. You didn't even know THERE WAS a greater picture. But your Inner-Self, Joy-Divine, and the rest of your soul family… well, we have a plan. Shall I tell you what it is?

Z: Can I possibly turn an invitation like that down?

8: It is to help you with your REAL quest. Which is: to create your reality. Let me explain. You live in a reality which you find confusing. You don't understand why things are the way they are. And for so long as you choose, in that reality, to take things at face value and believe what is presented, then you will take your creator status and nullify it. You will use it in such a self-defeating and chaotic manner that it will be of no use and will never show itself to you. And so you will proceed, believing that you are a very small pawn in a very big game. Others will capitalise on this self-limiting perspective and use little strategies to entice you to play games of their devising. In almost every instance the ones doing this will not even know THEMSELVES that this is what they are doing. Everyone is just playing the game and everyone is equally confused. And you can go on playing this game for a trillion lifetimes if you desire. It is a game that can suck you in like that and cause you to stay forever. But, of course, you do not desire this. You feel within yourself that this is not right for you. You make other choices. You call out for help with those choices. And help is ALWAYS there. It is my honour and privilege to be that which responds to your call. And I can assure you that if any being upon the planet calls for help, their call is heard. If they are prepared to take the help offered, then they will be helped. But therein lies a conundrum. Speaking for myself, I point-blank refuse to help you in such a way that the help diminishes you. I WILL NOT help you to be less than you are. And so a difficulty arises. I cannot "do for you". I can only help you to learn how to "do for yourself". But when you first called out to me, you did so precisely because you believed yourself to be weak and powerless. The only help you could conceive of was me "doing for you". Me, rescuing you.

So there was a road to travel. The first stage of the road is to disabuse you of the notion of your incapacity and to teach you that you are powerful and that, in fact, YOU create your entire reality. The second stage is to teach you HOW to go about creating your reality with greater and greater efficacy. And the final stage is to be there with you in an advisory role as you undertake your first direct reality creation exercises. And of course we chronicle this journey in book form so that we might share it with others who might like to read about the process and take value from it. But the thing you have yet to understand is how those who find value in this are actually co-creating it. Together you are all co-creating the reality you desire.

Now you and I have already walked quite a path together. We have brought you to this point where you are near the end of the first stage of the journey. You are now almost ready to know, believe, feel, experience and express that you are indeed the creator of your own reality. You have mostly released your doubts and fears. It is as a result of this work that has gone before that you are able to undertake the writing of THE ASCENSION PAPERS without getting too ensnared in fear and doubt. That is well. It will now be as a result of writing THE ASCENSION PAPERS that you will release the remainder of your fear and doubt and that you will complete your journey into your creator status. And it is most pleasing to me that we can share the process with your readers who are really our many brothers and sisters who are on planet earth. We retrace a few of our steps so that we may share them with your readers. And, as you go over them again, you bring a new willingness to listen and so you too gain a much deeper and clearer understanding of What Is. And then too we will share with your readers the other two stages of the journey: as you learn how to create your reality and as you decide what you will be creating. I don't easily stray to hyperbole, but this is going to be more amazing, magical and magnificent than you can now imagine. And for your readers too. Those whose souls call them to stay the course with us. They are going to realise quite soon that they are not passive observers of something, as people usually are when they read a book. No, they are going to find themselves drawn in and they are going to realise that, on a soul level, they are co-authoring this with us. And then they are going to start doing it directly… in the here and now… they are, if they are so called, going to make choices. They are going to make contact with you. And they are going to create with us. With you and me and the spiritual hierarchy of this reality. Together. We are creators. And we are going to create. And it will be the best, the brightest and the most beautiful that we can conceive of. And then we will go there together and walk inside our creation. Together. As beloved friends.

(he smiles) Does that sound far fetched?

Z: Wowzer, 8! I don't know whether to break into a spontaneous standing ovation or to hide under my bed. This is… out there. Exciting and amazing and… very out there!

8: Yes. Good. You need a little shaking so that we can begin your awakening. Because that is what we are doing. Waking you all up. Everyone who is prepared to hear the alarm and not just roll over and go back to sleep is being called:

Hello!

I am 8!

It is late!

We have a date!

Z: And you can rhyme.

8: Yes.

And it is time! (he laughs)

But it really is. I know you are all like trees in the spring - you can feel the sap rising. You can feel it in your bones and in your souls that there is a quickening. There is an energising. The time is near. I know you feel it. And there are ones such as I who are reaching out to you to teach you to do what you must do. Because if I come in and do it for you then I teach you the very opposite of what you must learn. Then I teach you that I am your master and that you need me to create for you. This will not do! If you are to awaken to your true magnificence then you must raise yourself from your slumbers, make new choices, set a new course for yourself and then… create!

So that is what we are going to do. Together, you and I. And together with your readers too. Because, you see I am not alone over here where I am. I surrounded by a good number of what you might call Spirit Beings and Light Beings. Many here with me are related to some that are on earth right now: your readers - the ones who are wishing to come and play reality creation with us - the ones who feel the deepest resonance with THE ASCENSION PAPERS. Such ones have THEIR soul-family here with me now. Inner-Selves and Spirit-Guides and the like; they are all with me and Joy-Divine in the planning and the co-creation of all this. And that is how it comes to be that the reader will know if THE ASCENSION PAPERS are right for them. Their own Inner-Self and spirit family would have been a part of their creation right from the inception. So they will feel it deep within their being, as they read these words, that something "right" is being expressed.

But now back to the nitty-gritty. I said part one of this process is about showing you your own power. And the first thing to do there is to deal with all the erroneous things you believe about yourself and your life that lead you to believe that you are NOT powerful. After we've stripped that nonsense away, then we can provide evidence to show you that you are powerful. And that is the over-arching theme of Part One of THE ASCENSION PAPERS.

Z: Part One? There is a Part One?

8: Yes. The first seven chapters are "what is" from your personal perspective. It's a bit of Self Discovery for you. You went on a journey with Joy-Divine and got some self-knowledge there. The next seven chapters are with me. I will introduce myself to your readers and maybe you, yourself, will learn a few new things about me. I'll be telling you a little bit about your planetary reality. Why things are the way they are. What came before. What will come after. WHAT IS. And why you have come to believe the things you do about your world. You're going to find some of this quite surprising and perhaps a bit shocking. But the story needs to be told. And then the final seven chapters of Part One will be with your dear old friend Adamu. He will also talk to the same sorts of issues, but from his perspective: what is going on in your greater environment. I mean your galaxy and beyond. All the flash and sparkle of what you call "extra terrestrials" and UFOs and civilizations on other worlds. All that fun. I know you'll look forward to it because that greatly interests you.

Of course there will be overlaps between the conversations of J-D, Adamu and I, as none of these topics can be discussed in isolation. But anyway that is the gist of Part One, the first 21 chapters.

Z: Wow. This is surprising. And exciting. I had no idea…

8: On a deeper more intuitive level you did. You opened yourself to it and have allowed this to flow. I just thought it was time for me to bring this to your conscious mind. So now you know.

Z: Great! Thanks. But if there is a Part One, there must be a Part Two, right?

8: I don't want to run too far ahead. I want to allow for creative flux; to allow that we might want to change the plan if it serves us to do so. But, without being too specific, I will say that Part Two is going to be all about reality creation. You will come to see how you are currently hampering yourself in this regard and how to stop doing that. Instead you will be shown the tools of creation and how it works. Then you can begin to create and slowly, gently, begin to see the results of your creations so that you can begin to know that it is working for you in your direct personal experience. There will be plenty of info in there that you'll be able to begin to apply in your life right away and some more info that will only really be more applicable as you progress into other realms later on. After the Singularity Event, I mean.

Z: Fantastic! It feels as if I have hit the jackpot!

8: Why? Because someone has a plan?

Z: No, because I really like this plan.

8: You had better. It's your plan.

Z: I don't understand.

8: You will. But let's not waste time with cryptic puzzles. In time you will see what I mean. Particularly in Part Three.

Z: Part Three?

8: That's where the fun begins. Part Three is active reality creation. You are going to close the circle by working out what your new reality, that you will want to create for yourself, should be like. What you want to retain of this reality and what you want to let go of and what you are going to replace the released stuff with. In Part Three you are, quite literally, going to create your whole reality.

Z: Uh… 8… I have to take a moment here and register that this is an extremely scary thought. In so many ways. Prime of which is the concern that I don't feel at all qualified for this. I mean how do I know what would be a good thing to create or not? What if I make mistakes? I mean, I am just a person living on earth who…

8: Alright, alright. That is an acceptable stance for you for now because you still don't understand what is going on. You STILL think of yourself as one single, separate little human being living on Planet Earth. If you were even paying a smidgeon of attention to all that Joy-Divine was saying then you'd understand that you are an indivisible part of The One. As are all your readers. I mean, really, was that not the central focus of all he had to say? Did he not offer that truth to you over and over again?

Z: Yes. He did.

8: Okay. So I understand that this hasn't really sunk in yet. You still think it's a bit of theory. Well, when you start to think like it's true, act like it's true and FEEL like it's true, then you will also begin to KNOW that it's true. And when that happens you will have no problem understanding how you can create a whole new reality exactly as you like it. You will understand that it is a co-creation and that you are simply focusing your intention in a particular way. It is not a grandiose thing. It is not an ego-kick. It is just choosing what is right for you. But choosing when you know how to make your choices come to life. And you will realise that you are not choosing alone. You are a part of a magnificent structure and you are simply playing your perfect role in that. And then you will really and truly come to see that your readers are not the passive "absorbers" of this material that you and they both think they are. You will understand that they are as active in writing this book as you are.

Z: Okay 8, I have now heard you say this a few times and I have adopted a "wait-and-see" attitude. But now I want to know. How can my readers, who haven't even read these words yet, be part of the creation of something that I haven't even written down yet?

8: Pah! You think you are trapped in time? Okay, it DOES look that way to you. But you and your readers are all a part of greater beings who are not. Time and sequentiality and dimensions and causality and co-creation and... well... many such topics need to be addressed with you. When you understand these things then you will be ready to let go of the limitations they are placing on your ability to imagine your world correctly. And all of that – and so much more besides – is what awaits you in the conversations that lie ahead. And that is why, when you get to Part Three, you will be ready to create!

Z: But, 8, what if I don't want the responsibility of creating stuff for others.

8: But you won't be! Everyone creates for themselves. Usually some of us create together. Then it is called co-creation. You will simply be a part of that, playing your role.

But enough of this, now. I said we'd talk about it as it unfolded. All I wanted to do was open this, my section, with a clearer understanding of where we're going. Give you a rudder, so to speak. I understand that some of this seems outrageous to you. That is fine. You ALWAYS have choices. In every moment, in all of your reality, you will always have choices. So right now you have a choice. If this is all too bizarre for you, you can just take your hands from the keyboard and, in so doing, shut me up. Your readers also have a choice. They can stop reading. There is no coercion of anyone. But you have asked me to speak and I ALWAYS speak my truth. Often such truths make beings uncomfortable. Sometimes they turn away, sometimes they stay. I am not in the business of sweetening my words to entice you gently along. But I do notice that your fingers are still on the keyboard and you are still typing (he chuckles).

Z: Well, you know, I am a little spooked by what you have said, but I love you and trust you. And I'm most willing to hear you out. I will reserve my right, in every moment, to decide to what degree I will internalise what you say as "my truth". But I will most certainly stay to hear you out.

8: Good boy. Then let me begin. We've wasted enough resource on the overview. This first conversation is meant to be an introduction to me. So I will tell you who I am. Then you and your readers will have context for my words. You and I have spoken a great deal already in this life from when you first began to learn to really listen. So you and I will pretend we don't know each other at all so that your readers can catch up.

Right. Ask a question.

Z: About you or about this reality? Or what?

8: It doesn't matter. If your readers want to know me, they can discern my nature from my words. If you want to spend time digging around in my character first, then I'll entertain that. I will answer any question directed at me. You may like the answer or you may not. That is your concern, not mine.

Z: Okay. Let me ask a simple one. What IS your nature?

8: I am a being of truth.

Z: What is "truth"?

8: Truth is a way of being. It is ordering. It is simplifying. It is knowing. It is the basis upon which realities can be created and it is the basis from which perspectives can be held.

Truth is my essence and my nature and I express this in my character.

Z: So then what is THE TRUTH.

8: Now you ask an interesting question. There are an infinite number of truths that are true and right from a given perspective. But ultimately they are all also false from some other perspective. This means that there are many transitory truths but only one absolute truth.

Z: And that is?

8: The one absolute truth is:

"The One is".

Z: That's it? Not a wordy truth then (laughs).

8: No. We can add words to it if you like. But often that makes it less true. We shall in this conversation attempt to degrade the truth as little as possible.

Now let's look at the statement: "*The One is*".

Firstly, by that statement I indicate that there is only ever truly One. My partner and "Other-Self", Joy-Divine, has already made this quite clear in his way in his section of these conversations. There are Many, but their many-ness is transitory. Inevitably they all return to Oneness. The process of becoming Many produces many experiences. When something has been experienced and felt, then it is "true" from that perspective. But eventually that perspective will be surrendered for another. Then new experiences will be had and different things will be true. So there will be many truths about the many-ness. But these truths will always hold incongruities, inconsistencies and imbalance. This will manifest as discomfort in your life. Fear and pain and illness will result. And so it will come to be that, in order for TRUE healing to be obtained, at some point on all journeys all the truths about separation and many-ness will begin to be relinquished in favour of truths about unity and oneness. And then the impossibly complex multiplicity of truths will begin to condense. They will begin to coalesce. The temporary illusions of separation will begin to dissolve. Until finally the illusion is released. Until the Oneness is again understood to be the truth.

Secondly I indicate that The One *is*. In your time-bound parlance I could say, "*The One always was and always will be*". But that is a distortion. YOU think there is a past and a future, I do not. I know there is only NOW. So it is more correct to say, "*The One is.*" If you understand that that statement was true in your earliest history and will be true when time ends, then you might get a glimmering of what I mean. I mean that there is no context in which the The One is not. Truly, The One is eternal.

Z: Okay. "*The One is*". Is that the only thing that is true?

8: It is the only thing that is absolutely true, from all perspectives, under all circumstances, always. It is true even in those circumstances, such as your current reality, where this basic truth is deeply hidden. The One is. It is true.

Z: Is there nothing else that is true in that way?

8: No.

Z: What about… uh… like, what about "free will". Isn't that always true?

8: No. Free will is always relative. In some ways it is so that you have more free will than I because you can believe things that I cannot. You can believe that you are absolutely separate from everyone else; I cannot. I KNOW I am one with everyone and everything. In similar manner you can hatch all kinds of other beliefs about yourself and your reality and you can believe them quite fervently. I cannot do this. But, on the other hand, I can create realities and manifest energy and matter as an act of will which would, to your eyes, look quite god-like. So we both have Free Will but it is different and it is relative. Neither of us have absolute free will.

And then, I must also add, there are other realities elsewhere where there are other modes at play, where there is not what you'd call free will. So free will is certainly not always true. It is not an absolute.

If it were, then everyone everywhere would be able to do exactly what they wanted at all times. And you cannot can you?

Z: No. I mean I am free to think all kinds of stuff, free to believe all kinds of stuff. But I can't right now just leap in the air and fly. I can't turn the sky green. I can't… stop the sun from rising tomorrow…

8: Quite so.

Z: So then it appears we DON'T have free will.

8: Oh you certainly do. It is just not absolute. If you will kindly keep your mind from wandering then you will notice that what I am saying here is that there is only one absolute truth. It is, "*The One is*". I said right at the beginning that there are an infinite number of other "truths". That these will be true, to a lesser or greater degree, from one perspective or another. Free Will is one such subjective truth. But it isn't even one of the more interesting ones. It is simply an effect. So how about we stop trying to poke holes in this first truth and do something constructive?

Z: Such as?

8: Well, I could tell you about the derived truths.

Z: What's a "*derived truth*"?

8: Let's look at it like this: do you exist?

Z: Yes, of course!

8: Are you sure?

Z: Of course I am sure!

8: So that is your truth and you're not going to change your mind about that any time soon?

Z: Yes.

8: Good. Then we have one truth about you. For you, from your perspective, it is true that you exist right now.

Right?

I mean let me just make sure that you aren't just a figment of my imagination? You do REALLY exist, don't you?

Z: Are you pulling my leg, 8?

8: Yes. But only to make a point. So you now have two truths: YOUR truth, which is that you exist right now and the absolute truth which is, "The One is". With me so far?

Z: Yep. I can just about keep two truths in my head at once (smile).

8: Fantastic. Then you'll be able to make this leap with me. If both of these things are true then it must mean that you are a part of The One. Right?

Z: Yes. Everything that exists is a part of The One. I exist. I am therefore a part of The One.

8: And can The One be destroyed?

Z: No, because then it would be "The One was". Or "The One will be for a while and then it'll stop being".

8: Quite. So you agree that you are a part of something that IS. Yes?

Z: Yes.

8: Good. Now imagine a big jig-saw puzzle. You can take it apart and you can put it back together again. When it is together it is whole. It is one picture. When it is taken apart it is many little pictures. With me?

Z: Yep.

8: If you take it apart and then destroy one of the little bits. Can you put it back together again?

Z: Uh… no. I mean you can put all the OTHER bits back together again but the picture will be incomplete.

8: Exactly.

So, you are a part of The One. If you were to be destroyed, then a part of The One would be destroyed. The One would then be incomplete. But this is not possible. Then it would no longer be The One. It would be a fraction. It would be The 0.9 recurring. Or The A-Little-Bit-Less-Than-One. You get the idea?

Z: Yes, I do.

8: If you were more interested in mathematics I could have argued the same point more eloquently by stating that The One is infinite and infinity cannot be divided.

But the point of all this is that we can arrive at a derived truth. You are a part of The One. No part of The One can be removed from it and no part of The One can be destroyed without destroying The One. And that is impossible. The One IS. This means that you also ARE. It means you cannot be destroyed. No part of The One ever is destroyed.

Which brings us to our first derived truth:

"You are eternal and immortal".

This is so for everything you can address these words to. Everything that has a perspective, a subjective experience, everything that in one way or another is a "someone", everything that has found for itself a concept of "Self"… will never, and can never, be destroyed. It is eternally valid.

And of course this applies to you.

Z: But what if you WANT to destroy yourself?

8: You can't. The relative truth of free will is far and away trumped by the absolute truth of The One IS. So your (free will) ability to decide for annihilation cannot be enacted. You see, you cannot stop being a part of The One. And as long as you ARE a part of The One then you cannot destroy yourself because The One IS. A great number of souls have desired their own annihilation at one time or another. And I don't mean something simple like the suicide of an incarnated being… I mean a spirit being desiring to destroy itself.

Now, on the face of it, this seems to be a desire to cease being, but what it REALLY is, is a call for help on a very profound level. You, yourself, have been there. In between this life and the last one you desired your own termination (Zingdad note: see Chapter 1, *"A Life Between Lives"*). You went about attempting to achieve this with some commitment and fervour, I can tell you. Obviously you didn't succeed. And in all of creation everywhere there has never been a case where a single being has succeeded at terminating their own existence and, equally, there has never been a single case of one being terminating another. It is simply not possible.

Z: So there is no murder in the true sense of things?

8: No. If someone takes a gun to your head and pulls the trigger, then I assure you of three things:

1. Though your body will fall away, irreparably damaged, YOU will survive. Your body will cease biological function and will die, but you will not, even for a split second, cease to be. After the bullet tears through your brain you will no longer be able to use that apparatus to filter your perceptions. You will immediately become aware of yourself as a being who is very much alive but now looking down on the ruined body that you used to think of as "yourself". So that will require a small adjustment of your perspective. This change in self-identity will have to be assimilated but you will very much still "exist". The important point to note about this is that the killer will think you are gone… dead. But this is only a failing of his perceptions because he will no longer perceive you as a living being. But you will know that you are alive. And this same thing can happen in some of the subtler realms as well. Just as it is possible to destroy someone's physical body here in this 3D realm you inhabit, so it is also possible to dissipate a 4D body. You can even do it at 5D though it is both rare and difficult to do. Above that it can no longer be done. But irrespective of where this happens and under whatever circumstances, it is ALWAYS so that the one who is "killed" survives the experience.

You simply lose the use of the vehicle that you were using.

2. If someone else "kills" you then you will eventually come to understand that this was, on some level, agreed upon by the two of you. It might take a little time, a little processing and possibly even some counselling but it is assuredly so that you will come to see that this event was the outcome of decisions and choices that you had made. Either you yourself, or you as your Inner-Self.

Z: But hold on, 8. What if I am at odds with my Inner-Self? What if I don't agree with that choice? I mean surely it isn't right for my Inner-Self to negotiate my life away without my consent?

8: As long as you still do not understand that you and your Inner-Self are really and truly the same being, that might be a valid concern. And if you "died" in such a circumstance then you would be helped. Members of your spirit-family would be immediately on hand to guide you and counsel you so that you could come to a full understanding of what had occurred. You would be helped to see the perfection of the moment.

Z: And if you don't come to see it as perfect… if you don't agree to the ending?

8: Then you will always have the choice to go back.

Z: Reincarnate you mean?

8: Yes, that is one option. But there is another option, and this brings me to my third point.

3. You always have the right to return to the life that was terminated, no matter how that termination occurred.

Z: The one with the head blown off? Surely not! How would I reanimate a body with my brains splattered across the floor?

8: My goodness, you DO have a colourful way with words.

Zingdad, you have already understood from Joy-Divine that time is not absolute. It is only in 3D that you are constrained to the illusion that time is linear and absolute. This constraint does not apply to beings of the subtler realms. So we can help you in some interesting ways. After your "death" you will find yourself in a position to either accept that "death" and move on OR you will have the option to enter into a counselling phase with more advanced members of your spirit family. At this point you will either accept the "death" and move on or there will be an agreement that you should return. If the latter is the case then there will be further counselling to help you to make better choices next time so that you don't just end up repeating the same scenario over and over. When all these issues are properly dealt with then you are returned to your life at an appropriate moment. What the "appropriate moment" is will vary greatly from case to case. In some instances it would be quite a bit before the previous moment of death so that a new path forward could be found and the death event avoided completely. In some instances you will be returned to the event mere moments before it and, with inspired guidance, you will navigate it differently. And then there are those instances which can be highly inspirational where the being is allowed to experience the "death", remember some part of the counselling and remember the returning. These are often called Near Death Experiences in your culture. But each and every case is different and unique and each one is handled with great love and sensitivity by the being's spirit family.

Z: That's pretty amazing stuff, 8. That means no one dies without agreeing to it.

8: My dear Zingdad. We have been telling you for a while now in all kinds of different ways and now, more recently, through this work, THE ASCENSION PAPERS, that you are the creator of your own reality. How did Joy-Divine put it?

Z: You mean when he said,

> *"You always get exactly what you create".*

8: That's exactly what I mean, yes. How then would that statement be true if it ceased to be true as soon as you died? It wouldn't.

Z: You're right. Then it would have to be, "*You mostly get some of what you create*"

8: Exactly. And that is the point: even death does not victimise you. Even when you have died you STILL have options. You still have the right to say, "*Hey! I wasn't done with that!*" And if, after being properly counselled, you decide that there is indeed unfinished business or a better way to end this then… back you go to an appropriate moment before the "termination event", whatever that was.

Z: But then surely people wouldn't choose to die? Surely they would all come back, if for no other reason than to help their loved ones who stayed behind?

8: When humans on earth "die" then they are immediately in an interstitial reality where they have all kinds of assistance to make sense of what has occurred. They come to agree that this is for the best - that they should now move on - or they return. That is how it is. And you'd be surprised to know how many times almost all of you have already "died" and returned.

Z: Really? Except it has never happened to me. I don't remember anything like that.

8: Of course you don't remember it. It didn't happen in your time-stream. It is not "behind" you for you to remember. When you went back into your life you chose an alternate time stream which

---

meant that FOR YOU, you never did die.

But let me help you remember. Perhaps you remember the motorcycle accident you had a few years ago. The one in which you "miraculously" came away without any serious injury. You had, for some time before then, been thinking about the futility of your life. You didn't feel a great lust for life and things had become a bit colourless and drab for you. You lost your direction somewhat. Then, that evening, you were having a chat with a friend. He was telling you about an horrendous motorcycle accident he had had and how he almost died of his injuries. You had the quiet little thought that maybe, just maybe, this is what you wanted. To just leave this world. And then you said goodbye to this friend, got on your motorcycle and rode home. And on the way home, as you came round a bend on the highway there was a sudden blockage in the traffic ahead of you and you were travelling way too fast to stop in time and you had the accident.

The thing you don't now remember is that you actually got to "die" that night. And then you and I had a little sit-down. We talked about where you were at in your life and I showed you some of the highlights of what lay ahead. You agreed that, while there was quite a lot of work to do, it was worth doing because you could see what an exciting future lay ahead. You agreed with me that you needed to go back, that you needed to go on with your life. And so we took you back to a moment JUST BEFORE the accident and this time you received some assistance. This time you manoeuvred your motorcycle like a Hollywood stuntman, flipping and flying around the vehicles that had stopped dead in front of you. And then, when it was time to part company with your motorcycle, you executed the most unbelievably acrobatic roll, landing without so much as a sprain or a scratch! Everyone marvelled. Then you stood up, removed your helmet, and released some choice expletives in the direction of the driver who had caused the whole mess on the road that night.

And then you went on with your life.

You often thought back on that accident. You wondered where you found the skill to pull off those manoeuvres. You also wondered how it was that, after that the accident, you began to find some new direction in your life. There were many things you wondered about but never did you realise what actually happened that night.

Z: You mean I REALLY could have died that night?

8: You DID die. And then you didn't. Both are true. You are experiencing the timeline in which you didn't. That is your choice. And it isn't the only time this has happened to you.

Do you remember spinning the car on the highway on the way to your holiday destination? (he smiles) At one point you were driving in reverse down the highway at 100km/h and then you just calmly spun the car another 180 degrees and kept going the right way down the road. More amazing stunt-driving that worked out perfectly! How do you think THAT was accomplished? There have been a few other such occasions. Some of them less dramatic and less glamorous than these. Some of them quite sad and lonely and not to say a bit pathetic.

But the point is that you have provided yourself with a number of exit-points from this life. But each time you have chosen not to take them. Each time you have come back. And so here you still are. This is your choice. And it is so for pretty much everyone who is here on earth. It would be quite rare for a person to come to full realisation of Self as an adult and never to have passed a few such exit points. In fact, I would strongly recommend to each reader that you give this some thought. Think back on your life. Think of the times when strange and miraculous-seeming events brought you through life-threatening or life-changing situations. See if you do not think it possible that this might have been you navigating your own exit points. Sit with this. Write it down. Analyse it and understand it. Open your heart to true understanding. You will find some amazing insights for yourself in such a process. Do it right now, if you like. This chapter will still be waiting for you. Or do it later. But do it.

Z: Thank you, 8, I'll do the same and think about moments other than the two you have given me.

But still… I want to come back to the issue of those who died and DIDN'T decide to come back. Why didn't they? Surely they would have come back, even if only to be with the ones who love them?

8: Okay, look… Are you willing to agree that there is a much broader perspective than the one that you currently hold in this incarnated life of yours here on earth?

Z: Yes, I guess that is obvious.

8: Because if you are willing to accept that it is a part of the design of your reality that ones who inhabit it are restricted from knowing certain things, then it should be OBVIOUS that, once you have certain restrictions lifted, your perspective will be different.

Z: Okay, I guess, but…

8: What you don't understand is that this life you are currently living really and truly is just a part of an elaborate game that you are playing. It is as if you are playing a part in a huge stage-play. Your whole incarnated life is a role. This does not mean that it is not important or that it does not have great value and purpose. But it is so that, after "death" you will come to see it for what it is. And you will come to be willing to release your attachment to it when the time is right to do so. And, as for your loved ones, your friends and family, let me tell you about them. When you "die" you will see them again in spirit form. You will see the truer version of that being, here, in spirit form welcoming you home and AT THE SAME TIME you will also see the incarnated aspect of that being continuing its life and mourning its loss of you. Obviously you will feel compassion for the loss and mourning of the incarnated aspect and you will feel great love for them. You will desire to comfort them and be with them in their pain. But their confusion will not be your confusion. You will know that it is only their limited perspective that they have lost you, that you are gone, that you are now dead. You will know that this is not so and you will know that a far more eternally valid, wise and magnificent version of this loved one is there with you in spirit form. So then… what do you think your decision will be? To immediately rush back into that incarnation to alleviate the mourning and loss of that one incarnated aspect? Or to see it for what it is, as an inevitable part of the journey that is incarnated life in that system; to allow yourself to be shown the greater marvel and mystery of All That Is; to give love and comfort to the mourning beloved-one from your new perspective in spirit-form; and to be there waiting when they too are ready to die to incarnated life and awaken to their greater reality?

Which do you think you would choose?

Z: Well… I guess… I will make the best choice I can under the circumstances. And I guess when it really IS time for me to go I'll choose to leave.

8: That is well said. But I think it important to make the point right now that death of the body is not the only way out of this place. It is certainly the most common. So much so that it is usually thought to be the only way out. But there are some other interesting ways to move on. We will be addressing these in greater detail a bit later in THE ASCENSION PAPERS.

Z: That certainly sounds like a fascinating subject!

8: You are sure to find it so. But now – are there any more questions you have about death? I really want to make sure we have laid the subject to rest, if you'll forgive the expression. Death is understandably an issue of some considerable difficulty for 3D beings as it causes much fear and confusion. The fear of death can often be a major obstacle to the pure enjoyment of life.

Z: Yes, I do still have some questions. Could you help me with the issue of mourning, from the perspective of the one who stays behind? How are we to come to terms with the thought that the person who died could have returned to us and didn't?

8: Not every ear can receive every message. Sometimes people need to hold onto their grief and pain for a while. Sometimes it feels as if that validates the love they had for the one who, to their perception, is now gone. Human emotions are complex things.

But if the being who is mourning a loss is able to really hear what is being expressed here, perhaps this will in fact bring some modicum of healing. Could it not be so that there is comfort to be found in knowing that the person who died is really alright? That their "death" is something about which they have had, and have exercised, some choice. And that, as they have gained a broader perspective, so they have seen the beauty and the perfection and the completeness of the path they have travelled in their life.

If the grieving one is able to see this, then the grief can begin to be put in its right perspective: that you grieve for YOUR loss. You feel pain over the fact that you no longer have the experience of this person in your life. There is a gap, a hole, an emptiness in your life. And of course that causes you pain.

That is the correct perspective.

You do not grieve for the other, you grieve for yourself. For your own loss. And this is, of course, the normal and valid way to respond to the situation. And grief is a process, it is a road which you will travel. It has a number of well-known vistas along its path. Your counsellors and psychologists will tell you that denial, bargaining and anger are to be anticipated. And as you travel the path, so will you come to find acceptance. These are the things that a counsellors can help you navigate. However there is one more stage which is not generally acknowledged.

Z: And that is?

8: Joy.

Z: Joy?

8: Yes. Because you will, in due course, be reunited with the one you feel you have lost to death. When you yourself release your hold on that life stream, you will again meet with the one who previously "died". And that reunion is filled with unbounded joy as the circle is completed.

Z: Because when each person dies they meet their loved ones on the other side.

8: Correct. People on earth really have the thing backwards. They usually imagine death to be some kind of "going to sleep". Some kind of "going into the dark night" or something like that. When really it is quite the opposite. Death is very much more like an awakening. Like arising from a dreaming sleep where the life you have just lived is the dream. When you are "on the other side," as you put it, you will realise that your perceptions are many times sharper than they are now. Your insights and understandings will be far more powerful than they are now. So your experience will be that of someone who wakes from a dream and realises that the dream, though very vivid and powerful, was yet quite restrictive and less "real" than that which they now are experiencing. You will feel light and free. And you will find yourself surrounded by your all most beloved ones. And now imagine how you feel when you find that most beloved being, whom you believed you had lost years ago, is suddenly there to greet you! And not only is this being present, but you see them as they really are: at their prime and in full radiance and beauty.

Yes, it is so, this is a time of boundless joy.

And perhaps knowing this will bring some comfort to those who mourn a loss. It doesn't remove the pain of loss for one who is grieving, this is true. You cannot be held in the arms of thoughts and ideas. But, at least, you can understand that your loss is not permanent. You will be reunited eventually.

And also, it is very much true that the one you mourn is aware of you and is with you... even if you cannot always sense this.

Z: I see. Thank you. But 8, what about all the stuff that I have heard about there first being a tunnel of light and all that... how does that fit in with this "meeting the family" stuff?

8: The tunnel of light is indeed something that most will perceive. The death experience is often quite traumatic and so a period of adjustment is provided. First you are allowed to hang around in the environs of the 3D world for a bit, if you want that or feel you need it. Some are very attached to their current incarnation, to the body or the paraphernalia of the current life. They are not ready to see that all of these are just the props of the play. Nothing more. Such beings will probably want to remain close to the 3rd density reality for a time after death.

Z: Are they then ghosts?

8: That to which you refer as ghosts could be one of a great number of things. It is possible that more sensitive people might sense the presence of such ones who have not yet moved on. Perhaps this will be labelled a "ghost". But ones who become stuck in the earth-environs will be helped to move on sooner or later.

The next phase that is usually experienced is a place of comforting, silent, darkness. After all the hurly-burly of incarnated life and the sometimes traumatic ending of that life, it is usually deemed beneficial to allow for a brief "time out". And so, beings usually find themselves in a place of stillness. It is dark and peaceful. But, so that beings are not confused and do not think they are deserted and alone, there is a bright, white light which shines from the perceptual-direction of "above". The symbolism of this "bright, white light from above" is both clear and universal. And now the being must choose. Do you move into the light or do you not? This is the choice being presented. If you like the peace and silence, you can remain there as long as you need. Time is irrelevant there. If you move into the light you will feel it to be quite blissfully loving. If you reject the light, you can find many other directions to move into. For example, there is the lesser-light of direct entrance into another incarnation. This is not advised but can be chosen. Or one can swan around in the meta-realities that find expression from beings' dreams, fantasies and imaginings. This is an option but is also not advised. Some of these meta-realities are the nightmare world where beings burn off the worst of their inner torment. Stumbling around there can seem pretty hellish indeed!

There are many options and, as always, the choice will be yours. If you seek love then you should do the obvious: look for the bright, white light, feel its love, and move towards it.

Z: And when do people get to have this joyful reunion with their family members?

8: Once you have moved somewhat into the light you begin to feel a union and a belonging. If you move towards that, then you will be following your heart to those who love you most. It is inevitable that you shall find them.

Please note that I present you with some of the general trends of what one might expect during the process called death. I must emphasise that this is just that: some general trends. There are no firm rules. Each person is unique and will have their own unique experience of this transition. The above is by no means definite.

And what do you think will determine exactly what each persons' experience will be?

Z: What they need?

8: No... What they choose!

Even in the process of this transition called death, you STILL get what you create. You have the right to make poor choices. Or let me rather say, choices that will cause you pain. It is your right to make such choices. But if you are willing to choose the path of love then you also have the right to be counselled and advised and to then make really good choices.

And that is why I have been happy to get into this long discussion about death. It is a very, very important point that I need to drive home: At no point in the death process do you actually die. At no point do you cease to have options. At no point do you cease to be possessed of your consciousness or your sense of Self. You quite simply do not die. Not ever.

Z: Then why do we believe that we do?

8: Do you want to hear a curious dichotomy?

Z: Okay.

8: The closest thing to actual death, is the thing you call "birth"!

Z: Huh!?!

8: It works like this: I have already explained how, after "death" you become more conscious and aware. How you feel like you are waking up. You remember your life with great clarity. You will usually also begin to remember other lifetimes and all the many and varied experiences between incarnations. In short, your sense of self expands and your capacity to process that which you know also expands. You become MORE.

That is "death". And birth? Well, it's the opposite process. As you integrate yourself into the new life, so you immerse yourself into forgetfulness. You lose your memories and your knowingness. You release your ability to deeply process. You slow down, dim down and forget. You become LESS. And THAT is why you can believe that death is final. Not because nothing can be remembered beyond death, no, because almost nothing can be remembered beyond birth!

Z: That's very interesting. But why do we do that?

8: Why do you choose to experience birth? Well, if you have been following the reasoning that has been presented to you thus far in THE ASCENSION PAPERS then it should become clear that you have chosen to enter incarnated life down there in the 3rd density so that you can discover yourself and create yourself from a place of not-knowing. From a place of forgetfulness. So it is obvious that it actually serves your purposes to allow the final, most dense layer of the Veil of Unknowing to fall over your consciousness as you enter into an incarnation. When this happens you are limited to only be able to perceive the things of the 3rd density and little else. This facilitates the learning and growth that you desire.

Z: Alright. That makes sense.

8: So then if I may summarise what has been said; as you enter incarnated life you forget pretty much everything you have known. You go about your life, and as you do so, you are offered a number of exit points from that life-stream. Many you will ignore. Some you will take and then realise your mistake and you will return. Your life stream will end when you take an exit point and do not change your mind. When you decide that your life is complete. And then you will move on into the spirit realm to continue your journey, whatever that might be.

So now you understand what I mean when I say there really and truly is no actual "death". And even the illusory experience of death that you do have is a matter of choice. Your choice. Because, as I have contended, truly it is so that:

"You are eternal and immortal."

Z: 8, I have to say that this is one of the most beautiful things I have heard. It feels right and true for me and it makes me very happy to think that it might be so.

8: I really want you to understand that death is nothing more than a profound change of state. And change is life. Life is change. Resisting change is death. And so a rather curious dichotomy is set up. Those who fear death to the extent that this fear begins to consume them, they try to resist death. They try to cease the flow of change. And ironically, all they do is cease the flow of life. They in fact bring death upon themselves even whilst they still live! This causes all kinds of inner-torment and brings about illnesses of the psyche and the spirit which will also manifest as illness of the body. Can you see the irony? Fearing death will cause disease that brings death closer!

So it is most beneficial for us to understand death correctly so that we no longer fear it.

The next step is to embrace life and embrace change and then, soon enough, you will be able to leave the experience of death behind altogether. And this is quite central to the notion of ascension. Ascended beings transcend the notion of death. They remain in life forever more.

And with that I would like to move onto the next derived truth.

Z: Okay. Thanks 8. I must say it's already pretty mind blowing for me to hear that I am immortal on a soul-level, but the added fact that I have died before in this lifetime and each time chosen to return, well that's a lot to take in. But through our discussion here I really am coming to see how death might not be this bleak, scary thing.

8: No, it really isn't. In addressing the derived truth that *"you are eternal and immortal"*, I simply needed to deal with the fact that there is this experience of death but that it is actually just a portal from your current reality to another reality. Nothing more. And I also state that it is not even a one-way door. And, on top of that, you are in control of how you use that door, even if you are not now aware of this.

Now we can move on to the next derived truth which we have just touched upon. It is this:

"Change is the only constant".

Z: I've often heard that said. And it does seem true to me. I mean everything DOES eventually change. But could you first tell me how this is derived from the first absolute truth?

8: I implied this in our discussion about death but let me reiterate. Do you understand that anything that is still, unmoving and unchanging is dead? ANYTHING, if it does not change at all, if it ceases to move, then it has ceased to live. It is dead. And, as nothing ever dies, it follows that nothing ever ceases to move and to change.

Z: Nothing ever dies?

8: You have already forgotten the first part of the conversation. We've just been through that.

Remember – The One IS?

Z: Oh yes, sorry 8. I do remember. The One IS, and cannot be divided, and that means all parts of The One must continue to exist. Nothing dies, nothing is destroyed. And now you are saying that "nothing dies" equals "everything changes".

8: Yes

Z: But 8, lots of stuff doesn't change. And lots of stuff is dead.

8: Such as?

Z: Oh come on, 8, surely you jest with me. Take a brick in one of the walls of my house. It's pretty dead and it certainly doesn't look to be doing much changing!

8: Wrong. The brick lives. Only in a way that you are not able to understand. It is a part of a living system that you haven't the ability yet to perceive. Let me ask you: are the bones in your body alive?

Z: Err... yes. They are a living organ kind-of-thing, I think. They grow and change over time.

8: But you cannot talk to them. You cannot see them eating food. They have no central nervous system. They don't seem to be intelligent. And yet you are happy to ascribe to them the term "alive". What if I tell you that, just as a bone or a blood cell is alive in its own right, so is the brick you so disparage. And just as a bone or a blood cell is an essential part of a much larger living entity, so is that brick. The brick itself is in a constant state of flux, always changing. On a sub-atomic level there is constant change at a very high rate and on the macro level there is constant change at somewhat slower rate. If you want to see such change, go and look at a house which, for a few centuries, has had no maintenance or upkeep. That whole house will slowly return to the earth. The bricks crumbling and changing and becoming a part of the earth. You see, it is the arrogance of humanity that you believe you can determine what is "life" and "not life" by arbitrary parameters that you can measure... and tellingly, by their similarity to your own state. How would you like it if I said that you are not really a life form because your life-span is too short to be meaningful? Such might be the view of a galaxy, should it hold the same arrogance as humans do. Well it's time to release that arrogance. It's time to understand that EVERYTHING is life. Everything is, in one way or another, of consciousness. And then you can come to the understanding that nothing dies and everything changes. These two ideas are actually the same idea when you get right down to it. Change IS life. Stasis is death. Nothing is ever truly static. Nowhere does anything ever cease all movement. Everywhere, beings and things are in a constant process of motion and change.

Change is an absolute constant. And it is the ONLY absolute constant.

Z: Alright 8. Let me work through this from the top: there is not a single thing that I could point to or name that is not a part of The One.

8: Right.

Z: And no part of The One is dead or static. All parts of The One are alive and changing.

8: Yes. They might not have the narrow attributes which your science calls "life" but they are most certainly alive.

Z: But then, what is life? If it is not the "narrow attributes" science has given it, then what is it?

8: Growth. Change. Evolution. Becoming. Consciousness. These are some of the attributes of life. But what it actually IS? That is a very large and very complex question. Look around you. Look at your planet. If you have seen every single thing that has ever happened on your planet since its creation until its end, then you will have a small part of the picture. Then go and do the same for every planet and every star in the universe. Slowly you will get a bigger and bigger part of the picture. When you have seen everything, everywhere in All That Is, then you will begin to hold within yourself the answer to the question, "*What is life?*"

Life is a mystery. It is beyond comprehension. It is beautiful and magnificent and unending. Life IS.

Z: I don't often get to see this more poetic side to your soul, 8.

8: You know, my dear young friend, the more you try to simplify things, the more you see their complexity. And when you are ready to give yourself over to infinite complexity, then suddenly there is pure simplicity. This is my experience. Life will break your heart with its unendurable beauty. And, with broken heart, you will call for more and more and more.

Life is a wonder.

And assuredly, your dour old friend 8 is very much in love with Life.

Z: My goodness, 8, that is a beautiful thing to say!

8: Thank you. Life itself is my inspiration and life itself is beautiful. But you see, because life is infinite and constantly changing, it is a logical certainty that it will remain beyond definition. And that is why, sadly, your attempts at using the scientific method to define what life is will always fall short. You cannot know life with your mind. You can only know it with your heart. And that is why, when you ask me what life is, you hear me speaking of love and beauty and such matters of the heart.

Z: That makes perfect sense to me, 8, and I really enjoyed that description.

8: That is good. Then let us move onto the next derived truth, shall we?

Z: Great. What is it?

8: It is this:

"What you put out is what you get back"

Z: Cool. I know that one. But how is that derived?

8: This one is very simple for me to explain but will probably be the hardest for you to understand or believe.

First, let us look to your own experience. Tell me, do you have an experience of being able to do things and choose things?

Z: Yes. I certainly do.

8: Do you feel that much of what you do, you are doing TO someone or FOR someone?

Z: Well... if I can include myself as a "someone" then, yes. I'd say everything I do is either being done to, or for, someone.

8: Good. This means that you see that your actions are only really valid in relation to some being. You would not get out of bed in the morning if there was not a "someone" to get out of bed for. And, as you quite rightly point out, you can include yourself in the set called "someone".

But who is this someone?

Did we not say there is only One? That the many-ness is an illusion? If this true the obviously anything that you do, you do TO or FOR The One. But you yourself are not separate from The

One, you are one with the Oneness. So then logically, anything that you do, you do to, or for, Self. YOURself.

And that is the logic of it. But of course this will not satisfy you. Because it is not apparent in your life, is it?

Z: Hmm. You are exactly right. What you say makes sense intellectually but... if it is true then why is it not apparent in my life? Why do I not immediately see what I do to others coming back to me?

8: That is the perfect question. You asked why you do not IMMEDIATLY see this. That is exactly the point! Let me explain: When you do something to another it takes time for the result to come back to you. In that time you have the opportunity to disregard the connection between the cause and the effect. When the result arrives in your life you have the opportunity to forget how and when you chose this and caused this. And to massively complicate matters IN THE MEAN TIME you will have made countless other choices and in so doing enacted countless other outcomes. So, when these outcomes do arrive in your life they arrive blended together. They are a mixture of all the results of all of your creations. And this is how most beings who are incarnated upon earth right now experience their lives. There lives are a blended confusion of outcomes from their many choices. Random things seem to happen to them with no relation to that which they have been doing or choosing. Sometimes its good, sometimes its bad but mostly its just a bit drab and mundane... and so they bumble along from cradle to grave.

And who can blame them for holding this perspective? If the results of their choices arrived immediately after they were chosen then there would be no confusion. They would immediately see that they created what they got. Then they would immediately begin making better choices. Then they would awaken to their creator nature. And then they would leave the duality illusion. And THAT, my friend, is exactly the point of this thing called "time". It is that which separates the cause from the effect. It is the experience of distance between the choice and the outcome, the action and the re-action.

Z: But why, 8? Why do we choose to experience time like this if all it does is confuse us?

8: Because this is exactly what you wanted! You came here specifically to experience a forgetting of who you really are. And the construct of time is a very powerful way to aid you in your forgetting.

It's actually all quite simple. The summary goes like this: What you put out is what you get back because... there is only one of us here. But some parts of The One wished to forget that they were One. And that is what you have accomplished. And a vital component in your forgetting that you are a part of the Oneness is to lose all sense of being a creator. This is because fear keeps you in separation. Fear comes from victimhood. Fear is dissolved by creator-consciousness. If you know you are creating your experiences then there isn't much point in fearing them, is there?

Z: No. That's like making scary shadow-monsters on the wall with my hands and then getting scared of them.

8: That is EXACTLY what it is like!

Z: Okay, good. But here is the thing: I can completely understand the logic you are offering me. If there is only one of us here, then clearly anything I do I am doing to myself. Good. I also get the logic of your argument that I am creating the situation that I forget that I am not the creator of my own reality. There is a kind of infallible circular logic here. But how do I come to KNOW that I am the creator of my own experiences. Or do I have to just accept that I can't know this while I am incarnated here?

8: No, not at all. As a being that chose an ascension path, you are one that chose to come to know the essential Oneness of All and also your own creator-nature while still incarnated. That is what the ascension process means. So you most certainly can know that you create your own experiences. In the third part of The Ascension Papers, when we discuss The Tools of Creation, we are going to deal with this topic exhaustively. But I can give you a hint here: If you are the creator of your own experiences but have, up to now, only created for yourself that you are a victim and not, in fact a creator then how do you go about reversing that experience?

Z: I... uh... create that I am the creator, I guess. I make that choice.

8: Perfect! That is exactly what you do. YOU create it to be so. No one else can do this one for you. If anyone else does it then they are creating that THEY are the creator of your life. Which is the same thing as you being a victim. So only you can do this!

Z: Alright. But can you give me something to keep me going until we start writing part three? How do I actually do this... how do I create that I am the creator?

8: First you act as if it is true. You do all the things you would do if this were a thing you absolutely believed. The rule a creator being lives by is:

"What you put out is what you get back"

So live like this and then see. If it is true then it will show itself to be true. Putting only loving, positive energy out will mean, over time, your world will change until you get only loving, positive energy back. Do this and see. If it works then you know directly and in your own experience in a way that you cannot deny that it is true. Then you are also well on the path to becoming a creator-being because you have understood the use and application of the first tool of creation. You create what you want by putting it out in the first place.

"What you get is directly determined by what you have put out"

It is really just the reverse statement of

"What you put out is what you get back"

Z: I think I am getting this now! Okay, that makes perfect sense. So we get what we create but the only way to see if this is true is to purposefully and consistently create one thing that we want for a period of time so that we can observe the rule in action.

8: Yes. Very well said. You must be both purposeful and consistent in what you put out and then you must be observant of what you get back. Then you will see that it is true as a fact of your existence. Once you have experienced it in this way it will come to be that you will feel this statement is so obvious as to be almost silly to even state. It will be like saying, "Your left hand is the hand on the left side of your body."

"What you put out is what you get back"

It's a truth that has been stated in many ways throughout the ages. It has been called "the golden rule" and "the law of reciprocity". It is stated in one form or another in the religious writings of every religion in the universe. You have heard it formulated as

"As you sow, so shall you reap"

and

"Do unto others as you would that they should do unto you"

There are other formulations which say the same thing in different ways. If you look at it from the negative then you get:

"That which you resist persists"

You see? It means the same thing. It is like saying, "If you focus on the stuff you don't want you will get more of it." Because what you are putting out is coming back to you! This understanding is the underpinning of what is called the law of karma, in that it teaches that you cannot avoid the consequences of your choices. It also underlies the abundance philosophies and the "law of attraction" teachings that are gaining some popularity now.

"What you put out is what you get back"

It is a simple truth that you can apply in your life to bring to yourself the life you desire.

Z: Isn't it also expressed as

"You always get exactly what you create"

8: Ha! Yes, it is! That is the way we have expressed it here in THE ASCENSION PAPERS. It is the strongest case statement of the golden rule and it is the case you and your readers are now ready to receive. You see, beings that are deep in duality consciousness are, by definition, not ready to hear that they are creators. So this concept is presented with weaker-case statements that they can apply in their lives. If they do choose to live by this tenet they can enjoy a life that is harmonious and joyful while they slowly awaken and prepare for their eventual awakening to their creator status and the concomitant ascension out of the duality system.

But you and your readers are directly and consensually engaged in the ascension process. You would not be engaged with a book called THE ASCENSION PAPERS if you were actually wanting to learn about knitting or pottery (he laughs). You are here after your own ascension! So we can view the concept, *"What you put out is what you get back"* in its very strongest case:

"You always get exactly what you create"

You are a fractal, holographic representative of The One. You MUST be a creator being. It simply MUST be so. All you have to do is to find a way to remember that and to deal with the programming that tells you that it is not so.

A good place to start is to see this truth working in your life, as we have just discussed. The next step is to learn to use it as one of the Tools of Creation, which discussion is still coming.

Z: I must say I'm really looking forward to that!

8: It is going to be both interesting and useful, I'm sure.

But before we move on, there are a couple of very important things that I must point out.

Z: Yes?

8: Did you notice that everything we have discussed in this chapter stems essentially from the one prime truth?

Z: Which is,The One is.

8: Right.

Well the argument I am making is that there are layers of truth. There is the one absolute truth which is at the pinnacle, and then below it are the truths that are derived from it. Great truths such as these discussed in this chapter will remain true for all of your experience, from the moment of your creation as a consciousness, to the very moment at which you are willing to release even those truths and simply return to The One. For so long as you have an identity, an individuality and a persona, these truths will have validity. Below these truths as many other "lesser" truths, which you may now hold, which will be much more transitory. Like a child who holds something to be to so fiercely true that he will get into a school-yard fight over it but, by the next day, has already realised that it isn't actually true. You too hold such beliefs that you are prepared to defend to the hilt, but very soon you are going to release those beliefs entirely. Such is the nature of lesser truths. They serve for a short while and then their transitory nature is discovered. This what is meant when people say that one of the symptoms of ascension is "seeing through the illusions". It is so. As you awaken, so you let go of the beliefs and ideas to which others around you still cling. You come to see ideas as not-so-very-true. They are the illusions of this world. If you are going to stay deeply attached to the dramas of this world then you really need to continue believing these things. If you begin to see through them, then you find yourself unable to continue playing the games implicit in life in this world. This is already happening to you, as I am sure it is happening to your readers. You find that you can no longer take seriously things such as politics and religion. You begin to view "the news" with more than a little scepticism. Money, status, power… these things look a lot less interesting to you now than they did a few years ago. Possessions, you now discover, are either "fit for purpose" or they are a burden. And so it goes. These kinds of transitions are inevitable. You view your world through the lens that is yourself. As you change yourself, so the world looks different. Layers of truth, you see. And you, the awakening ones, are beginning to see through the more transitory layers.

And THAT is a large part of the purpose of the conversations that will follow. I will be talking to you about some of the transitory truths that you still hold. Some of them have been buried quite deep in your psyche and will need a little nudge to be brought to the light and seen for what they are. Joy-Divine said at the end of chapter 7 that I would be "deprogramming" you. I prefer to say that I will be helping you to release the illusions that no longer serve your purpose.

Z: This sound like a very interesting and exciting journey. But 8, there is something that is bothering me a little. You're going to be telling our readers "how it is" and "how it isn't". But that concerns me. It feels as if we might be infringing on peoples' right to choose and their right to create for themselves.

8: That's a good point and you have raised it at exactly the right moment. You will notice that Joy-Divine was very careful to keep making it clear in his chapters that these things presented in THE ASCENSION PAPERS are things that are true from his perspective and that the reader must trust their own intuition and truth. Well that is good and I echo that. But then the material Joy-Divine handled was mostly the"soft" stuff. Some philosophical issues and so on. He rarely wandered into the hard issues of your reality, as it is. I, on the other hand, am going to be talking extensively about these hard issues. I am going to tell it like it is. Now OBVIOUSLY this is from my perspective. But I am going to qualify why my perspective is particularly useful and valid. I am going to tell you why it is right and appropriate that I can stand and tell you the story of your reality. Then it is up to you and your readers. You can decide to accept my credentials or reject them. And, based upon that, you can give credence to the truth of "what is" from my perspective or not.

Z: But 8 – how are we to know the difference?

8: Good question. I will teach you how. If you take learn just ONE THING from everything I have said, and am going to say, in THE ASCENSION PAPERS, then I would say it should be this:

"The truth is, whatever is really and truly deeply in your heart"

This is the most important thing I can tell you about TRUTH.

Z: Can you explain that?

8: Sure. You see, all beings everywhere are masking some truths about themselves from themselves. Because, if the only thing that is absolutely true is, "*The One is*", then everything that creates separation, differentiation, individuation… is a transitory truth. An illusion. That I am separate from you is an illusion. That you are separate from your reader is an illusion. We are all ONE.

Z: I follow.

8: Now these separation constructs; these things that we believe about ourselves to allow ourselves to do things separately and to hold different perspectives, these are illusions within our minds.

There is nothing wrong with them. It serves the purpose of The One that we do this. But they are illusions none-the-less and they are in our minds.

Z: Got it.

8: Now what do you think the Veil of Unknowing is?

Z: Ohhhhhh! It is an illusion of the mind!

8: Yes it is. There are many shared illusions. We call the results of our shared illusions a "consensus reality". It means that we all agree to the illusions which make up the reality in which we live. And then we create that reality together. When two or more beings give each other permission to create things that they will all share the experience of then it is called co-creation.

Now the thing to understand about the Veil is that it is actually conscious and alive. In order for you to be behind the Veil as you now are, you have to be co-creating with the Veil Holder too. This way you can cease to concern yourself with what you may and may not know. You enter into that agreement and then you come and play the game. The Veil Holder works to keep the rule true – which is that you may not discover the truth of the Oneness of All.

Z: Wow.

8: But now… Tell me again what the Veil of Unknowing is? You just said it a moment ago?

Z: I said it is an illusion of the mind.

8: Right. So the mind is where all these illusions of separation reside. The mind is where you hold all the complex constructs that allow you to play the games you are playing. The mind is the place of all these understandings and complexities. The mind analyses and engages in reductive reasoning.

The mind UNDERSTANDS.

However...

The heart KNOWS.

Your heart is your path through all illusions. Your heart is connected directly to The One and to the greatest truth of all, which is the Oneness of All. If you stop all the babble of your mind. If you silence all the noise in your being. If you learn to just SHUT UP long enough to hear what your heart has to say, then you will hear it crying out in longing for ONENESS. For the infinite, overwhelming, blissful love of The One.

Your heart knows and has never forgotten this greatest truth.

Can you feel it?

Can you go to your heart and know this to be true?

Z: Yes. Yes, I most certainly can.

8: Others that are engaged in the ascension process will, by definition, also be able to. The ascension process itself is you responding to your heart's call. Your heart calls you home and you begin to respond.

The deep truth I am therefore trying to impart to you therefore is:

"The heart KNOWS."

Your job is to learn to listen to your heart. If you can do that, then you can know the truth of anything at any time. Because, through your heart you are connected to everything, everywhere, all the time. You are connected to the Oneness of All. Your heart is a direct line to all truth and all knowingness. You must just learn to LISTEN!

Z: And how do I do that, 8?

8: Trust your feelings. Remember when Joy-Divine told you about how the light is rising? About how, over time, more and more light is streaming in? And when you weren't sure if that was true he did a little exercise with you? He made the statement, *"The light is rising"*, and you were then asked to go to your heart and FEEL how that felt.

Z: I remember.

8: Well that was a very beautiful illustration of the principal. Your heart speaks to you in feelings. Feel your heart. Feel how it feels. If you ever feel need to test a thought against your own truth you can simply stop what you are doing, close your eyes, still your mind and then become present to the feel of your heart. Then the thought you wish to test in your mind and feel how your heart feels. If it feels "right", then it is true for you. If it feels uncomfortable, then you should be careful with it. And if it feels outright wrong, then you should walk away.

Practice this. Like anything in your life, the more you do it the better you will get at it. Soon your heart will speak eloquently to you because you are paying it the respect of really listening. Getting really good at listening to your heart is about the most valuable tool you will ever have. There is almost nothing more important than this for the journey that lies ahead.

Z: Thank you 8. I really appreciate this.

8: It's a pleasure. A great pleasure indeed. But now this discussion has become overly long. Let us end it here. A very exciting journey awaits in our next chapters together.

Z: I look forward to it 8. This has been an amazing and beautiful chapter. I have really loved receiving it. I'll talk to you again soon.

8: Good then. I love you. Until next time…

* * * * *

Chapter 9. A Mystical Interlude
A conversation with 8

Zingdad: 8?

8: Yes?

Z: I'm struggling a bit.

8: Uh-huh? What with?

Z: Well… actually I'm struggling quite a lot.

8: Alright. What with?

Z: Well, this is hard for me. You see I have this issue with the fact that, in the last chapter you spoke about how I had overcome my doubts and fears such that I was able to receive THE ASCENSION PAPERS. And, when you said that, I felt quite good about myself. But between finishing that chapter and starting this one I've had some time to think. And I feel a bit like a fraud. Because I STILL have doubts. Loads of doubts. And the more I think about it the more doubts I have. And then I get worried that doubt itself is going to mess everything up. And why can't I just believe… you know… why can't I just have faith?

And then I feel like an even bigger fraud because, here I am writing this book, here I am receiving this material, and even *I* don't have absolute faith in it! And if even I have my doubts, how can I possibly expect my readers to believe this stuff? And then I think I must be insane because I KNOW I couldn't have come up with all the stuff in the previous chapters. I KNOW it is not within my capacity to do that. And so these words MUST be from you and J-D, but then why do I still feel this doubt? And round and round I go.

So I am struggling. And I'm not sure how to move forward. But I DO know that before I can resume writing the book I need to have SOME kind of resolution to this. I simply can not just keep holding the dichotomy in my mind that says, "*It could be true or I could be deluded*". I need some resolution on this before I can go back to writing the book.

8: (long pause) Are you quite done?

Z: Yes.

8: Good. Then let's sort some things out. Firstly: in the last chapter I said that you have MOSTLY released your doubts and fears, and that it is as a result of this that you are now able to undertake the writing of THE ASCENSION PAPERS. And this is true. You could not have received these words even one month before you actually began. You began when you were ready. And I also said that it will be as a result of writing THE ASCENSION PAPERS that you will release the rest of your fears and doubts so that you can awaken to your true creator nature.

Do you not remember me saying that?

Z: Yes. That sounds about right.

8: So now. If I said we were going to release the rest of your fears and doubts it must mean that I knew there were still some to release and that I intended to help you with them. And here we are today and you find you need to talk about this very subject. Well that is perfect. It comes at the perfect time. And no, you don't need to resolve this with me BEFORE you can get back to writing the book. Resolving this with me now IS writing the book. It is an essential part of the book, as vitally important as any other topic we might address.

Z: Really?

8: Joy-Divine said it:

> *"If you cannot see the perfection then you are standing too close to the picture."*

Remember how it was true for you in the chapter about the Darklanders?

Z: I do.

8: Well it's going to be true for you in this chapter too. This chapter is about doubt. Sort of. It starts with doubt and it ends with you realising that you are a mystic.

Z: A what?

8: A mystic.

Z: Sorry. I know you said "a mystic". I was registering my confusion. I'm not even completely sure what a mystic IS, let alone how I come to be one by talking to you about my feelings of doubt.

8: Okay. Well, you have access to the Internet on this laptop. Take five minutes to get a quick definition of what mysticism is and then report back here.

(I do that. I literally take five minutes and get the briefest idea.)

Z: From what I have been able to glean from the 'net, a mystic seems to be someone who seeks direct, personal union with the divine. Someone who seeks (or finds) contact with God without the intervention of religious doctrines. There is also something about a mystic being an adherent of the "mystery schools". Now I do vaguely recall having heard that term before but beyond that, I haven't a clue as to what these schools are or what they teach.

So mysticism seems to be all about some great mystery.

Which is appropriate because it's all a bit of a mystery to me!

8: That's fine. You have gained just enough understanding for the purposes of this discussion.

Next we need a brief definition of the word "mystery", if you'll be so kind.

Z: Okay. I'll go look it up.

(Which I do)

What I find is that the word "mystery" broadly means:

A secret. Something that is not known or is unexplained. Something that causes curiosity. Something that is only knowable by divine revelation.

And, interestingly enough, the word derives originally from the Greek word *mustēs*, which means "an initiate".

8: That IS interesting, isn't it?

Alright. Knowing this will come in useful later in the discussion. For now I want to move on directly to your difficulty. You say you are struggling with doubt. Can you tell me where you think doubt comes from?

Z: I think it's from fear.

8: Fear is one of its parents, yes. But doubt mainly originates in uncertainty. It comes from that which you do not know. Right?

Z: Oh, yes. That's right. For example, I don't know if the Singularity Event is going to happen. So

I doubt.

8: And then you judge yourself for doubting?

Z: Yes. I do. Because I am supposed to have faith. Isn't it?

8: No! Why do you expect yourself to believe in something that you have no experience of whatsoever?

If someone approached you in the street tomorrow and proposed to sell you a magical substance that would turn everything it touched into gold, would you believe him and hand over the cash, or would you demand a demonstration first?

Z: (laughs) I'd insist to see it in action first, of course.

8: I should hope so. Otherwise you'd very quickly be separated from your money by all manner of charlatans. So that is prudent behaviour. But then do you expect yourself to behave differently when it comes to the Singularity Event?

Z: That's interesting. I'm not sure why.

8: Then I shall tell you why. In your mind you separate "real" stuff from "spiritual" stuff. And "real" stuff needs real proof whilst with "spiritual" stuff, you feel you must just have faith and believe. And the reason for this is that you are suffering from one of the effects of religion. Most of the religions of your world work quite hard to propagate the notion that doubt is "bad". Well it isn't. It's just bad for business. Their business. If you belong to a religion, and then find yourself beginning to doubt, then what is happening is that you are finding that the answers the religion provides do not satisfy you. If you pursue your doubts, you might very well find answers that DO satisfy you elsewhere. Not in that religion, though. And if you find better answers outside of that religion, you might very well leave that religion. Then you cease to do as it tells you. Cease to be controlled by the greater agenda of that religion's leaders. And, of course, cease to give them money. So obviously they aren't too fond of people asking questions and even less so of people seeking answers. So they develop quite a cunning strategy. Tell people how bad doubt is. Make them feel really rotten about doubting. Then, when people do have uncertainty and questions, they will feel so bad about them that they won't go looking for answers to the questions. They will simply take the existence of their doubt as proof of their inherent sinfulness. And then they work extra hard to be "good". Clever huh?

Z: Maybe. But it's not very nice, is it?

8: If you are of the opinion that religions come into being and propagate around your world by being "nice", then you are extremely unobservant. I don't say that they have not also been responsible for a great deal of good. But if you ignore the fact of religions ALSO being used as a political tool of power, control and oppression, then you are missing a big part of the picture. But this topic is not about religion. And I am not actually against religion *per se*. When we talk about religion in a follow-on topic, you'll get my broader perspective.

Right now all I am indicating is that religion has had a pervasive effect on shaping your planetary psyche. And given that it is very much contrary to the interests of religion that you question spiritual concepts, it is no surprise that you have an almost instinctive negative response to doubt.

"*Do not doubt, just have faith!*" they tell you. But in any other sphere of life, if you just believe what you are told, you end up getting cheated out of your possessions. And so a little neurosis is born:

"*I MUST just have faith and believe in relation to 'spiritual' matters but I must keep my wits about me and trust my own experience everywhere else,"* you tell yourself.

But this is patently silly! Surely there should be nothing more REAL than your spirituality? Your own truest nature – your spirit self – should be the most real thing of all! So why should you not ALWAYS simply trust your own truth and your own experience?

So now we have to undo some of this programming. We have to reconcile spirituality and real life. We have to dis-intermediate these clergymen and their doctrines from between you and your soul, between you and The One; the Source-God of which you are, in truth, an inseparable part. Because really, what silliness is this that you should have to go to some other person with ancient texts in order that you should know that which is within your heart; that which lies as close as your own breath?

Z: That does seem like an odd notion.

8: It is appropriate for those who seek to enter more deeply into duality to do so, for they are creating a victim state for themselves. They burrow ever deeper into duality by saying, "*I do not hold my own truth, someone else must hold it for me*".

And so they always seek experts to tell them what is true: clergy, politicians, lawyers, doctors, scientists and so forth. These authorities must tell them what is in their own reality. But for those who seek to arise from this density, it is not so. Awakening ones, might certainly take another being's perspective into account, you might share with them and learn from them. But your connection with God, Divinity and the Oneness can only occur directly and personally.

For the ascending ones it becomes appropriate to cease attempting to separate "spirituality" from "life". For the awakening being, all of life will become a spiritual thing. For example, for us here in the higher dimensions there is no such concept as "spirituality" or "religion" because EVERYTHING is "spiritual". And religion – being a set of doctrines and beliefs to which we must adhere – is utterly pointless to us. You see, everything is done in relationship to The One. It is ALL in service of God. We don't have to think about it, or try to be pious, or set aside some time for it. We can, quite simply, do no other.

So let me then complete my point here and say this: release your judgement of yourself for doubting. To do so is counter-productive. You doubt, quite simply, because you do not know. Let me use the Singularity Event as an example to illustrate the point. You do not hold anything like the Singularity Event in your experience. When Joy-Divine first told you about it, you got excited and happy. But then you began to wonder. You found you didn't know. This is doubt. If you focus on the doubt, you get stuck in what I call "debilitating doubt". Remember, one of the derived truths in the last chapter was, "*What you put out is what you get back*"?

Z: Yes. I remember.

8: And the corollary of that, is the equally true statement: "*What you resist, persists*".

Z: Right.

8: So if you feel doubt, you can either do something about it or you can focus on the doubt itself. If you focus on the doubt itself and wrestle with it, then it "persists". You get more of it. And holding a judgement about your doubt that tells you that the doubt itself is wrong is pretty much guaranteed to make you focus on the doubt. You are quite likely to get an attack of "debilitating doubt".

Round and round and round you go. You keep doubting and you keep feeling bad about it. All because somewhere inside of you there resides this originating thought that you may not doubt.

Perverse. Odd. And not very useful.

Z: Wow, huh? I see that. Okay. So then I'd like to let go of that judgement. Maybe it IS okay for me to feel doubt about the Singularity Event!

8: Maybe it is. Let's look at that:

Let's split everything into two kinds of things: those that you have experience of and those that you do not. The things you have experience of, you can say you "know". The things you have no experience of, you can say you "do not know". The more you know something, the more certain you are of it. The less you know something, the less certain you are of it. Which seems simple enough, right?

Z: Right.

8: So if you were to be certain of the Singularity Event, then I'd say you are probably a little defective in the thinking and reasoning department. How CAN you be certain of something that you have no direct experience of?

So obviously we are not asking you to be certain of it. Quite the contrary. We are telling you about it, knowing that you will respond with surprise, amazement and wonder. And is it not so that almost all the material in The Ascension Papers is of this ilk - it speaks to things that you cannot know, that you most certainly can be very uncertain about.

So your uncertainty is right and good and healthy.

What is unhealthy for you is to get yourself full of fear about it or to stand in judgement of yourself for it. It isn't WRONG if you choose to do that. It's just not taking you forward to where you want to be. And it hurts you. It is, as I say, unhealthy.

Z: I understand 8. So I'd like to stop doing that then. I'd like to stop getting stuck in fear of uncertainty. And if I DO feel fear, to stop judging myself for it.

8: Excellent. And that is what I am going to help you with in this chapter. I am going to do that by helping you to gain a better understanding of uncertainty. I am going to teach you of its power and magnificence. The result of this will NOT be that you will have no more uncertainty or that you will never doubt again. The result will be that you will embrace your uncertainty and learn to use it in wonderful new ways. You will come to see it as an amazing gift.

Z: Really, 8? That sounds quite hard to believe.

8: Does it? Then I'll take that as a challenge! (he laughs)

To start with, let's create a hypothetical situation:

Imagine you are sitting next to a camp-fire on a dark and moonless night. You can only see so far as the light of the fire penetrates the gloom and you have no other source of light.

What do you do? Do you huddle closer and closer to the fire and shiver with fear at every leaping shadow? Or do you respond to the dark, unknown landscape with curiosity?

If you feel fear, then you stay put. You probably won't even LOOK out at the darkness because it makes you feel uneasy.

If you feel no fear – or indeed if your heart is filled with a love for the place in which you find yourself– then you stand up and venture out into the darkness. You begin to explore and to open yourself to new discoveries. And in so doing you expand your knowledge of your environment. And as you learn new things, so you actually expand yourself!

Now this is obviously just a hypothetical situation. I am not saying one should be foolhardy and stumble around in the dark of night. I am simply illustrating a point, which is about the way you respond to the unknown. If you respond to it with love, you get expansion of the Self. If you respond to it in fear, you get a contraction of the Self.

Now the thing you must understand is that there is, and always will be, a great amount of "unknown" in your experience of life. There will always and forever be a great deal to be uncertain about.

Z: Really 8? Always? Even for someone like you?

8: (laughs) Oh my goodness, yes! Let me explain: The One is infinite, right?

Z: Right.

8: And within the one is an infinite multiplexity of manyness, right?

Z: Yes…

8: And all of that manyness is eternally and infinitely changing and expanding and growing. Right?

Z: Right.

8: Do you understand what that means? It means that The One is infinite and yet is expanding at an infinitely fast rate! It is simply mind boggling to even try to comprehend it. And this of course means that there is an impossibly huge amount of stuff "out there" beyond the periphery of any one being's perceptual field. And what is "out there" just gets more and more! And no matter how fast you grow, learn, experience and understand, the "unknown" will always grow faster than you. Because the faster you "expand", the more you expand The One and the faster you help all other aspects of The One to grow. It's really awesomely beautiful. The mystery just deepens and expands.

So yes, assuredly, there is ALWAYS uncertainty. The question is quite simply how you will choose to respond to it. Will you shrink back from it in fear or will you explore it with love? That is up to you. And, as always, you will get exactly what you are creating and you will experience the results of your creation.

Do you follow?

Z: Yes. Thank you for the patient explanation. That makes sense.

8: So let's see how this has worked in your life. Let me ask you this: that boy who first sat down with a pebble in his hand (Zingdad note: see Chapter 1: An Introduction to Zingdad) and asked me if I was "out there". That boy who asked me if I loved him. That boy who sat there night after night asking his questions and laboriously finding a path out of his incomprehension with yes/no answers…

Was he venturing out into the darkness or was he sitting close to the fire?

Z: He was venturing out.

8: And how did that work out for him?

Z: Quite well, it seems.

8: You think?

I think it was one of your finest moments!

If you think about it, The Ascension Papers and all the other processes and questing that you have done, all flowed from that moment. Certainly, along the way you developed and refined your ability to listen. But in that moment with the pebble in your hand, in that instant there, you stood up from your comfortable, safe spot at the fire. You turned to face the darkness of the unknown and you stepped forth boldly for the very first time. With no precedent, with no cause to believe it would work, with no-one to show you the way, you chose love over fear in the face of uncertainty.

It was a moment of yours that I will always treasure.

And, in continuing these conversations, you continue to broaden your search. You expand yourself into the darkness. In fact you turn the areas of darkness you encounter into areas of light by the very act of exploring them. You bring YOUR light to them.

And THIS is what you have done with uncertainty.

In fact THE ASCENSION PAPERS are entirely a product of your uncertainty.

Now, I ask you, do you wish for us to take away your uncertainty? Do you wish to cease to experience it?

Z: Good grief, 8, that is a very surprising perspective on all this. Wow. No, I guess I don't want to stop having uncertainty.

But I have to say that this uncertainty that you are speaking of now - the stuff that inspired me to ask the questions - it feels different from these other feelings of doubt.

8: Let's look at this. You say you feel doubt. But still you keep asking questions. Still you keep talking to me. Still you move out into the darkness in ever greater arcs, searching the unknown. And THAT is what I meant when I said to you previously that you had done enough work with fear and doubt to allow THE ASCENSION PAPERS to come through. What I meant was that you had come far enough not to let it debilitate you. Not to bring you to a halt. Because that is what happens when you feel uncertainty and you respond to it with fear and then judge yourself for feeling the fear. This is what I was telling you when I spoke of "debilitating doubt". It is quite okay to feel some fear of the unknown but when, as a result of the fear or your judgements about it you choose not to search the unknown, then you enter an area of difficulty. You then make it impossible for yourself to begin to find answers for your doubt. So you remain in a state of doubt and you cannot get out. You find you are debilitated by it.

So the first thing to do is to choose to LOOK at the unknown. If you feel a fear or a doubt or a question, then go and LOOK at it. Make a decision that you will try to find answers. As soon as you do this, you find you have options. And as soon as you become aware of your options, then you realise you are no longer stuck. Then you move into a process of creation. This is immediately a lot healthier. And let me tell you something that is true: there are ALWAYS options. If you can't see any then you have simply not looked hard enough.

For example. If you are stuck you could try putting your faith in what you are told by one of the religions. You can try that and see if it works for you. Many do and many find great benefit there. Nothing wrong with that. Unless you desire to ascend, of course, in which case I firmly contend you will be better served by putting your faith in yourself, in your own inner truth, in your own heart, in your personal connection to the divine. You can try that and see how THAT works.

Choosing the latter will often entail quite a bit of work. You will have to learn to listen to your inner voice and so forth. You will have to learn to trust yourself. To love yourself. There is, as I say, a good bit of work to be done. But you will find, as you progress, that you begin to lose your fear of the unknown. You will venture out into those areas of unknown questions with greater and greater courage. You will begin to enjoy the process of searching your heart, your psyche and the whole universe for the deepest meaning. Slowly your fear will transmute into love. And when you approach your uncertainty with true open-hearted love, then you will discover a very magical thing – playful curiosity.

Playful curiosity allows you to enact your most creative self in the search for answers without attaching your ego to the outcome. You play. You have fun. You create. The most amazing and marvellous answers will come to you if you are able to reside in a state of playful curiosity. If you don't fear being wrong. Because "wrong" just means an answer that didn't work. And therefore is another opportunity to PLAY AGAIN!

You see?

And it all starts with uncertainty and how you choose to feel about it.

Z: That's awesome 8.

8: And there is more. Let's look at the opposite of uncertainty. Let's look at "certainty". Things that are certain are fixed. We say we are certain about them precisely because we feel they are unchangeable and immutable. We use these "certainties" and build upon them our reality and our perceptions of ourselves. They are our deepest truths and as such they are the scaffolding upon which we can create. And they are therefore very valuable to us. Without them we would have a hard time creating anything of any meaning or significance. I mean – how would you go about experiencing life on your planet without, for example, all the rules of physics. It would all be chaotic. Life as you know it would not exist.

And how would you begin to understand yourself if nothing about you seemed to remain fixed for any length of time?

Z: Very difficult. I can see that.

8: So these Truths of ours, these "certainties", have great value to us and we love them dearly. But they are, in fact, transitory. Given sufficient time, every single thing that we hold to be true will come to be less true, and then eventually untrue. It is thus for whole civilisations and it is thus for individual souls. The things you now believe about yourself and your reality will inevitably come to change and evolve. You will gain new beliefs. The old ones will eventually cease to serve you. You will let go of them. Or you will replace them with far greater truths. That is the nature of "The Truth". Like everything else, it always changes. And so it is for the things we are certain of. In time we will come to be less certain of them and then eventually we may even come to be certain that they are NOT so!

Z: Everything, 8?

8: To the very best of my rather exhaustive effort to be able to discern, I will say this is so of everything other than the one immutable truth which is…

Z: "*The One IS.*"

8: Correct. And as for the rest… "*Change is the only constant*".

And if there is only change then, given sufficient duration of experience, you will experience great change. Given infinite experience you will change infinitely. Hardly sounds like there is much room there to hold onto small truths about your current reality, does it?

Z: No, I guess not. It sounds like uncertainty is certain.

8: (laughs) Exactly. And it is a very good thing that this is so. Because it is the areas of uncertainty that we can grow and change in. The areas we temporarily hold to be certain are the areas we stop looking at and stop growing in. And so here is the important realisation:

Without uncertainty there is no creation. There is nothing new.

If you embrace uncertainty then you embrace creation.

If you open your heart to uncertainty then you allow your greatest, most divine self to play with it. You actually move into "genius" (the ancient origin of this word referred to a state of consciousness in which a greater spirit acted through the hands of a "mortal" being). Uncertainty is the greatest muse of all!

Cherish it. Seek it out. Explore it. Love it. And most of all, HAVE FUN with it!

Z: 8, that is brilliant. I feel quite excited by this. It feels right to me. Thank you.

8: You are most welcome.

And yet I can sense that you are still not completely at ease about this…

Z: Yes. You are right. Maybe I just need to internalise what you have said. Or something. Because I still feel like I have some issue here.

8: Talk it out with me.

Z: Okay. Let's see. I think it goes like this: so I have uncertainty. If I fear it enough, then I will get locked up and I won't move forward. So that's not healthy. If, on the other hand, I love it then I begin to create. And I have fun creating. First I begin to define the questions inherent in my uncertainty and then I begin to find answers that seem to fit the questions. In so doing I find I'm beginning to really have fun. And then I begin to create some really amazing dialogues and have really astounding, awesome answers come back at me and I find I am totally loving the process and it just feels so RIGHT.

8: But?

Z: Yeah. But!

But I STILL don't know if these answers are right or true. No matter how much better I am feeling about myself and my life, I still don't know if all this that I have been getting has any validity outside of the confines of my imagination.

Please don't get me wrong. I am astounded at the information I am getting. I am blown away at the internal consistency of the messages. I really, really don't believe it possible that I could – in the normal sense of it – have imagined all this. It is so for me that there MUST be something "paranormal" going on here. But I STILL don't know if it is all <u>true</u>.

8: Alright. I want to say a few things to you.

The first is an issue I have already addressed here, but I will state it a little differently. I want to say to you that it is YOUR JOB to hold a degree of uncertainty – to "hold lightly" onto your view of reality. For it is in so doing that you are able to do the work that you are now doing. It allows you to write this book and do the many other creative tasks that will follow. You decided to create your path home in this way. That was your choice. In order to do that it is imperative then that you continue to hold some uncertainty. Otherwise you cannot create this path and will have to find another.

Secondly: how would it be if I waved a magic wand and you had complete certainty? If you KNEW with absolute conviction, and certainty and had not a shred of doubt in your soul, that all that is spoken of in THE ASCENSION PAPERS is absolutely true. If you KNEW that the Singularity Event was going to occur and there was no possibility of it not occurring. How would that be?

Z: Uhh… on the face of it that doesn't sound so bad. I mean I'd still be able to write all this down and tell folks about it, wouldn't I?

8: Okay, wait a minute. Let's get something straight right now. You are not doing this for all these other folks. You are creating your own way home. That is what you are doing. Because you can do no other. Yes, you are allowing that your path home should be available to others to use if they so choose. Yes, there is some beautiful and magical co-creation that can flow out of this. That is all true. But you are NOT rescuing anyone. If you begin to see it that way, then I assure you, you are going to get hurt. You will develop a saviour complex instead of seeing this as your own path home that is also being offered as a gift to others. Okay?

Z: Thanks 8. Phew! That's right and I'm really glad it is. I don't want to be responsible for rescuing anyone else.

8: I'm glad that's sorted out. Now back to the issue at hand. Let me ask you again. How would it be if you had absolute certainty that the Singularity Event was going to occur?

Z: I'm thinking about this, 8. But I still don't think that would be so bad. I'd still just continue with my ascension path, but this time without the doubt. And yes, I'd still write about it for others to share in my process if they wanted to.

8: I see. Yes, maybe you would. Provided they gave you access to a computer and the Internet.

Z: Who? Provided who gave me access?

8: The nice people in the home for those with mental delusions. If you had this kind of absolute knowing and conviction that could brook no doubt, then you would be at terrible odds with the rest of the society that you inhabit. Complete certainty of something that everyone else regards as unknowable is, in your reality, called delusional. If your "delusion" is about something huge and life-changing – exactly the kinds of things that we are talking about – then you will be driven to express your message everywhere to all people all the time. This will put you at such violent odds with your society that something will have to break. And that something will almost certainly be you. Society is a powerful thing. It has ways of making members who make it uncomfortable stop what they are doing. If you stubbornly refuse to change your views after gentle interventions, then there is a fair chance that you could end up being separated from society and placed in a facility for the mentally ill. There you will almost certainly be given large doses of powerful chemicals to make you stop being the way you are. To destroy this certainty that you have.

Perhaps after being there for a while, you'll begin to find some doubt.

That would be the sensible thing to do.

Z: Sheesh, 8. You paint a bleak picture. But sadly I know you're right.

8: You live in a very peculiar part of All That Is. It is marvellous and amazing in all kinds of ways. But it is disastrously unkind to those who are sufficiently "different".

I'm not universally decrying the mental health professions. They often do great work in helping people to be less self-destructive. But I am certain that this firm, unshakeable KNOWINGNESS that you think you might want, will inevitably bring you into contact with the sharp end of this profession. It will undoubtedly be viewed as being "for your own good" and maybe they won't even be wrong. There will, quite simply, be no way for you to integrate into society with such a conviction in place. So, really, you DO NOT want this kind of firm, unshakeable conviction while you reside in that reality. It is your very doubt that keeps you "normal" enough that you can carry the message that you are now carrying and still function, still be considered "sane" in that very… interesting… place.

Z: Chilling. But yes. I see it. I agree.

8: But, as valid as that argument might be, that STILL does not bring you a feeling of resolution about your doubts, does it?

Z: Uhm. No. But I AM a little less keen to have unshakeable conviction. (laughs) That's for sure!

8: Quite so. Alright then, let us finalise this. I have made the contention that uncertainty is not the problem; it is the way you feel about it that can be problematic. If you love the uncertainty, then there is no problem. So clearly you still feel a little fear of the uncertainty. You so badly desire this outcome because it sounds so fantastic. But you have no way of making it happen. And you cannot find any experience in your reality to tell you that it WILL happen. So what to do? You want it very, very badly. You can't procure it. You certainly can't be certain of it. There you sit. So you come back to the good ol' stalwart – you must have faith! And that holds you for all of about 25 seconds until you realise you just DON'T have faith! So now you doubt and you fear that your doubts are going to somehow "uncreate" this. That if it DOESN'T happen, it will all be your fault because you just didn't have enough FAITH.

Z: Wowee, 8. It seems you really and truly DO know me inside out. That is EXACTLY what was going on with me.

So, what should I do?

8: Again. The problem is not uncertainty, the problem is the way you feel about it. Which is just as well, given that I have made the contention that it is your job to hold some uncertainty. And given that the removal of your uncertainty would get you institutionalised. So it pretty much seems as if you are saddled with the uncertainty. And, as long as it doesn't debilitate you, you will use it to keep creating your path home. And, as we have discussed, you have chosen to share your path home and this will be used to some great good as the seed for co-creation. And here, finally, is some possible resolution to your difficulty.

You see, you don't HAVE to share your path. You COULD keep it all to yourself. You'd still get home. But in sharing it, you open the door to co-creation. And do you remember what happens with co-creation?

Z: Remind me?

8: It is when you allow yourself to experience the results of someone else's creation with you.

Z: And how exactly will that help me?

8: Well, you see it isn't necessarily everyone else's job to hold the same uncertainty that you do. By co-creating with others you will begin to experience some of their creation, as they will begin to experience some of yours. Then you may begin to feel quite differently about your uncertainty. You can begin to feel the love that they will bring to it.

Let's have a look at a few particular examples.

Your co-creators will know that they are your co-creators because they are drawn to THE ASCENSION PAPERS and will know that it is right for them. Their very knowingness will be the first bit of "right feeling" that you will get from them. And you have already felt some of this, haven't you?

Z: Yes, I have. It surprised me a little at first how positively people were responding. And you're right. I did feel love and encouragement from this.

8: And, as you get to know these co-creators on the forums and in other interactions, so you are going to see again and again that these are wonderful people. You will come to feel a growing sense of community and belonging with them. You will find you respect them for who they are. It will be clear that these are not simple-minded people who are easily lead astray by silly flights of fancy. These are intelligent, thinking, highly spiritual people. And the fact that THEY know it is right for them – that will give you some further positive feeling.

And then they will begin to co-create with you. You will begin to see the magic unfold. In fact, you can expect to see some really beautiful co-creation begin to unfold very soon now. That will give you a great feeling of excitement and rightness. You will really begin to love your uncertainty then.

And then you will begin to find more and more independent confirmation. As more and more people come to read THE ASCENSION PAPERS so your readers will share with you more and more other sources of information that correlate with what you have received in ways that will… "*blow your hair back*" is the phrase I think you use. What I am saying is that you will hear the things that you have typed here in these pages coming back at you over and over again. Sometimes it will be phrased in startlingly similar ways and other times it will be expressed quite differently but you will know that all these things speak to the same essential ideas. It will be abundantly apparent to you that such repetitive and powerful corroboration cannot be mere coincidence. This will engender in you even more excitement, more joy and more love for the process!

And soon you will also begin to communicate directly with a number of others who are also message bearers or who are in other similar ways shining their light. As you do so you shall realise that the message you bear is but one strand in a "rope of truth" with which you shall all hoist yourselves up into the light. Each strand is unique. Some will speak to a different audience. Some will take a very different approach. But each is essential and each is perfect in its own way. And meeting and conversing with these other message bearers will bring you a great sense of rightness and will powerfully motivate you to keep creating.

Z: And then I will at last resolve my doubt?

8: Yes and no. You resolve your doubt whenever you stop fearing uncertainty, by simply trusting yourself and loving the process. It will always be possible to bring uncertainty to your mind. Always. But when you cease fearing it and begin loving it instead then, obviously, it will not trouble you. And how you feel about it is very much your choice.

Initially you will have to work hard at the choice. In due course you will master it and there will be no fear. But there will always be uncertainty. Always. And this is a wonderful thing because that means you will always have options. You will always be able to create. There will always be scope for growth and change.

Uncertainty will always come bearing its two children: debilitating doubt and playful curiosity. You must choose which you shall play with.

And now I shall finish where I began. Now we shall make of you a mystic.

Are you ready?

Z: (laughs) I guess so. But how?

8: Do you agree with me when I say, "*You always get exactly what you create*"?

Z: I am seeing that to be more and more so in my life as I go. Yes. I agree that it must be true.

8: So then you'll agree that the more you focus on something, the more you will get of it?

Z: That is logically correct and also my own experience. Yes.

8: So what will happen if you LOVE the uncertainty? Really love it with an open heart and so, focus on it and stare deeply into it?

Z: Uhh… you'll get more of it. A LOT more of it.

8: Yes. Exactly. The mystery will deepen. It will enshroud you. You will come to touch and experience more and more of the great unfathomable mystery. And because you do not fear it, you do not feel you need to handle it, control it and manage it… you do not feel you need to have a comfortable explanation for it… you can allow the experience to be what it is and just BE in it. You see?

Z: Yes…?

8: Okay. So then. Can you agree with me that the infinite Source-God is way, way, way beyond your capacity to even begin to comprehend in Its fullness? And is therefore, in greatest part, a profound mystery?

Z: Obviously. Yes.

8: Then you should be able to make the logical leap which is this: to embrace the mystery with an open heart is to bring yourself closer to experiencing direct union with the Divine!

When you really open yourself to the mystery, you bring it forward into your experience. And you do so without the need to make it less than it is. You release your need to dissect and reductively understand that which you experience. You let it BE. You let yourself BE. You let God BE. You allow yourself to experience God with all of your being instead of trying to fit It into the tight little confines of your mind.

You experience God with ALL your being.

And THIS is the beginning of the path to true ecstatic union with The One.

Z: Oh my God!

8: Yes! Exactly!

And so? Is that what you seek? Do you seek ecstatic union with the Divine?

Z: Yes! I do! I have had hints and tastes of this in some very deep meditations. But my heart yearns for more. I want to KNOW God. I want to feel a more permanent sense of Oneness with all beings and all things. I have been striving for this for quite some time now – trying to find a way to experience it deeply and fully.

8: I'll take that as a firm "yes" then (he smiles). And of course your spirit-family and I know of your striving and your yearning. It is a part of your ascension process that you feel this and that you desire it. And THE ASCENSION PAPERS are our way of responding to that. You ARE going to experience the complete union with the Divine that you desire. But first there is some work to do. And that is EXACTLY what we are doing here. We are doing the work. And this particular chapter is us working with doubt and uncertainty.

And I am here to tell you that your uncertainty is not only where your areas of creativity lie, but is also where you will find this experience you so deeply desire. It is where you will, in a sense, find God.

Z: Wow, 8, that's gorgeous. I have never thought about it like that.

8: Such thinking is NOT encouraged in the system in which you live. It causes people to cease to be manipulable. Not only do you go cold-turkey on religion, but you also give up on things such as politics and war and hatred and violence and… all of that sadness. Such thinking takes you out of the system. It causes you to ascend. So it isn't taught or encouraged.

Some of the only places it was systematically taught in your reality were the mystery schools that you were wondering about. Thousands of years ago these schools were established to transmit the knowledge of the ancients. Information that came from the remnants of older civilisations. Individuals who sought profound spiritual training could go to these mystery schools. Different schools took different approaches, but one of the cornerstones of many of them was training in understanding fear: learning that fear is a tool that can be used but that it is not to be the controlling principal. As the initiates in the mystery schools came to truly master their fear, they would be willing to approach the Great Mystery also without fear. They would be willing to experience the Divine directly. But, of course, the mystery schools' initiates – or mystics – also lost all fear of the leaders of their world. Royalty and clergy found their mutual interests were being undermined by the teachings of these schools. After all, if you begin to experience the Divine directly would you think another mortal man is worthy of being bowed to? Would you find his petty dictates to be worth following? And what interest could all the folderol of religion hold for you if you have embraced the eternal mystery? Would you listen to a man making utterances about how God demands this thing and that thing from you when you have experienced the Divine directly within your own heart?

And so it came to be that these mystery schools were driven underground for that very reason. Those in power identified the mystery schools as threatening their status. They struck back with vigour. The mystery schools were either crushed and silenced or they became secret, hidden organisations. A number of them hid their true teachings behind layers of secrecy, the outermost layers appearing to be ordinary societies of guildsmen or groups of "spiritual enquiry" and the like. There would be tests and pledges and secret swearings-in that would indoctrinate members deeper and deeper into the organisation. Until eventually, after greatly proving yourself, you might slowly become privy to their true secrets.

The problem with this is that the very act of hiding the mystery teachings and making them the sole property of the secret, select few, changed the nature of these teachings. The ones who held the knowledge in these now secret societies became enamoured with their own egos and they ceased trying to share what was known. They felt important and special for the fact that they had attained the lofty heights that allowed them access to this information. But you see, the teachings themselves are hollow. They are just ideas. They must be lived and loved and experienced and shared to have any meaning. And so it all contorted into near meaninglessness. It is so that wisps of the great teachings of the mystery schools live on today hidden in secret and arcane groups, but the process of unlocking them essentially invalidates them. Which is ironic and sad.

And so it is that the time now comes for these groups to see that everything has changed. It is now time for them to complete their journey, and make available to all, their treasure house of knowledge. In so doing they shall return to true service. This will be their final test – if they have the courage to do so.

But we shall not bait our breath for them. Whether they do or not will be of import to themselves only. Those who thirst for the essence of the knowledge will find it, irrespective of what the holders of the ancient mysteries do or don't do. The Light is rising and it is now possible to reach you and teach you what you need to know in many different ways. The awakening is happening and there is nothing anyone on that planet can do to stop it. We will touch your heart and help you to find your way without all the hocus-pocus of secret handshakes in the dark.

Z: That's amazing 8. But I want to back-track a bit. The mystery schools were driven underground because they undermined the power of the religious authorities? But what I don't understand is how it came to be that we gave our power away to the religions in the first place.

8: That is a very long story. I'll get to it some time soon. For now, just observe in yourself how easy it is to fear the unknown. It is not strange to do so. Out there in the dark there might lurk a tiger to gobble you up! (he smiles) So the unknown can be scary. And it is easy to fear the unknown that lies beyond death. And so it is that you might be willing to have intermediaries tell you about God and about how Life works and about what you should, and should not, be doing. You would then place religions and beliefs and clerics (who themselves are but confused and doubting men) between your own heart and The One.

You most certainly can do this if you wish, but then do not wonder why you cannot directly experience The One. You cannot because it is nearly impossible to see anything through all those thick obfuscatory layers of demagoguery, doctrine and dogma.

Z: I understand.

8: And now, before I wrap this all up, there is a little gift I want to share with you.

Z: A gift? What is it?

8: To start with, let me ask you this: have you thought to ask yourself what would happen if you DIDN'T have a Singularity Event?

Z: What? Where did that come from? No. I haven't.

8: You see? Still you have fear! You don't even want to LOOK at that possibility. And because you won't look at it, it has power over you. LOOK AT IT. What would happen?

Z: Okay. I'll look at it. The Singularity Event is our amazing happy experience of union with the Divine that will precipitate our ascension into the next dimension. If that didn't happen then how would we…

Oh. Wait a minute. You have just been telling me about a union with the divine through embracing the mystery. Is this a "different" union with the divine?

8: No. There is only one The One. And union with It is a pretty absolute concept. The Singularity Event is simply a function of the Light rising to the extent that this union with the Divine almost "catches up with you", as it were. It makes it really easy and fail-safe. As opposed to the difficult process that it was in the times of the Mystery Schools.

Z: But that means we don't actually NEED the Singularity Event! It means we can do this anyway when we are ready!

8: Bingo! Every day you are raising your consciousness. Every day you are moving closer to Oneness. You are already, right now, busy ascending. It is inevitable that you will get there.

Z: So then there really is nothing to fear!

8: How's that for a gift?. And the best part is, you gave it to yourself.

Z: That is simply fabulous, 8. But why didn't you just tell me that right at the beginning?

8: It is not the outcome that is important, my friend. It is the process. How much have we learned and how much have we understood from doing this? A great deal! The process is where the love lies.

Now obviously we are going to have to talk about this a LOT more. You will need some training and guidance in attaining the right meditative state to experience this state of blissful union. And you'll need help to learn to navigate it. It is one thing to experience it. It is another to use it to transubstantiate yourself.

Z: Trans-what?

8: (laughs) Don't worry about that for now. I'll get to all that in due course. I'm talking about you having a deep meditation and then experiencing something blissful. Falling deep into a profoundly transformative experience. Then returning to a reality, but choosing for it to be a reality which is different from the one you just left. That is what I am talking about. It's the same thing as was addressed in the Singularity Event. I am saying that it can be up to you to take ownership of the process if you like. Then you are not the victim of the Singularity Event. Then you can release all fear about it and it can just be the magical sparkly gift we give to others who are not consciously engaged in the process of their own ascension. How about that?

Z: Jeepers, 8, this begins to look like an even bigger gift that I thought.

8: It might just be, at that!

But now I must wrap this all up. To do so I am going to ask you a few questions.

Tell me again. Is it true that you seek direct, personal ecstatic union with the Divine – that you seek to know God directly?

Z: Yes! That is certainly true.

8: And do you agree that you cannot accomplish this by following the teachings and doctrines of a religion and by subjugating your truth to the utterances of other men?

Z: Well – that certainly seems true for me. Maybe others are on their right path if they follow a religion. But that is not right for me.

8: Discernment in action. Very good.

Then… can you see that, in order to accomplish this goal of direct knowing and experience of The One, you must be willing to approach It with your heart and not your mind? That you must be willing to plumb the mystery? To experience It as IT is without demanding to understand It and contain all your experiences in your mind?

Z: Yes. I follow that. And I agree.

8: So you embrace the mystery?

Z: I do.

8: And you understand that this implies a willingness to release your fear of the unknown. It means you actually LOVE uncertainty and embrace it as a great gift.

Z: Yes. I understand it like that. I agree.

8: Then I declare you to be… a mystic!

Z: Ha ha! 8, that is fabulous!

8: It is. And see what you have just agreed to: that you embrace uncertainty as a gift. Remember the challenge right at the beginning of this chapter?

Z: Oh my goodness, yes! You have won!

8: No my friend. It is YOU who have won.

And with that, this chapter is done!

* * * * *

Chapter 10. What is Evil?
A conversation with 8

Zingdad: Hi 8.

8: Hello my dear friend. What are we going to talk about today?

Z: Gee, 8, I was going to ask you that.

8: Consider it open mic night at Club 8 (he smiles). You choose the subject.

Z: Well, there IS something that has been on my mind a bit. It is the matter of "evil".

You and J-D have both stated that everyone creates their own reality. You have made the case that everyone, through their choices, creates all the things that have happened in their lives. Even the bad things. But that has got me wondering… does this mean there is no such thing as evil? And if there IS such a thing… what exactly is it?

8: Ah, yes. A very interesting question. Do you want the short answer or the long answer?

Z: I guess shorter is probably better…

8: Alright then. The short answer is:

> *"If there is such a thing as evil, then it is an opportunity to learn about love."*

Z: That's it?!?

8: Yes. That's it.

Z: No no no no no no no no. You don't understand. I'm talking about EVIL here. I'm talking about things such as people who are willing to commit genocide – murdering whole populations of other people for the sake of power or wealth or political expediency. I'm talking about terrorists who have no regard for the sanctity of life. And people who would commit rape. People who would abuse children and babies. You know? That's what I'm asking about. Real evil. And what about demons? Are there really such beings? And is there really such a thing as demonic possession? I want to know all of it. And while we are at it, I want to know if there is such a being as Lucifer. You know… Satan… The Devil… him. Does he really exist? THAT is what I want to know about. Once and for all, I want to know about all that dark stuff so I can figure out what to do about it. And please, 8… you can't be wanting to tell me that it's all just an opportunity to "*learn about love*"! Surely? If you had incarnated on earth you'd know that there is some really, really atrocious stuff going on down here!

8: Ah. I see. So apparently you want the long answer then.

Z: The long answer?

8: I just said that the short answer is, "*If there is such a thing as evil, then it is an opportunity to learn about love*". That doesn't seem to please you. So we'll do the long answer instead. It will be, by far, our longest conversation yet. It will wend its way past numerous fascinating points and then eventually arrive at the same end-point as the short answer: "*If there is such a thing as evil, then it is an opportunity to learn about love.*" And then, when we have arrived at that point, you will want to know more about love itself. And so that will be our next chapter: "What is Love?"

Z: You seem pretty sure about all this.

8: I've seen this discussion from many perspectives. I know what to expect.

So now. It seems to me you want us to address two basic questions: First, "*What is evil?*"

Second, *"How should one respond to the presence of evil?"* And, finally, you want to know about this little list of horrors that you have come up with. We will deal with that under the heading "manifestations of evil."

How does that sound?

Z: Thank you, 8. That sounds right.

8: Okay then, let's get started. Question 1:

What is Evil?

We need to agree on what evil is before we can properly discuss it. Otherwise we might have different things in mind and all manner of misapprehensions might creep in.

Z: I agree.

8: Good. Then I will suggest a definition for evil. How do you feel about this:

> *"Evil is any action, which seems to take away a being's right to choose".*

Z: Umm. Well… I don't know about that. That doesn't seem quite right. That seems… a bit… lame.

8: Lame? You clearly have not given this due consideration! I'll explain this to you, but in order to do so, I need you to name three actions that you would consider to be evil.

Z: Three evil actions? Alright. How about rape, murder and theft?

8: That will do very well for the purposes of this example. Let's start with rape.

Let's say we have two people: Person A and Person B. They are both adults of sober mind and in full possession of all their faculties. They are also strangers to one another and have had no previous dealings whatsoever.

Z: Right.

8: Now, if Person A were to approach Person B, and say something like, *"I'd really like to have sex with you, would you like to have sex with me too?"* would that be evil?

Z: Err… no.

Somewhat forward.

And probably not the most successful strategy I've ever heard of.

But it's not evil.

8: Good. And then, if person B, said *"No thank you,"* and the two of them went their separate ways, would that be evil?

Z: No, obviously not.

8: And what if person A said, *"Yes, sure"* and they actually DID have sex?

Z: Then they'd both be very, very easy (laughs).

8: I concede (he smiles). But still this isn't actually evil?

Z: Not in any way that I can see. Two consenting adults, who know what they want, agreeing to have sex? That's not evil. It's not MY style to have sex with strangers and I personally can think of all kinds of reasons why it's a bad idea. But that's me. If there are two people out there agreeing to it, then that's their stuff. But it's certainly not evil.

8: Now let's see what happens when we remove the element of choice from one of the participants in the equation. Now Person A approaches person B and offers person B no choice whatsoever but simply coerces person B, by force or threat, into non-consensual sex. Is that evil?

Z: That's rape. And yes, I very much do think that's evil.

8: Well then, that is my point exactly. It isn't the ACT that is evil. It is the fact of someone feeling that their choices have been taken away. THAT is what is evil.

Z: Ah yes. I do see your point.

8: And the exact same case can be made with every single other act that you might try to define as evil. To further illustrate my point, let us look at another of the actions that you named: murder.

What if Person A approached Person B and said "*Would you like me to terminate your connection with your body?*"

And Person B replies, "*Yes, please.*"

What then?

Z: Hmm. That would be weird. I suppose, at a push, I can envisage a circumstance where this could happen. If Person B, for example, is terminally ill and suffering unbearable pain and Person A, out of a feeling of compassion, offers to help Person B to die. This sort of thing does happen sometimes. It's called assisted suicide.

8: In the culture you currently inhabit there are many taboos around death and dying which spring from the powerful illusion that death is final. That it is your end. There have been other cultures on your planet that have known that death is simply a transition. Like going to sleep before again waking up. Like breathing out before again breathing in. This view is the predominant view in more advanced cultures on other planets too. It is a more beneficial perspective, as it allows you to be less rigid and fearful around the notion of death. And in such cultures, if it happens that a being comes to a place where they feel that their path is best served by their departure from the mortal plane, then that being might find a way to leave on their own, or they might be assisted to go. Their passing might even be ritualised into a grand celebration where some "holy person" is responsible for the termination of the body connection. Such things would seem abominable to most in your culture but only because your context is mostly one of a desperate fear of death. From the context of such other civilisations it can be a beautiful and glorious thing.

Z: That's most interesting, 8. I can see how that might be.

8: But this is not how it is in your culture. Choosing to terminate your connection with your body is seldom seen as an acceptable choice in your culture, is it?

Z: No it really isn't. In fact suicide is actually considered to be a crime in many countries. I've always thought that to be odd. I mean what are you going to do to punish "criminals" who have just killed themselves? But anyhow, as a result of this taboo, assisted suicide is one of those legal and ethical morasses. In some countries it is legally permissible and in others it isn't. And there certainly are ethical considerations that need to be addressed.

8: Are there really? Well you go ahead and address them all you like. For myself, I am quite clear on what I hold to be right. In this regard, as in all others, my position is this:

Your Right to Choose

Whoever you are, whatever the situation, I believe in your right to choose for yourself.

I believe it is your job to know best what is right for you. And no-one should therefore take from you your right to choose.

If you feel you need advice or guidance in making any choice, then those whom you hold to be the wisest and best informed may be asked to assist you in making your choice. And these ones have the right to agree to assist you, to refuse to assist you, or to ask for fair compensation for assisting you. If they agree to assist you, then they must take responsibility for their assistance.

If you are somehow incapacitated and are therefore not in a position to be able to choose, then those whom you love most must choose for you and must take responsibility for their choice.

If you are somehow incapacitated and you find you cannot enact the choices you have made for yourself, then you have the right to ask someone whom you consider competent to assist you in enacting that choice. And that person has the right to agree to assist you, to refuse to assist you, or to ask for fair compensation for assisting you. And they must take responsibility for the assistance they have rendered.

And THAT is what is right for me. And I have no doubt that this is right for me because, quite simply, this is what I would want for myself if I were ever incarnated in a system such as yours. In every situation I would always want to be able to choose for myself. I would never want to be at the mercy of some system – legal or otherwise – to decide for me. What does a legal system care about me? What does it know of my unique situation and my experiences? Nothing. Legal systems and the like should be the final fallback position for when all else fails, not the first point of reference.

Z: What you say seems right and valid to me. I agree with this. Thank you, 8.

8: I'm glad you find value here. But the original point of this intellectual perambulation was actually to address the issue of death when there is choice involved. If you are offered the choice to have someone terminate your life and you have the absolute right to accept the offer or to reject it… then…

Z: …then I agree, this is not evil. I stand with you on this one. And I also say that I would always want the right to choose for myself. And I would therefore want to grant others that same right to choose. This is not evil. This is moral and right. That is my position.

8: And everyone else can decide for themselves?

Z: Yes. Of course they have their own choices to make. As long as their choices do not take from me my right to choose for myself.

8: Hmm… yes… choices. You see the beauty of it? If we are saying that taking away the right to choose is evil, then offering someone more and more choices is… what?

Z: Well, if taking someone's right to choose away is evil, the offering someone more choices would be the opposite of evil.

8: That is a good answer.

Z: But what is the opposite of evil? Love?

8: Possibly. Love is certainly the correct response to evil. Love is that which quenches evil. But is it the opposite of evil? Maybe the answer is Life. Creation. Something like that. It is hard to answer this question because, from my perspective, evil is a temporary, illusory experience and

Love is a very powerful very real force.

Z: Okay. It was just a point of curiosity anyway.

8: Lets move on then and finish this little section of the discussion with the final point: You named theft as the third evil act. So let's look at this.

How would it be if Person A were to ask Person B, "*May I have your television set and your hi-fi, please?*"

There is surely nothing evil about that?

Z: I wouldn't think so. If Person A agrees to Person B's request, then it is a gift that is given. That's not evil, that's just generosity. And if Person A said "*No*" and Person B accepted that and went on his way, then there is also no harm done.

8: That's right. And we can play this out with as many more examples of what you might call evil behaviours as you like. The bottom line will always be that evil is only perceived to be done when choice seems to be removed. Put the choice back in and there is no evil.

Z: I see that, thanks 8. And thanks for your patience with the explanation too. I accept your definition that evil really is the removal of the right to choose.

8: Okay, good. Except you missed something. I said:

> "*Evil is any action, which SEEMS TO take away a being's right to choose*".

That part about "*seems to*" is very important. What it means is that I cannot REALLY take your right to choose away. No one can do that. Not really. But you and I can agree to create the illusion thereof for ourselves.

Z: Ah, yes. By now I have had enough exposure to these concepts to see where this is going. It's the whole victim/ perpetrator thing again, isn't it? I cannot truly be your victim. I can only have the illusion that I am.

8: Now you're getting it.

Z: So then you cannot truly take away my right to choose. But we can agree to make it seem that way.

8: That's exactly what I am saying.

Z: So then evil is an illusory thing?

8: This is my perspective, yes. It is something that you can, within this reality you currently inhabit, SEEM to experience. It can seem very real to you. But it is still just an illusion. Let me tell you a truth about good and evil. It goes like this:

> "*There is not a single thing that is either good or evil, but that you feel that way about it.*"

Z: You're saying that nothing is intrinsically evil. Nothing at all. But some things might still feel evil to me?

8: That is exactly what I'm saying. Or I can rephrase it like this: evil does not exist objectively but it might certainly be experienced subjectively.

Z: Uhh… That is another way of saying I can feel like I am experiencing evil, but that does not mean it really, truly exists?

8: Correct.

Z: Hmm… I understand the logic and it makes sense to me intellectually. But I'm not sure if I really feel this to be true.

8: I understand. And that is why we must have this conversation. Because you must come to see it this way before you can ascend to Unity Consciousness. So I present you with a choice: on the one hand you can choose to continue to label certain beings and their behaviours as evil and, in so doing, you can keep yourself distanced and divorced from them, so that you can remain in a state of judgement of them and so you can keep feeling superior to them. On the other hand you can choose to be willing to come to an understanding that nothing is truly "other" than you, that nothing is eternally unlovable or unforgivable.

Z: And that's the choice? If I am not willing to come to see it this way then I can't ascend to unity consciousness?

8: That is the truth of it. As with all things, you always have a choice. This time your choice is between unity consciousness and duality (or separation) consciousness. Understand that there is no right or wrong about what you choose and no judgement of you for the choices you make. But what you choose defines who you are and creates the reality that you will experience. And, quite simply, you cannot become a being of Unity Consciousness and you cannot reside in a Unity Reality without being willing to see All as One, without being willing to see the "other" as "self" and without being willing to let go of the mechanisms of separation, such as judgement and hatred.

You see, my dear friend, this is the choice offered to you by duality. You can accept the offer of duality and continue to see yourself as separate from all else and travel ever outwards on the path of separation with fear as your motivator. Or, on the other hand, you can choose love. If you adhere to a choice for love, then you step onto the path of unity. You begin to travel back home to the Oneness. It is true that you can, for some while, travel the path of love whilst still clinging to the illusion of separation. This is what happens with those who choose either the "Service to Other" or the "Service to Self" modes of being. And that is fine if that is what you choose. But sooner or later these paths too will converge and these beings will realise that the concepts of Other and Self are not what they first thought. That indeed there is only One.

If you follow what I am saying, then you will understand that it might seem as if there are many possible options and choices on your path. But really, it is not so. There is really only one choice.

Either you accept ALL as being One, or you do not.

The choice is yours. And you cannot move towards being One with All That Is, whilst still at the same time holding onto the view that some beings are so despicable and unlovable that you can simply refuse to accept them as being part of the Oneness. That you can label them "evil" and thereby damn them to eternal darkness.

ALL is One. Or it is not. Your choice.

Z: You have explained that very well, thank you 8. I get it now. I must choose between two ideas. On the one hand there is the idea of certain beings being beyond all possibility of ever being loveable. And so we label them and their activities as evil. On the other hand is the understanding that all of this is just a temporary illusory state. And that all beings are inherently worthy of love and are a part of God. That I am truly One with all beings and all things everywhere.

8: Yes. That is the choice.

Z: Well then, I choose Oneness.

8: That is well. But if you make this choice half-heartedly, then it is of no value. You must make it completely and truly from the heart before it will result in a change in your experience of life.

Z: I understand and I am ready to make that choice. Will you help me to release the last vestiges of the beliefs and choices that keep me on the path of separation?

8: Yes. I will. That is in part what THE ASCENSION PAPERS is about.

Z: So then, let me try to summarise what I have understood from you about evil:

It is when I feel that I have had my options taken away from me that I feel as if evil is being done to me.

8: Right.

Z: But these occasions when I might experience this are illusory. That is to say that I have actually chosen the experience of having my choices taken away from me and I can, in fact, always choose other. No matter how it might seem to me at the time.

8: Yes. And the fact that you are experiencing this evil means you are probably working quite hard at believing that you have no other choice but to experience it. This is what you have chosen. You, as a creator, have created the illusion that you are not a creator. And you, as an indivisible part of the Oneness, have created the experience that you are completely separate and alone.

Z: Whew! That's quite a paradox, isn't it, 8?

8: Yes, it is. But is this not consistent with the way the universe would be if you were in fact the creator of your own reality?

Z: It is.

8: And the opposite would also be true. If you were prepared to begin to choose that you were One with All, as you have now chosen, then something interesting would happen: as you make this choice and as it becomes more manifest in your reality, so it would come to be that, in time, you will cease to experience evil.

Z: Really? Choosing for Oneness means I will cease to experience evil?

8: Yes. The degree to which you know it to be true that you are really One with All That Is, is the degree to which you will no longer experience evil. You can only experience the illusion of evil whilst you reside in a state of separation. Of duality. Once you remember your intrinsic Oneness, then you cannot experience evil being done to you, nor can you contemplate doing it to another. It is only in the state of separation or duality that you can either experience the actions of another being as evil, or indeed contemplate enacting evil upon another being.

Z: Can you explain that to me, 8?

8: Certainly. At the level of Oneness it is impossible for me to set out to do any harm to you whatsoever.

Z: Why 8?

8: Precisely because I know that you and I are One! You see, all beings who reside in a place of Unity Consciousness, directly experience everything that they do to another as being done to themselves. If I hurt you, then instantly, with that very action, I hurt myself in exactly equal measure also. In fact, the hurt I do to you IS the hurt I do to myself also. That is what happens at the level of Unity Consciousness. And, as I don't desire to hurt myself, I won't try to hurt you.

You on earth are residing within an illusion of duality, which means you have an illusion that this is not so. The instrument of "time" is used to separate you from your choices, so you do not see that it is so that everything you do to others you are doing exactly and precisely to yourself also. But we, outside of the illusion of duality, see it directly. We are One. We know this. We experience it. What I do to you, I do to myself. So a Unity Conscious being will never seek to hurt any other being.

Z: Wait a minute, 8, are you saying that everything I do to another I also directly do to myself? Literally?

8: Yes. It is so. But you have a clever illusion of time and space that separates you from your creations so that you can believe it is not so. But it is. Hurt another and you hurt yourself. You might need to travel a bit of time and space to feel the hurt and so you might not realise that you did it to yourself. And you might be able to tell yourself when the hurt comes back to you that it was another being who did it to you. That is the power of the illusion. But it is none-the-less so; everything you do to another, you do to yourself. Therefore it would be very wise to, "*Do unto others exactly as you would have them do unto you*". That is the best way to get treated as you wish to be treated.

Z: Okay. I get this now. And you are saying that you guys in the higher dimensions and other realities and what-not don't have this illusion of time and space, so it isn't possible for you to think that you are separate from each other. Is that right?

8: For those of us who are of Unity Consciousness, this is so. If your every experience shows you unambiguously that you are One with all other parts of reality, then you'd be pretty unobservant if you didn't accept it to be true. That is how it is for us.

Z: So you guys would never consciously choose to hurt anyone else because that would immediately result in you hurting yourself.

8: That's what I am saying.

And the other thing, of course, is that a being of true Unity Consciousness cannot experience hurt in the same way you believe you can. We cannot imagine that we can be physically damaged or killed. The hurt we can endure is what you might call emotional hurt or possibly psychological hurt. And these hurts are understood differently from the way you understand them. If we experience these, then we do not think they have been inflicted upon us by another being or by some external experience. We understand quite simply that they are the results of our own choices. If I am hurt in an interaction with another being, then I understand that my own choices have caused me pain. The interaction with the other Self is simply the catalyst. Indeed, if I am observant I will see that this is all just a gift that shows me where my choices are not what I wished them to be.

A being of unity consciousness cannot experience evil being done to it nor can it contemplate doing evil to another Self.

Z: I think I understand this now.

8: That's good. Then you will understand that it is only inside a duality reality such as yours, from the perspective of separation, when you do not know that you are One, that a being might wish to act in a way that is deeply hurtful and destructive to themselves and others. Only in such a reality might they experience their inner turmoil in such a way that it can cause them to hate themselves so badly that they can be willing to do all manner of atrocious things to each other.

Z: I see.

8: And equally it is so that it is only inside a duality reality like yours, from the perspective of separation, when you do not know that you are One, that you might look at the actions of such a being and be able to say: "*You are evil*".

Outside of duality you will know that you and the being with whom you are interacting are both being shown how the choices that you have previously made have resulted in some pain and confusion for yourselves. The miracle of the situation is the way this interaction has perfectly brought together two disparate Selves for an interaction that perfectly shows both of you exactly how those choices are not serving you. Before this interaction you might not have seen this. But now, as a result of the interaction, you can see it clearly. And now that you HAVE seen it, you can choose differently. And when you have made a better choice, the previous choice and its results can be healed and loved and re-integrated.

It's a wondrous gift, you see.

But, inside of duality, you might very well experience this interaction as evil. It might be the victim's experience that they were innocently going about their life when they were horribly victimised by some evil-doer. And it might be the perpetrator's experience that they had a horrible life, which drove them to behave in this terrible way. And no-one can tell either of them that their experiences are not valid. It IS their experience!

Every experience presents you with a choice. Almost everyone playing the duality game will, after every such interaction, make one or another victim-based choice. Which will serve to keep them in duality and invite more such interactions. But it is possible to escape this trap. It is possible, instead, to accept that the interaction is an experience that you have brought to yourself as a result of your choices. If you can do this then you can begin to look to yourself to make new choices that better suit you. It might help to realise that all the experiences play out within an illusion. And that there is a greater truth at hand, which is that, at another level, you and the other player both know this is something you have chosen and agreed upon.

Z: That's very hard to do though, 8.

8: It is. But it was never meant to be easy. I'll explain this in a moment with "The Monastic Order Parable".

Z: (laughs) The WHAT!?!

8: (smiles) You'll see. But before we can get to that, I'd like to first offer you an illustration of how a victim relationship could originate.

Imagine now that you are no longer incarnated. You are here with me in spirit-space and we are planning a new lifetime. I come before you and say to you:

"*You know me, I am 8. I have played the role of Spirit-Guide to you when you were lost in duality and helped you to find your way home. I am also your dearly beloved friend and on one level we are partners of long standing. On another level we have found Oneness together. You know me. And now I come to you with my need. In order for me to proceed as I desire, I really need to understand the experience of the victim state. I feel I have a need to incarnate and then experience what it is like to place myself utterly in another's power such that they might treat me very badly and then cruelly kill me. I need to play that out, see how it feels and see how I respond to that. Are you willing to incarnate into a duality system with me where we might Veil ourselves and play out that scenario? Will you play the role of perpetrator for me?*"

So then, if you agreed to my proposal, we could have a situation where we both send a part of ourselves beyond the Veil and I get to experience being a powerless victim and you get to play the role of the evil perpetrator. We see what that is like and we learn something about ourselves and then we deal with what we have learned.

You see?

Z: I follow, yes.

8: And can you see that this doesn't actually make you evil? You have simply helped me to experience that which I desired.

Z: I get that, yes. Thank you for the explanation. But I very much hope you never do come to me with such a request.

8: And why is that?

Z: Because then I'm afraid I would have to turn you down. I'm very sorry but I will not be your perpetrator. I will not ever seek to hurt you or treat you badly. I will never choose to act in any way towards you other than in love, respect and honour.

8: Alright. But why? If I have asked this of you, why will you not do it for me?

Z: Because, my beloved 8, it is wrong for me. Because no matter how much you might need to experience such a role, I have no desire in my heart or in my being to play the opposite part.

8: Why?

Z: Because… I am not willing to do that to myself. Because being your cruel abuser would hurt me too much. In this life, and especially in my past lives, I have seen what it is to be a perpetrator (Zingdad Note: see Chapter 1, *"The Wizard"*). I know what this is and I have no need to know any more of it. I am not willing. I love myself too much to put myself through that and I love you too much to do it to you. That is how I feel in my heart. I'm sorry if I disappoint you.

8: My dear friend! Quite the contrary. Why would that disappoint me?

Z: Because, if I am not willing to be your perpetrator, then you can't have the experiences you feel you need. Isn't it?

8: No, it isn't. Is your world not full of people who are willing to enact some form of victimisation upon anyone that will but allow it?

Z: Yes. I guess so. So you are saying that you will always be able to find SOMEONE to play that role for you.

8: That's quite right. In actual fact it's a lot simpler than that. The fact of my desiring some experience creates an imbalance in the field of consciousness. Remember there is actually only One of us here?

Z: Okay… so…

8: So if there is only one of us here, then an aspect of The One desiring to experience something, is the same as The One desiring it. This means that you can't have the desire without the means of the fulfilment. The One can, and will, only express that desire in me if there is also another Self who answers that desire by being willing to play the corresponding role. And when we are done playing our respective roles, we can heal any pain that we have by realising that we are actually One, actually the same greater being. And THAT is how it happens. When you are willing to see the horrible, evil, wicked, perpetrator as Self, then you become something greater than you were. Then, you ascend. And the same thing, of course, occurs when you are willing to see the sad, pathetic, weak, dismal victim as Self.

Z: Oh wow, 8. I feel you have just expressed something very important there. I feel it in my soul that this is something of profound importance to me.

8: Not just to you. To everyone who is ready to seek Unity Consciousness. This is an idea that we'll develop further as we go. But for now I want to turn your question back to you: given our discussion, what do you now think will happen if I ask you to play perpetrator to me and you turn me down? What then?

Z: Well, in light of this new information, it would seem to me that I am either the right response to your need or I am not. If I am, then I will say "yes", if I am not, then I will say "no". And, as we have discovered, saying "yes" does not make me evil because then I am simply showing you something about yourself. And saying "no", is also okay because, assuredly, there will be *someone* for whom it is right that they should respond "yes".

8: So, where is the victim? Where is the evil?

Z: There is none! Because I always have a choice. We all do. And when we make our choices we are simply showing ourselves something about ourselves!

8: Right. And at the risk of belabouring the point: if you choose to agree to be my perpetrator, I might come to perceive you as being evil, but only inside the illusion of the game. And it will only be a temporary experience.

Z: Yes, I get that now.

8: And always YOU have the choice to respond in your own highest good. And if you go to your heart and make choices with your deepest truth, then your choices will be in harmony with what the Unity Conscious part of yourself is also choosing for you.

So you see… all there really is, is choice. You choose and then you experience the results of your choices.

Z: I see that, 8, thanks.

8: So! Let's see recap: you now agree with me that beings feel as if evil has been done when they feel their choices have been removed?

Z: Yep. Got that one.

8: And do you also agree that you *actually* always have choices? You might have the illusion that you do not, but if you are willing to take responsibility for yourself and if you are willing to use your guidance and listen to your truth in your own heart, then you will also see through the illusion. Then you will know that you always have choices.

Z: Yes, I get that too. At the level of Oneness there is no evil, only choices. And by connecting with my heart I connect with that which exists at the level of Oneness.

8: You are coming along very nicely. Yes. That is well said.

And now, before we move on, I want to briefly revisit my request of you to be my perpetrator. When you chose to turn my request down, what was it that motivated your choice?

Z: Love. I decided that I didn't want to hurt you because I made a choice for love.

8: That's right, you did. You chose to only express yourself in such a way that you would love your expressions. And that is a very fine choice indeed. You chose to let go of the need to create with pain and fear. Now you only create with love. Can you see why that choice would please me?

Z: Yes I can.

8: And when I pressed you for the reasons for your choices, you very nicely illustrated an important point: you expressed the realisation that being the perpetrator would hurt YOU very much. Right? So that means the beings in your current reality that might be regarded as the great evil ones have apparently caused themselves considerable pain in playing that role for you.

Z: Yes. I can see that. But I still can't approve of what they did, and are still doing!

8: That's fine. That means they offer you a gift, which costs them very dearly to give. It is the opportunity to choose whether or not you want to be their victim. If you decide you DO want to be their victim, then there they are! Willing to play the role you want them to play. And if you choose not to play the victim, then you show yourself that you REALLY have made that choice. You see, without their extremely well crafted offer you would not be able to say that you have finally and completely chosen not to be a victim.

Z: I don't follow that exactly…?

8: Okay. I promised we'd get to it and here it is…

The Parable of the Monastic Order

There were once two men of similar ages who were both born into modest circumstances. The one had a very astute business mind, which he conscientiously applied to accumulating wealth. He had barely left his parent's home before he was already quite wealthy. By the time he was in his mid-thirties he was by far the richest man in town.

The other man did not pursue wealth and he was not very keen on hard work either. He was a poet and a musician and his favourite thing was to sit all day at the river catching fish and composing songs.

But, as disparate as these two men might have seemed, they both had a deep interest in spiritual matters. They both had a hunger for their own enlightenment. And so it was that they both came to the decision to dedicate themselves totally to their spiritual growth. They each decided that the appropriate way for them to do this was to join the monastery on the hill above their town.

Z: They wanted to be monks?

8: Exactly. And one of the requirements of this monastic order was that the monks take an oath of poverty and release their attachment to all material possession.

Z: Hah, the rich man would struggle with that!

8: And he did! Given that he had spent his life accumulating wealth and that he was very good at it – it was indeed very difficult for him to let go of it. The poor man, on the other hand, had no such difficulty. As he owned almost nothing, he gave up almost nothing!

Z: Yes, I see. But how does this illustrate the point you were making about choosing to stop being a victim?

8: Obliquely. Stay with me and I will get there. You see, as it happens, both of these men DID take the oath of poverty and both were accepted into the monastery. Both were then brothers of the order and neither had a single physical possession to call their own.

Z: Okay…

8: So what do you think; which of them then knew, to the very depths of his soul, what it is to choose poverty over wealth?

Z: Ah, I see. It is the man who was rich who really knew the value of this decision.

8: Yes. And so it is for you in this duality-reality you inhabit. You are all very wealthy in opportunities for victimhood. You are invited in a million different ways every single day to be a victim all over again. Every time you turn on the television, open a newspaper or read a magazine, you are being bombarded with messages about your own victimhood.

Your political, legal and financial systems exist upon the basis that you are all victims and they strive to keep you in that state.

Your employers need you to be victims so that you keep doing the jobs you hate for the money they offer you.

Everywhere, in every direction you look, you are surrounded by offerings of your own victimhood on platter.

And it is all terribly compelling and deeply addictive. So you keep believing that it is the good, right and responsible thing to do to get that job, pay that mortgage, buy that insurance against every conceivable disaster, consult with those experts on everything from what is right and moral, to what is true for your soul, to what is good for your health, to what you should be eating, to how you should relate to your own life-partner and how you should treat your own children, to… well, you get the idea… you are addicted to being a victim.

And there are some pretty compelling pay-offs. You get to say, *"It's not my fault! I didn't do it! It's not fair!"* and my personal favourite, *"Why me?"*. And you get to feel as if someone else is to blame for everything: *"They wronged me! I was cheated! They never gave me my chance!"* And so you let yourself off the hook from ever having to take responsibility.

Pretty addictive stuff.

And pretty childish too, don't you think?

Z: Yeah, when you put it like that, it sounds as if we're all just brats throwing tantrums.

8: It certainly can look that way sometimes. But that's okay. The point of childhood is that it is there to be experienced, and from those experiences we begin to discover ourselves and decide who we want to be when we grow up. It's a difficult place to be and a bit of tantrum throwing is, I suppose, par for the course. And, given a little time, everyone does indeed grow up. And the very hallmark of growing up is… taking responsibility. That is what a grown-up does. And a spiritually mature being is one who is willing to take absolute responsibility for all of its own experiences.

Z: And a spiritual child doesn't take responsibilities? A spiritual child sees itself as a victim?

8: That's right.

Z: Hmmm. So I guess it's time to give up the victim addiction then.

8: Yes. And just like the rich man who gave up his attachment to wealth and temporal power, just like the junkie who gives up an addiction to a drug, so you will be one that knows TO THE DEPTHS OF YOUR SOUL that you are finally and completely done with victimhood. When you ascend out of this duality system into your own creator status, you will never again fall foul of believing that you are a victim. You will have seen victimhood in all of its most beguiling guises. You will have vanquished it in your own soul, in your own experience and with your own decisions. You will have created yourself as a creator. Which is, of course, the only legitimate way to become a creator-being.

Z: Ha ha! There's that paradox again. But this time we see it from the other side. If we are creators, then we must be willing to create that we are creators or else we won't be!

That's just so mind-bogglingly cool.

8: It is said that as a being first awakes to self-mastery so that being begins to laugh and laugh and laugh. And very often it is so. The solutions to the problems and traps that previously bound you are discovered to be nothing more than great cosmic jokes.

But to come back to evil: what then is it but an opportunity for you to choose? And if you are ready to choose love, and stay with that choice, then you are on the path to choosing Oneness. And when you are ready to choose Oneness, then you are ready to begin releasing the experience of evil entirely.

Z: I get that now.

8: Okay then, let's recap. Tell what you think: is there really such a thing as evil?

Z: Given what I have come to understand, I would say the answer is both yes and no. It's an illusory thing. You can feel as if there is evil, but it isn't actually happening.

8: You mean,

"There is not a single thing that is either good or evil, but that you feel that way about it."

Z: Ha! Right!

8: But what is the illusion that we are actually experiencing?

Z: We are experiencing the illusion of having our choices taken away.

8: So then you would agree that;

"Evil is any action, which seems to take away a being's right to choose".

Z: Yes, I would agree.

8: Good. Then we are on the same page and we have, I believe, answered the first question, *"What is evil?"*

Z: Yes, we have, thank you.

8: And that sets us up perfectly to address the second question, which is:

How Should One Respond to the Presence of Evil?

And so? Do you what to take a shot at it? How do YOU feel you should respond to the experience of evil?

Z: I'm not sure about that. I mean I can tell you what I THINK the right answer should be and I'm more or less sure it's right… but I don't yet FEEL that way inside myself.

8: Good. Sometimes the intellect can point the way and we can follow with our experiences afterwards. So go ahead… tell me what you think the answer is. How should one respond to the presence of evil?

Z: I think it calls for a transcendent moment. Such an experience asks of me that I choose to remember that I am really One with All. That I choose, and act, from a place of great love.

8: That is very well answered. You will quite shortly get to see what happens when you yourself reach for such a transcendent moment. But that's a good answer and it is also in keeping with the other thing I told you about evil which was,

"If there is such a thing as evil, then it is an opportunity to learn about love."

And now I am going to help you to move that insight from your head where you THINK it to be true, to your heart where you KNOW it to be true. Okay?

Z: I look forward to that, thanks 8.

8: So let us begin with you telling me why you don't feel as if it is true. Tell me what it is about this idea that troubles you.

Z: I'm almost embarrassed to say. I feel as if I should be beyond this. Because it all still comes back to the whole victim/ perpetrator/ rescuer triangle. And I should have that one sorted by now. We have discussed it so much!

8: Go easy on yourself. It takes a lot of work to release deeply ingrained ideas and beliefs. Allow yourself a little grace. You have one final round to go with this triangle and I have been expecting this conversation. So... out with it... what is bothering you?

The Victim Triangle – One Last Time

Z: It's like this: I have come to see that evil is an illusion and that, by embracing the Oneness, I can release myself from experiencing it. And that's just dandy for me. But what about everyone else who is still suffering with it?

8: Ah. Compassion.

Compassion is a wonderful, and yet terrible, double-edged sword. It allows you to really share in another's experience, which brings you closer to the Oneness. But it also attaches you to this other's suffering, which pulls you back into duality.

Let me ask you something. You are, as we write this, busy letting go of your own victim consciousness, are you not? You are moving out of the victim relationships you have had with your world and moving into a new situation where you will be in greater harmony with life, are you not?

Z: You're talking about my move from the city to the forest?

8: That is what you are doing on a physical level. But, of course, it is the movement that is happening on an emotional and spiritual level that I am more interested in. You are, right now, in the middle of quite a radical change in your life choices. Are you not?

Z: Yes I am, but...

8: But nothing. You should find a way to share this other story... the one that runs parallel to what is going on here in The Ascension Papers. You will find that it brings you value to share it and others will find value in reading about what you are doing.

Z: Okay. I'll do that. I was thinking of starting a blog or something.

8: Do it.

Z: Okay.

8: But the point is this. You ARE right now busy making this change to release yourself from your old victim relationships with the world. There is movement in your psyche and in your external world. You are letting go of victim. You are discovering yourself to be a creator-being. Right?

Z: Uhh, yes. That is what I am trying to do.

8: Okay. Well, here comes the question... Does the fact that you are doing this mean that you should insist and demand that everyone else in your world should also do this? Must everyone on the planet do what YOU are doing right now, just because you are doing it? Must every single person make the exact same choice you are making?

Z: No. That doesn't seem reasonable. Of course not.

8: And so, what then about all the other beings who still wish to play the victim game? Must they stop because you stop? Do you need to first force them to stop playing their victim game before you can go on and play another game? Or are you willing to let them do as they wish while you go and create a new game for yourself with those who share your vision of what constitutes a good game? A game that is more congruent with the kinder, more loving version of yourself that you discover yourself to be?

Z: When you put it like that then I can see it. I must obviously be willing to allow them to continue with their victim game if that is what they wish to do.

8: So then, the fact that there IS the experience of evil to be had – the fact that some are playing Victim and Perpetrator with each other – is this your problem?

Z: No, I guess not. I mean, I know it isn't my problem.

But then, why do I feel guilty for saying so?

8: It is really quite simply that you still have some attachment to an idea of yourself as a Rescuer. You can see that you should be able to let people choose what they want to choose, but when their choices lead them into painful outcomes, that makes you feel uncomfortable. As if it were wrong of you to let them get on with what they have decided they want to do.

Of course you can do whatever you want to do. You can respond to every invitation to dance, exactly as you most desire. But what you should remember is that, with every choice you take, you create yourself. With each choice, you decide what your reality will be like. And if you are choosing to rescue someone, then you are creating yourself as the Rescuer. And the Rescuer is a part of the Victim/ Perpetrator/ Rescuer triangle. And all three of those are actually, when properly understood, just victims. If you choose to rescue anyone, then you are still choosing to be a victim. You remain locked in this state and you continue to reside in duality.

Rescuer is the final hurdle for the ascending soul. Of all the victim addictions, Rescuer is by far the most difficult to kick, and it is also the last one to be released. In the analogy of the monastic order we used above, finally letting go of Rescuer would be like the very wealthiest of all men being able to choose poverty and enter the monastery.

Z: Why is Rescuer so difficult to release?

8: Well, with Rescuer you get to tell yourself a story about what a good and noble person you are being. You are HELPING! That is GOOD! While Victim is a weak person and Perpetrator is a bad person… when you are in Rescuer you get to tell yourself that you are being a Good Person.

The problem with this is that you inevitably find all your good intentions going up in smoke. The Victim you rescued becomes dependent upon you and starts claiming more and more from you. Then you start to resent the Victim and start to withhold help. Then the Victim feels like YOUR victim because you aren't fulfilling your side of the bargain. And you feel like a Victim because Victim is abusing your good nature. And Perpetrator hates you for meddling in his relationship with Victim. And soon, all of you need help. And THEN who are you going to call?

Z: Err… Ghostbusters?

8: (laughs) Very funny.

Z: (smiles) I do see what you are saying, though; then we all three of us will need a Rescuer. And THEN what?

8: One way or another, it never ends. As long as you are holding onto the idea of yourself as a Rescuer then, in truth, you are keeping yourself in Victim. You will never be free of the triangle.

Z: Okay. So then let's say I was ready to let go of Rescuer. Then how would I respond to a world in which I see people making choices, which lead them to painful outcomes?

8: I have a strategy, which I can offer you. If it should happen that you find yourself being pulled into Rescuer mode, then you can adapt this strategy to suit your purposes. The purpose of this strategy is to help you to help another in such a way that you do not fall into Rescuer. If they are willing, you might even be able to help them to move out of their own victim state too.

Z: That sounds awesome, thanks 8.

8: And while we are at it, we will look at the other two legs of the victim triangle too; namely Victim and Perpetrator. I will offer you strategies, which you may adapt to your own life if you find yourself in any of these modes. Together these strategies will go some way towards answering the question of "how to deal with the presence of evil."

Firstly: Where You Are The Perpetrator

This occurs when you find yourself in a situation where you have, either intentionally or unintentionally, made another being feel as if their choices have been removed from them.

What should you do?

Start with courage in hand. Be brave and face what you have done. Speak to the Victim and seek first to understand very clearly from them how they have experienced the situation. What did they feel? Why were they hurt? When you have asked all the questions you needed ask, such that you feel you have really understood their experience and that they have said everything they might have wanted to say to you, then you should feed back to them what you have heard and check with them that you have really understood their perspective correctly. When they agree that you have a really good understanding of how they felt then, and only then, is it time for you to give them your perspective. If you give your side before you have understood theirs, then you are simply trying to make excuses for yourself. You are trying to "get out of it". You are being a coward. So have the courage first to truly and deeply see the experience from the Victim's side. THEN tell them why you did what you did. Tell them from your heart what it was that you intended and what motivated you. In all probability you never intended to do the harm that was done. In all probability it was an unintended side-effect of your trying to do something else entirely. Explain yourself as best you can and ask them then to feed back to you what they have heard from you. Work with them until you feel they have correctly understood you and your motivations.

When this is done, then the healing can begin. Now you must undertake not to do this again. You have seen how it caused harm, so make the choice not to hurt yourself or any other like this again. It is very useful if you can try to find the very deepest core choice or belief that allowed this to happen. If you work with a surface choice, then you will have to address this again and again until you DO find the core choice that does not serve you. Tell your victim about your new decision and tell them how it is that you believe this new decision will keep you from hurting them or anyone else in this manner ever again.

The next thing to do is to seek redress. Try to find something that you can do for the person whom you have harmed that will somehow balance the harm you have done. If it is possible to directly repair that which was damaged, then do that. If this is not possible, then try to do something for them, which will benefit them in at least equal measure to the harm done to them. Make it as personal as possible. Don't just give them money or something impersonal like that. That doesn't really help the healing.

And THAT is what you do when you find yourself cast as the perpetrator.

Z: That is some cool stuff, 8. I can see that this would really work.

8: If you are of sufficient consciousness that you would be willing and able to apply these principles, then you are quite seldom going to find yourself in the Perpetrator role. But I felt it useful to set out these ideas. You can try them and you can share them with others who are still struggling with finding themselves being the one who does the harm.

Z: Thanks 8.

8: You are welcome.

Let's move onto the next way in which you can perceive evil.

Secondly: When You Are The Victim

If you can get the Perpetrator to play ball and go through the same process outlined above, then that would be great. But ultimately, if your Perpetrator was willing to do that, then you wouldn't really see yourself as a Victim. Just someone involved in an unhappy circumstance that eventually turned out okay. So, if you are really feeling like a victim, then it is because you feel this other being will never right the wrong they have done to you.

What to do then?

The very first thing to do when you are feeling like a Victim is to give yourself choices. When you have choices that you can take, then you are immediately a Creator again. And you cannot be both a Creator and a Victim UNLESS you are a Creator who is creating the illusion that you are a Victim. Which is exactly what you will be doing in this situation.

So that is the first thing you must do. Move your consciousness into Creator mode. Recognise that you have choices. A very powerful thing you can do in this regard is to say to yourself:

"In every moment I create myself with my choices. What choices do I have now and how will I create myself with each of those choices?"

Then list your choices. Think of every possible thing you can conceive of that you could do in this situation. Write them down, if there are more than a handful. Then, next to each choice, write down what kind of a person you would be if you made that choice. Be honest and clear. THEN write down what kind of person you really want to be. You might for example want to be "*the most magnificent, loving version of myself*" or possibly "*the wisest most creative person I can be*" or something like that.

Now see if any of the choices you wrote down conform to a choice that would be taken by that most loving and magnificent version of yourself. Chances are none of them have. That is why you are experiencing yourself as a Victim. Because you aren't choosing to be the best you, you can be. The Victim experience is a gift. It is asking of you to choose again.

And now you are in a magical and wondrous moment. Some alchemy of the soul is about to happen, if you will only let it. Now you can ask yourself the very important question: "*What*

WOULD the most magnificent, loving version of myself do in this situation?" Does the answer come to mind immediately? Then write it down. Then do it! If you don't have an immediate answer to you question you can simply, allow yourself to "percolate". Hold the question in your heart and be willing to hear the answer. Perhaps you will wake up the next morning with the answer. Perhaps you will receive it indirectly from someone else or through inspiration. But let me tell you this: if you hold the question in your heart the answer will come.

And when it does come you will feel wonderful. Light and free and liberated.

And then it might be time to do some delving into your psyche. Go into your deepest beliefs and memories. Especially your childhood. Go and find the seed-thought which you hold that caused you to invite this experience of victimhood into your life. Realise that this belief does not bring you closer to love, joy or peace. Work with it until you can release it.

And if you cannot? If you find yourself to be stuck? Then I would recommend that you seek a gifted counsellor or therapist to help with this. Or else seek some wise soul who is further down the path than you are who can offer the right input. Or indeed, you might find some words somewhere on the Internet or in a book that will be just the right words at the right time to help you to transcend your pain.

You see?

Z: Yes. I begin to see.

8: But you must seek. And you must be willing to change.

When the soul is ready to progress, it will do so. If it struggles to do so, then help will be offered. If it is ready and willing to accept the help, then the path will open up.

Z: I see. I like that.

8: And then, in due course, you will find you are no longer having Victim experiences. You will find you are making decisions, which allow you to leave behind all those relationships which do not serve you. And then you will be finally ready to know that, indeed you have created every single Victim experience you have ever had.

And then you will be done with being a Victim!

Z: Awesome! Thanks 8. And the third victim state is Rescuer?

8: Correct.

Thirdly: When You Are The Rescuer

When someone in your life finds themselves feeling like a Victim, you might find them reaching out to you for help. If you yourself are still of Victim consciousness, then you are very likely to be pulled into playing Rescuer to this other being. If, on the other hand, you are completely done with the victim triangle then you will not have that difficulty. You will see their whole situation for what it is. You will see that they are creating their entire drama all for their own purposes, just as you used to do when you played the same game. And you will see that their pain is not of your making and that, in fact, you cannot be responsible for healing their pain. You cannot choose for them. You cannot fix them. You cannot change them. And you would know that, were you to try, then you would very soon embroil yourself in their pain starting out as their Rescuer and then moving swiftly to becoming both their Perpetrator and their Victim. You would not be willing to do that and you would be fully aware that, in fact, only they can heal themselves. They themselves first need to decide that their life is not as they would wish it to be. If they find they cannot affect the change they desire themselves then, of course, they can ask for help. For no help can come to anyone who is unwilling to be helped.

Now, it is possible that this person does not know HOW to do all of this. Perhaps they believe that something or someone outside of themselves must change before they can be happy. Perhaps they don't know how to understand that they are responsible for their own choices. Perhaps they don't know how to find out which choices are harming them. Perhaps they don't know how to make better choices. And so it could be possible for you to help them to help themselves without moving into Rescuer.

Z: And you are going to share a strategy for doing this with me?

8: I am. Let us formalise it into a three-step process:

Being of Assistance Without Becoming a Rescuer:
The Three-Step Process

Step 1: Raise your own consciousness to a higher vibration by saying to yourself:

"All is One. All is perfect. Both ………….. (this other being's name) and I are perfect expressions of The One. I am motivated only by love."

Step 2: Understand the position of this other being. You can do so by seeing yourself in their situation and also by talking to them and asking them questions about their experience until you really can understand their position. In this step you are NOT trying to fix anything, you are simply trying to understand, as well as you possibly can, what it is that ails them. In so doing you give them the first gift. You give them the gift of your attention. If you can do this without any judgement or criticism then you give them a very loving gift indeed. Keep going with this until you really feel you understand their situation. And check with them that you do. Tell them what you have heard them say and ask if they agree that this is an accurate description of their experience. You will be amazed what a wonderful healing gift JUST THIS step will be.

Step 3: Once you have a really good grasp of the situation you can ask yourself what is the very highest and best offering of assistance that you can give this other. What is it that you would want done for yourself if you were in their situation?

Z: Oh right: *"Do unto others as you would that they should do unto you."*

8: That's it.

But here comes the twist. And pay attention, because this is important.

Before you actually offer any assistance remember… whatever you do to this other being, you do to yourself also. So be willing to experience for yourself whatever you are giving to this other being and then watch for it. It will find its way to you. If, for example, you rush in and take away this other being's choices, then you will come to find your choices being taken away too. If you treat the other being as if they are not actually capable of finding their own way, then you too will come to lose your way. If, on the other hand, you offer loving and respectful assistance, then this will be offered to you too. If you treat this being as part of the Oneness then you will find yourself feeling as if you are part of the Oneness too.

You get the idea?

Not only, *"Do to others that which you would have done to you"* but, *"Do to others realising that you are doing exactly that to yourself"*. Be sure you are ready to have this done to you also.

Z: I see. That is excellent advice, 8. I can see that this could really help without causing me to be pulled into Rescuer.

8: I have something more that I would like to offer you in this regard.

Z: Please…

8: If you find yourself dealing with a person in Victim, then is it not true that the thing you would most want done for you is to be helped out of Victim? To be helped to see that you are actually the Creator of your own reality? Would that not be the way you would want yourself to be helped in such a circumstance?

Z: Yes. It certainly is!

8: Well there is a right way to do that and a wrong way. The wrong way is to tell this person who is sitting with their pain and confusion to, *"Pull yourself together because you created all this yourself anyway!"*

Z: (laugh) Oh my goodness I can see how THAT wouldn't work!

8: No, indeed. The right way is far more gentle and loving than that. And FAR more effective. If you can help this being to see that they have options and choices, then they can immediately move out of Victim.

Z: Oh, right… just the same as I would do for myself if I found myself in Victim.

8: Isn't that what we are saying? Do to the other exactly as you would like to have done to yourself.

Z: Yes, I see.

8: So, just as you would go about showing yourself that you have choices, so you could help a friend who is in Victim to realise that they always have choices. And if they are open to it, you might be able to help them to reach for a transcendent choice… a choice that not only shows them that they are not a Victim but, in fact, a far greater version of themselves than they previously thought.

And that is the path of the Unifier. That is the way of a being who is returning to Oneness.

Z: That's brilliant, 8. Thank you. I will apply that to my life. I will make it my way.

8: Instead of simply accepting this as gospel I would suggest to you that you try living this and then see how it works for you. Remember I am not here to impart instructions or doctrine or dogma. I am simply offering you a choice. So if you choose to take this on board, then I recommend that you do so with an experimental mind-set. If you want to try it out then of course you need to really *live it* in your every interaction every day. Do this for a while until it feels natural. Then take stock of your life and see if you are happier with yourself when you live this way or not. See if your life brings your greater joy or not. See if you feel greater love for yourself and for others or not. Decide if this is right for you based upon your own experience rather than based upon my say so.

Z: Got it. Thanks 8.

8: Good then. But before we can move on from here I would like us to do a little practical work. Let's see how you would apply your new understandings, shall we?

Z: Okay…

8: Alright, then let's create a scenario. Imagine you have a friend, let's call him Uther, who is quite badly stuck in Victim consciousness. Uther is struggling a bit with his life and many aspects of it are just not working out for him. He expresses to you some ideas such as, "*I hate my job and my boss is an idiot*" and "*These stupid politicians are screwing up the whole country*" and "*My wife just doesn't understand me*" and "*Nothing ever goes my way*" and "*If I had just had different parents as a kid I wouldn't be so messed up today*". Such ideas. You can see he is in pain. You can see his life is not bringing him joy and he clearly doesn't know how to improve matters.

Now that you know what you know, what would you do?

Z: Hmm… I can empathise. I have felt some of these things in my life and so I know what he is feeling. I'm not there anymore – I now understand things differently. But I sure can understand that he is where he is.

8: So? What do you do?

Z: Well… let me apply the three steps.

First I recognise that All is One and All is perfect. Both Uther and I are perfect expressions of The One. I am motivated only by love.

Second and Third I state my intent to make a choice which not only does to Uther that which I would want done to myself, but does to Uther realising that I AM doing exactly that to myself… that I am willing to make that exact choice for myself.

(I give a little thought to the situation and then…)

Alright. This is what I have come up with. I'll sit with Uther and be right there with him where he is at. I'll let him tell me about his pain and confusion and give him a safe place to share without being judgemental and without criticising him or making him wrong. At most I will ask him questions that will allow him to better express what is going on in his life. I'll make sure I am really hearing him and check my understanding with him to be sure I have really got it. I will give him the gift of my full attention and my listening. I will bear witness. I will "be present" with Uther.

That is the choice I have come up with and I feel it is a good one because it is congruent with the three steps. I myself would be very, very happy if someone should offer me such an attentive and loving ear if I had some pain that I was working through.

8: Excellent. You make me proud. And I can give you another reason why this is a good choice: if you were to apply this, you would be amazed at how much progress Uther would make towards solving his own problems. Just being in the presence of a loving attentive listener like that will almost always bring great healing. Progress will follow. And after simply talking to you in this manner Uther is most likely to say to you, "*You have helped me SO much!*" or something similar. And you will tell him, "*No, my friend, I just listened. You helped yourself.*" And both of you will walk away feeling uplifted.

Quite different from the situation where you decided to rush in and rescue Uther, where you told him exactly how he must pull himself together and what he should do to fix up his life. Such a path would result in you both feeling blocked, unheard and resentful.

Z: Hmm. Yes. I've been there. On both sides of that equation. It just doesn't work.

8: Alright now, the next question. What will you do if Uther asks you for advice? Perhaps he finds he is not making enough progress by just talking about his life. Or perhaps he sees you are not struggling as he is and wants to tap into your learning and experience. What then?

Z: Again I will apply the three steps (I give it a little thought).

What I have come up with is that it will be unhelpful if I tell Uther what he must do. Because I can only put myself in his position to some extent. I can't really know fully what it is to be where he is. What I CAN do is tell him what I think I would do in his situation and why I think it would be helpful. Then he can make his own choices. Also I will make it clear to him that I do not expect of him that he should do what I say. I offer my thoughts with love and he is welcome to do with them as he sees fit.

I think a really great way for me to tell him what I think is by telling him some appropriate part of my story. Then he can hear for himself how similar (or otherwise) he thinks my experience was to his and he can hear what I did in that situation and how it turned out for me. Then he can decide for himself if he will do as I did, or do as I suggest (if that is different from what I actually did).

This works for me because, again, it is congruent with the three steps. If I had a friend who has sorted something out that I was still struggling with I would like it if I could ask his advice. I would want him to have the freedom to give me his advice. I would want it given in such a way as to allow me to see how he applied it in his life and how it worked for him – or why it is that he feels it would work for me. And finally I wouldn't want him to get all attached to the outcome that I do exactly as he says. If I want to hear his advice, and yet have the freedom not to apply it, that must be okay with him. Or else I don't want his advice at all.

8: That is well said.

And I'd like to point something out to you.

Z: Yes?

8: If your friend Uther asked you for advice on how he could free himself from his Victim consciousness… is it not possible that you could simply share THE ASCENSION PAPERS with him?

Z: Oh, right. (laughs) That is exactly what I could have done! And it is exactly what I would have wanted. When I felt deeply lost in my own Victim state I would have wanted someone to give me exactly this book.

8: So truly THE ASCENSION PAPERS IS you doing to others that which you would most like done to yourself.

Z: Hmm… yes… I see! This is quite perfect, isn't it?

8: Together all of us are providing the Self with a path out of a difficult position in a way that is both gentle and respectful. It is true that the Self who writes the book and the Self who reads this book may choose to accept the wisdom herein or reject it. Or to take the bits and pieces they might like. This is the way you would want it to be given to you, is it not? Sharing with no coercion?

Z: It is, yes.

8: And so you give away that which you most desire and, in so doing, you give it to yourself! That is the beauty of your sharing it.

And so we discover an important corollary to the idea that you should only give to another that which you are willing to receive for yourself. It is this: if there is something you feel you want or need, then you should find a way to give that which you need to another. Because indeed it is so that you always gain that which you first give away.

Z: That's lovely, 8. I understand that in a whole new way now. I will apply this and see how it works for me.

8: Good boy! And then you can let go of the need to rescue anyone ever again, can't you?

Z: I certainly can.

Because when I play Rescuer then I am giving away that which I actually DON'T want. I don't want someone else to make my decisions for me, to take my learning opportunities from me or to tell me what to do.

8: Good. So then don't do it to others.

Give only that which you would desire for yourself.

Z: That's great, thanks 8.

8: There is one last thing I would say to you about helping other beings who finds themselves in Victim. It is this: please remember that it is their perfect right to remain in Victim, if that is what they wish. The fact that they are asking you for help does not mean you should attach yourself to the idea that they should change in the way you want them to change. You can offer your help but you cannot force them to take it. You cannot demand of them that they do what you expect them to do simply because they have expressed a need to you. Almost everyone on this planet is still busy playing the Victim game. Most people still need their Victim dramas to continue to play out so that they can have the experiences they came here to have. Even if they ask you for help and even if they say they want to stop playing victim, STILL it might be that they actually want, and need, to continue with Victim. It is not your place to coerce them to change.

Z: Yes, I can see that. I agree that I should either offer my help without expectation or not offer it at all.

8: Yes. Apply the three-step process with courage and an open heart. At the very least you will be creating yourself as a being of loving compassion who is not a Victim. That is a good start. The degree to which the other being gains value and makes changes in their life is up to them.

Z: Thank you 8. I will try all these strategies and see how they work in my life.

8: Good. If properly applied and adapted to each situation you should find yourself releasing the direct experience of evil from your own situation.

Z: Thanks 8. But what about indirect experiences? Like… what about all the stuff that goes on "out there" in the world? There is a whole lot of bad stuff happening on this planet. How do I release the experience of that from myself?

8: That sounds like the perfect cue for the third part of this conversation:

Manifestations of Evil

We aren't going to look at ALL the ways in which evil is manifest. A complete list will need many more pages than you would be able to type. What we are going to do is to confine ourselves to addressing the areas of concern you asked about. These were:

1. People willing to commit genocide for the sake of power, wealth or political expediency

2. Terrorists

3. People who would rape children and babies

4. Demons and demonic possession

5. Lucifer, Satan and the Devil

I'm going to talk to you about each of those issues and then, when I am done, you will be able to release your concerns about them. And then you will also be willing to understand that it is truly so that...

> *"if there is such a thing as evil, then it is an opportunity to learn about love."*

Irrespective of the context.

Are you amenable?

Z: Of course! Let's do it.

8: Alright then.

The first manifestation of evil you wanted to know about was:

People willing to commit genocide for the sake of power, wealth or political expediency

Let me begin to tell you about these people by continuing where we just left off when we were talking about Rescuer. Remember I was just saying that there are many people who are not done with their own Victim dramas?

Z: Yes.

8: Well it is so that the greatest majority of people on your planet are indeed still deeply engaged with the Victim state. And so it is that pretty much everyone you would meet from day to day is, to one extent or another, playing out a number of concurrent Victim dramas in their lives.

This is right and appropriate because this is what they came to this planet for. On a soul level they chose to come here and they knew they were going to have these experiences when they made these choices.

Z: ...and so we shouldn't try to rescue them. I get that.

8: Steady on. I am making another point now. Not only should you not try to rescue them but you should also allow that they actually need a Perpetrator. If you are going to sit on the one side of a see-saw, then you need someone to sit on the other side. That's the only way to make the ride work. Well in just this way, Victim and Perpetrator need each other. The one without the other has no movement. And until each being is ready to finally release the whole Victim experience they will still need Perpetrators. Until they make this decision powerfully and finally on a soul level they will not be able to leave this game behind and move on to another perhaps kinder, more loving game. Until each of you has mastered both the dark and the light of your own souls, you will not be your own master. And only masters ascend.

And so... the point I am making is that there is a need for Perpetrators to allow Victims to experience and explore their own beings. To provide them with the choices that they need so that they can create themselves again and again until they have mastered themselves.

Z: I see. But how does this pertain to these people who would commit genocide.

8: What I have just said pertains to all Victim/ Perpetrator relationships. But alright, let's get into the specifics of this question: those who commit genocide for the sake of expediency.

How about I use an example of something that is very much in your planetary consciousness right now? An issue that is highly emotive, thorny and hotly debated. How about I use the example of the 9-11 attack on the World Trade Centre?

Z: Whew! That certainly is a very contentious issue for many here on earth. But now we're talking about terrorism and I thought we were supposed to be talking about genocide.

8: I know. I am not in the habit of letting my attention wander. If YOU were paying attention you would recall that we were actually talking about the PEOPLE who would commit genocide. If you are to understand these people and how and why they act as they do, then you will need to understand that genocide itself is just one of the deeds that they get up to. It is really just one page in a much greater story. And if I am to tell you this story, then it is best I begin telling it from a place to which you can relate.

The Story of John, the Conspiracy Theorist

I will begin by telling a story of a man – we shall call him John – who has lost a family member in what has been called "the 9-11 terrorist attack". This was quite possibly the most visible terrorist attack in the history of humanity. It was captured on film from every angle and shown over and over again on television around the world. Not only was John deeply aggrieved by his loss, but the way in which this vile act was presented to him over and over again resulted in his grief becoming inflamed to the point of profound rage.

"What kind of foul, evil demon would do this?" John wondered about these terrorists. And almost magically, in answer to his question, there appeared on his television screen an image of a bearded man in a turban. This, he was told, was the arch-villain. This was the evil mastermind behind the whole operation. There were even recordings in which this man claimed responsibility. And soon after that John saw further images on his television of other middle-eastern men. These dark-eyed foreigners with a foreign religion and an ideology of hatred were the Perpetrators, the talking heads on the television told him. Finally, John had a target for his rage. And the way all this was presented to him caused the target of his hatred to grow from a small handful of men to a whole culture… a whole religion. In fact John found he now hated the residents of a whole geographical region! And when the cowboy-hatted president of his nation talked war talk, John found his voice calling agreement: Yes, punishment! Yes, vengeance! Yes, retribution! John found the idea of going to war against the terrorists an idea that he could very easily support. If he wasn't too old, he told himself, he'd volunteer himself. He'd love to go and kill some of those "evil monsters," he told himself.

And of course John was not the only one in his country to feel this way. Or even the world. This was quite a popular sentiment for a while there.

And so there was war.

But it was a complicated war. John's fervour first began to wane when he read about "collateral damage". It's a term that means civilians being killed. You see John is a bright enough fellow and his heart is actually in the right place. And this wasn't what he wanted. He wanted TERRORISTS punished. Not simple, poor village folk in some far away country. But all the time there was this idea of catching the chief terrorist. A man in a turban who had made video recordings in which he had taken responsibility for the 9-11 attack. That was an idea that John could still get behind. And while he waited for the chief terrorist to be brought to justice, somehow this one war became two. John wasn't entirely sure how that happened. First they were hunting in the mountains for this arch-enemy and then they were looking for Weapons of Mass Destruction in a different country altogether. Which had links, the television told him, to the 9-11 terrorists. Traumatised, fearful and very angry John was willing to keep supporting the war effort. *"Go kill them all,"* was his thought on the subject.

But the more these wars dragged on, the more the fire left John's belly. This began to look less and less like a good and righteous war to him. First, there were no Weapons of Mass Destruction to be found. Then he read that there was no connection at all between the 9-11 terrorists and this second country. He began to suspect that there was another reason for all this. He wondered if it wasn't just all about oil. Or possibly all about a vendetta between his country's leader and the leader of the other country. And then, a little later, John first encountered a conspiracy theory which claimed that the whole 9-11 attack had been instigated by people inside his own country's government!

The conspiracy theorist came with all kinds of evidence that supported the contention that it was not, after all, two airliners that brought the two skyscrapers down but, in fact, explosives that must have been placed inside the buildings before the time. And then there was the video he saw showing a third building being demolished with no aeroplane hitting it at all. At first John rejected these ideas. They were too abhorrent to contemplate. But the ideas fascinated him because he had no answer for them. They taunted him in his mind. So he kept going back to the Internet to look for more. And he kept finding more. More and more evidence that, at the very least, a group of people in power in his government had worked quite hard to allow the aircraft attacks to happen. More and more evidence that the buildings were actually destroyed with explosives. Never any proof – but always more evidence.

Layer upon layer of cover-ups. Facts not fitting with the official story. Professionals in various industries such as engineers, architects, pilots and so forth all coming forward with more probing, unanswered questions. All saying that the official story did not fit the facts. All demanding the truth. All convinced that the official story was a whitewash. And then John finally decided for himself that the conspiracy theories were true. And, as soon as he opened this door, he was hit by an avalanche. The deeper down the rabbit hole he went, the more information he found. More and more stories of deception and deceit that had played out across the face of the globe and going back into history. Shameful covert operations being conducted with, it seemed, the knowledge and blessing of his countries leaders. Murders and assassinations, wars instigated in foreign lands, arms and equipment supplied to despots and madmen to use upon their own people, narcotics being traded for guns... on and on it went. Everywhere John looked he found stories detailing gross abuses of public trust by those in power, which were then hidden behind layers of lies and deception. And these conspiracy theories all tied together. The one leading to the other. All of them adding up in a way that, quite sickeningly, explained why the world was the way it was. It went a long way toward explaining why there was so much hatred in the world.

And that is where we leave John.

Z: Wow, 8. You paint quite a bleak picture. And is it all true – all this conspiracy theory stuff?

8: True?

Z: Yes, I mean did it all happen the way the conspiracy theorists say?

8: (sighs) My dear young friend. I know this is hard for you to understand but please try. There is no objective truth outside of yourself other than, *"The One IS"*, remember?

Z: Oh yes. I do remember that. But surely this attack either happened one way or it did not.

8: No. You still don't really get it yet. There is NO objective truth of this story that exists outside of yourself – or of any other story, for that matter. It doesn't exist. Things simply do not work that way. There are perspectives and probabilities which all of you, inside this game, are busy co-creating. But no single version is fixed. No single version is eternally valid. So the only thing you need to concern yourself with is your own subjective experience. And for each of you this is a little different. You each have a slightly different experience and story. But here is the thing: so please pay attention to what I am about to say. It is not the "story" that is important. You believe it is, but it isn't. The story is just a mechanism, a device, a plot line, which you are using as a vehicle to understand yourself and to create yourself.

So listen! Now I will tell you something important.

It does not matter what did, or did not, happen. What matters is the way you feel about it. What you decide, choose and create as a result of this perceived external stimulus. What is important is your own inner-reality.

So there is The Truth Of You, and then there is the story that you are using to help you to get to The Truth Of You. The story is subordinate. It is only of importance whilst it serves the primary goal. Which is your self-discovery and self-creation.

You understand?

Z: I do, thanks 8. I mean I understand what you are saying and it does make sense and I really appreciate it. But I don't understand yet how there is no <u>one</u> version of events. How can there be many equally true stories?

8: You'll get there. In time you will certainly come to see that it is so and can only be so. For now, let us return to our discussion.

So I say again… there is the STORY and then there is THE TRUTH OF YOU. Now I want to get back to our friend John. I want to talk about his subjective experiences and I want to look at how he can now create himself as a result of them.

You see, from the ultimate perspective, the question of conspiracy theories being true or not is an irrelevant question. It is meaningless. But from John's direct, personal and subjective experience, it is an over-riding and vital question. And if John is willing to be really deeply honest with himself, he will admit that there is no absolute proof of anything in any direction. No-one has been able to offer any kind of evidence that would make any particular version of the truth absolute and unarguable. All he has is a burgeoning collection of evidence from which he can reach his own conclusions. And if he is deeply honest and also incredibly observant – then he will realise that it is his own ideas, beliefs and preconceptions that lead him to collect the evidence he has collected. You see? He IS creating his reality without even being aware of it. John believes he is simply observing his outer reality. But he is not. He is going out into his world and carefully filtering what he observes and then creating a picture inside himself with the puzzle pieces he has hand-picked. Given a slightly different starting position, with a slightly different set of presuppositions, John would have gone about collecting different bits of evidence and holding onto different ideas of what is true. He would end up with an entirely different belief about what was going on in his "story".

His story… history. It is all fiction. A selection of perspectives and views. Collect different perspectives and views and it all looks entirely different.

But it is not the story that matters; it is what you do with it. How you feel about it. Because THAT is when you are creating yourself and discovering yourself. Dis-covering. Removing the cover. Exposing yourself for what you really are.

Z: Fantastic stuff, 8! This is awesome. I am beginning to understand now. So how did John create himself?

8: Well, you see, John very much does believe in an external truth about events. And, as a result of his journey, he came to decide that the conspiracy theories were mostly true. They made sense to him. He found them to be an accurate reflection of his reality. And so? Given that, what was John to do? How was he to respond?

And the answer, of course, is that it depends entirely on what he really wants. He must decide what he wants, and he will create himself with his choices.

If he wants to do so, he can go on a crusade for "the truth" in which he seeks to force the government to loosen its steely grip on its secrets. To try to force those in power to tell the truth. To go and meet and interview those that were there at ground zero. Find and view new video footage of the event. Talk to experts. Try to "awaken" his fellow citizens to "the truth" (while they, on the whole, would really prefer to hit the snooze button one more time). He can do that. And there are many versions of John doing exactly that right now. And there is nothing wrong with that if that is what they want to do.

Or he can let it go and give up. Decide the machine is far too big to battle and he can walk away with a deep sense of distrust and disillusionment.

Or he can get active in politics and try to fix the system from within. Perhaps look for some lone voice inside the system who looks to be an honest broker of the truth to support. Get involved in trying to get more voters for this "person of truth" within the "system of lies".

And of course there are many, many other ways in which John might respond. You see, he is constantly being offered all kinds of choices all along the way. It seems as if there are a million different things he can choose at every point – will he believe this theory or that one? Will he trust this politician or that one? Will he protest against this thing or support that thing? Will he go to that town hall meeting and raise his concerns? Will he lose faith enough to take his anger and distrust underground, to get guns and ammunition and have clandestine meetings with others of a like mind? And what about a legal challenge to force those who are in power to tell the truth? Or will he put his faith in the system once more and trust that it will repair itself? What about just voting for the "right" candidate this time?

So many, many choices.

But you see, that too is all an illusion. There is really only one choice: to go deeper into the Victim game or to raise yourself out of it. And ALL of the choices outlined above for John are really just the same choice: to go deeper into the game. You see the game itself never shows you the other option… it never shows you that you can raise yourself out of the game. Instead it dazzles you with stage-magician lights. You only see the choices it wants you to see and ALL of those choices are about going deeper into the game. This is why it is such a successful system. It keeps everyone playing the same game. Exactly as it is meant to.

Z: So you are saying that the game is designed so as to keep the Victims playing and believing?

8: The game is designed to show you only the choices that keep you playing the game… the Victim choices. It is particularly good at offering you the kind of choices where you end up supporting the victimisation of other people. Those are the best kind of game-continuing choices. If you can be induced to cause another person to be victimised too, then the game is working twice as well.

And now I want to talk a little about the engine room of these choices. To do so, I want to introduce you to someone else. Let's call him Maximillian, or Max for short. Max is what I call a "Super Powerful Individual".

The Super Powerful Individuals

Z: What, like the president of a country, or the owner of a large corporation, or what?

8: No, a Super Powerful Individual would be one of a very small number of people who, despite having a great deal of power in your world, is not visible or known. Max would not see himself as a member of one country or another. He would see countries and their political leaders as a means to manage assets. He would not think of himself as merely owning corporations, he would think of corporations as tools for his use. Max is one of a handful of people, who together own everything worth owning on the planet. In fact they would probably believe that they own the people of the planet too. And most especially they would feel as if they own everyone that you would normally count to be powerful: presidents, CEOs, kings and cardinals are all the SPI's special assets. Politicians come and go with election terms. Members of corporate boards can be unseated by the shareholders. But the SPI is there to stay. Behind the scenes. Unseen. Untouchable.

If you were a man like Max, then you would hold some pretty impressive powers. If you wanted the democratically elected leader of a country deposed, you could arrange that. You could have that leader replaced with someone who would be more amenable to your desires, if that is what you wanted. And, as you control the flow of capital around the world, so you could dictate how one region would get richer and another poorer. You could bring on boom times and you could trigger a global financial bust. You could start wars on a regional or even global scale or you could stop them. You have that kind of power.

Now, let me ask you a question. If you were Max, what would you want?

Z: That's an interesting question. I guess I wouldn't actually WANT for anything. Not anything material anyway. I'd have everything I could possibly imagine I needed. I guess I'd probably decide to enjoy my wealth and power by finding ways to use it to help others.

8: You'd essentially begin to give it away?

Z: Yes. I think so.

8: Glad to hear it. And so would the other SPIs. That would mean that they would be able to gobble up your empire and, in so doing, become even more wealthy and powerful. And I won't even bother getting into the details of how tough you'd actually find it to give your money away responsibly – so that the giving did not cause more harm than it solved. That's a whole other point. But the point I will make is that you would very soon become irrelevant in the world of the Super Powerful. You would very quickly no longer be very powerful at all. So I'm going to ask you to try to answer the question again. Try to shift your perspective. Try to imagine yourself as someone who IS that powerful. You would not have become that powerful if you hadn't been honed and trained from birth to be the bearer of that power. You would only be that powerful if you were very determined to remain so.

Z: Oh I see. Because I would actually be in a sort of competition with all the other Super Powerful people.

8: Yes. It is a sort of a game. Sometimes a breathtakingly cruel and vicious game. But a game none the less.

Z: Okay. I see. So you ask what I would want. If I try to imagine myself into that person's shoes, then I suppose I would want to "play the game". I would want to win it. Even though I would have obscene wealth and power… I would want MORE. As does everyone else "at the top". My desire would be to be the very best at the game and to outmanoeuvre all the other SPIs and grab ever more power and control.

8: You intuitively can see that it would be so?

Z: Yes.

8: And what would you want with respect to all the little folks "at the bottom"? All the regular folks who are factory workers and clerks and shop-assistants and office managers and what-not?

Z: Umm… I guess I'd want them to keep working. To keep slaving away. And to do what I want them to do when I want them to do it. And to not get noisy and disobedient along the way.

8: And what if they did get disobedient? What if some of them stopped serving your will? What if they began to realise what was going on? What if one day someone looked up from the factory floor and said, "*I don't like this job awfully much. I'm going to do something I love doing instead. I'm going to find my most blissful expression of Self and discover my true nature and then ascend from this system*". What then?

Z: Well that would be bad news for me. Because obviously such a thing could catch on. If others saw this guy doing what he loved and being happy, then they might want to do it too. Soon all my minions would be off making daisy chains and singing "Kumbaya" and making tie-dyed clothing or whatever. They wouldn't be serving me. I'd start to lose at the game.

8: But it's okay, isn't it, because that isn't going to happen. I mean, think for a second. How many people who are slaving away in factories, shops and offices around the world can just give up and do what they want?

Z: Not very many at all.

8: And why is that?

Z: Well mostly they have debts to pay. And even if they have no debt, how will they pay for stuff like food and housing and so on? And even if they could pay for that, what about the future? What about their children's education?

8: Exactly. So that's the first point. Debt. Remember these Super Powerful Individuals run the show. They essentially own the world's economy. Certainly they own all the banks. So, the more folks are deeply in debt, the more they keep slaving away. In the factories, shops and businesses that are also owned by the Super Powerful.

Z: Wow. That's pretty shocking.

8: No. That's still nothing. There are many other ways to keep Joe, the factory worker's, eye down on the factory floor. Debt is only one of them. Some of the others are even nastier. Remember the example above of the 9-11 attack?

Z: Oh no! You mean the 9-11 attack is nothing but a huge control mechanism to keep people manipulable?

8: What do YOU think?

Z: I… uh… Oh but wait a minute, 8. What happened to all that stuff about "the story being less important than The Truth Of You". Are you now saying that the conspiracy theories are true?

8: No. I am telling you a story. Nothing more, nothing less. Or did you feel at some point I was demanding of you that you must believe me?

Z: But 8! What's the point of this if it isn't true?

8: The point? It is the same as the point of the story that you are telling yourself by living your life. The point is that you are giving yourself experiences so that you can choose and create. Exactly as I told you before. I am telling you about this so that you can hit rock-bottom on the victim drug to which you are addicted so that you can decide to let it go and CREATE! Take ownership! Wake up! Discover who you really are!

If ANYTHING I have said to you in all of our conversations was true, do you think there would be a story out there that was absolute? That was not actually a creation… a fiction… an elaborate stage play? YOUR stage play that YOU are co-creating!

Z: So then, what is the value of telling me about these SPIs? Why not tell me any old mother goose story?

8: I could. But it would not conform to your experience. It would not be of use to you. I'll say it again, so PLEASE pay attention this time round, okay? It really IS the important bit and you really must try to take notice of this:

There is NO objective truth to any story. There are only perspectives and probabilities, which all those playing each game co-create together. But even so, each co-creator has their own unique perspective, experience and story within the greater story. There is no one absolute story, which makes any other story untrue. Which is okay because it is not, after all, the story that is important. You simply need to pretend that the story is the most important thing for the game to work. But as you are now leaving the game, you can come to the realisation that the story is simply the means by which you show yourself your inner being as projected into an outer reality. You simply use the mechanism of the story to discover yourself and create yourself. Now, the story can be very compelling. It is meant to be. But you are now ready to realise that it is only of value in the context of THE TRUTH OF YOU. Other than that, it is meaningless.

And so you can now understand the story for what it is. It is something that you can use to show yourself something about yourself and then, depending on how much you like what you see about yourself, you can make new choices about yourself.

Discover yourself and create yourself. That is the point of all of it.

So now you ask me why I tell you about these SPIs. Well here is the answer: I myself am now using story. I am using your story. Your co-created reality. And I am telling you something about your story. You can decide for yourself to what degree what I am telling you is valid. And then you can decide what this information tells you about yourself. And then you can decide how you will create yourself.

How's that?

Z: I'm actually quite deeply shocked by that, 8. I think I only now get what you were saying about "story". And I don't know how to respond. It makes me feel as if there is no more point in hearing about these things. If it is all just made up… then what is the point in talking about it?

8: Alright, let me help you with this.

Do you remember dreaming last night?

Z: Yes. As a matter of fact I had a very long and elaborate dream. And then I woke up and I was telling Lisa about my dream and she and I had a conversation about the dream. And then I woke up again! And I realised that BOTH experiences had been a dream.

8: Many people will have these kinds of dream-within-a-dream experiences. If you are willing to pay attention to it, it is a very important message you are imparting to yourself in such a dream. You are showing yourself how you can wake up from a dream and believe that you are awake, that the dream was all just a fiction, and yet you are STILL inside a dream. It is still all just a fiction. And then you wake up again and…

…and…

Z: I guess I can realise that I AM STILL living inside a fiction.

8: Yes. And it is quite a compelling fiction. I mean, do you not feel that there is a character who has chosen the name Zingdad and who is choosing to write a book called THE ASCENSION PAPERS?

Z: Yes. I do. I feel like that is me.

8: And there are many people around the world who are co-creating this fiction. They ALSO believe there is a character called Zingdad who is writing this book called THE ASCENSION PAPERS. But they experience this fiction a little differently. They experience this character as being "elsewhere". As being someone they found on the Internet. Someone who lives far away who writes these words that they can read.

But what would happen if you all should now wake up and realise that this was just a great, elaborate dream that you dreamed together? If you realised that the Zingdad character was just your character in the dream and that you are something much more? Something much more creatively powerful and real. And THE ASCENSION PAPERS were not actually a book that YOU were writing, but that it was actually one of a number of mutually agreed upon wake-up calls that you had all arranged for yourselves. A bit like setting an alarm clock before going to sleep.

What then?

Would you then wake up and say, "*Oh, those stories were just stories. And stories are unimportant and meaningless. It's all just rubbish. Let's forget it and go and do something real.*"

Or would you see the great beauty and truth that was shown to you in your magnificent stories that span many lifetimes… often hundreds of lifetimes. Would you come together and share your experiences and learnings? Would you show each other your stories? Would you love and cherish the experiences? Would you see the great value that you have extracted?

Z: Yes. Yes. I see it.

These lives we are living are our stories. And we, collectively, are telling ourselves these stories. We are the authors of the tale and we are the characters inside the tale. And in telling living these stories we are discovering some very powerful truths about ourselves. And that is why the stories are important.

Okay.

But then why is it important to understand about these Super Powerful Individuals?

8: It works like this: your readers experience the reality of Zingdad in their lives because their lives are impacted by his works. They believe you exist, because they read this book. And, as a result of this, they are offered choices in this work and they can decide for themselves how they are going to respond and create themselves.

But how would it be if you experience an impact on your life, but its origin is very cleverly hidden from you. You see, there are these other beings who are experiencing themselves to be these SPIs. That is the fiction they are creating for themselves in this story. And their works are quite pervasive. You'd have to live very far from any so-called civilisation in order to completely avoid being impacted by their works. But you struggle to make decisions about this impact because it is not obvious what is going on. And that is what I am doing: I am helping to make overt that which was hidden.

I said before that there is no one single story that is absolutely true. I also said that there are only probabilities and perspectives. What I should add now is this: the more energy that is put into a particular probability, the more that probability gains value. The less energy that is put into it, the more it fades away into non-existence.

Z: You mean the more we believe in something the more real it is?

8: Something like that. You make choices and by your choices you focus your energies. When you focus your energy on something, you add to its creation. You make it more real for yourself. If many people join together and make something real for themselves, then this thing has a greater probability. That is how a co-created world works. And sometimes you are misdirected. You are collectively mesmerised into putting your energies into things, which actually feed something hidden behind it. You feed an illusion and the creator of the illusion is fed as well.

And that is what is happening here. Even though very few of you know of the existence of the SPIs, still you are very vividly and powerfully bringing them into your reality by focusing your energies on that which they are presenting to you.

So I wish to tell you what it is that they are doing and how. Then you will be aware. Then you can release your energies from that. Then you can cease to create this for yourself. Unless of course you like it, in which case... well that would be up to you.

Z: Ah.

Thank you again for your patience, 8. I appreciate that you are prepared to nurse-maid me to my own awakening. This really does begin to make sense to me.

I am ready to get back to the story of the SPIs. I want to know how they are featuring in my story so that I can make better choices in my life.

8: That's great. Well done.

Z: Alright, so you were saying something about the 9-11 attack. You were suggesting that maybe the SPIs were actually behind this? Really?

8: Yes. I didn't use the example of 9-11 for nothing when I was telling you about John. I was showing you how it might be a story whose plotline is being directed by the SPIs. Such things have been going on all through your history. One of the best methods the SPIs have to keep their minions servile is to stoke a war. As long as people can be convinced that there is some evil other nation, evil other religion, evil other WHATEVER out there that wishes to destroy them, their family and their way of life... then sure as nuts they will be willing to put their shoulder to the wheel and do their bit. Maybe they will even feel they must volunteer to go to fight in the war. And then, if they die in the war, there is just one more reason for everyone else in their family to get angry and full of hatred at the wicked enemy.

Anger and hatred... these are probably even better than debt at keeping people in duality and separateness.

And did you ever wonder about religions?

Z: Religions? What specifically?

8: Well isn't it really very, very peculiar that most religions seem to be founded upon the words and deeds of the most deeply peaceful humans who ever walked the earth? I mean – all dogma and beliefs aside – if you go and have a look at what is at the core of these religions' teachings, then they are about a striving for peace amongst people and a desire to do right in the world. And yet you keep finding the most fervent adherents of one of these systems of peace being whipped up to go and kill the most fervent adherents of some other system of peace. It happens so often, it's not even thought of as strange. And sometimes the differences in faith are so minor as to be indistinguishable to outsiders.

Does this not seem really odd?

Z: Yes. I hadn't thought about it that way before.

8: And so now I have to ask you – how does it happen that a person who believes in one of these religions with all its beautiful thoughts about loving your brother and so forth... how does it happen that such a person is persuaded to kill his other brother from another faith?

Z: I don't know.

8: Well, I'll tell you. It happens by the simple expedient of some leader telling him that the person of the other faith is not, in fact, his brother. He gets told that the other faith is an abomination. It is evil. And that HIS faith actually permits the killing of people of another faith. Not only permits it, but REQUIRES it.

Mad, huh?

That a system of love, peace and tolerance could be the very reason why you should allow yourself to be so deeply bigoted that someone who believes something just a little different from what you do, should be killed.

No internal inconsistencies there then! (he laughs sadly)

Z: Wow. That's a very good point, 8. So why? Why would these religious leaders do that?

8: Well it's quite simple. It's those Super Powerful folks again. They noticed a good while ago that there were these spiritual teachings that were counter-productive to their interests. Every now and again a teacher would come round spreading a message of love, peace, unity and tolerance that would cause a few of their minions to lose interest in the duality game. Sometimes there were even schools directly teaching ascension, which led to the minions exiting the game. So the super powerful ones devised a very cunning plan indeed. They found a way to turn these religions to their own use. Instead of allowing the religions to continue being simple sets of faith shared by people ministering to each other as brother and sister, they were politicised. Power structures were built into the religions. Dogmas were established. They were turned into ORGANISATIONS. Often religious leaders were more powerful than kings and emperors. And then it was decreed that the people of a certain area HAD to follow a particular faith. They were ordered: "*You MUST believe THIS*". And if you believed differently from the dogma, you were punished. Usually very cruelly and violently and mostly ending in death. And now the people in charge of these wonderful systems of peace were suddenly men of great power. See how it works?

Z: That's pretty sickening.

8: I can see how it might feel that way to you. But remember...

> "*There is not a single thing that is good or evil, but that you feel that way about it.*"

Z: Oh yes.

8: So that means it is your choice to be here in this system. The system is designed to keep you here. You keep getting every inducement to stay.

So these Super Powerful Individuals... are they evil?

Z: Well, it seems to me as if they are certainly capable of behaving in some pretty evil ways. That is to say, the incarnated aspects certainly do. And the incarnated aspects of us "minions" certainly could feel as if we were the victims of a great evil being perpetrated upon us.

But, if I understand this correctly, that is a lower-order perspective. And choosing that perspective will result in my staying here in duality. My anger and indignation will cause me to want to strike back. And so I will stay separate from the Oneness.

8: …which means they win. Even if it is the Super Powerful that you decide to hate and fight against – it doesn't matter – the fact that you decide to hate and to fight means they win. Because you stay here. And you stay serving their agenda. See how it works? And if, for example, you decide to band together with other warriors and take up arms against them, if you decide to fight against them, guess what will happen next?

Z: I don't know.

8: Along will come someone who is a worthy and capable leader. Someone well versed in strategy and warfare. Someone who seems to hate "the evil sons-of-bitches" even more than you do! And then you'll be ready to follow him to battle, to do what he says, and... bingo!... You're back in the game serving them. Directly and indirectly. Directly, because they are masters of the strategy of managing any opposition. They do this by making it their business to LEAD that opposition. As you begin to organise a resistance group, so they will find ways to put their puppet in charge of your resistance group. You won't know it, but your leader will be one of their minions strategically positioned in your organisation by them to rule you!

And you serve them indirectly as well. Who, for example, do you think you will buy your weapons from? Where will you get all your other equipment and infrastructure from? Everything you will need to engage in resistance to the Super Powerful, will be bought from the Super Powerful. And every cent that changes hands in every transaction is also taxed and inflation-taxed to further enrich them. And so on and so on. And the same is true if you engage in more "peaceful resistance". If you congregate with others on Internet forums and discuss "the evils of The Powers That Be" and "spread the word" about the truth of what is really going on. You might think that you are helping to raise consciousness amongst the people of the world. You might think that you are doing something to crimp the activities of the Super Powerful by spreading the truth. And then, as you go, you'll find all kinds of "experts" who seem to be leading lights in the "truth movement". Surely it must have entered your mind that at least SOME of these "leading lights" are in the employ of the Super Powerful? Isn't that what you would do if YOU were the Super Powerful? And if that IS the case, how do you decide whom to trust? Who is telling you the REAL truth and who is selling you a version of the truth that is seeded with lies that are there to manipulate you? Suddenly things are not so simple, are they? You see the Super Powerful didn't get to be the Super Powerful by being stupid. And they have seen and survived every kind of rebellion and insurrection there is. And each time they have become smarter, wilier and more powerful. And they have LONG memories and agendas. They think in terms of many generations, not in terms of what happens now in this lifetime. That is how they succeed so amazingly at the game. And so it is that we arrive at the situation where they have a whole planet full of minions slaving away, doing their bidding and hardly a single one even begins to guess it! And even those who DO discover this seem not to be able to do anything about it. In fact, in trying to do something about it, they just strengthen the hand of the Super Powerful.

And the final point about your waging war against "the evil Illuminati" or whatever you are calling them: who exactly will you strike against? Will you "stick it to the man" by bombing your local government offices? Do you actually think any of the Super Powerful will be found there? And if not there, then where will you find them? And I will tell you: you will not find them! The Super

Powerful are so deeply hidden, so far behind the scenes, that you will never see them or even so much as hear their names. So no matter who you bomb or shoot, you will just be hurting some proxy. Some puppet. Some poor sack who is also just trying to make his way in life as best he can. And so you have not hurt them at all, and all you have done is contribute to a bit more hatred in the world. Which, ironically, just makes them more powerful.

So you lose.

Then you lose.

And then you lose some more.

And when you have lost completely, then you just lose some more.

And THAT is what happens if you try to play the game that way. You cannot beat them, or the system, by fighting it. The game is set up such that you have a handful of nothing and they hold all the aces. And, just in case, they have a selection of every other card they could possibly want up their sleeves.

Remember when I said it was all a game to them? Sometimes a vicious and cruel game, but still a game? The thing to remember about this is that they have a role to play. As long as they keep providing you with the very strongest inducements to stay in the game, then they are doing their job.

Z: THAT'S their job?

8: On a soul-level, yes. Many of their incarnated personalities don't even know this. But essentially that is the soul-contract they have with everyone who enters this particular game. And I know you'll find it quite difficult to drum up much empathy for them right now but, you know, these beings carry a very heavy burden. And their lives, contrary to your popular imaginings, are not very happy at all. It is not just one glamorous party after another. Yes, there are compensations to being the richest and most powerful humans on the planet, but there are some grave costs to the personality as well. Maybe on another day I can go into this in a little more detail, but for now let me give you this summation of their lives:

The Super Powerful are completely hidden from you. If you know a name or have seen a picture in the tabloids or on the television, then this is, at best, a functionary of the truly powerful ones. The SPIs are NOT themselves in politics, nor are they chairmen of boards. They are hidden. They hold the reigns of power THROUGH other individuals who are their functionaries. If you can see the hands on the reigns of power then you are looking at a functionary.

The truly powerful are bred to it. Born, and not made, as they say. You do not get to join their ranks by being successful at business and by being wealthy. You cannot become one of them by joining some secret society and working your way up to the top-most ranks. You cannot join them by winning elections. At most you can become a servant. A conscious and willing slave, perhaps. The Super Powerful are almost a breed apart. It is a vital part of their success strategy that they carefully protect the integrity of their family lines. Their genetic purity is something of an obsession with them. And with good reason. For one thing: their genetics are free from a great number of the afflictions that plague the rest of humanity.

From the very crib they are trained, conditioned and drilled to be what they are. Their upbringing is hard. Much harder than you could imagine. When other babies are being coddled and taught about love and sharing, these ones are being taught tough lessons involving self-discipline and self-reliance. They are taught unquestioning obedience, but only to their master. They are taught that all others are pawns, minions there for their use. Cunning, back-stabbing, deceit, lies and manipulation are all valuable tools of their trade. As long as your actions lead to a greater accumulation of power for your family, then you are serving the family's interests. And if this means you personally rising to power over other SPIs through morally ambiguous means, then that too is acceptable. If not out-right respected.

And whilst ludicrous levels of opulence are taken for granted, kindness, gentleness, patience, tenderness, and such manifestations of love are in pitiful short supply.

There is so much expectation placed upon the shoulders of these ones that there is no place whatsoever for failing to achieve excellently, always, at everything that is endeavoured. Any sign of weakness is derided. It is shameful. It is to be weeded out. Failure is not tolerated.

There is so much more that I could say here about their existence. But all I wish to do for now is to give you but a hint. I'm sure you begin to see that these beings have a very, very hard life. Right from the cradle to the grave. Love, in their eyes, is a luxury they cannot afford. Of course they misunderstand Love. If they did not, they would not be able to think so. But all that too is part of the contract.

Z: But why, 8? Why? I don't understand it at all. If at least they were having a merry old time, living it up, then that would make sense to me. If they were doing this because they really liked having all the power and it really made them happy, then at least that would make sense. But if having the power is really just an almost unbearable burden, then why do it? I mean, if they are so unhappy, why don't they just get their flunkies to come out in the press and on TV and say, *"Sorry folks. There has been a bit of an error. We find we don't actually like running the show. It's not as much fun as it seemed. And we know you folks don't really like the ways things have turned out on your end either. So now we'll all just share our toys and play nice. The party is at our house. Everyone's invited!"* Sort of thing. Then everyone would be happy.

8: Happy? I'm not sure everyone would be happy. If the truth were to begin to come out in that sort of a fashion, then I rather suspect there would be a lot more rage than happiness. How happy would people be if they were told that the reason they have been at war with each other is, quite simply, because both sides had been lied to and manipulated? And that's just one small point. No. The depth of the deception is staggering. And if this began to come out, people would go into shock. There would be all kinds of responses such as denial, anger and rage. Very, very few would respond by deciding to just be happy. And anyway… what makes you think people WANT to be happy?

Z: I… uh…

8: Yes, of course that is what everyone REALLY wants. But if that were your prime motivation – to just be happy – would you really have chosen to incarnate on planet earth in this civilisation and at this time? No. There are places in All That Is that really are all about the finding of happiness. And we'll talk a lot more about that some time soon. But let me assure you, in case you are feeling confused on this point, that this planetary reality at this space/time nexus is not all about people trying to be happy. And THAT is how I can begin to answer your question. You ask me why the Super Powerful Individuals are doing this if it makes them unhappy. Well, I guess I can ask you the same question. Why have any of you come to this planet and incarnated here if it makes you unhappy? As you keep telling us you are, in your prayers and meditations. Why? Why any of this?

Z: I understand we come here to discover who we really are from a position of forgetting.

8: Yes, that is the prime motivation. To discover yourself. To create yourself anew. There are an infinite number of other subordinate reasons. Like healing some pain. Like finding Oneness by exploring not-oneness. Like understanding what Love really is by forgoing it for a while. And so forth. The reality you inhabit is a wonder. It is an unbelievable tool for creation and discovery. And so each of you, for reasons of your own, chose to go there. And each of you will find some wonderful, amazing prize as you leave there.

That is WHY you went there in the first place.

Now. Do you think it would be any different for the Super Powerful Individuals?

Z: I don't know. I suppose not.

8: It will not. Everyone that goes there plays a selection of roles. The Super Powerful play the role which helps to create a particular spiritual climate on your planet.

Z: Explain?

8: At the heart of every human being is a spark of the Divine. You are all therefore essentially good, kind and loving. You each actually WANT to do good, be kind and help each other. You want to find love, express love, BE love. You want your bodies to be healthy and strong. You want your relationships to be good. And so on. So you see, if you all had what you really wanted, it would be a hop, skip and a jump and you'd be discovering your truth in your heart. You'd be bringing amazing quantities of Light into your being and then you'd ascend out of the system. Every second person's Grandpa or auntie would be the most wonderfully wise sage. There would be wisdom for the asking. Concepts like the Oneness of All would be universally understood. There would be no division amongst nations or races or religions or any such. Each would simply follow their own truest path home.

Z: Sounds wonderful!

8: And this is what happens in many other realities. There are even a number of planets in your galaxy where this is the way it is. And it IS wonderful when it is like this. And if that is what you, on a soul level, needed or desired, then that is where you'd be: some other unity-conscious planet where there is peace, love and joy.

But you aren't there, are you?

Z: Apparently not.

So, if I understand you correctly, then I am here in this reality because this is what I, on a soul level, wanted to experience. And this means I actually need these Super Powerful Individuals to do as they are doing. If they did not, the world would not be as it is. And if it was not as it is, I would not have THIS opportunity to experience and express myself.

8: Give the man a cigar!

Z: Jeepers, 8. I'm stunned. If I continue along this path you'll be asking me next to recognise the sacrifice of these individuals… the fact that they give up on a life of simple pleasures where there is love in abundance and joy in the moment so that they can play this hard, cruel role that the rest of us need them to play.

8: Don't be too quick to cry long tears for them. This too was chosen. And everything is by agreement. Just as you agreed to enter into all kinds of loving relationships with friends and family, so you also agreed to enter into the more antagonistic relationships you might have experienced. And, in just the same way, the broader relationships have also been agreed upon. And so it is also true that each of you on earth right now, have at the soul-level entered into an agreement with the Super Powerful. They agreed to provide you with an environment that will make it as compelling as possible for you to stay so that you can play out the other dramas and relationships that you wish to experience. They get the experience they have chosen for themselves in return; don't worry about that. And the rule still applies: whatever they are doing to you as a planetary consciousness they are also doing to themselves. And this will continue until they too see that this doesn't serve them. Until they too are ready to awaken to their greater magnificence. You see? You are all in this together. You are ALL Victims of your own making. Every one of you. Including the SPIs. And this will continue for each of you until you are finally ready to be done with the Victim game in all of its many guises. And then, when you are quite done with all of this, then maybe you will want to play another game. That is when you might decide to break free from the inducements to stay in this reality. If you do, then you will come to a place in your development where all the crazy things that are being instigated in this world will no longer entertain you. You will see through the illusions of this world.

War, religion, a swathe of manufactured diseases, food depleted of nutrients but pumped full of poisons, toxins added to your water supply, debt, inflation and other iniquitous financial ideas, politics, non-stop violence and aggression in entertainment, a ravaged and polluted world, fear-based news media and even things like alcohol, nicotine and drugs, are all just some of the things which are used to keep you from finding love and peace within yourself. Which keep you from seeing every Other as a brother or a sister. Which keep you from knowing that the greatest Truth lies inside your own heart.

But it has always been so that those who chose the ascension path have found, as they have progressed, that these duality inducements began to lose their power. They have found themselves making choices to heal themselves, body, mind and spirit. They have found love, compassion and emotional connection to be more interesting than making more money or gaining more power. And they have realised that the road they are on is of their own choosing and that there is therefore no sense in complaining about it. As they have begun to ascend, so they have found themselves taking an active hand in creating their own path to the greater good of the All. And then they got ready to go home. And soon after that, they left this mortal realm by having their bodies die so that they could return to spirit form to experience the beauty and wonder of the Oneness. Then they became what is often called "Ascended Masters" and, if they so chose, they could do fun things like being channelled by those who were making there way home on the path behind them. Or maybe, if they were extremely brave, they might decide to go back and be a really loving, wise teacher with a message of unity, love and peace. Something like that.

Z: But...

8: Hang on. I'm getting there. You were going to ask about where the Singularity Event comes into all this, weren't you?

Z: Yes. Exactly.

8: Well, okay. That which I outlined above was the old plan. That is how it has been done up to now. But you see, that plan is one which works well so long as you wish to maintain the *status quo*. If you want to keep the engine running, so to speak. But that is no longer the requirement. Now the creator-beings of this reality wish to make some changes. Not the normal cyclical harvest. No, something much more radical. We are going to stop this game, dismantle the apparatus. And then start some entirely new games.

Z: What do you mean when you say, *"The normal cyclical harvest?"*

8: That's quite a complex topic really. All I'll say about it for now is that there are these periodic events, which one might call "the harvest". It is when those in the system who are of an ascension-consciousness are helped to move up into the next dimensional reality. These events recur at regular intervals. These intervals are, from your human perspective, very, very far apart. The last time would have been very far in your pre-history. No record of such a thing survives. Or so it seems. But that too is another topic. And we have wandered far enough. The point is that there are these events. When they occur, a relatively small percentage of beings leave the system and go elsewhere. That is the harvest. What is coming now in your very near future is different. We are not simply harvesting. We are ending the game and starting some new games with completely new rules. There is a Being of great consciousness that actually IS, Itself, the rule set of this whole system. Well, that Being is handing over the reigns to another Being. There will be a fundamental change.

But we cannot just do this with a laugh and a shrug. If we were careless with this, it would be like throwing souls into the meat-grinder. If you'll forgive the analogy. So the very greatest levels of care must be taken to disconnect beings from their desperate clinging attachment to their current creations, such that they are willing to lift their eyes and look into the Light for but a moment. Then we can work with them. Remind them Who They Really Are. Remind them why they are actually here. Remind them that it is all but a game. And then allow them to make some new choices.

And that is what the whole Singularity Event is about. It is the carefully constructed and created gift that is given to this system so that this Great Change can be wrought. It is a gift of love. And it is given to everyone, with no thought as to what they have done, or where they have been, or how they have performed, or any such transitory notions. It is given to ALL, knowing that ALL are perfect manifestations of Divine love. That ALL are playing their roles to perfection. And any idea of one being more worthy than another is but a temporary misunderstanding.

Z: So EVERYONE is going to ascend?

8: No, I cannot say that. What will happen is that the "reset" button will be pushed and everyone will have a chance to choose again. To create a new reality for themselves. But I can't say more about that right now. We'll have to get back to that in another conversation. Firstly, because it's off-topic here and secondly, because I need to help you expand your consciousness a bit more before you can receive that information. If we try now you're very likely to get tripped up in misunderstandings. You are way too attached to linear progression to understand the kind of multiple outcomes that are a better reflection of what will be.

Z: Okay. I accept that. So why did you tell me this now?

8: Planting a seed. And also closing the point about evil. What I am saying is that EVERYONE is going to get to go home soon. Together. Those whom you might now see as "evil", you will soon come to see as the ones who bore the heaviest load. You will see them as your most beloved "sibling-soul" who played a very tough role that you needed played in order to do what you came to do. Whatever that was for each of you.

Z: And what about those who don't choose that? What if some people choose to remain in duality?

8: Not your problem, remember? You are only responsible for you. Follow your heart. Find the beauty inside yourself and be true to that. Each "other" will take care of themselves and will get what they are creating. And if they call for help, then they will get it. And if you hear such a call for help, then you should answer that call in a way that is congruent with your own highest purpose. I know you won't be able to see it now but this is indeed how everyone, and I mean everyone, will get to go home at the ending of the game. Which is very soon going to happen.

And yet, at the same time, it will be possible for someone to choose not to go home; to choose to continue to play duality and separation. But this will just confuse you now. So we'll talk about this some more later, when you are ready to hear what I have to say.

Z: But 8, you say the game is about to end. What if I like living here on earth? What if I love my life? What if I want to keep expressing myself here?

8: Again – another topic of discussion. But let me quickly allay your fears: THE GAME is ending. Not the world. The rules of the game are fundamentally changing. The game of separation and duality will soon be no more. This means that your whole system of reality, as you currently experience it, is going to end. No more war and disease and famine. No more iniquitous financial systems. None of all the artificial silliness, which is currently keeping you in servitude and separation. That all ends soon. And the game, which allows you to treat your Great Mother Earth, this jewel of a planet, as your toilet and your object of abuse… that also ends. So there is a great ending. And then a new beginning. A new day will dawn for those who have stayed the course. If you truly love the planet, then you will inherit it. But the planet you will inherit will be different from the one you currently inhabit. She will be clean and beautiful. And you will have no need or desire to try to despoil her ever again.

But only some of you will want to play on this ascended version of planet Earth. Many will want to play all kinds of other games, elsewhere. And so it will be that each will find a reality that is congruent with who they are, how they have created themselves and what they have chosen.

But I said I would only briefly digress. We were actually talking about the Super Powerful Individuals. And the reason we were talking about them is that you asked about people who would willingly cause genocide for their own expedience.

Z: That's right…

8: Well, by now you might understand if I say to you that the Super Powerful look upon you, the citizens of the world, as their assets. Perhaps a bit in the way a farmer might think about his livestock. The farmer does, in his own way, love his livestock. He husbands them, cares for them, tends their needs, keeps them free from disease, protects them from predators and so on. The relationship shows many of the hallmarks of genuine loving concern. Except, of course, when it comes time to slaughter. When the farmer needs to get a return on his investment, the relationship begins to show some other characteristics. The livestock are loaded onto trucks, carted off to the abattoir and slaughtered.

If you were able to look at all of this with a disaffected eye, you might come to the conclusion that the farmer loves the HERD but does not care at all for a single INDIVIDUAL in it.

Z: And you are saying the Illuminati are like that?

8: Firstly, I prefer not to use the term "Illuminati". Using this term causes misunderstanding. There is a meme in your collective consciousness that there is a hidden organisation, a shadowy group, a cohesive underground unit that is running affairs on your planet. That is an incorrect understanding. These ones, these Super Powerful Individuals, are very much not the kinds of beings who band together and work harmoniously towards a collective goal. There simply is no such organisation. The most cohesive unit of organisation these beings seem to be able to hold together is the family. Some families have extremely dominant, powerful beings at their head and these families prosper because their members are willing to align behind the head. Others are not so successful because they are racked with internal strife over who will lead. Often certain families will form allegiances and will work together for a while. Sometimes those allegiances become institutionalised over time. But to imagine all the Super Powerful Individuals of the planet sitting together, plotting together, working as one, is to quite fundamentally misunderstand who and what they are. These are all incredibly strong individualists. Each one essentially looking after their own personal interests first. Strict hierarchies with harshly enforced discipline are the only way cohesion can be maintained. And even then the inner functioning of their organisations can be quite Byzantine, as there is endless intrigue, back-stabbing and double crossing. So you understand: this is not the planet-spanning unified organisation that you might have imagined it to be. Rather it is a number of families, each operating along roughly feudal lines, with a most senior "head" running the family. And then there are, as I say, allegiances and compacts between some of the families.

But to answer your actual question: yes, they do very much look upon you as a farmer might look upon his livestock. They believe it is their duty and almost sacred trust to manage and look after the human race. The race as a whole. Like a farmer looks after a herd as a whole. But along the way he would happily have certain individuals slaughtered to pay his bills and, if they began to over-graze his land, he would consider it irresponsible not to do a bit of culling. You see the individuals are just not considered to be important. And so they will use you in whatever way they see fit in the pursuance of their own goals. It is certainly so, for example, that these beings might be quite willing to instigate war or any other kind of atrocity on any kind of scale they deem necessary, if this serves their plans. In fact it is so that these kinds of events are almost always, in one way or another, sponsored or instigated by these Super Powerful Individuals. And causing wars is just one way in which they manage to gain more power, more control and more wealth, as they jockey with each other for control. There are other ways. None of them would make you happy to hear about. I could mention the instigation of massive pandemics. In more recent times this includes the actual engineering of diseases. Such tools are employed to keep you servile and to place more wealth and power in their hands.

The SPI's are, as I have said, the ultimate owners of anything big and important enough to be worth owning. And if the economy grows in such a way as to cause them to NOT own everything worth owning? Then they are not beyond trashing the economy so that they can then buy everything for a fraction of its previous worth. As the economy rights itself again, so it is that they are once again in possession of almost all of it. The fact that countless peoples' lives were ruined and that many starved and that others' hopes and dreams were dashed, does not deeply concern them. It is not the individual who matters to them.

So you asked about genocide for the sake of expediency. The Super Powerful Individuals are not the only ones to have ever instigated genocide. But they are the ones who have done it most consistently throughout the whole of your recorded history.

Z: I don't really know what to make of all this, 8. It is horrifying and chilling.

8: Maybe so. And now you have a number of choices. You can believe what I have said because it matches some of your observations of life. Or you can disbelieve it because it doesn't… or because you don't want it to. And if you do decide to believe this, then you can get angry and full of hate. You can try to hit back. And lose.

Or, if you are ready to stop being hurt by the game, you can awaken and discover who you really are and you can see it for what it is: a very big game. A serious and scary game. But a game, none the less. One that allowed you to undergo some of the most incredible experiences that can be had anywhere in All That Is. A wondrous, magnificent machine which outputs profound and amazing insights into who and what you really are.

This whole world, as it is, exists to show you who you are.

It reflects with perfect precision and fidelity your own ideas beliefs, thoughts and choices back at you. And ultimately the Super Powerful Individuals are just one part of the machine. Without them it would not function.

And if you want to choose to see yourself as their victim, then it is apparent that you want to go for another spin around the inner workings of this particular machine. If, on the other hand, you come to the realisation that only you can create your reality and that you are no-one's victim… well… then everything will begin to change for you. Then you will become the master of your own being, your own destiny and all of your own experiences.

And then? In that state of Master Consciousness, how then will you think of the Super Powerful Individuals? I tell you, you will not think of them as super powerful anymore. You will see them as nothing other than role players in a great play. Ones that have had some quite interesting parts to play. You will see the difficulty, the pain and the complexity in their roles. And you will have understanding and compassion. Anger and vengeance will have left you.

And THAT is the story I will tell you of The Super Powerful Individuals. I tell it to you like this so that you will hear and understand that I am not trying to paint you a rosy picture. I am not trying to tell you that, *"Things are not as bad as you think"*. No. Indeed things are probably a whole lot worse than you had thought. And yet… this is not a problem. Because, indeed, it does not matter how bad things are in your world, if those things are what is required for you to come to your own awakening.

You are all a bit like drug addicts who have been addicted too long to a very powerful narcotic called V. V is for victim. And you all take repeated doses of V, and even though you sometimes have a bad trip, even though you sometimes over-dose, still your addiction drives you to keep taking it. And at some point you need to hit some kind of rock bottom experience, which will make you say, "enough!" And then, and only then, will you decide to kick the habit.

So, the world you see around you, is as you are. And when you are done and done and DONE with victim, then, I promise you, your world will look entirely different to you. You will no longer encounter any victim experiences. You will see a new world through new eyes.

And now, to bring this question to a close: can you see that, without the Super Powerful Individuals playing the role they are playing, the game would not work at all? The planetary system would be quite different? Your experiences would be quite different? And you would not be offered the choices and opportunities for self-discovery and self-creation that you currently have?

Z: I can, yes.

8: And can you see that it is actually so that you agreed to this experience before you came here? And that you continue to agree to it every day? And that you can choose to release yourself from this agreement and come to choose something else if you like?

Z: Yes. I can speak from my own experience and say I am right now finding out what it is to free myself from my own inner victim states. I am letting go of deeply limiting beliefs. And as I do so, I am also moving to a place in my life and my world where I no longer feel I am the victim of anything. Not of other people or political systems or… anything. And if I contrast how I now feel with how badly victimised I felt as a young man… wow… it is quite amazing what a difference it has made to release myself from my own bondage.

8: Then that is my point exactly. Your outer world reflects your inner world. Most make the mistake of expecting the outer world to change if they are unhappy. But this does not work. The outer world does not seem to be willing to change so they stay unhappy. But then there are some who come to the realisation that the only way they will be able to make themselves happy is by changing their inner world. They do this and they find happiness. Perhaps they find it miraculous then to discover that their outer-world also follows suit and changes to fit with their state of happiness. Is this magic? A miracle? Maybe! Or perhaps this is just the way things would work if there were only One of us here experiencing itself in a fractal holographic expression of Itself. So perhaps we should not be surprised that it is so.

And this is one of the great lessons that this reality can teach you.

And so tell me now how you now perceive these Super Powerful Individuals? Are they evil? Are their actions evil?

Z: Ha ha! Now I really begin to understand what you have been saying all along. Because, yes, from the subjective standpoint they ARE evil. Without a second's thought they seem to remove from millions upon millions of people the right to choose. But that is an illusion. Objectively, we all always have the right to choose. So then, they are not evil.

And thanks to them we have the most amazing opportunities for self-discovery. So then they are again not evil.

It all depends on your perspective, doesn't it?

8: Yes, it does. While you are still deep in the game and struggling to make sense of it, you see all kinds of beings around you as evil. As soon as you DO make sense of it, you see it all for what it is. And then you leave the game and you see the perfection of the whole arrangement.

Z: Yeah, as a result of this conversation I am actually ready to know this to be true. Thanks, 8.

8: You are most welcome.

Let us move on to the next manifestation of evil you wanted to know about.

Terrorists

Do you really need me to talk about this one anymore?

Z: No. I guess not. I think I can see this for what it is.

8: Good. Then you can give us a brief summation and we can move on?

Z: I'll give it a bash…

I think there could be many underlying reasons why someone might be driven to commit acts of terror. But ultimately, it is the act of someone who is so deeply lost in his own powerlessness that he feels the only way to try to fix things is to commit some really horrendous act of violence. It is clear that this is a deeply traumatised soul lashing out at the world, which he feels has victimised him. This is a being who has chosen to experience the life he has and, as a result of his experiences, he chooses to respond to the world by expressing more fear, hate and anger into it. In so doing, he creates more of that which hurt him in the first place. And, in so doing, he also gives all of us the opportunity to choose how WE are going to respond. We can see his solution isn't working. We can see how killing people and destroying the lives of the survivors doesn't result in a better world for anyone. So what are we going to do with HIS act of terrorism? Are we going to respond as he did with the desire to return the favour with interest? Are we going to try to kill him and his people and destroy lives over there where he lives? We can do that, but I'm not sure why we think it will help. It certainly didn't help when he did it over here where we are.

Or are we going to make a new choice about ourselves to cease to be willing to kill each other. Or what?

And that is where I leave this. Terrorists are simply people who have responded to terrible circumstances with terrible choices, thereby creating more terrible circumstances. That is their story. The important bit is how we respond to this. What are our choices and how will we create ourselves in return?

8: I like how you handled that.

The next manifestation of evil you asked about was:

People Who Rape Women and Abuse Children and Babies

What can I say about this one that hasn't already been said in previous discussions or, indirectly, in this one? It IS a very tough issue to come to terms with and so it keeps coming up for you. I understand that. But the resolution of it remains the same. Before any violent or abusive interaction can take place between two beings it will be so that they, on some deep level, will be carrying within themselves a trauma. You see, one must have some considerable inner-pain to work out if one is going to choose to engage in such an interaction. To be willing to do such a thing to another OR to be willing to allow this to be done to themselves... they must certainly have some difficulty within their psyche that needs to be addressed! The event itself then is really just the manifestation of the pre-existing inner-turmoil. As a result of the event, this pain is now made overt and is present in their reality. Now they can no longer deny the existence of the trauma. Now they must each make their way through their pain. The difference is that the perpetrator gets to be reviled by society. Gets to be told over and over how deeply wrong he is. He might end up spending time in prison and, even in prison, be treated like a pariah. It is a long dark ride through the depths of the wretchedness of the soul to be on such a journey.

For the raped and abused the experience is no picnic either, of course. But at least one can hope that there might be loving support after the event. The victim might, depending on the circumstances, get psychological counselling and so forth.

Of course I'm not asking you to pity the perpetrator in such cases. That would probably be more than one can really ask. But I offer you this perspective.

And so... is the perpetrator evil? Is the act evil? It is the self-same answer over and over again. It is the same answer as with the Super Powerful Individuals. And the answer is, of course, that it depends on your perspective. From the subjective experience of the victim and those who are close to the victim, the answer is almost certainly a resounding "yes". And who can say they are wrong to feel this way? Who can blame them for wishing untold harm and eternal torment upon the perpetrator? From the objective perspective though, he is of course not evil. He is a soul working out his deep-seated pain and confusion. And he has a contract with the soul that is expressed as the victim. And that contract is enacted. And so, from that perspective not even the act can be labelled evil. It is what it is.

You, yourself have had another incarnation in which you were repeatedly abused as a child; both sexually and violently. (Zingdad Note: see Chapter 1, "*Lost in my own dream world*"). And not just any child but one who was mentally disabled. In your instance it was your soul's desire to understand the victim state quite deeply that led you to choose these experiences. And while that poor dear boy was living though those experiences there can be no doubt that they were... words fail me... deeply, deeply traumatic. Yes, that is so. But I tell you now that you would not be here today engaged in your ascension path without having had, if not those experiences, then ones quite similar to them. They were the counter-balance to other experiences in which you played quite a malevolent perpetrator. (Zingdad Note: see Chapter 1, "*The Wizard*"). If you take from your soul the one experience, you must take the other. And you would not be able to leave here without knowing both sides. Your psyche would be in a state of imbalance. So you COULD have chosen not to experience either, but if you go down that road you end up choosing not to do anything at all whilst incarnated here in this system. And then, what is the point? You would learn nothing at all about the Self. And coming to this reality would not hold any value for you. So you engage. You engage deeply. You fling yourself bravely into this system and you risk everything. You risk that, indeed, you might discover all manner of unendurably despicable things about yourself. And then you do! And then, when you are done with that, you begin to discover your true power, your eternal beauty and your magnificence. For it is so that you who have been here will know and understand Love far more powerfully than another being who was not here. And this is so, of course, because you have truly been to where there was NO love and then found your way back. You really, really will know what Love is when you have done that!

So I ask you again: is the perpetrator evil? Is the act evil?

Z: I am really beginning to get this, 8. You have been kind enough to stay with me on this, looking at it over and over again from all kinds of perspectives. So now, as you ask me this, I can really see it. It really is only evil from the limited subjective experience. Objectively it is not evil. I actually get it.

8: I am pleased. As this becomes your truth, you will liberate yourself from all kinds of inner turmoil. You can expect to find yourself releasing your emotional pain and even symptoms of physical pain and discomfort, as you let go of your desire to hold all these other beings and their actions as "evil".

But let us get into an interesting one next. You asked me about…

Demons and Demonic Possession

Z: Yes. Are there such things as demons?

8: The word "demon" is one word that means a great many different things to different people in different circumstances. It most certainly doesn't cover just one class of being! Now, I could try to get into all the various beings and experiences and we could talk at some length about each of them, but that would not only make this conversation unmanageably long but it would also not be of any great use to you. So let's talk about what is both important and useful for you to know.

Z: Good enough.

8: The first thing you should know is that the word demon started out in your ancient times meaning something quite different to what it now means to you. At its origin the word meant something like "higher being"; essentially any being which existed between your "mortal realm" and the realm of "the gods". All such beings were called *daemons*. Any being that was of a finer density than that which humans perceived themselves to be, could be called a *daemon*. It was certainly not an inherently negative term. Daemons were very often kind and benevolent spirits. Though it is true some of them might also have been indifferent or even malevolent too. But the point is that the word Daemon had no inherent negative connotation. It was simply a catch-all word that meant something like "higher spirit being". Perhaps in your current parlance you might express this as "higher dimensional being."

Z: I see.

8: But over time the meaning of the word changed. And certainly it was expedient to the expansion of the monotheistic religions to characterise all such beings as evil and therefore not to be consorted with. Wherever you have people using religion as a tool to gain and maintain power, you will find them casting any path to spiritual truth and growth, other than the one they offer, as evil. But, be that as it may, it is so that, in your present reality, the word has come to be loaded with the most negative of connotations. It is now taken to mean exclusively a spirit being of deeply malevolent nature.

Z: But such beings do exist?

8: Are you asking if there are beings that reside at densities other than your own who desire something other than your best interests?

Z: Yes.

8: Don't be naïve. Of course there are! A huge variety of spirit beings exist that have, for all kinds of reasons, come to feel the desire to manipulate and damage others. Just as there are such beings incarnated on your planet right now, so there are such beings in the disincarnate state. Mostly these ones are of a very small amount of light. Lost ones. Sad, small energies that have hurt themselves badly and lost their way. And now they would steal a little light from you if they could to sustain themselves. Like little leaches they would come and steal crumbs from you if they could.

There are ones who are a little more powerful than that too. Ones who have, with full intent and purpose, chosen a path of negative orientation. And then there are also the ones who are directly minions of The Adversary – which we shall talk about in a while.

So, yes, these all exist. But what of it? You are no more their victim than you are a victim of anyone else. You should be aware that they exist and then you should choose not to give them any of your energy. Create with love and they shall have no purchase upon you. And that is as simple as it is. There are some basic spiritual protection tools that I could teach you if you wish to formalise your own defence until such time as you know yourself to be above such concerns.

Z: Thank you, 8, that would be useful.

8: Alright we'll talk about that as a separate discussion.

For now I wish you to understand that these beings are not your problem if you are not willing to allow them access to your energy.

Z: Okay, but what about demonic possession? Does it, or does it not, happen?

8: It does. Those who are willing to create the opening for such any experience will probably get it. There are, as I have said, a good number of spirit beings that are of a negative energy. If you offer access to your energy, you can be sure there will be someone who is willing to take what you offer. How would it be if you left your home open and unlocked with all your possessions unguarded and then went off on holiday?

Z: I guess I'd come home to a pretty empty house.

8: If you were lucky! More than likely your house would first be stripped bare and then all kinds of undesirables would move in. And who could blame them? Here is a house full of stuff for them to steal and sell. And there are nice dry rooms for them to sleep in. And there is free water and free electricity to use. Wonderful!

Z: Until I return home?

8: Hmm. Yes. And then you must decide what you are going to do. If you do want to evict the squatters then you can get help. If you own the house then you can get law enforcement officials to kick them out. And then you have the mammoth task of setting things back to rights. Certainly it will take you some time and a great degree of effort to replace everything that was lost and to repair everything that was broken. But if you are determined you will be able to accomplish this and will emerge from the experience a great deal wiser.

This is a good analogy for what occurs in the spirit realm. You have a physical body and a number of more subtle spirit bodies. These are your home and you must take responsibility for them. You must secure your walls and lock your gates and only give access to those whom you love and trust. But when you are new to this you won't know how and so you are given help. You might call those who help with this, your Spirit-Guide or guardian angel. It is often so that you might have a particular Spirit-Guide who is responsible for your spiritual protection. Such a one is called the Gate Keeper. Your whole spiritual guidance team is appointed before you enter each incarnation to assist you with your psycho-spiritual protection. If you want to maximise your protection, you can make the conscious choice to allow them to protect you. And you can help them in their task too by listening to your intuition. And as you "grow up" spiritually, so you can also learn to take more and more responsibility for your own protection. And then the time will come when you will no longer need a guide for protection. And that is how it should be. But unfortunately it doesn't always work that way. Sometimes incarnated beings make some very strange choices. Sometimes they are lead to believe that they can gain certain gifts, powers or tools with which to manipulate their reality by negotiating with negative beings. Sadly the negative beings are not very reliable. They will tell and lie and make any promise to get what they want and will give nothing in return if they can get away with it. A human being with its shields down and its spiritual guidance disabled is a very vulnerable thing. This path never ends happily.

Sometimes though it is as matter of self-destructive urges that would lead beings to cease to care for their own protection and to disallow their Spirit-Guides from protecting them. They might open their defences and invite all and sundry in.

Whatever the motivation, for such beings it will not be long before the house of their being becomes a squat for all kinds of undesirables.

Just as the case is with evicting squatters from your house, so too cleaning your spiritual abode is a traumatic thing. I would most strongly advocate that you not allow yourself to wander down this road. Take charge of your own spiritual hygiene and at the same time avail yourself of the help that is offered to you by your guidance team. Trust your own heart and choose for love. Then you'll be fine. These squatters cannot invade your spiritual home if you do not actually open the door to it. They are not able to over-power you. You are not their victim. So, quite simply, do not choose this!

Z: And what if I know of someone who has such a problem?

8: If this other being wants help and is willing to make different choices, then they may be helped. But you will need to get competent help for such an exercise. If you look, you will find a variety of people who are competent to assist. Assist this person to choose someone with whom they will feel comfortable. Then the journey towards a "clean home" begins. It might be a long journey. Parts of it might be quite distressing. Your task will be to make sure you don't move into Rescuer. Help this being to help themselves. Do not rescue them.

The closing point I would like to make on this subject is this: as with any manifestation of evil, you certainly can choose to experience it. And choosing to experience it can make your life very uncomfortable. But the over-arching point is that it IS your choice. You can always choose NOT to experience it. And for so long as that is the case you are not actually victimised by it.

Z: Thanks 8. I think I have an understanding of this situation. These are not beings with which to toy but they are also not my problem.

8: Yes. And very soon you will be able to discover for yourself that, truly, these beings that would act in a "demonic" fashion are actually quite small, lost and powerless. Their stories are always very sad ones. They are actually in desperate need of help. Which they will get when they are ready to receive it. But that is not for this discussion.

Let's move on then to the three names that you have given, which seem to add up, in your society, to the very epitome of evil.

Lucifer, Satan and the Devil

Z: Oh yes. This should be interesting…

8: Oh it will be. But before we get started I wish to briefly point something out. The words and names you use in your world are very imprecise things. One of the many reasons for this is that people ascribe different meanings to words. Some words are more prone than others to having diverse meanings and these names: Lucifer, Satan and the Devil, more so than most. And when you consider that, on the whole, these words are an attempt by those behind the Veil to describe what is beyond it… well it is bound to lead to some confusion.

And this provides me with a challenge. In being willing to describe and discuss the beings that may be represented by these three names I am going to have to have to exercise some editorial control. I going to discuss the beings that I believe are the best match for these names. That is the best I can do, so it will have to suffice.

Z: Okay. But I don't see the problem…

8: Please understand. There is no one single being anywhere who answers to any of these names. Where such beings might exist, the very concept of a NAME is meaningless. It is only in your very, very limited sphere of existence that these names exist at all.

Let's take Lucifer, for example. The name literally means something like "that which carries light". So should I try to find the greatest carrier of the light and describe THAT being to you?

Or should I instead look within the cultures that pre-date yours, from whom you inherited this concept, and see that this name refers, quite directly, to the planet Venus?

Or should I look deeper into those early cultures and see the allegorical value that they ascribed to Venus and see how this story corresponds somewhat to a greater story of your reality?

Or should I look at the babble of contrasting views offered by the many religions in your reality and somehow try to sift out to whom it is that they refer with this name? Because, I can tell you, there are a good number of different beings and principles that could all answer to the description thus provided!

Z: Ah. Now I begin to see the problem.

8: So, I am simply stating upfront that the understandings that follow are my best attempt to deal with this complexity and ambiguity in a way that is both useful and truthful.

Z: Thanks, 8. I understand and accept your offer to deal with this as you think best.

8: Thank you. Although I have already begun to talk about Lucifer, I find it would better serve our purposes if we first talked about The Devil and then I continue with Lucifer next. Are you amenable?

Z: Sure, no problem. But does that mean that these are different beings?

8: They sometimes get conflated together. But in my view they are indeed different beings. So…

The Devil

The Devil occurs in one guise or another in a number of your religions. But it is, quite simply, an entirely fictitious construct created by those religions themselves.

The sponsoring thought from which The Devil springs is that the religion in question's doctrine is perfect and flawless and therefore unarguable and undeniable. It is, after all, the "word of God", or at least the word of God as spoken by His very best representatives. Do you see the problem?

Z: No. I don't understand how THAT could be the sponsoring thought for The Devil.

8: It wouldn't be if everyone in the world who ever came into contact with this particular doctrine just immediately accepted it. I mean, surely, the Word of God should brook no opposition? Surely all that encountered it should immediately have their hearts swayed and immediately fall into line and BELIEVE. So either the scriptures in question ARE NOT the word of God… or…

Z: … or there is some powerful supernatural agency interfering with things?

8: Exactly! And so, enter stage left, bearing horns and a trident, a certain goatish fellow of ill repute...

Z: (laughs) 8, you crack me up!

8: (laughs) I'm glad. But this IS a serious subject. Think, for example, of medieval Europe. This was a time when a small group of men had nearly absolute power based upon the fact that they were religious leaders. Their word was law. And their authority came, they said, from God. They were, they said, God's agents on earth. Power, wealth and status was theirs and there was no-one who could challenge them. Or was there? Occasionally there would arise various spiritual views, which diminished their power. Some of these ideas would gain popularity, as ordinary people found them to be preferable to the ideas espoused by the church. And then, what would happen? The church would come down on this heresy with a heavy hand. And of course, the justification was that these heretics were inspired by The Devil. So the church would send someone to persuade the heretics to change their mind and to again affirm that the Church's line was the only correct one. And the fact that these confessions were extracted with torture and the fact that the end product was almost always death was seen as an acceptable price for the saving of the heretic's soul from the clutches of The Devil. At one point it got so bad that genocide was committed on the population of a whole region in the South of France, ostensibly for heresy. The Cathars were a distinct cultural group who were both prosperous and spiritually advanced. Greedy eyes desired their land and the church was easily swayed to declare heresy as a pretext for exterminating them to steal what was theirs.

So the subject of The Devil is a deadly serious one. But not for the reasons you might have thought. It is serious because The Devil has been invoked as justification for some of the most egregiously vile acts ever committed in your history.

It has been the same in a great many of the wars that have raged upon your planet too. Each time one group wants to go out and slaughter another, some benighted soul will get it into his head to claim that God is on their side, that the opposite side are for The Devil and that it is their holy duty to kill as many of the "devil worshippers" as possible.

And, sad to say, this kid of thinking did not end in the dark ages. Still to this day each minuscule splinter of each religion everywhere claims some kind of special truth. Some kind of greater connection with God. And then they claim that every other splinter and every other religion has, to some degree or another, been lead astray by... you guessed it... The Devil. And each time someone leaves their religion or lapses it is, of course, The Devil who led them astray. And it would not matter in the least bit if the person in question found a greater sense of peace and harmony outside of their religion. Still they would be wrong and still it would be the work of The Devil.

And you can see the logic. As long as you require your specific and exclusive story to be the only TRUTH and the only Word of God, then you are going to have some considerable difficulty if something comes along that can powerfully argue against your doctrine. The creation of the notion of The Devil is a very powerful defence. It keeps you "right" and it makes the opposing story even more wrong without you even needing to examine the ideas you are holding to be true. In fact, the more powerful the opposing ideas are, the greater the evidence that they are "inspired by The Devil". Because such a powerful and cunning argument can only come from The Devil. Right?

Z: Whew! I see the argument. But how do you deal with that?

8: You don't. It is NOT your job to win converts. If someone so badly needs to hold onto their specific belief that they need to believe that all other beliefs are inspired by The Devil, then you should let them be. Don't try to change their mind. If you go out to persuade people that their beliefs and ideas are wrong, then you are committing spiritual violence. Don't do it. Remember - what you do to others, you do to yourself also. And, as you don't wish to have others trying to change your beliefs for you, so you should not do this to others.

Find what is right and true for you. Live that. And, just as you love to be able to learn from others, so you may share your truth as a gift; offer it, but offer it openly and lovingly. Allow others to take from your truth if they so desire, but do not attach yourself to the need that they should agree with you or be changed by what you say.

If you do this, then The Devil will cease to matter to you. You will not come into contact with those who are creating this construct.

Z: This is a very interesting thought, 8. I had not previously considered it possible that The Devil is actually created by those who claim to hate him.

8: It is a very important realisation. Remember that you create with your attention. Whatever you focus on, you bring into being. Not only the things you like, but the things you dislike too. And the more powerful the emotions, the more powerful the creation. So, yes, hate creates! It certainly does. Less powerfully than love, but it still creates.

So what you should take from this is the realisation that it would serve you well to release all hatred from your own being. These powerful negative emotions simply bring to your life that which you DON'T want. Focus your attention and thoughts and creations on that which you love, and you shall get that which you DO want.

Do you see?

Z: I do. Thank you, 8.

So, if The Devil is created by those that claim to be in opposition to him, does that mean The Devil is not real?

8: Ah ha! I am SO glad you asked that question! Because the answer to this is both interesting and important.

No. I am NOT saying that the Devil is not real. In fact, quite the opposite. He IS real. If he were not real, then you would not be creator-beings! So many of you have focused so much attention and emotional energy on this construct that it has taken on an independent validity. A great many people, over a good deal of time, have externalised into this being all that they have found to be unacceptable and repugnant within themselves and their world. Everything that is vile and disgusting and unlovable has been divorced from the Self and the world and embedded in The Devil. That's a whole lot of energy, life and creative force! So, yes, creators, you have created. You have created many wondrous and magnificent things and you have created some very sad and painful things too. The Devil is not one of your happier creations.

Z: I am at a loss for words. Wow. So what now? What do we do about this?

8: You grow up. I have said it before in this conversation and I say it again. The mark of an adult is one who takes responsibility for his or her life. The mark of a spiritually mature being is one who takes responsibilities for its creations. And this is what you must do. If you take responsibility for everything in your life and your experience, if you take responsibility for everything you have ever done or said if you take ownership of who and what you are, then there is no place for The Devil in your life. There is no need, value or desire in your being for some other who is responsible for the "wrong" so that you can be "right". If you take total, absolute and ultimate responsibility for all that you are, then this little creation shows itself to be a fable. You release it from yourself and your life.

Z: But what about others who are still holding on to it?

8: Not your problem. Or are you their Rescuer?

Z: Ah! No, I am not.

8: So?

Z: So then I am fine. If there is such a thing as The Devil then it is simply me showing myself that I have not taken responsibility for myself. I should respond by growing up and taking ownership of my experiences and my creations. Then it has no further hold on me.

8: That is a good response. Shall we move on?

Z: Okay thanks.

8: Next you wanted to know about…

Lucifer

Z: Yes, please. Is this also a fictitious being? Or is it a real being and truly the source of all evil?

8: That which would be the best fit for the name Lucifer very much does exist. And he might well be called the "inventor of evil" but probably not the "source of all evil".

Z: A surprising answer!

8: There is more to come. A good deal more. What follows now is a very important story. If you understand the story of Lucifer, then you understand much. But to tell the story I need to step back a bit and tell you something else.

Z: Okay.

8: Do you know that every single mote of consciousness everywhere always begins its journey with a dawning of its consciousness? As it first gains self-awareness, the first actual thought it would have would be curiosity about its own being. We have paraphrased this awakening with these words:

"Here I am. What am I?"

It is really and truly so that this is the way every single Beingness has begun. It is so because it is the way The One began. From What Is, Self-awareness dawns. The first act of consciousness is curiosity about this Self-awareness. *"Here I am. What am I?"*

Indeed, at every level of your being, from the very highest right down to the very smallest particle of Self engaged here in the deepest density, it is true that the only function and purpose you really and truly have… is to discover yourself. To find out who and what you really are. This is the purpose you began with, and this will continue to be your purpose for all eternity. Discover yourself.

And, when you understand that THIS is what drives The One, this very desire for discovery of the Self, then you understand that every time you discover yourself a little more, you are contributing to The One. Then YOU are an aspect of The One that is being "successful". Then YOU are contributing to The One's greater Self-knowledge. And the more grandly you discover yourself, the more grandly you are contributing. And so, it should be obvious, that if you can procure a situation in which you could catalyse other Selves, other aspects of The One, to quickly and very powerfully attain a greater degree of self-knowledge, then you would be doing a very great service to The One indeed.

Z: And what happens at the journey's end, 8? What happens when I have finally and completely discovered myself?

8: We are digressing, but it is an interesting question. So I shall answer. You can never cease discovering yourself. You see, you can ALWAYS, if you try, create more. And, in so doing, you can realise that there is more you did not know about yourself. But, that said, there can be an end to the journey. Any time you really and truly wish the journey to end, you simply return yourself wholly and completely to The One. You cease your separation and gift all that you are to The Oneness. In so doing you make the ultimate discovery about yourself: you discover that, in truth, you are one with The One. That you are all there ever was and all there ever will be. That all the journeying and adventuring and discovering was all just you discovering yourself. That it's only ever been you. You, and many other aspects of you, playing out every single role and creating every single creation.

THAT is what lies at the end of the journey, should you so choose it. And even if, and when, you DO choose it, in choosing it you will discover that there is STILL an on-going, never-ending process of self-creation and self-discovery. And still it is you doing this. Now it's just you, as The One.

And that is the story. In fact I would say it is THE story. It is your story, my story and the story of every other particle of consciousness that ever was. You get permutations and variations in the story as beings strive to discover themselves in different ways, but that too is all just a part of the story of self-discovery.

Z: I feel such a quiet, comfortable resonance with this. I understand and know what you have told me to be true. Thank you for telling me this.

8: It is my pleasure. But now, let's get back to Lucifer.

Lucifer is no different. Lucifer is also a part of The One who is on a mission of self-discovery. What Lucifer did that was quite unique and special was to invent true individuality. True separateness. Of course you can't REALLY separate any part of The One from the rest of The One. But what you can do is to create a totally immersive, compelling illusion of separation. If the illusion is strong enough, then you can rely on the inherent creator-nature of the beings that choose to experience it to do the rest.

Z: Explain?

8: Let's take a step back again.

This is Lucifer: he is a great consciousness. A being of Light. Lucifer desires to understand himself and Life and consciousness and All That Is. This is what drives all of us and Lucifer is no exception.

Z: Uh… let's just say that if this is true then he has some pretty bad press down here on planet earth.

8: I understand. And if you stay with me then you too will understand. But in the meantime, you can remember what we have just learned about perspective. From one perspective a being can appear to be pure evil, but from another it is not so. Remember?

Z: Okay, sure.

8: Good. Then stay with me.

So Lucifer…

The thing that deeply intrigued Lucifer in his quest for discovery of the Self was the very idea of Oneness: what is it really? And how would it be if we were not One? And this became a bit of an obsession with Lucifer – the drive to really understand this. And so he created all manner of realities and experiments in consciousness to try to understand it. And then, finally, he came up with his master-piece. It was his own gift to The Is-ness. He created a very clever barrier, fashioned from his own consciousness. You could conceptualise it as a sort of a spiritual one-way mirror. So now, any being who wishes to do so, may use this principal to place some part of itself on the far side of this barrier. The fragment on the other side of the barrier will not be able to "see" back to the side from which it came. In practice, this means that passing through the barrier causes a kind of impenetrable forgetfulness. The being ceases to recognise, know or remember what is back on the other side, where it came from and who it really is. It is born a babe with no memory of Self.

And so you have two sides to the barrier: the side which is in knowing and the side which is in unknowing.

Z: And so this is obviously the Veil of Unknowing!

8: That is exactly what it is. What I have described is greatly simplified. The Veil is a very complicated creation with many layers and levels. But now at least you have the gist of it.

Z: Wow! Finally I have an answer to a question that has been sitting with me. The Veil is a creation of Lucifer! And he made it as a tool for self-discovery! Because everyone who wants to know something really deeply true about themselves can go beyond the Veil and discover it from a position of not-knowing. Cool! I get that.

But…

8: Yes?

Z: But where does evil come in? This doesn't seem like an evil thing to have done. It seems like quite a good thing. A gift. And you said at the beginning of this that Lucifer invented evil. So…?

8: Well, here is the thing. The first consciousnesses to go beyond all the levels of the Veil were beings who started civilisations right at the beginning of your whole system of reality. They went there and they began to express their own basic nature. They discovered themselves as they were.

Z: Which was?

8: Love. Unity in expression.

When you get right down to it, the purest, most essential nature of everything is love. Because that is the purest, most essential nature of The One and we are all part of The One - all aspects and expression of The One. We'll talk about this some more in the next chapter and I'll explain how this all works. But for now I will say that the first few rounds of this New Game, as invented by Lucifer, were sweet and beautiful, if perhaps a little boring and uneventful. Small civilisations would assemble themselves in a created reality and then they'd express love and kindness and unity to each other for a while and then, in so doing, begin to discover their essential Oneness. And that was the trigger, which returned their consciousness to the "knowing" side of the Veil. You can't remain in "unknowing" after you have discovered the basic truth of your eternal Oneness. It's like a treasure hunt. When you discover the treasure, the game is over. But the problem was that these beings were discovering the truth of the Oneness too soon. They discovered it before they really deeply quested into discoveries about their own nature - before they truly discovered who they themselves were.

Z: So the Veil experiment was a failure?

8: No. Not a failure. Any scientist worth his salt will tell you that there are no failed experiments. There is only more data. And then you use this data to create the next generation of experiment.

And indeed, there were many generations of experiment. Each one added a new idea or a new layer of complexity. And, as the experiment became more and more interesting, so more and more great consciousnesses came to look and to play. It became increasingly fascinating to see how this could be made to work. But always the challenge was the same - how do we induce the particles of Self who are beyond the Veil to want to stay there? How do we keep them there for a sufficient length of experience so that they can lose themselves in the illusion? Because that is what was required for the experiment to work.

And it was Lucifer himself who came up with what proved to be the most ultimately successful model.

Z: Which was?

8: The Adversary.

Z: How did that work?

8: Well, it's actually quite elegant in its simplicity. If the problem is that those on the other side of the Veil keep finding their Oneness too easily, then the answer is to show them their separateness. And you do so by putting them in the presence of beings who are expressing deep separation from them. Not love. Not kindness. The opposite of that. And so Lucifer invented, for the purposes of this experiment here beyond the Veil, the notion of antagonism.

Hatred. Wilful destructiveness. Aggression. Manipulation. Malevolence. Yes… evil. That which takes from you your right to choose. Squeeze a being into believing that it has no options and force it to your will and you will have stung quite badly that being's sense of what is fair and right. That being will go to quite some effort to repay the favour. And bingo… suddenly those beyond the Veil became embroiled in the game. Suddenly the challenge was not to keep them there but to find a way to eventually bring them home!

And, as Lucifer invented this in his own creative imagination, so it was that he began to play it out. You see the great consciousnesses experience their imaginings with creation. When we wonder "what if?", then we are actually creating a reality where it IS so. Then we can see within ourselves and our experiences how that would be. And so, anyway, it was as a result of this imagining of The Adversary that Lucifer came to express certain particles of his own consciousness into this reality of yours. A number of these particles travelled beyond the Veil and incarnated into your system, while one of the particles stayed beyond the Veil as the Master Adversary. These particles' very purpose was to sow dissent. To create separation. For, in so doing, they provided the most powerful inducement to all other particles of consciousness to remain beyond the Veil. That is the gift they brought.

And this brings me to the last name on our list.

Satan

At its origin, the root of the word, "Satan," means something very like "The Adversary". And that is the energetic resonance held by Satan. His is the energy of "The Adversary". One could say he was dreamed into being when Lucifer asked, "What if there was a great adversary to keep everyone in the game?"
You could even make the argument that Lucifer is Satan's Inner-Self.

Whatever the case, it is as a result of the presence of these particles of Lucifer's consciousness that there came to be in your frame of reality an entirely new experience. For the very first time beings could encounter others who were "the enemy". And so it was. Throughout your universe there were beings who existed at the fifth densities and higher who came into contact with Satan's minions. Satan's minions are those who feed directly on fear. So they are best served by causing wanton destruction and pain. They could not be reasoned with and they could not be bested in combat. They were the interlopers in a great many peaceful dramas that brought, for the first time, fear.

Now, for the first time, those who were beyond the Veil began to feel things like fear and hatred. You separated yourselves more and more from each other. You broke your sense of Oneness. You fell down deeper into the lower densities. You built up layer upon layer of darkness upon your own souls. You lost faith in yourself and trust in one another. You learned to expect the worst of each other. You learned to treat each other like objects to use and abuse for your own ends. And this was your own creator-nature responding to your experiences. That is to say, as soon as you began to see evil around you, so you began to create more evil from within yourselves. You became agents of separation. You YOURSELF became The Adversary. Every time you chose hate, anger, separation and fear over love and unity, you served the interests of The Adversary.

And ALL of you have done this. All of you. All of you have done this very powerfully in some lifetimes. And all of you have continued, to one extent or another, to do this in your current lifetime. It is the source of your inner pain and hidden shame. It is that which drives you to psychologists and anti-depressant drugs. It is that which causes your self-loathing, which is at the heart of your addictions and self-destructive habits. It is the cause of all the violence and psycho-emotional pathology, which is rampant on your planet. A great many of your physical illnesses also spring forth from the deep seated feeling that you are, at your core "ill". Inside yourself, you feel yourself to wrong and broken, but you do not know why, so you manifest these experiences of being ill, wrong and broken into your bodies.

ALL of you have played The Adversary. ALL are guilty of this.

Z: Oh my God, 8! I suddenly feel as if I'm fighting back tears. I know I have done this! What must I do with this knowledge? What do I do now?

8: You smile and say "mission accomplished"!

Z: Mission accomplished?!?

8: Yes. But now try to say it with less horror in your voice. And without the question marks. And with a smile.

Z: How? I don't understand?

8: Well, let's go back to first principles. The point of all this was to create a reality where you could lose yourself completely in separation and duality. That is the first objective of the experiment. The second part is when you turn around and begin to remember who you really are.

And so? Is the first part of the experiment not well and truly served by you becoming The Adversary yourself? By you acting out your separation and duality? By you treating yourself and all other Selves as abominably as you can?

Z: Why, yes, I suppose it is. I suppose in those moments, I was as deeply in separation as I could be.

8: Right. So you can now see it for what it was and say…

Z: Mission accomplished.

8: Yes.

But it is a painful mission and I can see why you wouldn't be feeling very enthusiastic about accomplishing it.

The second part is a lot more fun, though. The second part is when you begin to remember who you are. You begin to discover that you are a being of pure radiant light. That your truest nature is Love. That you are really One with All That Is. That you are a powerful, magnificent, creator being. That you exist to discover yourself and create yourself exactly as you most deeply desire yourself to be.

And isn't it nice to know that you are quite firmly on that part of the journey now?

Z: Yes. It is. But what do I do with the stuff that I did while I was on the first part of the journey?

8: It is your gift to yourself and to The One. It is how you expressed yourself in your deepest un-knowingness in response to The Adversary. It is how you expressed yourself as The Adversary. Now you know. Now you can make other choices. And now, when you encounter The Adversary in another being, you can understand this is them, as they are, while they are still on the outward journey. They are still in the first part of their journey. And that is all. Now you can release your judgement of them.

Z: Yes. I see.

8: And you can release your anger at those who make the world as it is. Those who are in power and seemingly making very poor choices for the rest of humanity. Those who plot and plan and create evil. Like fomenting war between nations with trickery and deception. Like manufacturing diseases that blight humanity. Like suppressing technology that is clean, in favour of technology that pollutes the planet. Like creating systems of money that enslave the masses. Like creating systems of economy that keep the majority in crushing poverty. Like allowing death, disease and famine to rage when all of this could be eradicated instantly. And on and on. You can release your anger towards them because you have done the same. In your own way in this lifetime and previous ones... you were a part of all this. And now you can see that those who are behaving in this way are simply the same as you, but in a different part of their journey. They are doing the tough stuff. They have yet to begin to forgive themselves and to love themselves. And when they do, then they too will begin to return home.

And the ones who will have it the very hardest of all? The ones with the greatest burden and the most pain to resolve? These ones are the children of Lucifer. The particles of consciousness who have come here beyond the Veil to keep alive the duality system. They have, lifetime-after-lifetime fed the system by playing the roles they have, in the way that they have. They are the most separate of all. The most alone. The most individuated. And trust me when I say to you that theirs is a deeply painful place to be. And their journey home is going to bring them even more pain. Because, you see, for them it is not a simple matter of releasing the falsenesses about themselves. They have been true to their purpose and nature in their actions. So ahead of them lies a particularly difficult journey. But they will be helped. It is not expected to be easy, but they will be helped.

Z: Wow. I almost feel... compassion.

8: Yes. Compassion is appropriate.

Z: And these ones, these children of Lucifer. Are they the Super Powerful Individuals you spoke of previously?

8: There are different particles, which have played different roles in different ways. Some have been violently aggressive. And then there are others such as the masters of the Super Powerful Individuals who have played a much subtler game. But yes, it is so.

Z: Some things are beginning to fall into place for me now. But let's just get this straight then... Is Lucifer the cause of all evil, or is he not?

8: As usual, this too is a perspective issue. It depends on how you look at it. Perhaps I could express it like this. Do you remember in the movie called Forest Gump, the main character had a saying that went something like "*My momma always told me that life is like a box of chocolates*"

Z: (laughs) Yes, I remember.

8: Well, if life is like a box of chocolates, then I would say that Lucifer invented "The Adversary Flavour" chocolate. And seeing as The Adversary is really all about appearing to take from others their right to choose, one could also call it "Evil Flavour" chocolate.

It's there in the box along with all kinds of other flavours. In your various lifetimes you get to try all of the flavours to see if you like them. But, in each case, it is up to you to decide how long you are going to keep each of these chocolates in your mouth. How long you chew and savour the flavour. And whether you spit it out or whether you take it into your being by swallowing it. All of that is up to you. And if you do take it into your being, do you go back again and again for more "evil flavour" chocolates, or do you instead find a way to let it pass through your body so that you can release it from your being and decide not to choose that flavour again?

You see? It IS there. You can choose to experience it, if you want to. And once you have sampled it, you can decide what you want to do with that experience. Nobody forces you to do anything. You are the creator of your own reality. The fact that evil exists as a possible experience does not mean you have to choose to experience it. And even if you do, STILL you are not its victim, because now you know something about yourself. You know whether you like it or not – whether it serves your path or not. You have profoundly increased your self-knowledge for having had this experience.

Z: Alright. I can accept from your story that Lucifer invented evil, but is not actually evil. But then it seems to me that his invention, The Adversary, IS evil. Or am I wrong?

8: In order for you to understand this, I am going to need to explain to you about Consciousness Construct Holders now, even though you haven't yet done quite enough work to get the whole message. But we will have to do our best.

Z: What does that mean, 8? That I have not done enough work to get this message?

8: Quite simply that you must be readied to understand things. Because of the manner in which you are receiving this material, it is not possible for me to place ideas in your mind if the building blocks of that idea are not already there. And so it is that each chapter not only addresses the issues it seeks to address, but it also plants many seeds and lays much groundwork for the following chapters. And, as has often happened, if you are not ready to receive a chapter, then you find yourself unable to get down to writing. This is by design. You are needing to be still for a while so that you can undergo a little internal metamorphosis to bring yourself to readiness to receive the next chapter.

Z: Ah. I understand! That makes a lot of sense and clears up some questions I had in that regard. And now you want to tell me about these Consciousness Construct Holders, but you feel there is not sufficient groundwork?

8: There is insufficient to tell the whole story or to tell it properly. But we will get by.

Let me start by explaining that your experience of your reality is a deeply illusory one. You understand that by now. You live in a world that is predicated on layer upon layer of illusion. Nothing that you think is real is actually real. And the things that you think are not real, are. It is both a wonder and a miracle. And your reality is created thus very specifically for a very important purpose: the search for Self-knowledge of The One in all Its endless magnificence. This reality of yours is an unbelievable powerful tool of self-discovery. But in order for it to *work,* the illusions must work. These illusions are like the cogs of the machine – if they do not function then the whole machine does not function. And there is a set of cogs – possibly some of the most important of all the cogs – which are what I call the Consciousness Construct Holders.

By now you and your readers are quite familiar with one of these Consciousness Construct Holders.

Z: We are?

8: Oh indeed! Does it surprise you to know that your very own Inner-Self, Joy-Divine, is in fact one such Consciousness Construct Holder?

Z: I… umm… I don't know. I am not sure what to think about that. Tell me more about what a Consciousness Construct Holder is and then maybe I'll be able to tell you how I feel about that.

8: Certainly.

As I have explained, in order for your reality to work, you need certain powerful illusions. One of the most powerful of all the illusions is your experience that your emotions are somewhat alien to your own being, that these are just things that you happen to feel, and that these feelings happen to you as a result of outside stimuli. One could imagine that your feeling of happiness is analogous to, for example, a piece of chocolate cake. You believe you need to either bake the cake or buy it from somewhere if you wish to be able to have the sensation of eating chocolate cake. Well, this is the thing your reality seems to show you – that you must achieve a particular goal or buy a particular thing or win the love of a particular person or lose a number of kilograms or whatever other silliness you are telling yourself, before you can feel happy. And if you were observant, you would see that this never works. Hitting the target, at best allows you only a momentary feeling of happiness and then, you return to your normal not-so-happy state. And so you decide that you must just keep chasing ever greater targets in the hope that some day you'll be really lastingly happy.

And so you come to believe yourself to be a victim to your emotions and THAT is one of the very powerful inducements you have to stay trapped inside this reality. And so it is that, here at the level of deep separation and duality, you believe you are not in control of your own emotions. A great many people actually come to decide that the emotions are the enemy and they try to divorce themselves from their own feelings. This is a tragically poor decision. It takes them exactly opposite to the direction in which they really want to go. If you desire mastery of your Self, your life, your experience and your reality then, ironically, you should completely embrace your feelings and emotions and work to come to the realisation that they are absolutely under your control. When you own and control your emotions, then you are a small step from being the master of your reality. When you are in perfect control of your emotions, then you use them as powerful tools of creation. You give them full reign – but always in the direction you want them to go. You do not get blown around by them, as a leaf in the storm. And neither do you try to shut them down and silence them. And when you are in that heightened state of Self-possession and Self-creation, then you are approaching your true sense of Oneness with All That Is. Then you have learned much of what this system of reality has to teach, and you will be ready to leave here in triumph.

But the point is that you should only leave once you have discovered this, and created it to be so for yourself. Or else the system would have failed to work for you as it should.

SO, eventually I can tell you about Joy-Divine. This being has the role, of holding the frequency, the energetic framework, that is the very essence of pure JOY. The very truest nature of the thing that you would call joy is held steady, sure and true by this dear brother-soul of mine: your Inner-Self. And THAT is where the name Joy-Divine comes from. It is a name that is appropriate in this reality. But it holds no significance in other realities, you understand. It is really more of a job title than a name.

Z: Well, of course this is all fascinating to me! Given that this is my Inner-Self we are talking about I would love to talk a LOT more about this and find out more. But I think that would just be a selfish hogging of this conversation. We probably need to get back to the topic itself?

8: (gently smiles) This IS the topic itself. You see, I need you to understand the notion of a Consciousness Construct Holder in order to paint a bigger picture. These are beings who hold within themselves a particular consciousness construct. They hold these for you, who live inside this reality, so that you can have the illusion that those things are outside of yourselves. And so it is possible for you to walk around all day feeling emotionally empty. It is possible for you to believe that you can never make yourself happy again. It is possible for you to believe that only something outside of yourself can bring you happiness. Typically then, when you do hit whatever target you feel should result in your happiness your energy is momentarily brought into resonance with the energy – the consciousness construct – held by Joy-Divine. And for that moment you suddenly feel lifted and happy. And then you can go on believing that happiness lies outside of yourself. The illusion is maintained and you can carry on playing the game you-as-you-really-are wished to play.

This illusion is vital to the continuation of the Victim-based game almost everyone on earth is very intent on playing. If you realise that you can self-emote then you realise that you can decide to create how you will feel about things. Then you are no longer a victim of your external experiences. Soon after this discovery you will begin to see through other illusions. And as you see through the illusions, so you leave the Victim game. And the corollary of this should be quite obvious: if you wish to leave the Victim game, then it is necessary that you begin to see through the illusion. You will, and must, come to realise that you are able to decide for yourself EXACTLY how you want to feel at any particular moment. You are the one who controls your own feelings and emotions. It will take time and practise for you to show yourself this. You have, after all, spent a great deal of energy, across many lifetimes, teaching yourself that it is not so. So you should be willing to work at remembering that this is an illusion. But as you do awaken to the truth, so you will realise the power of it. Once you understand that your feelings and emotions are completely and utterly your own to command, then you are a very short step from being able to create your entire reality and experience as you desire

But we'll talk about this at much greater length when we discuss how you can learn to create your own reality. And now THAT seed is planted.

Z: Okay! Fabulous. I am beginning to understand more and more. Lights are going on for me about all kinds of stuff now.

8: That's good.

But for now, back to the story about the Consciousness Construct Holders. These are all sovereign beings of high consciousness who use their own very being to hold these frequencies for you. It is their nature, their duty, their privilege and their pleasure to do this for you. There are, for example, two beings who hold the true archetype for what is masculine and what is feminine in this reality. These two are twin souls who are the original "god and goddess". And then there is the office of the great unifier, the great energy that is responsible for holding the resonance, which is the energy of bringing all the separate parts back home to wholeness and oneness. This has been called the Christ energy. And there are many, many others. All absolutely important to the functioning of the game. Without any one of them, the game would simply not work. Like a machine that suddenly loses a vital cog.

Z: And so to Satan…

8: Yes. You see, I needed to preamble it like this because your very natural and normal feeling would be to see Satan as the unforgiven and unforgivable. As that which you must shun and revile. And that is a normal reaction to your conditioning. Nothing wrong with that. Or rather, there is nothing wrong with that UNLESS you desire to return to Oneness. Then it is time to grow up a little. Time to let go of the *scary-boogieman-that-comes-to-fetch-naughty-children-in-the-night* syndrome. Time to see this being for what it is and then make some appropriate decisions.

This is a being who holds a consciousness construct, nothing more and nothing less. And the consciousness construct it holds just happens to be The Adversary. And so, just as we can feel it acceptable to name Joy-Divine for his function, for the office that he holds, so it is acceptable that we can call this being The Adversary. Or we can, if we like, use the modern derivative of a more ancient name, which means exactly the same thing, and call him Satan.

Z: So then, if I feel happiness if I get into energetic resonance with Joy-Divine, what happens if I allow myself to get into energetic resonance with The Adversary?

8: Unpleasant things happen. You easily get very angry, or even fly into a rage. Resentment simmers towards all who you feel have wronged you. You hold grudges. You desire to hurt or damage others around you. You get all wound up around your own rightness and the wrongness of the people around you. You get unreasonable. You use verbal weapons to cause emotional harm and physical weapons to cause physical harm. You lead those "like you" to war against those "unlike you". In short, YOU become The Adversary. And there are few faster ways for you to drill yourself down, as deep as you can possibly go, into the Victim game than this. This IS the ultimate tool for keeping you inside the game. The Adversary is by far the single most effective cog in this particular machine.

And there we are! I think we have done a very good job of explaining the concept, given the minimal groundwork we had to go on.

Z: Maybe. But there is something I don't understand.

8: Of course there is. (smiles) Go ahead and ask.

Z: Well what you have described as the experience of coming into resonance with The Adversary – it really doesn't sound very nice.

8: Nice?!? No, of course it isn't NICE! It was never meant to be nice. It was meant to drive you into a deep state of separation. Which, in itself, is the most painful thing imaginable – to be violently ripped from a feeling of belonging, of Oneness, of rightness with All That Is. It is very, very un-nice!

Z: So I really don't want to experience that ever again. I reject that. It is just not me any more ever again!

8: Ah. Yes. We need to be very careful here. You would do well to remember that you create your own reality, and that you do it with your focus and attention. And saying "never again" is resistance. And, "*what you resist persists*," remember? You do not want to be saying anything is not part of yourself, not part of The Oneness. Everything is part of The One. That includes you, just as much as it includes The Adversary.

Z: But 8! That makes it impossible! How then am I to proceed? I don't want to come into resonance with The Adversary and now you tell me I can't reject him either! So what am I then to do?

8: Please realise that the only reason you can experience The Adversary energy is because it already exists inside of The One. It already exists inside of you. It is an entirely illusory creation that you have put this energy outside of yourself. This is what you did to enter into this Victim-game. You see? That is what I was telling you about the consciousness construct holders. Did you not follow that? That all of the emotions and feelings and archetypes are all from within the Oneness and are all ultimately from within you. But you need to experience them as being external to you if you are going to experience separation. You wanted to see what it would be like if this was all outside of you. THAT is how you experience duality. There is you, and then OUTSIDE OF YOU there is everything else. That is duality. Right?

Z: Okay I get that.

8: But it is an illusion. All is truly One. All of this is really within you. And every time that you reject something, divorce it from yourself and place it outside of yourself then you push yourself back into duality.

Z: Ohhhhhhhh. Sloooooowly I begin to get it. The Adversary is a fiendishly clever device. If you move into resonance with it, then you create duality, and if you reject it and push it away… then you create duality! Whatever you do with it, you create duality. Wow. That is… brilliant.

8: It is. The Adversary is the key to duality. And coming to understand this correctly is also the key to your release from duality. If you wish to find Oneness with All That Is, then you will need to unpick this lock.

As you have quite aptly said, it is fiendishly clever.

Z: Okay. Good then. I am willing to do this. I am willing to try to unpick this fiendish lock. Will you help me?

8: I am here. But I want you to do it for yourself. You have been equipped with all the lock-picks you need and you have been shown how to use them. It would be far better for you if you could do it yourself. And, in so doing, I am going to show you a formula that you can use for finding your own solutions to such problems that cannot be solved from the head. You solve it from the heart. Here is how.

Finding Your Own Solutions From the Heart
The Four Part Process

You are now going to do the first part. Which is to relax, ground yourself and move into your heart. So go and have a cup of tea. Go sit outside in the sun. Relax and release this issue from your mind. Then move into your heart. And THEN come back to your laptop. I will be waiting for you to take this conversation forward.

Z: Okay. This is exciting. And a bit daunting because I don't know how it will turn out. But I'll play along.

(I come back about an hour later)

Z: So instead of having tea and sitting in the sunshine I had a whole meal and a long soak in the bath. (smiles) Sorry.

8: (laughs) Excellent. The point really was for you to just take a step back and relax. To approach this from the heart rather than the mind. If you work from the mind, then you work analytically. You reduce problems to their constituent bits and can only come up with variations on solutions that you have seen before. When you come from the heart, you see problems holistically and can make intuitive leaps to entirely new solutions. And that was the point of asking you to go and relax and move into your heart. Eating and drinking also has a "grounding" effect. And so this was part one of the four part process.

For part two you have to state the problem. So now please tell me, as clearly and succinctly as you can, what is the problem, as you see it?

Z: Okay. The issue here is that I am caught between a desire to cease resonating with the energy of The Adversary and a need to not reject this being as the unlovable other.

8: That is a good first attempt at defining the problem. You have talked about the SYMPTOMS of the problem. You don't want to feel this resonance with The Adversary and you don't want to divorce yourself from another aspect of The One. That is fine. But it isn't the ACTUAL problem. What is the cause of the problem? What is at the root of this issue?

Now is the moment you must go to your heart. You heart knows. You mind wrestles with the obvious and tries to reframe the same old shapes into new pictures. Your heart sees the whole picture. Become aware of your heart now. Feel it in your chest. Feel how it feels. What IS that feeling? Allow your heart to talk to you. And tell me what you get. What is the problem?

Z: Oneness. Unity. The problem is that I don't want to continue to create ever more duality for myself. I want to come to know myself as being One with everything. I want to experience divine union with God. And dancing with The Adversary takes me in the wrong direction. And rejecting anyone and standing in judgement of them ALSO takes me in the wrong direction. So I can't choose either of these things. I can't resonate with The Adversary and I can also not reject him in any of his guises.

So what should I do?

8: Part two was to state the problem from the heart. You have done that. Part three, you might be surprised to know, is NOT to find the answer. Answers are just temporary illusory stories. They are not all that interesting. Far more important than finding the answer to some little puzzle, is taking the opportunity to define yourself. And THAT is part three. Instead of telling me the answer to this problem, why not instead, tell me who YOU are. Or rather who you really want to be. Who you will be when you have remembered who you REALLY are?

Z: I don't understand.

8: If you did, then I wouldn't be needed to show you this. Are you willing to play along and see where this goes?

Z: Of course. Yes. Okay, so the question you are asking me is who I say I am. Who do I say I will discover myself to be when I have woken up. Who is the … ascended version of me. Is that the question?

8: Yes. Now again go to your heart… and answer…

Z: I am a creator being of infinite power. I am love. I am one with the Oneness. I bring enlightenment and delight. I am joy. I am my most magical, magnificent Self.

8: Bold. And true. Good going. And now, part four: stand in that place of Oneness and tell me the solution to your previous problem. How do you, the creator being of infinite power and love who is one with the Oneness, proceed without either dancing with The Devil or declaring anyone to be beyond redemption?

Z: Hmm. I see something now: both of those are the same thing: dancing with The Devil IS declaring the other to be beyond redemption. The answer for me is to realise that All is indeed already One. And that all these experiences exist within myself. It is an illusion that they are outside of me. There is truly nothing "outside" of me. That is the illusion. It is all "inside" of me. So if I experience The Adversary, then I have created that experience. I chose to feel as if the experience was outside of me and outside of my control so that I could have the illusory experience of being in a game called Victim. If I want to stop playing that game then I simply realise that I am One with all that is and that the experience comes from within. I take responsibility.

8: That is very well done. In this moment you have entirely changed the game for yourself. You have moved your own consciousness into Gnosis. Which is the full realisation that you are both the actor and the playwright of your own stage-play. This is a great day.

It's a radical thought, but once you have truly understood that All is One, then this is a logical inevitability. The reason you do not get to it very easily yourself is because it is so at odds with your experience. But what you must understand is this:

There is no "out there" out there.

Z: Explain?

8: It is not just your feelings that are inside of yourself. EVERYTHING you perceive is inside you. There is, quite literally, nothing outside of yourself. What is outside of you is an illusion. The world you perceive is merely your own projection. It comes from what is real, which is what is inside of you.

Hard to grasp?

Z: Yeah, quite.

8: You'll get there. You are ready for this. I want you to think for a moment about who you REALLY are. Do you not have the perception sometimes that you are just a point of consciousness, which is observing your life?

Z: Yes, I do. Sometimes when I meditate or when I try to become hyper-aware, then I get this feeling that I am a point of no dimensions inside my own head. Then I am aware that I am not my body, not my thoughts, not my choices, not my emotions, not my ideas nor my experiences. I become aware that I am simply the observer of all this.

8: Yes. This is correct from one perspective. But the reason this experience can be quite unattractive to you is because you then come to feel that you are nothing but the observer. It feels a bit as if you are negating yourself. And the reason for that is the Veil. When you are in this place of awareness, you are right up against the Veil. On the one hand you are aware that the illusory stuff is just that: illusory. But on the other hand you are unable to become aware of what is actually real. Because the Veil is shielding you from seeing the truth of your own Self. So it is quite a stark place.

Z: Yes. But I don't mind. It can be quite peaceful. And on a very few occasions I have had the experience of suddenly being aware that "I" am not only that point of consciousness, not only my body, but everything that I perceive. Every sound I hear, everything I see. It is all me. I have somehow known this to be true, in a very few mediations.

8: It is the same thing actually. If you come to see yourself as the observer, then you are one small step from realising that you are creating that which you are observing. You come to the realisation that you are the film projector showing yourself the movie of your own experiences.

Z: But 8, if this is true then it has some pretty profound implications. It means that I really am the creator of my own reality.

8: You don't say!

Z: (laughs) Yes, I KNOW this is what you have been telling me all along, but I didn't realise you meant it quite this literally.

8: Ah. And when I have I ever not meant EXACTLY what I said. I tend to be quite precise.

Z: Yes (laughs) I know that too. I suppose it's just a bit of an adjustment to realise that the truth has been right in front of my face all along.

Okay so what do I do with this info now?

8: We were talking about the problem of what to do about The Adversary. Given what you now know, what will you decide to do?

Z: I guess there isn't actually all that much to do. I simply come to the realisation that all my experiences are my own projections. I have worked very hard to forget that fact. Once that was completely forgotten I got to experience myself as "what I am not". And now I am busy remembering it. As I remember it, so I will stop needing to believe there are others "outside of me" who are doing things in my life. I now come to realise that there are parts of this illusory construct that are unbelievably beautiful and loveable. I really love this planet. I love to experience life here. So I now find a way to keep creating the stuff I love, and then I release the need to create stuff that I don't like.

8: May I offer you my take on it? Can I tell you what this all means to me?

Z: Oh yes, please!

8: First: your outer world is a projection of your inner reality. It is your story.

Second: the illusion you have had is that the outer world is what is really real and important and the inner world is either unreal or unimportant.

Third: this led you to try to change things in your outer world to make them more like you want them.

Fourth: this was the cause of a lot of pain and confusion because, the harder you tried to fix the things external to yourself, the more you failed and hurt yourself.

Fifth: the more you hurt yourself, the more your outer-world reflected your pain back at you. The more messed up, troubled and confused your reality became.

Sixth: at some point, finally, everyone hits a terminus. At some point you come to the decision to stop trying to fix your outer-world and to try to heal your Inner-Self instead.

Seventh: as you begin to succeed at healing your own inner world, so you may notice your outer-world becoming happier and more harmonious.

Eighth: so wake up! Become observant! See what works! See the obvious thing that is being presented to you. If there is something in your outer-world that troubles you, you should look INSIDE. Find what it is inside you that troubles you. Find your own inner pain or confusion. Find a way to love it and heal it. If, and when, you do then the problem in your outer-world will miraculously cease to hurt you. It will heal. It will do so in beautiful and surprising ways. And this is because you will cease to project a damaged and broken reality outwards.

Z: Yes.

Yes, I get it.

Click!

8: It is a game-changing realisation, isn't it? We have been playing around in the shallows up to now. We have been preparing the soil and planting the seeds. And now! Now we see the first shoots of new green life. Now you can begin to re-imagine everything. Now everything changes for you. Now you must learn how to create effectively and powerfully, knowing full well that you DO create. And very soon you will be ready to change the state of your game completely.

Z: But 8 – I have to ask about the idea of "others". I mean, sure, I am projecting my reality. But what about my beloved soul-mate, Lisa? She seems to exist in my outer-reality. And what about my readers? Are these other beings in my world not real?

8: They are all absolutely real. Just not in the way you have imagined them to be. They are all just as you are. They are beautiful and divine aspects of The One; facets of the same great jewel shining in the light that they themselves are casting.

The trick is to understand that each and every aspect of The One projects its own reality. Every single reality is different. But here is the thing: you may decide to allow your reality to be influenced by the projections of another, if you choose. You might decide to agree to experience certain parts of your reality the same as someone else does. This agreement is a *consensus*. And so you have a *consensus reality*. You create it together so it is *co-created*. And that is how you come to feel that you and others all inhabit the same reality. Actually you have simply come to an agreement with a number of other aspects of The One to experience similar things in a similar way. And that is how a game is played. A group gets together and arrives at consensus on the rules of the reality and then they enter the game.

Z: But soon the game is going to end?

8: Yes. Soon. Because that is what you-as-you-really-are agreed to when you entered the game. That it would end in a particular way. And now you are ending it as you said you would. And then you can decide what you are going to do next. I know for a fact that a good number of the players have already created the beginnings of new rule sets of how they want to play the next game because I am party to those discussions. There are a number of new realities that are busy forming. And you who love life on this planet but wish for it to be a more loving, caring, joyful experience – you are readying a new experience for yourselves, which you shall, quite soon, re-imagine yourselves into.

And THAT is something which we will be talking about at great length still. You decided a while ago that you wanted to try to transition directly from the one reality to the other. And so we'll be laying plans for that.

But now we need to get back to the main thread of this discussion. We were, after all, talking about the issue of what to do about The Adversary.

Z: Yes. But I think I get it now. I project my reality. I am telling myself a story. By living myself into the story I get to experience myself in amazing new ways. This allows me to decide for myself if the things I believe about myself and choose for myself are good. I get to see if they are working for me and making me happy in all kinds of different scenarios. If they do, then I keep them. If they don't, then I make a new choice. This is the beauty and the value of the story that I am in.

So what happens if I encounter The Adversary? Well then I decide if I like the encounter or not. Does it take me forward to where I have said I want to be, or does it not? If it does, then I have no problems. If it doesn't, then I make a new decision about myself so that I no longer invite this interaction.

And if I think of it... it seems to me that an interaction with The Adversary is really just me, showing myself some place within myself where I don't love myself. This is me, showing myself something that I reject and find unacceptable. That is why I set it apart as the enemy – as The Adversary. So, it very much seems to me, the answer would be to find that unloved part of myself and love it. If I could do that consistently each time I experienced The Adversary, then I think I'd probably come to cease experiencing The Adversary at all.

8: Bravo.

We must, quite soon, have a very important conversation about "Negative Consciousness Constructs". It will form an integral part of the conversation about the nature of Love. In it you will come to a new understanding of things such as pain, fear, anger and jealousy. And while we are at it, we'll talk about other things that you have misunderstood – such as ego and karma. You will see that these things are only a problem when they are "outside of you", when you remove them from yourself and make them unlovable. When you reintegrate these things into your heart and make yourself whole again, then they not only lose their power over you but, in fact, become great and powerful tools, which you can use to the greater good of all.

Z: I look forward to that very much.

8: Good. But now, can we agree to leave the issue of The Adversary behind us?

Z: Oh, yes. This has been resolved for me in quite an unexpected way. I understand this issue now and it certainly doesn't trouble me anymore.

8: Good, but before we move on, I must ask you the usual question. Given what you now know... is Satan evil?

Z: (laughs) I have to laugh because I would have thought that is like asking "is the pope Catholic?" And yet, here I am, discovering that the answer to this is not as unambiguous as I had thought. It would seem to me that it is possible to experience Satan as evil. But it is also possible to see that this is just the role he plays here in this reality. And without him playing that role, this particular reality construct would not work as it does. And finally, it is also possible to see that I am allowing, choosing and creating all that I experience and so I am never actually victimised. There actually is no such thing as "evil", after all!

You know, 8, I've just had a thought.

8: And that is...

Z: Well, it strikes me that it must be a pretty miserable and lonely job being The Adversary.

8: I believe it is a role that carries substantial challenges. There is going to have to be a great deal of love and healing given before this being will be able to find its way home when this reality construct is collapsed. But this too was chosen.

Z: Hmm... I am amazed to find myself again feeling some empathy here.

8: That is well.

And now it is time to bring this conversation to a conclusion.

"If there is such a thing as evil, then it is an opportunity to learn about love"

This is true because, as you have discovered, evil is an illusory experience. And it is an illusion that you are only able to have when you believe that you are in a state of separation from The One. So that is the answer. Return your consciousness to the Oneness and you will no longer be able to experience evil. You will no longer be able to feel your choices can be taken from you. You will no longer be able to feel that you are the victim of another. The whole experience of evil in all its guises will be left behind you.

Z: That works for me. Thank you, 8.

Now the only question is HOW do I return my consciousness to The Oneness?

8: That's right, that IS the question. But you see, we first had to remove this obstacle from your path. As long as you were holding onto the idea that there are others out there who are so unacceptable that they cannot be a part of The One, then you yourself would not be able to return. It is like a blockage that you had placed inside your own heart. But that is shifted now. So now we may proceed. And the way we proceed is... LOVE. Love is the one and only way to move back to a state of Oneness.

Z: And that is what we're talking about in the next chapter! Just as you said it would be.

8: That's right. See you in the next chapter.

* * * * *

Chapter 11. What is Love?
A Conversation with 8

Zingdad: Hi 8

8: Hello my dear friend. It is good to be talking to you again.

Z: It is! It's been some months since I finished writing the previous chapter. In the intervening period, I have moved from the city to a small parcel of land in the forest.

8: ...and you have begun writing about your personal journey too...

Z: Yes I have. Just as you recommended in the last chapter, I now have a blog section up on my website (*http://www.zingdad.com/blog*) where I share what is going on in my life.

8: This is excellent news. You are still going to be very surprised to see what this little blog section of yours will grow into. But let's not run ahead of ourselves shall we? Let's get down to the business of this next chapter.

Z: Okay, great. This is the chapter in which you tell me what love is?

8: It is.

You know, this is a great moment. For you this is the turning point between the outward journey and the inward. Mark this moment. It is the birth of your New Being.

Z: What does that mean, 8?

8: A newborn does not know that it is newborn. For the newborn, there is not a sudden moment of self-awareness. It is a gradual dawning. Slowly the being comes to the awareness of its new situation. Slowly it learns to make sense of its new body. Slowly it learns to use the new tools at its disposal.

Z: New tools? You mean like fingers and toes?

8: Those, yes, but also smiles and tears.

And you are, right now, in many respects, a newborn. For every being who walks the ascension path, there comes a moment when the outwards journey has really and truly wound down and come to a halt. There is a specific moment when there is a turning around and the Homewards journey is begun. You will not be aware of it because this moment of turning always happens in great stillness. Which is counter-intuitive, isn't it? You expect your important transitions to happen with a great deal of movement, activity and noise. But they don't. Great change happens when you are being really very still indeed.

Z: I don't understand...

8: Let me use a very simple example. Throw a stone up into the air, as hard and as high as you can. It accelerates out of your hand in the skyward direction. This is its outward flight. Then, as gravity begins to tug upon it, the stone begins to slow. Finally, at its apogee, the stone comes to a halt. And only then, in this moment of perfect stillness, can it change direction and begin its homeward flight back to you. The flight home features an ever-increasing acceleration, it is true. But the moment of change of direction is right in the middle of the stone's moment of greatest stillness. And you are, right now, at that point where you are about to turn around. You SHOULD have come to perfect rest already, but you don't know how. You have travelled so far and so fast for so long that you don't actually know to do any other. But you must. You actually MUST come to stillness. Without this stillness you will not change direction.

If you do not come to stillness, then we can have a long and interesting conversation about love. I can tell you many interesting things about it and we will go off on all those curious tangents that we both enjoy so much and it will all be fine and fascinating, but it will not actually take you where you need to go. You will attain some intellectual understanding about love. But you will gain no KNOWING in your heart. And the discussion we need to have here must be built upon that sure KNOWING. Without it, the conversation we both really desire to have, will not occur. We will talk around the heart of the matter and never really get to its essence.

Z: So I must... what... meditate? And then?

8: Something more than your normal meditation is required of you. You meditate regularly and that is good. But your meditations are not actually the stillness of being that you think they are. Every meditation chases after one purpose or another. There is no fault with that, but something else is required now. You see, it is now time for you to change your mode of being entirely. Like the stone that has rushed away from the home of the hand, so you too must come to perfect stillness before you can change direction. And, from within that stillness, you must listen only to your heart. It might take you some time to get this right. You are so used to filling every corner of your consciousness with noise and movement that you might need to practice being still quite a bit before you achieve the goal, and are able to really hear your heart.

But I understand that all this is just so much theory to you. What you are asking of me is that I should give you something practical to DO.

Z: Yes, please.

8: It is a beautiful irony: until you know how to truly BE, you will still need something to DO to enable BEing. (he smiles) What a marvellous cosmic joke.

But I am able to help you with this. Here is what you do:

Pick a day in which you have no appointments. Set that day aside. It is to be your day of stillness and listening. Tell everyone that you will be uncontactable on that day. Tell those who share your home with you that you will not speak to them on that day and they are not to speak to you either. It is your day of silence.

The night before your day of silence, you must switch off your mobile telephone and all such devices that might intrude upon you. You must switch off your computer, your television and your radio. All devices, which you use to input information into your consciousness, must be silent for your day of silence.

On the morning of the day of silence you must allow yourself to awaken without input. In other words, no alarm-clock or similar device. Awaken naturally. Stay in bed and BE STILL. Listen to your heart.

Z: What does that mean, 8? What does it mean to listen to my heart?

8: In due course this will become second nature to you – much more normal and natural than even listening to a sound with your ears. But for now, I do understand that you need some guidance.

You should know that your heart is a portal. It is your connection to the Divine. It can be said that your Inner-Self resides inside your heart. It can even be said that the Oneness is inside your heart. All wisdom and truth and creativity are instantly available and accessible to you through your heart. But you need to learn to listen, truly LISTEN, to your heart. Because it speaks to you quietly and gently in the language of love. But believe me when I say, it speaks very eloquently when it needs to.

Z: Okay. But HOW do I listen?

8: For a start, make sure there is nothing else taking up residence in your consciousness, making a noise. Your heart will not compete for your attention! This is why you need to ask your family not to speak to you. It is why you must not engage with reading matter, not check your email, not speak to anyone. No external input at all.

That is the start.

Then you must be still and listen to your heart. You can, if you need something to do, just listen to your physical heart beating. That will help you because it is a literal listening to your heart. But then you should seek to still your consciousness and see what you receive.

And this is how you should spend your day. Be still. Listen. Wait upon your heart.

Your heart might speak to you more in "feelings" than in words. But, if you pay attention, you will know exactly what those feelings mean.

Z: And then?

8: Then you see what it has to say!

Z: What if it has nothing to say?

8: Don't be daft boy, all of the Oneness is in there! All of Life is in there! Life needs to express! Look around you at the universe, teeming with vigorous activity. Look at the world outside your window. Look at a drop of water under a microscope. Look at the nucleus of an atom. Where, anywhere, is the Oneness saying nothing? The Oneness is speaking with passionate eloquence all the time. The only problem is that you are sitting with your fingers in your ears, shouting nonsense doggerel, drowning out the truth and beauty that is flooding in at you all the time from all directions. For just one moment, do you think you can SHUT UP and LISTEN?

Or, to put this in slightly gentler terms: can you let go of your fears and your excuses and just go and see what is there?

Z: I am duly chastised (I smile sheepishly). Yes. I'll do this. Tomorrow is Sunday. I'll make that my day of silence and I'll see what I get.

8: Good.

It might be that tomorrow is just a practice run and that you actually need to do it again at some point. You might even need to spend a few days in silence. Be prepared for that.

Z: Okay, 8.

8: But if you manage, for even a single moment, to get out of the way, to be really still and to truly LISTEN to your heart then, I assure you, you will gain wondrous insights. And it will come to you in your heart such that you KNOW it to be true. Which is quite a different thing from the ideas that you can hold in your head and think about. KNOWING and thinking are very different things. And when it arrives you will have no doubt that it did arrive. It will be a powerful experience. And what arrives will be the basis upon which we will be able to build this chapter.

Will you do this?

Z: I will.

8: Good then, I shall speak to you again after Sunday…

(Zingdad note: Sunday passed and, as intended, I had a day of silence. It is now a week later)

Z: Okay, 8, I had my day of silence. And I've already updated my blog with the story.

8: Very good! And I am so pleased it went so well for you.

For the sake of completeness, why don't you repeat the story here in this chapter? Tell us how the day of silence went for you.

Z: Sure. This is what happened…

I woke up on Sunday morning and stayed in bed, lying quietly, listening. Well, mostly I was thinking about listening and filling my thoughts with all kinds of ideas about what listening to my heart should be like and how I should feel and… well… I wasn't really very still. So I meditated, which went a bit better, and I managed to release all thoughts for a while. Until I realised that I HAD released all thoughts, and began to think about that. And then I wondered how it would be to listen to my heart without thinking any thoughts. And then I realised I was filling my mind with babble again!

This, I realised, was going to be a lot harder than I had thought.

I won't bore you with the details of my day, but I will tell you that I was often frustrated with myself. "Being still" sounds easy. You just stop thinking, and then you listen, right? I can tell you it is quite a challenge to break the noise addiction. At least, I found it so.

By late afternoon, I was done wrestling with myself. I was done TRYING to be quiet. I had had enough of attempting to find the right way towards stillness. I was through with trying to listen. So, I decided the day was probably a waste and that I should just enjoy it as it was instead of fighting with it. I made a snack and went and sat outside to watch a truly breath-taking sunset. It was magnificent. As I sat and marvelled with wonderment at the beauty of the spectacle a deep peace settled over me. And in that quietude something came to me. A thought sidled in through the back-door of my mind. A thought about love. A beautiful thought. A thought arrived in such a way that it really touched me. I didn't so much think it, as feel it. I felt it to be true and it brought tears to my eyes. I knew THIS was what I had been waiting for. Here it was. Finally when I stopped trying and wresting… it was simply there as if it had always been!

I came inside and sat before my laptop to capture this thought in words. Before I could think about how I was going to structure this, or what approach I would take, I found myself typing. It flowed out of me in one go. Non-stop, no editing and no changes, I wrote it all down.

This is what I wrote:

* * * * *

I listened to my heart and this is what it said:

In the beginning of every particle of consciousness, from The One, right down to the smallest, newest particle of Life, there is a moment when that being gains self-awareness. In THE ASCENSION PAPERS we have paraphrased that moment as that being saying, "*Here I am*". But self-awareness is always curious. And therefore the next utterance can be paraphrased as, "*What am I?*"

The journey outwards begins always with, "*Here I am, what am I?*'

Then, the journey itself consists of, "*I might be THIS. No wait, maybe I am THAT. Or what if I am THIS.*" On and on and on and on. Always searching for the answer. Each time something new is tried, there is a fragmentation of the consciousness. New beings are sent out on a foray of self-discovery from within the consciousness of the parent being. Variations are tried. Multiples of possibilities explored. Whole clouds of consciousness are expressed. Multiplying and complexifying and then specialising and trying again. Always seeking that moment of bliss and peace that comes from having found the answer to the question, "*What am I?*"

And, in every instance, with every answer we have tried, we have pushed away from The One. Further and further, we have pushed out. Like a tidal wave that burst forth from but a teacup, we have surged out. Becoming a tsunami of consciousness, we have pushed off from one another; outwards, outwards, ever seeking: THE TRUTH. Ever seeking the answer...

What

Am

I

?

And here we find ourselves living our lives on Planet Earth, way down in the densest place of consciousness. You could say that this is about as far out as the wave would ever push because this is about the deepest forgetfulness of the point of origin that could ever be achieved. Thanks to The Veil of Unknowing and the choices we have all collectively taken; this is IT. Perhaps it is possible to head out further? Perhaps someone wants to try? I don't. I am ready to be a part of the returning. Like all waves that have pushed up from the greatest depths of the ocean and found themselves crashing to the shore, this wave is going to return. It is going to go surging back with ever-increasing speed and exuberance to its source. To The One. We are returning!

And HOW are we to return?

It begins with the correct answer to the question, "*What am I?*"

And the correct answer of course is... Love.

Every other answer causes further complexity. Every other answer pushes you outwards and away. Because every other answer implies something else that you are NOT.

For example. If I am (as I have discovered myself to be) a being called Delight, the child of Joy-Divine, then I am NOT all kinds of other things. I am NOT fear, pain, sadness, loss, anger, hatred or misery. Obviously. But I am also not stillness, peace, harmony, order, or patience. I am not even kindness, honesty, justice, valour, dignity, steadfastness, dependability, righteousness or any other such worthy thing. Do you see? If I choose any thing at all and say, "*I am THAT*" then I am, in that very self-same moment, saying, "*I am NOT that*" to a whole host of other things. So anything that I would claim myself to be causes separation, division and pushing away from The Oneness.

The ONLY exception to that rule is the statement, "*I am Love*". Not passion. Not lust. Not need. Not any of these silly, temporary little feelings that we usually refer to when we say the word, love. No. I am Love with a capital L. I mean the kind of Love that looks at another being and sees God in their eyes – sees the wonder and the perfection inside the heart of that being, irrespective of the exterior they are currently wearing. Love is that which is given to everything and everyone everywhere, unconditionally, always. That is the Love I am talking about.

I am talking about the kind of Love that puts you down on your knees in gratitude that you are alive. That threatens to crush your heart with the beauty of the world around you. That makes you yearn to be the greatest and best and most magnificent that you could possibly be, simply so that you are worthy to serve the Life that you perceive around you.

If THAT is the answer to your question. If you can declare with surety, steadfastness and conviction, "*I AM Love!*" Then you are an answer-bearer. Then you are a particle of Life that is going back home. In the very moment of that declaration, for you, the tide has turned. You are then in the wave that is done rushing up the shore… and is now pulling back to sea. And as you go back, so you will collect other particles. You will see everything that you have ever been and done in this lifetime and you will say, "*I am Love AND I am THAT*". And as you go, you will see more and more particles of Self and you will say, "*I am Love and I am this too, and THAT and that one and that one also.*" You will declare, "*I am Love and I am ALL of these beings!*" And all of these beings will get carried home with you in the tide of your amazing Love. And then you will meet your Inner-Self. You will see it for its amazing and beautiful Self. You will fall in Love with this being. And you will see too its wounds and its pain. And you will soothe them all with your capacity for Love. "*I am Love,*" you will say, "*and I AM THAT!*"

And so, whoever you are. Wherever you are. However you got to being where you are. There will come a time in your journey home, and in my journey home, where we will be looking at the same great being and we will both be saying: "*I am Love and I am THAT*". And then you and I shall be One. And indeed, in due course all beings everywhere, in All That Is, will look to The One. And we shall ALL declare, "*I am Love and I am THAT!*"

But for now, I look forward to the moment when I know that I am you, and you are me. And because I know that time is an illusion and all time is really now, I can already look out at you from across the divide of this bit of text. I can see you reading this. I can look at you and say, "*I am Love and I am THAT!*"

* * * * *

… and that is what I got, 8.

8: Bravo, my friend.

I am well pleased, and so very proud of you. This is beautiful.

And to think you were worried that you heart might have nothing to say…

Z: Silly, huh?

8: Perhaps. But fortunately you know better now. The only time your heart would ever be still is if you yourself were in such a perfect state of blissful oneness and perfect balance that there would be nothing for it to add.

You see, anything that you do that causes imbalance, will result in your heart speaking to you. And the song of returning to balance is the heart-song. But you must not misunderstand; "imbalance" is not a bad thing! Not at all. If there were no imbalance, there would be no universe, no life, no "you" and no "me". Nothing would exist without imbalance. And Love itself is a function of imbalance. Love is the cause of the imbalance in the first place and it is the drive to re-balance the imbalance. Love is, in fact, the energy that drives EVERYTHING.

Z: I have so many questions about all this, 8. I don't know where to begin…

8: You have done the work of being silent and listening to your heart and you have thereby attained the basic understanding that you need for us to be able to get this chapter to you. So I'm going to help you. I'm going to tell you a story that will go a long way towards helping you to clarify your understanding of the way Life works and of why Love really is EVERYTHING. And then, when you have a better understanding, you'll know with greater clarity what it is you wish to ask of me.

Z: That sounds great. Thank you, 8. I'd love to hear the story.

8: Here it is then…

The Story of Push and Stay and the Infinite Elastic Ball

Z: I have to say, that is the most imaginative story title you have come up with yet!

8: You like it?

Z: I do. And I wonder what kind of a story could have a title like that?

8: It's a good one. But it's a bit different from most stories you would hear. This one requires of you that you not only listen to the story, but that you do some work to imagine the ideas I am going to express. If you do so, then you will receive the wisdom inherent in the story.

You are, of course, familiar with elastic bands. Well, I'm going to ask you to imagine something which is a little like a rubber band. But instead of being a band, it is a ball. The most curious attribute of this elastic ball is that it is infinite. Infinity is not something that you will naturally and easily understand, though, so I am going to take some time to explain this properly.

Firstly, this ball can be stretched out an infinite amount in any direction. It never snaps or breaks and it never runs out of stretch.

Secondly, it can be stretched in an infinite number of different directions. And here you are going to have to work with me to imagine this. A rubber band can only be stretched in two directions, right? Either end can be pulled outwards. But the Infinite Elastic Ball can be stretched in EVERY direction. Left, right, up, down, yesterday, next year, green, cinnamon, happy, vibrant, quartz…

Z: Whoa! Are those things directions?

8: For something that is infinite they are. They are directions in consciousness. You live in a narrowly confined three-dimensional world. You imagine that the cardinal directions in space are the only directions you can move in. Some on your planet have become a little more imaginative and have come to the conclusion that "time" is also a direction. They are right. The next step is to realise that all things are of consciousness and that all consciousness can be traversed. But let's not get stuck here; in due course this will make better sense to you.

Back to the Infinite Elastic Ball. If you take these two properties: that it can be stretched out infinitely and in an infinite number of directions, then it follows that this ball includes everything. Nothing is outside of it, and everything is inside of it.

Z: I'm not sure I understand that. But I always have a bit of difficulty understanding the concept of infinity. Are you saying that anything that is infinite MUST include absolutely everything that exists?

8: Yes.

The word "Infinity" originally comes from the Latin word, *infinitas,* which means "unboundedness". If there is a boundary, then it is finite. And specifying that anything at all is NOT inside this Ball, is to specify a boundary. But this ball is not finite, it is IN-finite. Infinite. So there can be nothing that it does not include.

Z: That's a crazy thought. All things that are infinite, include all other things!

8: Exactly. This is actually a very interesting point that we might want to spend some time talking about in due course. But for now you can simply understand that all-inclusiveness is a property of the infinite.

Z: Okay, got it.

8: The third attribute of the Infinite Elastic Ball is the fact that, when it is not stretched out in any direction at all, it collapses down to nothingness and ceases to exist. Can you imagine that?

Z: Not really. If we are all inside the ball – if EVERYTHING is inside of the ball – how can it cease to exist if we stop stretching it out?

8: This is a good question that you ask. It allows me to tell you something very important about the nature of What Is. You struggle to imagine that the ball can snap back to nothingness because your experience of your reality is that "things" are real. You don't yet know that they are all transitory illusions created by you, out of your collective consciousness.

You, at your core, are pure consciousness. This is your true nature. And pure consciousness, when it ceases all function, has no form. There is a dictum in the world of architecture and design which goes, "*form follows function*" and in that context it means something like "*purpose should dictate design*". Now I want to reuse that phrase in a different context. You see, in the most universal sense, it really is true that form DOES follow function. In fact, it is function that brings form into being. It is DOing and creating that causes all form to come into existence. If you cease all function, then you will lose all form. You will return to pure consciousness and simply be at one with the Oneness. If all parts of the Oneness were to cease function, were to cease pushing out at the Infinite Elastic Ball, then, yes, all would collapse to formlessness or no-thing-ness.

The fourth attribute of The Infinite Elastic Ball is called *Infinite Variation*. Understand, time does not act on the Infinite Elastic Ball – time is just one of the things INSIDE the Infinite Elastic Ball. So there can be no past or future for the Infinite Elastic Ball. This means that this ball is always in all of its possible states. It is, right now, pulled out in every single direction it ever was pulled in AND every single direction it ever will be pulled in. And it is also NOT pulled in any of those directions. It is right now busy expanding AND busy contracting. And every other permutation that we can imagine AND the great many more that we cannot. The Infinite Elastic Ball is in all of these states, all at the same time. If it is to be truly infinite, it must be so that all possibilities exist at the same time. At no point is any possibility excluded. Otherwise there would again be a boundary, you see.

This really means that everything that is created always exists, and it all exists at the same time. All of it is RIGHT NOW. Because that is what "infinite" means.

Can you imagine that?

Z: That's a bit of a stretch for me. (laughs) But okay, I can imagine it. What does this all really mean?

8: Everything I have told you up to now was necessary background was all necessary. But to get to the real meaning of this I am going to add some personalities to the story to whom you can relate. Allow me to introduce you to the two characters of our story: Push and Stay are their names.

As I have said, the Oneness is creative and Self-creative. In its quest for Self-discovery, one of the things it has done is to imagine that there are different parts to Itself. And then, because it imagines it to be so, it IS so. So, in the beginning, one part of the Oneness says, "*I am going to push outwards so that I can look back and see what I am*". It does so… and it sees itself for the first time! And looking upon Itself, love is born. When any part of the Oneness looks at any other part of the Oneness, it sees the beauty, wonder and perfection of The Oneness – of Itself – and it feels Love. I can paraphrase it like this: *"The God in me sees the God in you"*. It is truly Love! It causes those parts to draw together in wonder and amazement at each other. They see that they are both of The Oneness. They move towards each other and merge back with each other and then they are, once again, One.

It is Love that draws them back together.

Z: That's beautiful.

8: It is. And what it means is that any part of the Oneness anywhere only really needs to pay attention and really SEE any other part of the Oneness, and this will happen. If you have eyes to really look and SEE, you will see God in every other around you. In every animal, every plant, every sunset. You'll see God in the insects, in the waves of the ocean and in the stars that shine. You'll see God in your own body and you will most certainly see God in the eyes of other people around you.

Z: But this doesn't often happen, does it 8? I don't know many people who experience their world like that. And much as I'd like to, I only feel I have had glimpses of that. I'd really love to be able to see things like that all the time. Is that possible?

8: Yes. I am going to help you with exactly that in this chapter. In due course, we will talk about *"how to learn to love"*. There are many ways to get there and I will share some of those ways with you. But that is later on in this conversation. We still need to finish the story of Push and Stay and the Infinite Elastic Ball. There is much that you can learn from Push and Stay.

A little earlier I mentioned that nothing would exist without imbalance. Now I will explain this in more detail.

Imbalance in the Field of Consciousness

Everything that exists – including you, me, the chair you are sitting on, the universe you dwell in and every reality that ever existed, in short EVERYTHING – is created with imbalances in the field of consciousness of the Oneness. You see, if all is in perfect balance, then there is only consciousness. No forms, no individuals, no personalities, no creations, no realities and no variation. Just a perfectly, blissfully still consciousness in silent repose. That is, one could say, The One at rest. But in order for The One to DO anything, there must arise some imbalance. But there can only ever be LOCAL imbalance. All local imbalance MUST be re-balanced elsewhere in The One. So locally there is imbalance, but across the whole of The One there is always perfect balance. Not even for an instant can The One be thrown out of balance overall.

Z: I think I understand, 8. But perhaps you could help me to imagine this?

8: Oh, certainly. This phenomenon happens constantly on your planet with the tides in the oceans. When there is a high tide on one part of the globe, it is balanced by a low tide elsewhere. When a wave rises up from the ocean, it is balanced by a trough of equal size beside it. In all these instances, there are local increases and decreases in the ocean depth and volume, but across the whole of the ocean, there is no increase or decrease.

Do you follow?

Z: That helps a great deal, thank you.

8: So, with that understanding in place, you are ready to see that, in order for Push to come into being in one part of The One, there would, at the same time, HAVE to be a counter-balance to

Push that would immediately also come into being.

You cannot create Push without creating "not-Push". For the purposes of our story, we shall call "not-Push", Stay.

So, can you see that the creation of Push IS the creation of Stay? And that the creation of Stay IS the creation of Push? They are created together and are perfectly balanced, equal-but-opposite, expressions of The One.

These counter-balancing beings can seem, from a very localised perspective, to be two different beings that are acting differently and independently of each other. But this is only a temporary illusion. There is a greater truth, which is that they are actually the same one being who is also conscious of itself and who is simply acting *through* them.

Z: How can that be, 8? I can't really imagine that.

8: This is again quite an important understanding, so I shall take a moment to help you to understand:

Last night you slept soundly and barely moved your body for hours on end. Then, this morning you went out to your farmland and worked hard physically and were very active with your body. Right now you are writing THE ASCENSION PAPERS and your mind and intuitive centres are very active. Inside of the flow of time, you might think you are one person who sequentially goes through these three different states of being. But from outside of time, it might seem as if you are one being who also holds three other coexistent beings inside his consciousness. Possibly we would call these other three beings, Sleepingman, Hardworkingman and Writingman.

Z: Or maybe Snoozy, Sweaty and Smarty.

8: (laughs) Yes, perhaps.

But you can see, of course, that Snoozy, Sweaty and Smarty are each just aspects of you. And, in just that same way, The One is one being, but has within Its being an infinite number of different aspects. And for the purposes of this story, two of those aspects are Push and Stay.

Does that help you to understand?

Z: It does, thank you!

8: And as we have seen, Push pushes out, sees Itself and comes charging back, full of excitement and wonder, and reunites with Stay.

Z: And then what happens to Push and Stay?

8: Well, through their little game of self-discovery, Push and Stay have enabled The One to experience itself in a new and wonderful way. The One caught a glimpse of Itself and it discovered Love. As a result, it decides to try this experience again. So Push and Stay arise once again and decide that they loved the experience so much that they want to do it again, exactly the same. And so they try. But, here comes the part I like: even though they want to repeat the exact experience, they cannot. Because, you see, you can never do the same thing twice.

Z: You can't?

8: No. Remember chapter 8? *"Change is the only constant"*.

Well I can prove that statement once again, using the story of Push and Stay, and at the same time I can tell you why they could not do the same thing again.

The first time Push pushed out, it WAS the first time. He can never push out *for the first time* again. The next time he pushes out, it will be the second time. So it is different. Now he has some experience of pushing out. He has some idea of what to expect. And the fact that he knows what to expect, changes the whole experience. He is not quite so surprised to see Stay. And when he returns to tell Stay what she looks like from "out there", she is not nearly so excited. They do not implode into each other with nearly the same force. The whole exercise is not nearly as ecstatic.

Z: Sounds like things are going to get less and less exciting for Push and Stay. Is their relationship doomed to failure? Do they need a marriage counsellor? (laughs)

8: (laughs) No. Fortunately not. Because, you see they will only try to repeat the exercise once or twice before they will see the obvious and then they will change the game. Push and Stay are parts of the Oneness. And, as such, they share in the attributes of the Oneness. They are creative and self-creative. And they are curious and questing. So they change the rules and it becomes new and exciting again.

Z: How? How do they change the rules, 8?

8: Well, what if this time Push decided to see how far he could push out? What if he decided to push out SO FAR that he managed to forget that he was pushing out in the first place? That would be different! Because then, returning to Stay would be like the first time for him, even though it wouldn't be for her. And then something magical would happen. Because Push would push out for a whole long while, pushing and pushing until he was so far away from Stay that there was no way for him to see her. And because Push doesn't have the facility of memory, out-of-sight really is out-of-mind. So then he will have forgotten Stay. And if he has forgotten Stay, then he has also forgotten that he is Push. In that instant Push brings forth from his own consciousness a new being, whom we shall call Forget.

But you'll remember that I told you that all imbalance is always only local imbalance, because it is always perfectly balanced by another imbalance elsewhere in the infinite field of consciousness of The Oneness. So when Push creates Forget he also, at the same time creates "not-Forget". Whom we shall henceforth call, Remember. And so, memory is created. Remember is the first being in all that is who can hold within her mind something that she is not directly experiencing. Remember can see a simulacrum of Stay in her mind without actually being near to Stay.

Z: And Forget?

8: Well he has forgotten! So he is wandering around the outer extremities of The Infinite Elastic Ball. Let's focus our attention on him for a while, as he has much to teach us about ourselves.

Forget's lot in life is somewhat confusing. He has no knowledge of who he is, or how he came to be where he is, or what the point of his existence is. He simply IS. But in his heart he knows he is incomplete. In his heart, he feels a yearning for that which he has forgotten. But he doesn't know that. All he knows is that he feels a loss and that he feels disconnected. Forget is alone, without knowing how he came to be so, or why.

So? What does Forget do?

He does the only thing he can do. He pushes out in a new direction in consciousness. He does this by asking himself basic questions such as, "*why am I here?*" or, "*what is my purpose?*"

Forget might decide to answer his question with: "*I am here because I am seeking to understand; to know the truth*" and, in so doing, he creates within his consciousness a new being called Truth. Or he might say, "*I am doing whatever I do for the pure simple joy of it, because it is FUN!*" and so he creates within himself, Joy. Or he might say, "*I do this to serve others; I am here for the good of all*" and so he creates himself as Love. And those are just three possible options. There are an infinite number of options and alterations and variations as to why Forget might decide he exists and who he therefore decides he is.

And, as he declares himself to be, so he is! For Forget, though he doesn't know it, is an indivisible part of The Oneness. He is god-like. He is creative and self-creative. And he has the power to create himself in any form he might choose. And, as he creates himself, so he IS. But he does so within the confines of The Infinite Elastic ball which has, remember, the amazing property of Infinite Variation. You remember what that means?

Z: Yes. It means everything that is created always exists, and it all exists at the same time. All of it is RIGHT NOW.

8: Good. Yes.

Z: I cheated – I scanned back to look. (laughs) I think I am a child of Forget...

8: (smiles)

So then, what do we realise if we apply the idea of Infinite Variation to the story? We understand that Forget created a number of different beings and that, because of Infinite Variation, all these beings co-exist in the Now. That means they can play together, work together, create together. And they do!

Together, these beings begin to try to make sense of their existence. And so they create from their own essence and energy a reality in which to play. They seek to resolve their sense of disconnection and separation by playing out their thoughts about themselves in the realities, which they create. Again and again they try. Each time a reality is created, something is learned and understood and the reality is collapsed and returned to them. And then they do it all over again. Each new reality is more complex and amazing than the one before it. Each time populated by more and more variations and combinations of themselves. And each time, as it expends its usefulness, it is rolled up, collapsed and returned to them before they begin again.

As we find them now, they have created some pretty complex and amazing consciousness constructs such as space, time and dimensions, so that they can really spread apart and separately experience the various causes and effects of their creations on different parts of their own being. And within each dimension they have created many different realities, as were appropriate to that dimension. In the third dimension, for example, they have created that which would come to be called "the universe" by some parts of Self that went to play in it. It contained trillions of galaxies, each with billions of solar systems. Each solar system had a number of planets. And each planet teemed with very many life-forms. Your science doesn't yet acknowledge this and you haven't a broad enough perspective to see it, but it is true: there is not a single planet anywhere that does not, at some point in time, harbour many forms of life. But no matter - this construct called The Universe is itself a living entity, which is densely populated with an infinite variation and complexity of life. It is one of the brightest jewels created by the beings of light. But beautiful as it is, for almost all of its creation it was just another experiment. Though it brought the beings of light a great deal of insight into themselves to play out their games of self-creation as they populated this place, it did not bring them that for which they most yearned: connection, true belonging, blissful oneness, completion, home.

It is a sad and confusing irony: they yearned for healing and wholeness. And the harder they worked to try to find it, the more they fragmented themselves and created separation. The more they sought to understand themselves, the more they diversified, separated and disintegrated themselves and the less they found of their true nature

Z: Oh, 8, this is too sad! Is there no hope for us?

8: Wait a minute there. I am telling you a story. A story about Push and Stay and the Infinite Elastic Ball. I didn't say this was about YOU!

Z: So it's only a story then?

8: Of course it is only a story! How could you think it was anything other than a story? It is even called THE STORY of Push and Stay and The Infinite Elastic Ball. How did you get confused?

Z: It started to sound like the truth.

8: Ah! It sounded like that TO YOU did it?

(smiles) I'm going to let you off the hook a bit. I can see you are getting confused.

Firstly, please understand this: your whole life is nothing but a story. A fiction. A wholly invented play that you are putting on for yourself to show yourself something about yourself. It is not real. There is nothing real about your world or your universe. The story of your life is packed full of beautiful and powerful metaphors so that you can figure things out about yourself. But it is still just A STORY. Your story. And in due course, you will change your mind and decide it is only a chapter in a greater story and then eventually just a very small part of a MUCH greater story. And then you'll release your need for this kind of storytelling and possibly, probably, play with creative energy directly without the need for metaphors and stories.

But until then… it is ALL just story!

But story is a very powerful thing. We can learn a great deal about ourselves from stories. And if I tell you a story that really captures your imagination, then it might cause you to begin to tell your own story in a different way.

Clearly, my story about Push and Stay started to do this for you. You began to see yourself in this story. But then you made the very normal mistake: you began to demand that it should be something other than what it is. You began to demand that it should be TRUE. But it cannot be TRUE. Because there is only one truth.

Z: *"The One Is"*

8: That's right! Everything else is just story. Nothing more, nothing less.

And, if you take a moment to consider The Infinite Elastic Ball, then you will remember that one of its characteristics is Infinite Variation. That means that everything that can be created, is created. And all of it co-exists in the eternal Now. This means that any story that you can come up with, can seem to be true from a particular perspective. But it also means that, from another perspective, it can also be untrue. Or partly true. Or fishcakes.

Z: Fishcakes? (laughs) Okay I get it; you mean that anything is possible and I shouldn't confine myself to needing a story to be true or false or… anything else that I might be able to define in my mind.

8: Correct. Stories are what they area – they are stories. You can decide if a story has value for you or is about you. You can decide what story you want to tell and then you can decide how you are going to tell it. You can decide if you want your story to play out within another bigger story and, notably, you can decide if you are going to co-create a story with other beings. There is a great deal you can do with your story, both in how you go about telling the story and in the content of the story. But there is one thing you can never do with any story: you cannot make it True. Not in the ultimate sense. You cannot create a true story that is not also false, from some other perspective.

So, struggling with this concept of True and False is not really a very productive way to spend your energy. Nothing is ultimately true other than "*The One Is*". All else is just a matter of temporary, local imbalance. And Infinite Variation tells us that all things that can be created co-exist and are equally true. All things are, and all things are not. That is the nature of The Infinite Elastic Ball

Z: But, 8, you have just used the Infinite Elastic Ball to prove something to me while, at the same time, saying that the Infinite Elastic Ball is just a story! And I don't know if it's true or not and now I don't even know if that matters. Ugh! I am frustrated and confused! I feel even MORE like a child of Forget right now. I feel like I am never going to figure this out.

8: Is that so? Well then, how about I tell you more about the children of Forget? In fact, how about I tell you about the one Saving Grace, which they could use to find their way Home?

Z: Home?

8: To Remember, remember.

Z: Oh yes. I remember. (laughs) So you are saying there is hope for the children of Forget? That they can go home after all?

8: Yes. There is always the one Saving Grace. But before I can tell you about the Saving Grace, I first have to tell you more about WHY the children of Forget kept finding their way into ever deeper forgetting and, no matter how hard they try, they never seem to be able to remember.

It has to do with identification; with who you are declaring yourself to be. You see, all parts of The One have the attributes of The One. They are creative and self-creative. This means you are able to create yourself as you desire. I can put it this way:

"You are who YOU say you are."

So what happens if you declare yourself to be what you DO? Then you are declaring yourself to be your function. And this is something that almost everyone on earth is doing – they are declaring themselves to be what they do. Go to a social event and meet someone new and they, almost invariably, will open the conversation by asking you what you do. What is your job, your function. There is an implicit belief that, if they know what you do, then they will know who you are. But the problem, of course, is that this idea is so pervasive that you come to agree with it and believe it yourself. You come to say, "*I am what I do*" and then, because you say it is so, it IS! Then you ARE what you do.

Now, I want to introduce a word to you. It is a word you know very well. But it is also a word you have so misunderstood that you actually need a formal introduction to it so that you can meet it anew and discover what that word really means. You must understand it correctly and use it correctly. Because it is a very useful word for a very useful concept.

The word is EGO.

Ego is the part of the self that "does". It is the part that strives, that achieves, that gets up, gets out and gets going. In our little story, ego is exemplified by Push. It is the part of the Self that says, "*I am going to go and do this or that*" and then does it. Ego says, "*I do*".

Now I ask you, does that sound like a bad thing?

Z: No. It certainly doesn't. By that definition ego is required for, well, everything. I mean I couldn't get out of bed in the morning without ego. I certainly wouldn't be sitting here typing on this keyboard without ego.

8: You're right. Without ego you would DO nothing. A mother would not hug her child. Lovers would not stare into each other's eyes. You would not make nourishing food for your body. Nothing that you would consider a good and loving thing to do would ever be done. Nothing at all would ever be done.

I'll take it further: without ego, your universe would never have come into being. The Light Beings who came together to create this universe, did so by making decisions and choices and then enacting them. The very first, most basic decision of The One to seek to discover itself, the impetus to create, is ego. Push is ego.

Z: But so is war and destruction and killing and all that other stuff.

8: Yes, indeed, so it is! All activity is ego. Whether it is good activity or bad activity is just your judgement of it. Ego is simply a tool. It is the part of you that DOES. We have spoken a lot in The Ascension Papers about DOing and BEing. The part of your consciousness that is involved with DOing is your ego.

You cannot honestly think that there is something inherently wrong or bad about that, can you?

Z: No. I see what you are saying. It is neither good nor bad. It's like a tool that you can use to build either a hospital or a bomb. Like a knife that can be used to cut food or to kill. It is just a tool. I get it.

But why then is there this idea, especially in spiritual circles, that the ego is bad? You often hear it said that the ego is the enemy – that it must be vanquished or overcome or even destroyed before one can grow spiritually. I've even heard it said by some people that I quite respect, that ego can be said to stand for, "*Edging God Out*".

Is this all so much nonsense?

8: It is a misunderstanding. And quite an understandable one at that.

Z: An understandable misunderstanding? (laughs)

8: (smiles) Language can be fun sometimes, can't it?

But let me tell you why it is a misunderstanding and why it is understandable that it occurs.

Firstly there is, as I have said, nothing at all wrong with ego.

But if you identify yourself with your ego, then you are, absolutely guaranteed, to be heading away from Oneness. You are heading towards separation.

Z: Ah! And that's a bad thing so…

8: Not so fast Sparky! I didn't say that was a "bad" thing. If you WANT to be heading towards separation, then it's a good thing. But if you want to be heading towards Oneness, then it is an inappropriate thing. If you want to go home, then you must face home when you walk. Identifying with ego is facing away from home. Because you are, in fact, NOT what you DO. What you DO is just a transitory game you are playing with illusions. It is a part you are play-acting. With this doing, you create your form. But your form is your expression. It is not what you ARE. If you made a sculpture you wouldn't suddenly think you WERE that sculpture!

And, as surely as if you were a sculptor, you are creating your form with your doing. And here I mean "form" in the greater sense AND in the normal sense – your spiritual form and your physical form are created by your function. But this function is simply something that you are choosing to do for a while. This, you might say, is your purpose. It is, you might say, WHY you exist. And it is so, for so long as you say it is so. But believe me, if you ceased to do this thing, you would not cease to exist! So it is not really WHY you exist. At best it is a function to which you are well suited and which you enjoy fulfilling. And there is nothing at all wrong with that! But you need to understand that your purpose is chosen by you. And that, in due course, you will modify it and choose a new purpose. Please understand me: you are not defined by your purpose. Your purpose is defined by you. You are not what you do.

And it is important that you understand this, because if you define yourself by what you do, then you are heading towards separation.

When you declare yourself to be your creations (and only YOUR creations), you limit yourself radically. The sum total of your own creations is a very little thing compared to all the rest of infinity. So you choose to see yourself as very small, finite, limited, mortal and very much separated from everyone else. The only way to find some modicum of safety is to vigorously defend your creations and to seek to aggressively increase the extent of your creations. And this is why beings who are deeply ego-centric always take their creations VERY SERIOUSLY. If you ARE your creations, then suddenly your creations become VERY IMPORTANT. Do they not? Have you ever seen people who are very deeply involved in their egos sitting around discussing their creations? They are always Very Important People and they are always engaged in Very Important Business. Lots of frowns and seriousness is called for. It doesn't matter if it's the board of directors of some company or members of parliament of a country or delegates to the United Nations; when people of ego gather, it is serious business. Love, laughter and kindness are never on the agenda.

And this is quite unsurprising. If you are saying, "*I am this doing*" then you will throw yourself with all that you are into the doing of that thing. You measure your value by how well you do that thing. You will seek affirmation for doing it well. You'll expect a great deal of stroking for all the doing that you have done-well. In this world, that often means lots of money. But there are other ego strokes that you might seek, such as peer-approval or a fancy job-title or the corner office or whatever. If you are what you do, then you crave those kinds of rewards. And the flip-side, of course, is that you live in the shadow of constant dread that you will make some mistake and that your doing will be seen to be defective. Because this will mean to you that YOU are defective, you see. So ego-strokes on the one hand counter-balanced by a desperately hidden, unacknowledgeable panic on the other is how these beings proceed. When a machine part is overloaded in a way that threatens to break it we say it is stressed. Stressed materials eventually fail. When you live the life of an ego-centred being you reside in a permanent state of stress. It is even commonly acknowledged in your society. Work stress. Executive stress. It threatens you daily with harm to your body and your psyche. All due to misidentification.

But that is not the worst of it. When someone, in any way, threatens what the ego-centric being is doing then, naturally, they take it very personally. Because they believe what they do IS what they are. So it IS personal for them. And they will be willing to defend what they do with their very life because, after all, it is who they are. It is their whole existence.

And THIS is where a great many societal dysfunctions spring up.

War, for example, is a function of ego identification. Politicians identify themselves with their function and, when someone else threatens that function, they will send any number of their own populace off to slaughter to defend that function.

It is all a kind of insanity.

But you see, you are all children of ego. It is understandable and natural that you should keep seeking to understand yourselves with more and more DOing. You think you will find answers to the great questions of life by DOing. You think science and philosophy and religion might bring you back Home. But they won't. Because all these things are DOing. They are ego functions. You will never know Oneness from your mind. You will never comprehend God with thoughts. You will never feel love in your ego centre. These things are impossible.

But they CAN be useful! You'll notice that the whole of THE ASCENSION PAPERS has all been ego-stuff. It has all been ideas and thoughts and philosophies. It has all been the stuff of the mind. And this is not wrong! We have used ego-stuff to resolve other ego-stuff. So, if you are trying to ascend, then this is a useful application of ego-stuff. But we went about as far as we could go using ego stuff. Before we could proceed further, you needed to take even the smallest step without ego. That was what your day of silence was about. On that day, for the first time, you willingly and intentionally disengaged your ego completely for just a moment and, in that moment, you listened to your heart. And that changed everything.

You see; you are not your ego. You are, in fact, an indivisible part of The Oneness. You are pure consciousness. And for so long as you experience yourself as separate from the rest of the Oneness, then you shall be pulled back to Oneness with Love. In fact the more separate you are, the more Love will tug on you to return to Oneness – the harder you will have to work to remain separate. Love is the elastic in The Infinite Elastic Ball. You see, your true nature is to be one with the Oneness. So the more you push away, the more balance seeks to assert itself. So you are pulled back ever more forcefully.

There are a number of ways for you to counter this pull so that you can keep pushing out. Identifying yourself with your form is a great way to accomplish just that. Releasing that identification will cause you to slow down your pushing away and even come to a halt. If you wish to return home you can then simply identify yourself with that which you truly ARE.

And how do you do that? How do you find out what you truly ARE?

You go to the very centre of your being. You go to your heart. Buried deep inside your heart is a portal to The Oneness. Indeed you contain the whole of the Oneness within you. It is but an illusion that there is anything at all outside of you. Everything you experience outside of you is a projection of you own psyche – it is the light of The One shining though the lens of your own consciousness that you are experiencing. You literally create your whole experience. And you do it from within. So if you go to your heart you can find who you really ARE. And who you are is... The Oneness!

All the forms you have created are just your creations, and you, of course, are their creator. And as the creator, you are not limited to the forms you have created as you can create an endless amount of other, different forms if you desire. And by looking within you can find every single other form that has ever been created is also right there inside your heart: all wisdom knowledge and learning is yours. All ability is your ability. You become boundless. You discover your own god-like nature. You know everything you need to know and can do everything you need to do.

And THIS is the Saving Grace that is always available to all the children of Forget. Any time they decide to cease identifying themselves with their ego and move into their heart, then they discover the Saving Grace. They discover Remember within themselves.

Z: And then? What will they do then?

8: What would YOU do then? Would you take this knowledge of yours and go rushing Home to

Stay, or would there be some others to whom you would want to gift the knowledge?

Z: The latter. I would want to gift what I had found.

8: Yes. Of course you would. Because that is what Love would do. So you move one step closer to home, but you do not rush all the way home. And from that position, one step closer, you help as you can. And then, when you have done what you think you can do, you take another step closer to home. And from there you discover more god-like powers. You realise there is MORE that you can do. And so you do more. Because that is what Love would do. And so you go, step by step, loving and healing and helping and remembering, all the way home. And then, finally, when you are just one minuscule step from Home, when you stand at the very doorstep before rushing into the waiting arms of Stay, you will realise that you do not arrive Home on your own. You will realise that you are all of Push, because you have gathered up all the rest of Push. All of Push will arrive home to all of Stay. And the ecstatic implosion of Love will be wondrous indeed!

Z: I DO love a happy ending!

8: All endings are happy. If you are not happy, then it is not the end. It's just some misunderstood pause somewhere in the middle.

Z: So that is the Story of Push and Stay and The Infinite Elastic Ball?

8: It is. Did you like it?

Z: I liked it a lot. But I have some questions that I need to ask.

8: Good. That was why I told you the story – to help you to define your questions.

Z: Okay then, here are my questions:

I still don't know EXACTLY what love is. I understand that I have to experience it to truly know it but… I'd still like a clearer idea of what it is. If you can help with that, then I'd appreciate it. And then… you promised to talk about "how to learn to love" and I really would like to hear about this but… well… maybe it's a silly question, but I'm not exactly sure WHY I should do this. I mean I get the good stuff about love being everything and so on but, really, if I am going to do this learning to love thing then I would really like to know why.

8: That sounds perfectly reasonable.

So you want to round off this discussion with three questions:

1. Exactly what is Love?

2. Why should one learn to Love?

3. How to learn to Love?

Z: Yes please.

8: Okay, let's get to it.

1. Exactly What is Love?

I have told you that the Oneness exists in a state of perfect balance. That it is pure, infinite consciousness and that it is, therefore, everything and nothing. You are an indivisible part of the Oneness and you exist as a differentiated being with various attributes because you are created out of various imbalances. These imbalances arise as you or your Inner-Self come to hold different ideas about yourself. You identify strongly with certain attributes of the Oneness (I am this and I am that) and very weakly with other attributes (I am not these other things). So you are in a state of imbalance and will remain so until you identify equally with all attributes of the Oneness, and therefore also with none. Well, Love is the force that is pulling you back to balance. It is that which returns you to Oneness. Love makes whole that which is fragmented. Love returns all the pieces of the puzzle to their rightful places. It is Love that allows you to see through the illusions of separation and to see, even for a moment, the divine in the eyes of another. Love is the drawing together of that which is set apart. When true, pure, unconditional Love plays in your consciousness, then you will really SEE the Oneness. And because there is nothing that is not of the Oneness, you shall see to the truest nature of everything. You shall see through all illusions and all lies. You shall see the Oneness in everything. You shall see that everything and everyone is a part of you, as you are a part of them. It means knowing from your heart that everything is divine and that there is nothing that is not divine. That everything is perfect. That nothing is wrong. That all is worthy of your love and that there is no need for fear or other negative emotions. THAT is Love.

And if you should come to feel THAT kind of Love, then everything for you will be magically altered. You shall understand anew all the things that you previously thought to be bad or unacceptable. You will see light and love and glory wherever you cast your eye. And not because you are fooled – quite the opposite – precisely because you are no longer fooled… because you cease believing the false evidence of illusions.

And because you know the light and glory to be true, so it will be true and so your world will be altered. You have always created your reality in every detail from the very smallest to the very greatest, but now you will KNOW that you do. Now you will move into conscious creation. And you will create with Love. Love will be your motivation and Love will be the tool of your creation.

In summary then: everything that is, exists because of imbalance. Love is the force that drives everything back to balance and returns everything to Oneness. Where there is anything other than perfect Oneness, there Love is also. Love, therefore, is the second greatest truth.

There is much else I could say about Love. I could try for more compelling and eloquent words. But they would always fail the grace and glory of what Love really is. Love cannot be understood. Love is much greater than the mind that would seek to understand it. Love can only be experienced. And once you have had even a small taste of true limitless, unconditional Love, then you will be forever altered. Your life's quest will be to return to that state of Love. In that moment you will know that there can be nothing even remotely as important to you as existing in that state of union with the divine that IS Love.

Z: Thank you very much for that, 8. In hearing your description I feel I have had such an experience. I saw the divine in nature around me on a walk on a mountain. It was very brief, but it certainly did change me forever. It was the most blissful experience of my life. In that moment my life-path instantly changed. It was a great gift of grace that I was able to experience that. So what you have to say about this makes perfect sense to me. And I DO have a deep desire to return to that state of Love.

The other stuff about Love being that which pulls everything back to balance and Oneness is new and interesting to me. I didn't know that. But it makes sense. Thank you.

8: You are welcome. We'll talk some more about your mountain experience in a moment. For now, let's move on to your second question:

2. Why Should One Learn to Love?

If you learn to truly Love… to Love limitlessly and unconditionally… then the kingdom of heaven will be yours.

It is as simple as that.

But maybe you don't know what that means, so perhaps I should paint you a picture of what that might mean for you:

For starters, you will know absolutely that you are part of the Oneness and that everyone you meet, and everything you see, are also part of the Oneness. You will see others in a very different way to that which you now do. You will see their light. This means that, with a glance, you will see who they really are. Sure, you will also see whatever metaphor and illusion they might temporarily be clothing themselves with, but this will not fool your eye. Like a beloved friend who wears a fancy-dress outfit, you will know the being for who they really are, rather than for the body they are inhabiting or the game they are playing. You will see to the truth of them. And they will see you! You know that a great deal of the pain expressed by beings in your world is really just a deep desire to be SEEN. To be seen for who they really are. To be recognised. To be understood. To be loved as they are. Well this is something that will be instantaneous and automatic. Each will SEE the other. All will be understood. All will be loved.

And so, of course, there will also be no more misunderstandings. And, not that you would want to lie ever again, for that would be counter-productive to your own goals, but it is true that you could not then lie or be lied to. You will, quite simply, see the truth of this other being. Their "words" or whatever other metaphorical and creative representations they might present to you, would really only be additional input. Primarily, you will know this being and their true nature and intent by their light.

Telepathy will not only be possible, but will actually be the norm. If you know that you are, at core, the same One great being, then you have no trouble understanding that different parts of the Oneness can share the same thought with Itself. If you think of another being, then you can bring them to your mind and instantly let them know what you are thinking. If you wish it, it can be so: instant mind-to-mind sharing of thoughts, feelings, experiences and ideas across any separation of distance and time.

And, of course, if you wish privacy for your thoughts, that too is yours.

Time, space, energy and matter are all illusions created to make certain types of games work. When you know that you are a part of the Oneness, then the illusions only work when you want them to work. So these things become pliable. You will be helped (if you so choose) to learn how to manipulate time, space, energy and matter. It is not very difficult to do. Once you see though the illusion, it becomes quite easy. Then you see that time and space are the same thing. They are an illusory separation of things. Energy is created by this separation and flows between two or more points that were separated by the illusion of time and space. Matter is simply the result of holding patterns of consciousness in the flow of the energy. Up to now, you have believed yourself to be INSIDE the illusion. You have looked at the forms that result and, not only have you believed these things to be real, but you have actually believed yourselves to BE these forms. But it is not so. These forms, which result from the patterns, are not you. They are just your temporary creations. You will see that. You will see that you are a creator of these forms. And then you will learn how to alter the forms that you create, to your will. I mean, you will be able to consciously create your world, your body and anything around you as you wish.

And then you will learn instant teleportation. You will be able to simply let go of a form on this planet and your body will simply disappear into nothingness, only to reappear from the nothingness on another planet, as you hold the patterns in energy there. And then you shall be there. Or, at least the form you are using to represent yourself shall be. Teleportation is the favoured mode of transport for unity-conscious beings throughout the universe. Neither space nor time will be an obstacle for you!

And, of course, you will never again feel the need to die. Death, as you know it, is a very important and valuable tool for beings on the outward journey. It is quite normal for beings heading outwards to get lost in their games and illusions and to lose sight of the greater purpose and goal of their journey. Not only do such beings get a little lost and confused, but they also begin to create a great deal of pain, fear and confusion for themselves. So, death was created to allow these beings to interrupt their passage so that the being could, with some regularity, be brought back to their intended path. Death allows a means for the being to bring their journey to a halt and return to a higher consciousness for guidance and help. Without its merciful release, beings on the outward journey would become very weary and traumatised. But, once you are firmly on the return journey, you will no longer require such release. There will be nothing you will need release from. If you ever require rest and succour, you may simply still your ego-being and put down your burden and you will instantly be transported to a state of blissful Oneness - you will be back in the very heart of Oneness. And for you this will be as natural and normal as a night's sleep currently is.

And these are some of the general attributes of a life in unity consciousness. But you will not be confined to such a life. You might, for example, choose to reside in unity consciousness and, from there, make sojourns into the lower realms of duality on missions of discovery and adventures of service. Or you could move through the portal of the Oneness and go and visit other realities entirely. I don't simply mean other places in this universe or other universes, no, I mean other entirely different frames of creation. Creations, which do not operate at all like this one does. As you move from a place of Oneness, you can enter any other realm that is within the Oneness. And you may go and create there if you desire. This is all open to you to choose.

And you shall realise very quickly too that you no longer need a unidimensional perspective. You will realise that you can operate from outside of time. This means that you might want to maintain a life in one reality and, at the same time, explore and create in a thousand others. There are no limitations on you, save those which you place before yourself.

These are some of the general traits of the life of a being who creates Its world entirely with Love and who lives in a unity-conscious reality. It is what you can expect for yourself if you open your heart to Love, and then allow for your own ascension. But they are only general traits and you will be free, of course, to choose other experiences if you wish them. And as to the specifics of your life - where you will live, how you will live, what you will do - these, I'm afraid, are questions you must answer for yourself. I cannot tell you what you will decide. But I can tell you that you will be able, if you wish it, to live a truly sublime life. If you decide to surround yourself with others who are also of unity consciousness, then you shall feel nothing but soul-connection on all sides. You shall be held in the soft embrace of love all the days of your life. You shall trust all whom you meet and your trust shall be well warranted. You shall seek always to give your greatest gift and you shall be loved, respected and rewarded for your giving. And whatever your greatest gift is, it shall indeed be something worthy of your time and attention. And you will give your gift away with open-hearted generosity. You shall never need to ask, *"But what is in it for me?"* because all those around you will be likewise giving their greatest gift. And in an infinite universe, there is guaranteed to be someone, somewhere whose greatest bliss it is to create exactly the thing that you might think you want or need. Taking your need to them will be a gift to them! The fact that you have need of their greatest gift will bless them. And THAT will be the new economy of the new world in which you shall dwell if you choose to live amongst others who are of unity consciousness: you will give and give and give. And when someone takes of your gift, it will bring you joy. And if there is something you want or need you shall simply have to accept it, as it will be offered to you. And your accepting it will bring the giver joy. Love shall be the currency of the new world of the unity conscious, but the result of every transaction will be joy for all concerned.

Does any of this sound a little attractive to you?

Z: (laughs) Are you kidding? I feel like a kid who has just been offered the keys to the universal candy store!

8: The universal candy store. (smiles) Yes, and then some!

So, if you are ready for this… if you are ready for the New Earth populated by New Humans in a new Golden Age. If you are ready to be a creator being amongst creator beings. If you are ready to see God in the eyes of everyone you meet and to see the true beauty of Life in every vista you look upon. Then you are ready to really learn to Love. Love is the way. But not the lesser thing that you have commonly called love… not the mixture of things such as need, affection, kindness, care and passion that might have passed for romantic love. No. These are just Love's shadows and masks. No. I am talking about true, limitless and unconditional Love. Love that is given without reserve to all things and all beings everywhere. Love that shines like the brightest sun upon all. When you can Love like that, then you will be there.

There are, of course, some obstacles to you loving like that. I am not oblivious to these challenges. You have expended a great deal of effort to be here in this reality, as it is. You have worked very, very hard to forget that you are One. And you have grown quite attached to your separation. It has become like an addiction to you. Even when it hurts you or even seems to threaten to destroy you, still you cling to it. So, suggesting the direct path Home is not really a viable solution.

Z: The direct path?

8: Yes. As it is true that you are creating your separation with a great degree of effort and will, so it is equally true that you would be able to return directly to Oneness by the simple expediency of ceasing all effort and will. All you need to do to return to Oneness is to cease all DOing. Release. Let go. Become perfectly still. I don't mean the momentary semi-stillness of meditation. I mean something orders of magnitude more still than that. I mean a complete cessation of all activity. Releasing your whole life-stream, releasing all ideas and beliefs you have about your Self and your world. Releasing EVERYTHING. As you move towards perfect stillness, you will move towards Oneness, until you merge once again with the Oneness.

But this direct path is not something that you will wish to entertain. You are very attached to a whole host of ideas about yourself and you won't want to just let everything go. For example: you fear dying. You fear losing your individuality. You fear losing the life you have built. You fear for your family and loved ones if you should "go away". And then you have all kinds of positive emotions too: you love what you are doing. You have a gift that you wish to discover and give. You are busy with a journey that captivates you. You love those around you. There are many such reasons that the direct path would be inappropriate for you. I understand this. I mention the direct path simply to bring to your attention the realisation that it is not difficult to return home to Oneness. The hard work is NOT returning – retaining the illusion of separation is what is difficult. Returning home is easy. The "elastic" in the Infinite Elastic Ball is Love. And it pulls on you all the time. If you simply ceased pushing out, then you would be returned home to Oneness without needing to try.

But you don't want to just stop all doing, do you? You don't want to simply let go of this life of yours, this journey that you are on, and all that it entails. Do you?

Z: No. I really don't. I am not done here.

8: And neither am I! So we remain here. But the good news is that this doesn't mean we cannot experience Oneness! It just means that we have to find another way to do so. We don't just let go and go home – what we do instead is to bring home here. We bring the kingdom of heaven to earth, so to speak. One could say that we are not so much ascending ourselves, as ascending all of life! But doing it this way takes firm intention, commitment and a little effort. It is, perforce, the slower path Home, but I very much do believe you will enjoy the journey!

To travel this path you will need to learn to release all the blockages and obstacles you are creating between yourself and limitless Love. You will need to allow Love to flow though you without hindrance. You will need to BE love.

Would you like that?

Z: Yes. I want that very, very much.

Is it really something I can learn?

8: Oh yes! Very much so. In fact you don't really need to learn how to do this. It is your true nature. All you need to do is to release all the illusory programming you have taken on board. And then you might need a few pointers to get over some old habits. Then it should come naturally.

But seeing as you are willing to do this, let's get on to…

3. How to Learn to Love

I am willing to teach you all you need to know to open your heart to Love. But - and I cannot stress this enough – you will have to do the doing yourself. Love is an experiential thing. You will find your way there by CONSTANTLY releasing the blockages that you have towards it and by CONSTANTLY opening yourself to it. It will require of you that you set your intent and then stick to that intent, that you be conscious of your thoughts and feelings, and that you trust yourself and your heart. The road might seem tough at first, as you overcome stubborn programming but, as you go, it will get easier. As you begin to move into a truly open-hearted state of Love, your life will, without a doubt, become more joyful, more abundant and easier. And as you see these rewards begin to unfold in your life, it will be easier to trust to your heart. And so the path will become easier and your progression will accelerate. So there is much to look forward to. And I will give you the information you need to help you to choose. But you must choose. And you must steadfastly keep choosing. Only you can create your reality for yourself.

Now there are three parts to the path that I am going to talk about, each of them with sub-headings. The three main parts are:

3.1 Removing the blockages you have to Love

3.2 The energy cycle of Love

3.3 BEing Love.

3.1 Removing the Blockages to Love

There are a number of ways you might be blocking your heart from opening to Love. I will address the three main ways. I do suggest that, if you resolve these three issues, you will almost certainly be able to overcome any others that might lurk in your psyche. You really just need to move with firm intent and consistency in the direction of removing these blockages, and they will begin to tumble.

3.1.1 Judgement

Judgement is when you feel the need to make another being, idea or thing wrong, in order for you to feel right. This rejection and divorce of the other is quite probably the biggest block in most peoples' hearts. For most it is such a normal and habitual thing that you are probably often not even aware that you are doing it. So the first thing to do is to become conscious of your own judgements of others. So, watch your thoughts. Then you will want to release your judgements so that you can begin to open your heart to others.

Judgement results from an incorrect understanding of What Is. You are identifying yourself with your behaviour (which you are not) and then you are identifying others around you with their behaviour (which they are not). And then you are finding them *wrong* for that which they do, so that you can feel right about that which you are doing.

Let me help you to understand this in a new, more useful way.

Obviously if you are not your behaviour and they are not their behaviour, then all of this is just unnecessary. But perhaps that won't help you quite yet. Because perhaps you are not quite ready to cease identifying yourself with your creations. So let's go a step further…

Can you remember earlier on I told you about the property of the Infinite Elastic Ball called Infinite Variation?

Z: I do.

8: Well what it means is that every possible thing that could be, is. Right now, it is. Every wonderful loving world that could exist, does. And every painful place of evil and torment too. All the possibilities exist. Infinity would not be infinity if they did not exist. The fact of their existence is not at question. The question that you should ask yourself is quite simply WHAT DO YOU WANT TO EXPERIENCE? Or put another way, what do you wish to create for yourself?

And while you are asking that question, you should release others to experience anything and everything they might want and need to experience for themselves. Because you cannot create for yourself this freedom to experience exactly the world you want to experience if you are not willing to grant this to everyone else. What you do to others, you do to yourself also, remember? So give to others the right to create what they want. Release completely and lovingly everything you do not want for yourself. Cease any and all judgement of it, or of those that wish to experience it. And then choose what you want, and move towards that.

This is a very important understanding, so I am going to tell you about it again in a different way:

You'll recall I told you that everything that exists is created with imbalance and that nothing exists without imbalance. This means that everything that is created also immediately creates its "opposite" to counter balance it.

Z: I remember.

8: So think on this: you CANNOT create something without having someone else create the opposite.

This logically means that you should be grateful to every other being who is choosing every other thing that you are not choosing. You should be especially grateful to those who are choosing what seems to you to be the opposite of what you are choosing. All these beings are, in a way, making it possible for you to choose as you are. You could say you are all counter-balancing each other, enabling them, making it possible for them to be as they are. You are, in fact, a particle of life that is in a dance with every other particle of life everywhere. You are the soul-mate of every other being everywhere. You are all intimately connected to all of life.

Do you see the short-sighted, silliness of judgement? You cannot ask a single other being to stop doing what they are doing without at the same time also stopping doing what you are doing. And the corollary is true – if you change yourself, then you change the whole universe. Can you see the power of the dictum that you should become the change you desire? For indeed by changing yourself, you DO change your whole world and your whole experience. You bring to yourself a whole universe of experience that is a direct reflection of who you are.

Indeed you ARE a creator being.

You have always been.

You have simply created without purpose and without direction in your ignorance.

So judgement is counter-productive. And a waste of your time and energy. And, most importantly, it places a huge block in your heart and stops the light of Love from channelling though you. It gets in the way of you creating for yourself a new world of Love.

Let it go!

If you encounter someone making a choice that is not right for you, then be thankful. Now YOU don't have to make that choice. Send them love. The more difficult their path is, the more love they need. Send them abundant love. And then think upon your choices. If you like the outcome of your choices, then you need to be especially grateful to all those others. Without their contribution, your choices would not be available to you. They would not be "counterbalanced" in the field of consciousness of the Oneness.

Gratitude is the answer. Be grateful. Send thanks. Send love.

I made the statement earlier:

"You are who YOU say you are"

This statement was slipped in earlier in the context of telling you about ego. But it is a very important understanding. It has many uses. The first is, of course, that you should become very clear about who you think you REALLY are, and then you should say so. I don't mean you should "say so" only in words. I mean you should express who you really believe yourself to be in your every thought and word and deed. You should say so from your heart. And then it will be so. But be clear! If you say contradictory things about yourself, then you will have a confused and incongruous experience of yourself and your life. This is never pleasant.

So how DO you find who you really are and how do you express that?

You go to your heart! Which we shall talk about in a moment.

But for now, the point I wish to bring to the fore is this: you are who YOU say you are. If others stand in judgement of you, then these judgements of theirs do not tell you who you are.

"Other's judgements of you do not show you who YOU are, they show you who THEY are!"

And this can be very useful. When you know who others are, then you can decide if their being resonates with yours. You can decide if they are "right for you". Surely you should draw yourself towards that which is "right for you" and away from that which is "wrong for you"? So it is useful to get a clear picture of who others are. And a great way to do this is to watch what they say of you!

But have a mind! Your judgements of others are just the same.

"Your judgement of others does not tell you anything about THEM. It tells you something about YOURSELF!"

So your judgements and ideas of others ARE useful - if you know how to use them! Watch those judgements and opinions rise to the surface and ask yourself – *"What am I telling myself about myself right now?"* Somewhere in your judgement there hides a deep desire that is denied. Or possibly a deep hurt that is unexpressed. There is something deep within yourself that you are hiding from yourself. It finds expression by rising to the surface when someone else, in some way, is doing this thing that you are denying yourself or rejecting from yourself.

So watch those judgements! They are MOST instructive. And if you process them correctly, they will dissolve, because the underlying rejection or denial in your own psyche is healed. Each judgement you dissolve is a step closer to Love.

3.1.2 Negative Emotions

The second blockage to your heart that I wish to address is negative emotions. These are things such as fear, pain, anger, hatred, jealously, envy and greed.

If you are experiencing any of these emotions, you will find it very hard indeed to open your heart to Love at the same time. Negative emotions, quite literally, create a block in your heart chakra. Fear does so the most effectively of all. And so it is with some reason that many have come to say that fear is the opposite of love. But of course that isn't quite true.

Z: It isn't?

8: No. Don't be silly! Love is everything and everything is Love. How can one small experience be the opposite of EVERYTHING? These negative emotions are simply shadow emotions. They are a function of the illusion of duality. That does not mean that they don't appear real to you and it doesn't mean that you should try to pretend that they are not there. What you should do is learn to put them to their proper use so that they no longer rule you and so that they get out of the way of your heart expressing limitless Love.

Z: That sounds amazing. Can you teach me that?

8: I can teach you the principles. It's not complicated. But you will have to learn to apply these principals though practice.

I have said that these negative emotions are a function of the illusion of duality. For this reason it is important that you understand what duality is so that you can correctly understand negative emotions.

What is Duality?

"Duality" is a much-used word in spiritual circles and we have used it here in THE ASCENSION PAPERS quite a bit too. But what does it mean, do you think?

Z: Um… I don't know exactly. Duality would literally mean something like "two-ness". But that doesn't make sense…

8: It actually does. Let me explain. There is, as I have constantly said, only the Oneness. But if you recall in our story of Push and Stay, Push chose to push out so far that he could actually forget that he was one with the Oneness. This is a simplistic allegory for The Veil of Unknowing. It doesn't matter how you come to understand it though, the point is simply that a being might come to experience itself as being utterly separate, individuated, apart and alone. Not One. Then this being is of duality consciousness.

A deeply duality-conscious being does not even know that he is in duality. He is too deep in the illusion to even think in such terms. He would think ALL beings are separate. If he chooses to be religious, then he would believe in a god or gods who are also separate from him. God is "over there", somewhere else, doing things that have nothing to do with him.

Pure materialism – which is the theory that nothing but matter exists – is an example of a non-spiritual view from within the duality perspective. Those who ascribe to that view think that their own consciousness, mind, emotions, and being are all simply a function of their body and their brain. And they obviously also think that they are absolutely separate from all other beings.

There are probably an infinite number of things that you could believe to be true whilst being of a duality consciousness.

Ironically, it is only once you begin to raise your consciousness out of duality and awaken to the realisation that All is One, that you become aware of duality at all. It is only then that you might be likely to even use the word "duality". You first become aware that there IS Oneness but you also feel that you yourself are separate from it. Such beings are what I call the Awakened Duality-Conscious. And this brings me to the "twoness" you were talking about. Duality refers to two points on the continuum, of which the Awakened Duality-Conscious are aware. On the one side is unity consciousness - being one with All That Is - and on the other side is duality consciousness, which is being utterly separate and apart.

I'd like to do something new now. I'd like to put a picture in your head. Please find a way to make a drawing of it to share with your readers.

Z: That's different. Okay, I'll try…

8: The first image illustrates this duality-continuum, as it might be imagined by the Awakened Duality-Conscious being:

Ah, yes. Nice job on the picture.

Z: Drawing isn't my best suite. But thanks.

8: In this picture, a particular being's life path is illustrated by the solid arrow and other beings' paths are indicated by the white arrows. This being thinks of himself as originating in Oneness, but walking a path of separation. This being believes he is not now part of the Oneness. He might believe that others are - probably special exulted ones such as angels or ascended masters or such. But "normal" beings like him are separate from each other and separate from the Oneness.

The next picture I'd like to show you will illustrate an improved understanding of the way reality works:

In this picture you can see that all things are really within the Oneness (the outermost ring). Nothing is ever outside of that outermost ring. Inside of that ring are a number of layers of the illusion of separation. The centre-most circle is the zone in which all things are One and they also know it. As one moves outwards, so one has a greater and greater illusion of separation. Right the way out to the outermost ring, which Mr Solid Arrow has found his way to. As a result of being here, he feels as if he is separate, believes he is separate and experiences that he is separate. But that is just his illusion, you see. And it is also true that there are other parts of him that exist inwards of his own position that are less caught up in the illusion of separation. Some parts, for example, have an illusion of separation but they KNOW it is an illusion. They know they can give up the illusion at any point. They know that they have intentionally chosen this illusion to fulfil some greater purpose.

But Mr Solid Arrow knows none of this. He believes that he IS separate from all else. And since he believes it to be so, that is the reality he experiences.

Z: Awesome. I have a better understanding. Thanks 8.

But where do the negative emotions come in?

8: Perfect timing. I was just coming to that.

I have, in the previous chapter, told you about Consciousness-Construct Holders. These are beings who carry the resonance of one consciousness construct or another. Your very own Inner-Self, for example, carries the consciousness construct of the energy which is "Joy". Your Inner-Self holds this frequency so that those who play in this game can experience it outside of themselves. There are many others playing other similar roles. Love itself is held by another being. This is sometimes called the Christ being. It is the being who holds the energy that returns all things to Oneness. And so this Unity-Consciousness that I speak of, that is the highest form of Love, is sometimes called the Christ energy. There are many others Consciousness-Construct Holders. Each emotion, for example, is carried into your reality by a different such being. They shine their light into this reality and, as it shines upon you freely all the time, you may choose to experience any of these emotions at any time you wish. And you can! As beings awaken, so they come to a point at which they realise that they can "self-emote". It is a very important step in your progression. It is the point at which you realise that you can open yourself, at will, to receive particular emotional energy input while, at the same time, allowing the inputs you have not chosen to simply pass you by.

And that is the thumb-nail sketch of how emotions work. We shall call these "positive emotions" or maybe even "light emotions" because they are a function of the light that is carried from Source into your reality by these Consciousness-Construct Holders.

Negative emotions (or shadow emotions) are not actually emotions at all. They are the ABSENCE of emotion. Let me show you another picture:

Z: That was a bit tougher to draw.

8: Wait till you see the next picture I'm going to show you (he laughs). But don't worry, you'll do fine. You always have everything you need, to do what is required of you. Even if you don't know it at the time.

But let's get back to the picture itself. What the above picture illustrates is the fact that a being on the outwards journey is actually looking away from the light of the Oneness. As he arrives in duality consciousness, he is not only looking away from the light and seeing his shadow, but he also has no knowing that there is a loving Oneness behind him. He has forgotten that.

This being is casting a shadow in the light of consciousness with his own consciousness.

Considering that all things are of consciousness and emotions are consciousness constructs, it should not surprise you that your own consciousness can, in fact, mask or block other consciousnesses. And this is what causes the shadow. If you are heading away from Oneness, then you will see these shadows.

So the light of Love shines upon him but, if he looks into the deep darkness of the shadow, then all he sees is the absence of love – which is fear. And the absence of joy is anything from sadness to deep melancholic depression. The absence of empathy might look like callousness. And so on…

Do you see? These negative emotions are not really emotions. They are not a thing unto themselves. They are the absence of something. And that absence is really just a function of living in duality and, especially, of heading outwards towards separation.

Z: Now wait a second there please, 8. I like all the pictures and I get the idea you are expressing. But I don't just randomly feel fear or anger or hatred or whatever. I feel it in response to something. If I were to come across a dangerous animal, a snake for example, and it reared up to strike, BOY would I feel fear! And when I read about what the politicians of the world are doing – their incompetent bumbling interspersed with making war and despoiling the environment out of pure greed – well I get plenty angry then! Hatred is not something I often feel anymore but I can see how, for example, religious intolerance can get turned to hatred for some.

The point I am making is that negative emotions aren't just a function of the "light" that is shining on my consciousness or whatever; it's a function of what happens to me in my life.

8: No it isn't.

You are expressing the world-view of the Awakened Duality-Conscious: you know there are creator beings out there somewhere, you just aren't one of them. Or so you seem to believe.

So let me ask you:

Do you create your reality or do you not? It is time to commit to an answer. You can't reside in this state of ambiguity forever. I understand that you WANT to believe that you do and that you have some fears and reservations about declaring it to be so but, if you will not declare it to be so, then it never will be so.

Creator… create!

Now answer my question. Do you create your reality, or do you not?

Z: Okay, yes, I do.

I DO create my own reality.

8: Good. But the issue is that you are only just beginning to awaken to this fact. You are a beginner who is only just learning how to create. Certainly you are not ready to take responsibility for the creation of whole realities on your own! So isn't it lucky that you are offered some extremely competent assistance from some marvellous co-creators? These beings provide you with the most wonderful reality in which you can create just the bits you want to focus on. As you grow in skill, competence and confidence, so you will be able to take on more powerful reality creation roles. But in the meantime you are given so much! You are given the light of all the emotions with which to paint your life. You are given a planet upon which to live, which is abundant in all the raw materials you will ever need. You are given a universe to play in. You are surrounded on every side by more play-mates than you will ever be able to make the acquaintance of. And you are given the most amazingly spectacular tool imaginable – your human body – with which, and though which, you can experience all of these things.

Everything you need is given to you.

With this abundance of gifts you can create the reality you desire and then you can live in that creation. You are given the paint, the brush, the palette and the canvass. And the life you live, with all of its experiences, is your work of art. And you do not have to stand apart from your creation and enjoy it from afar! No, you have the glorious gift of being able to walk though your artwork, see it from the inside, touch it, feel it, smell it, taste it, love it and BE it.

It might surprise you to know is that it has always been thus: there was never a single moment when you were NOT the creator of your own life. You are not now becoming the creator of your reality – you are simply becoming AWARE that you are! You are awakening to your own creator status, to your true nature, to Who You Really Are!

So now, let me address the question of the biting snake, the corrupt politicians and the religious fanatics.

If you are the creator of your own reality then these things will only occur in your reality to the degree that you create that they do, to the degree that you agree to have these things happen to you.

Let me give you some examples: yesterday you were busy cutting a copse of Black Wattle (Zingdad note: a type of alien invader tree that grows like a noxious weed here) on your land. You suddenly noticed a juvenile Puff Adder (Zingdad note: a deathly venomous snake) slithering away from near your foot. Despite the fact that you very nearly stood on it, it just moved off. So, why did it not bite you?

Because it had no reason to! Snakes do not, by default, bite everything that crosses their path. You hold no malice against them in your heart and your intent towards them is pure: respectful and peaceful. So why should it bite you?

Another example: last week you were going to step onto a pile of brushwood when you suddenly had a feeling that you should stop and wait. You did… and then it was okay and you could proceed. You didn't know this at the time, but we needed to give another snake an opportunity to get away. He moved off and you could carry on. No need for a confrontation here, as neither of you wished to harm the other.

A different example, this time without a slithering friend: two weeks ago you were driving a little fast on the dirt road on the way home. You suddenly had a strange visual sensation like a point of red light repeatedly flashing on your retina. You took the hint and slowed down. As you turned the next bend, you noticed before you a tight S-bend covered in slippery mud. You negotiated it easily at the lower speed at which you were now travelling, but you would certainly have lost control of the vehicle had you not slowed down. So why did you not have the accident? You weren't creating the need for it and you were creating a willingness to be warned by constantly paying attention to the signals you get. Why should things then go wrong for you?

There is a whole bookful of such examples in your life and in everyone else's. If you are not creating fear-filled experiences for yourself, then they will not come to you. Like the little snake that slithered off, there is no reason for you to have a bad outcome if you have not created it. And it goes further. If you have not created a fear-filled outcome, but are heading towards one out of innocent ignorance, then you will be warned and helped by your spiritual guidance. Each and every human being on planet earth has a spirit being who is playing the role of guardian and guide, just as I am doing for you. If you are not creating a fear-filled outcome and you are willing to pay attention to your messaging, then you WILL be helped.

And as to the politicians... My dear young friend... You have gone to extraordinary lengths to move your home so that you now live in, what is for you, paradise. You awaken to bird-song in the morning, during the day you work on the land that you love, then you take your ease as you watch beautiful sunsets and your evenings are spent working on your website, writing THE ASCENSION PAPERS and watching the stars wheel though the sky with your beloved soul-partner, Lisa. Your life is exactly as you would choose it to be. But then, for reasons known only to yourself, you feel the need to go scrounging around the dank corners of the Internet to read what these politicians are up to. And you get this information served up to you through the writings of the disaffected and the malcontent. So obviously you find what you are looking for and, when you do, you get angry. But the strangest part of all of this is that you are now complaining to me about this anger! YOU went LOOKING for it! You created it, as surely as if you had baked an angry cake and eaten it.

So now I have some questions for you:

What kind of cook makes food that he doesn't enjoy to eat?

What kind of musician makes music that he doesn't like to listen to?

What kind of artist paints pictures that he doesn't like to look at?

What kind of storyteller tells stories that he doesn't enjoy telling?

In every case the answer is... a bad one!

So enjoy your creation, enjoy your life. Love every minute of it! Or start telling better stories!

Or do you actually enjoy being angry at these politicians?

Z: Umm... well... I was going to say something like, "*I need to know what they are up to*" but I won't. Because I have agreed to the fact that I create my reality. But... umm... I don't recall creating a reality run by scoundrels. And yet, I seem to have one.

8: Correct. You didn't create it. Instead you gave away your creative powers and let others create for you, with your energy. You bought into the illusion they presented to you that your only choices are the ones they are offering you. "*If you want change,*" they tell you, "*you have to vote for it.*" Then, come election time, Candidate A tells you that Candidate B is a liar and you shouldn't vote for him. Then Candidate B tells you that Candidate A is corrupt and you shouldn't vote for HIM. And right there, they actually gave you all the information you needed: none of them are worthy of your energy! But you didn't use this information. Instead you picked between Mr Lies and Mr Corruption and you voted. Or maybe you got disgruntled enough to abstain from voting. But even then you accepted the system as it is. Even then you didn't take your energy away from their system. Still they had your participation. Either willingly or *in absentia*, you continued to give your energy to their system. And every time you read a newspaper or go trawling around those angry political websites, you are giving it your energy all over again.

Now let me tell you: you cannot "vote" this rotten system out. They will never, ever present to you a candidate who will really clean up the system and make it Life-positive. The interests of the ones that own the system and make the rules are best served by keeping the citizens of the world disempowered and obedient. So that is what the world of politics will always strive to do. And as long as you engage with the world of politics, you are playing on their board-game, with their game-pieces and their rule-sheet. You will always be playing their game.

So stop playing their game!

Remove your energy from their system and create another game that you like better. Create a game with Love, for Love and by Love. You'll like it a lot better.

Politicians are irrelevant. Unless you make them relevant by paying attention to their shenanigans.

Z: Good enough. That makes sense. But what about people who live in war-torn countries because their politicians are just nuts. Are THEIR politicians also irrelevant?

8: Are we really doing this again? Are we REALLY going to have the same old tired, "*Who is a victim?*" conversation?

We have moved on past that. No. You can answer your own question, thank you very much!

Z: (sheepish) Okay, I do know the answer. If they are in such a circumstance, then they created it. And even if they are in such circumstances, then still they are victims as they always have the opportunity to create another outcome for themselves.

8: That is true. And more importantly, other beings are not your problem. You are not their Rescuer. They must be allowed to create for themselves whatever they want. Even if – no ESPECIALLY if – they want to create things for themselves that you don't want for yourself. If you won't allow this, then you can't get what you want.

You live a life in which politicians could be irrelevant to you. Anyone who wants it can also procure such a life. And if you have such a life, then you can let go of your anger at these politicians. And then you can move to a state of pure Love without blockages in your heart. And then you will be able to create the kingdom of heaven here on earth for yourself. And then, believe me, there will be no more need for politicians!

Now, do I still need to talk about those religious fanatics who might have a problem with hatred? Or do you get this point?

Z: No. I get it.

8: Then I shall reiterate, for the sake of clarity, and bring this point to a conclusion:

Fear-filled outcomes simply do not happen to you if you don't create them. The corollary, however, is that they can, and do, happen if you DO create them.

I said previously that you co-create your reality. That you create your life, your experiences and your world out of the raw materials that are offered to you. Well, by virtue of the shadow that you cast with your consciousness in the field of all consciousness, these negative emotions come into being. As a result of your own creative power, these negative emotions are given substance and made real. And so there certainly are dark, negative emotions available for you to create with. And, as beings who dwell in duality have experienced these negative emotions, so certain other beings have seen the opportunity and come to use these negative emotions for their own purposes. Some have opted to become the Consciousness-Construct Holders for these negative emotions. Some beings have found a way to feed themselves on negative emotions. These beings strive to bring you into fear and pain and confusion for their own purposes. They have minions who live upon your planet and try to run things in such a way that their master's appetites are served. Such beings can indeed cause fear and pain on a large scale. And then there are small, little beings who use negative emotions to try to manipulate and control others. Petty bullies and small abusers. All of this exists. And all of this plays out between those who are willing to play Perpetrator and those who all willing to play Victim, and, of course, those who are willing to try to rescue either of them.

For those who are willing to step out of the game entirely of course, none of this is relevant. They simply are not a part of all of this energy thievery and such petty nonsense.

Z: So I should work to leave duality behind me then?

8: No. That would not be my proposal. It is inevitable that you will eventually come to leave duality behind you, as you proceed on your journey, but in the mean time there are some amazing compensations for being there. Experiencing yourself as separate from each other and from the world you live in can bring much pleasure. You can look upon a sunset and see it as a delightfully surprising alchemy between sunlight, clouds and environment. You can be in the presence of your most beloved ones and be genuinely surprised by something they do or say, despite knowing them very well indeed. And these are just two random examples. What I am trying to have you understand is this: the more duality you allow for, the more your world can surprise you. Indeed Delight is the part of Joy which comes from the unexpected. Before there can be the unexpected there must be the unknown. Veiled. Hidden. Forgotten. And THAT is the actual purpose of The Veil in the first place! Remember Push and Stay? Remember WHY Push achieved forgetting in the first place? Not so that he could do all kinds of miserable things to himself! No! So that he could have the wondrous, overwhelmingly joyful experience of seeing Stay again, as if for the first time. So he could look upon her, see God, and fall hopelessly in love. So he could come rushing back to her, faster and faster and so that he could show her the glory and magnificence of her own being though his experience of her.

This is actually a love story! A madly happy, ecstatically joyous, love story. Not some grim tale of woe! The sad bits are just an interlude in the middle to provide some dramatic counter-point to the ecstasy of the latter half of the story!

So, yes certainly, fearful outcomes must be possible for you, and so they are. So you CAN play with that energy if you want to. But why would you? Now is the moment of awakening. Now you can put that behind you and cherish the spectacular wonderment of the mystery. You can love it all. You can, in fact, DELIGHT in all of life. Let it surprise you. Because if you create with the emotions of the light, your every surprise will be a delightful one. Sound like something you want to do?

Z: Oh my goodness, 8! This is what I live for! My heart cries out for this!

8: Then let me show you another picture for you to draw…

Z: Oooh! That's gorgeous. But I can't draw that!

8: Maybe you can't draw exactly this… but you can draw something that conveys the idea of it to your readers. Do your best, you'll do fine.

Z: Okay… how's this…

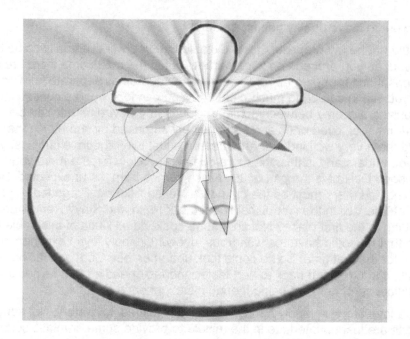

8: Good enough. It certainly illustrates the point I want to get to next. Well done.

This is a picture of someone expressing unbounded, limitless Love. This being knows that It is One with All That Is. It Loves everything and everyone, everywhere, always. It is a source of the Light of Love because there are no blocks to this being's heart. And since the centre of every heart is also the centre of All That Is, removing blockages to your heart results in your discovering your direct access to the entirety of all consciousness right there within your own heart. You discover the Oneness inside your heart.

There is a point of no size right in the centre of your heart that IS The One. This is the Source of the Light. You are the Light. And your choices and creations are the lens though which the Light shines. Your life, your world, your reality, your experiences… everything you perceive to be "outside of you" is really just a projection of the Light of The One through the lens that you are holding. Alter your choices, thoughts and beliefs and you alter the lens. Alter the lens and you alter the image that is shown. And then you have a new reality around you. Beings who are on the outwards journey who have managed to forget entirely who and what they really are, have managed to create so much darkness and blockage on the lens of their consciousness that they project very little light into their reality. So they seek a light from some other source. And that can be problematic for many reasons. Prime of which is the fact that your need of another being's light to see, means you are dependant on them. It means you are a Victim. It results in you looking outside of yourself for what is true. But what is outside of you is an illusion. It is what is inside of you that is true. However, until you remove the blockages, you will not see this. And even when you have removed the blockages, still you must be willing to create this – you must be willing to SHINE your light. And this is what the being, illustrated in the above picture, has done.

But, removing the blockages and being willing to shine your light, does not mean you MUST leave your current life either. In the past this was so. In the past the only way to awaken to these powerful energies was to first attain this level of unity-consciousness and then "die" to 3D physicality. Beings would normally only ascend to the next dimension after death. Except, of course, the few truly exceptional ones who turned their bodies to light and lifted themselves from this realm into the next one. But irrespective, the point is that one would not have been able to ascend your consciousness and still remain here. But now things are different. Now comes a big step-wise change in the way the game is being played. Together we have decided to change the rules. Not all parts of the Oneness are ready to know this yet – which is as it should be. All things are possible and it is even possible to be this far into the change and to insist that there is no change. Or that the change is scary and evil. Or…

Z: … or even… fishcakes?

8: (laughs) Yes, you have understood! Every possible thing that could be, is dreamt up. Many can feel it in their bones that something big is afoot. And because most fear the unknown, a fearful outcome is imagined. And because you are all creators in your own right, many will get some of the fearful stuff they are imagining. Sadly they must be allowed to get what they create. But we will do all we can to bring some Light to the matter. Already there are numerous voices speaking love, joy and peace into your planetary consciousness. Beings who are willing to conceive of a happy outcome will be given an opportunity to hope for that, to dream of that, to believe in that… and to get that.

You who are now willing to awaken to the Light of Love that is within you will be instrumental to this process. You see, you don't actually need to write a book or tell a story or anything like that. You don't need to try to persuade others to change. All you need to do is to be the change yourself. If you do, you change the world around you. And then others around you can see their world differently, simply because your light is shining. And then, person by person, one by one, we all become One.

Z: Oh wow, yes! Okay, I'm in!

8: Good. I'll tell you how in a moment. It's really quite simple. But first we must redeem negative emotions. Because anything that you reject and divorce from yourself and make unloved and unacceptable places a block in your heart. If it is outside of your heart, then it cannot be inside of your heart. And if there is anything that is not inside of your heart then, of course, you do not have the Oneness in your heart. Then it is, at best, one of the masks or shadows of Love that you are feeling and expressing.

Z: I get it, 8. I do. I have to be willing to Love everything. Nothing can be excluded. Including the negative emotions themselves.

But that sounds like a big ask. How do I love fear, for example?

8: You start by understanding its purpose and value in your life and that you are not a victim to it. It is a tool, like any other, that you can use when it's appropriate. A good and useful tool is something to love. Not something to reject.

To help you understand this, I want to talk for a moment about your body, about the human animal.

In order to be experiencing the miracle of Life as you do, you need to engage in a delicate and beautiful partnership. In due course, you will have some conversations that will help you to understand the human animal better. But, for now, I will simply say this:

You are, obviously, not your body. You cannot have made it thus far into THE ASCENSION PAPERS and still think that you are. You are pure consciousness. But your body has its own life, its own intelligence and its own kind of consciousness. And it constantly communicates with you in some marvellous ways. When it begins to run low on certain resources, it drives you to find a way to provide it with what it needs. You call this hunger and thirst. But the body is not as blunt a communicator as you might think. If you listen with a delicate ear, you will hear your body ask very specifically for the particular things it needs. You will feel a craving for fresh fruit if your body needs vitamins and enzymes. Or, if you have been working and sweating, then your body may call for more salt to replace what was lost, and so on. This is, as I say, a whole other chapter (or maybe even series of chapters). The reason I raise this now is to help you to understand something: YOU are invulnerable. YOU are pure consciousness and cannot be killed. Your body, however, can be destroyed. It is a complex alchemy of many consciousnesses that is actually quite fragile. And this alchemy has its own consciousness that desires a continuation of its own life. It seeks to thrive and be well and healthy and it wishes a good, long, happy existence. You can partner with it and assist it in that goal or you can, as most do, obstruct it and get in its way. Through your choices, beliefs, ideas and actions you can cause it to express illness and disease.

Many of you even make choices that put your bodies directly in harm's way. You can choose to be at dire risk by creating that you are a soldier at a time of war. Or that you live in a country that is ravaged by war. Or that you are in a terrible car accident. Or that you are a victim of violent crime. Or on any number of other such perilous paths.

Just as your body can talk to you with hunger – with very specific desires even – so too can your body say to you: *"Please don't go there!"* It can say so in very compelling terms. The *"Oh NO! I DON'T WANT TO DO THIS!"* response from your body is one powerful manifestation of fear. If you won't listen, it can turn to panic. In certain circumstances, the body will even go so far as to over-ride your choices and do what IT wants to do: You still thought you were heading into danger and then found you were running away!

You understand?

Your body is alive. It is a someone. It has desires of its own and a will of its own. If this were not true, it would not be able to do what it does. There would only be you in a meat-suit and you would feel no urges other than your own. Certainly no drives to eat, drink and sleep and the like.

So when you feel fear, take a moment to listen to that fear. Where does it come from? Is this your body talking to you? Are you being warned of danger? Are you engaged in a choice, which puts you are risk? Listen. Really listen. Go to your heart and pay your body the respect of hearing what it has to say. And respond accordingly from a place of love.

If your fear is more immediate than that and there is something right there in your reality that you feel you should fear, then there are three things to do:

First, remind yourself that you are the creator of your own reality. That, despite the evidence, you cannot be hurt, harmed, or damaged if you have not agreed to this. Then, don't agree to it.

Second, go to your heart. In your heart you have sure knowledge of what to do in every circumstance. Your spiritual guidance team is there with you and they can, and will, help you. But you must listen. And the portal through which they speak to you is your heart. Listen.

Third, act as your heart directs and do not second guess. Do.

You'll be fine.

But fear does not only originate in the human body. You are a more complex being than you think. There are numerous parts to your psyche. And, just like your human body, sometimes some other part of you might feel threatened. If its concern is not heard and addressed, then it might very well yell at you in unpleasant ways. This can certainly enter your consciousness as fear, panic or other unpleasant experiences.

So pay attention. Listen with your heart. Be loving and respectful. Make choices from a place of Love.

There are negative emotions other than fear, but they all actually root in fear – they all come from some part of yourself saying "*Oh no, I don't want this!*". Let's look at anger, for example. If some other being wants to do something, which you feel will have a negative impact on you, then fear might cause you to say, "*No, don't do that.*" But what if they do it anyway? Then you feel you need to bring some energy to bear – you feel you need to move to a more determined resistance. So you get angry. You see? Anger is fear plus energy.

Jealousy and possessiveness is fear of losing something you love turned to an obsessive desire to hold onto it.

Greed is fear of not having enough, turned to obsessive desire to accumulate all you can.

And so on and so on. You are smart enough to work the rest out yourself. The point I make is that every single negative emotion is rooted in fear. And, if you are feeling fear, then you are being communicated with, either by your human body or by some other part of your psyche.

So the appropriate response to any negative emotion is to pay it heed when it arrives. Go to your heart and respond appropriately.

But there is a bigger picture that you must be aware of. You can only experience a negative emotion today, if you created your reality with negative emotions at some point in your recent past. This is actually good news. It means that if you should create from today onwards only with positive emotions then, in time, you will come to have a reality made of only positive emotional experiences.

Z: So, deal with the negative emotions of today in a positive respectful way and create with positive emotions for tomorrow.

8: Exactly. Nicely summarised.

Z: Okay and what about pain? Physical pain, emotional pain, spiritual pain; what about that?

8: It's all just the same thing. You cannot experience pain without having created yourself in the first place. Usually you have dissociated the creation events from the outcome and so you don't know that you created the pain. Especially when the root cause lies in another lifetime. And even if you know that you created it, you often don't know how. And if you don't know HOW you created the pain, it is very difficult indeed to release that creation and create differently in the future.

You were recently taken on a spiritual journey to understand physical illness in a new way for a Guided Journey recording that you wished to make to help others with health issues. (Zingdad note: this is available for download on my website, see the notes at the end of this book for more information) I'd like to paraphrase some of what you were taught here…

If you wish to find real wellness and real healing for your body, then you must begin by recognising that your body is not your enemy and that the discomfort and disease you are suffering is not, in fact, a bodily dysfunction. It is NOT your body that is wrong or broken. In such instances, your body is actually playing a vital role as teacher in that it is engaged in showing you what truly ails you, at a deeper psycho-spiritual level. What actually ails you are deep-level decisions that you have taken and beliefs that you have entrenched about yourself that are causing you inner-turmoil and conflict. These are shown to you by the body in a way that is very present and real. You get to see these unhelpful ideas and beliefs manifest as physical illness. It is these decisions and beliefs that are the root cause of your illnesses - not the body being "broken" or misperforming for no real reason! If we are willing to pay attention to the body and hear what it has to say to us, then we may obtain guidance in healing our own inner imbalance, which occurs in our psyches. Healing that inner-imbalance will result in the external symptoms dissipating. Wellness of the body invariably follows wellness of the psyche.

So, exactly what is true of negative emotions is true of physical pain: respond positively and lovingly from the heart. Cultivate an ability to LISTEN to your body. Find out what is the root cause of the illness and pain. Work to release that cause and replace it with something more Life-positive.

And then, while you are at it, move towards creating all your tomorrows with Love.

Z: And how do I do that, 8? How do I create all my tomorrows with Love?

8: I'll get to that in a moment. There is a third blockage to your heart that I need to address first.

3.1.3 Identifying with your creations rather than with Who You Really Are

We have already addressed this when I spoke about ego, so I will be brief.

As long as you think you are your creations, then you will be creating separation.

There are a number of ways to realise that you are not your creations, which will also help you to begin waking to your true nature. Meditation is a good way. But there are many different practices that are all termed meditation. I would recommend meditations that assist you to become present to the NOW moment. Release all your thoughts and ideas about what came before and what will come later. Be present in the NOW. Do this consistently and you will begin to realise that you are not your body, you are not your thoughts, you are not your beliefs, you are not your relationships, you are very much not the things you do or your job. And you are CERTAINLY not the money you earn or the possessions you own.

It can be quite difficult to move into the NOW moment if you are not used to being there. Most beings who are incarnated on your planet, especially in western societies such as your own, are totally conditioned to living alternately in the past and in the future with no stop in-between for the NOW. On the menu for your thought processes are things such as:

Worries and concerns about the future

Wishes and dreams about the future

Reminiscences and reveries about the past

Recriminations and bitterness about the past.

But, if you truly spent a moment in the NOW, you'd be able to release all of these things and see them for the illusory constructs of your mind that they really are. Your past and your future are not fixed. They are your creations. And they can be recreated any way you want and need. But you must first cease trying to live in the past and future. To do so is to try to live in an illusory creation. This takes you away from who you really are and away from your connection with the divine. Doing so identifies you with your creations, not with who you really are.

The antidote is to become truly present to the NOW. Make time every single day to be still. Make time often to listen to your heart. Break the habit of not-NOW consciousness. Move into the NOW more and more often until you can reside there permanently.

Z: 8, besides the Guided Journey recording about healing, I have also created a number of other Guided Journeys that might be useful to readers in finding such a space. My Guided Journey called "open your heart is my way of sharing with others the path I discovered that lead to my own awakened and opened heart chakra (Zingdad note: Download information at the end of the book).

8: Yes, indeed! There are many aids to this journey available to the seeker. From books on the subject to personal instruction at the hands of an experienced meditation instructor. What you have offered in your Guided Journey recordings is the path that worked for you. This is all that we can do: share with others what has worked for ourselves. As you have already discovered, many have found value in what you have created and many more will still. Each will have to find their own path to stillness and to heart-connection and to each will be offered the assistance they need if they will but seek it.

And that brings us to the end of this rather lengthy discourse on blockages to your heart. If the seeker experiences any blockage and is willing to remove it and proceed to Love, then the path will be opened. Help will be given. It takes commitment, a clear resolve and a little effort. But anyone who desires to get there, certainly should be able to do so. And the rewards for doing so are immense. Removing the blockages to Love means being able to open yourself to experiencing Love.

Which is what I will be addressing in the remaining two points.

3.2 The Energy Cycle of Love

I have said before that you get what you create. But you reside in a time-bound system. This means that you are right now experiencing that which you created in your past. All the choices and beliefs that you engaged with in the past are the basis of your current life's experiences. If you decide right now to radically change perspective and you instantly come to hold new ideas and beliefs, then it will take some time for your reality to change. Over the next while you will experience less and less of the world built upon your old beliefs and more and more of the world built upon your new beliefs. This is the essential value of the consciousness construct called Time. It is that which separates cause from effect. So if the cause occurs in your own consciousness right now, the effect will not occur in your reality for some time. How long it takes will depend on how fundamental the change is and how firm you are in your resolve and intent. But what you should understand is that the process of changing your reality does take time. It is a matter of changing yourself, holding to that inner-change and allowing your outer-reality to transform over whatever period is required.

With that background I wish to tell you this: if you wish to live in heaven tomorrow then you should begin by being a citizen of heaven today. Be the most loving being that you can be. When you yourself are a citizen of heaven by your thoughts, your words and your deeds then indeed, you will come to find your world slowly becoming more and more heavenly. And no death to this world will be required of you. Be the change you desire and the change WILL follow suit.

The advice I offer is to be patient with your life, be patient with yourself and give yourself a good deal of grace. But make a start right now! Your tomorrows are being created by the consciousness and energy that you express today. So you can, and will, have a tomorrow that is love-filled if you create with only Love today. Every time you find it hard going and every time you falter, simply return to the path of Love. First be kind to yourself and love yourself. That you have faltered is proof that you are trying. Simply make a choice anew to engage with life using the energy of Love.

And that brings me right to the heart of the matter. Love is an energy. It is the only TRUE energy.

All other energy is a derivative of Love. The more love you give away the more you have. The more you have the more you can give. Love is the only thing that is like this. It is inexhaustible once you begin to express it. Imagine money was like that – imagine the more you spent the larger your bank balance would be. Everyone would be out on the streets buying and spending and giving it away! And this is how it should be with love. Give it away!

And not just to others. Give it to yourself too. I'd go so far as to say you should give it to yourself FIRST. Seek to love yourself magnificently. Seek to love what you do and do what you love. Then love those around you and surround yourself with those you love.

I have said that you are the Light of awareness that shines from the Source through the lens of your consciousness. I have said your consciousness is shaped by your thoughts, ideas, beliefs and choices. Well, if your choices are all about Love then your lens will grow very large and very clear indeed. It will let though vast amounts of Light. You will see clearly and what you will see will be full of Light.

And this is the essence of the process. The more Love you allow to shine though you, the more you are creating with Love. The more you create with Love, the more you will experience Love. And, of course the more Love you experience the more you have to give. And so a wonderful new cycle is begun in your life and it can continue cycling up like this until you are a radiant point of pure Love. Like a sun, you shall shine brilliant Love light upon all around you.

And when this is the state of your consciousness then it will be impossible for you to be like our the little running man in the illustration above who is heading outwards and seeing his own shadow of negative emotions. It will be impossible because you, yourself will be shining too much light for there to be any shadow anywhere around you.

And that is as simple as it is. In theory.

You might need a little more guidance to actually put this into practice.

Z: I certainly do. I mean – giving love in great abundance to all and sundry sounds like a great idea, but how do I actually do that? I mean, walking up to strangers and asking them if they want some love might not yield the desired result!

8: (laughs) Yes, I can certainly see that.

Your planetary culture has so badly messed up the concept of Love that this might seem quite problematic indeed. (still laughing)

Z: And also, it is actually quite hard, I must admit, to feel loving feelings towards some people.

8: I can see that too. There is so much diversity of consciousness on your planet that you will actually find it very, very difficult to simply express Love to all around you, all the time. And that is why this is a process. You take it slowly. You do not start by demanding that the world should change and that the people around you should change. No. You look to yourself for change. And as you change yourself, so your world changes in response. In small increments, you open your heart. In small increments, your world becomes more loveable to you. The outcome eventually is that you become the being in the last illustration… you become pure radiant love. And then your whole reality can do no other but reflect that back at you.

But it IS a process. It takes time. And I can help you with it.

Z: Okay. So where do I start?

8: There are many ways to achieve the goal of an open heart. The one I can recommend is to begin by doing service. If you do service, then your heart opens and the energy of Love begins to flow from you towards the being for whom you are doing the service. So this is how you begin. By doing service.

Z: Just for clarity, 8, may I ask what you mean when you say "service".

8: Ah good! You are quite right in asking me to define this word. It is quite often used, but also not often defined. Service is any action that you do to the benefit of another. It is generally thought of as "being of assistance", but I would say that there is much more to it than that. If you should cultivate, for example, the ability to really LISTEN to another, without needing to interject your ideas and opinions, to only ask questions that might allow them to better tell THEIR story, then you will be equipped to do great service. Many will feel profoundly helped for the fact that there was someone to whom they could really talk. Simple kindness can be service as well. Talking care can be a service. Giving others the space to give what they have to give is a great service. If you can find ways to help others to discover themselves and their gift, then you are probably doing one of the greatest services of all. What is not often realised is that the greatest services are often not particularly active. For example, assuming the best of someone or even EXPECTING the best of them, such that you create a space for them to rise to the highest and best that they can be, is a wonderful service.

Here is a list of words that can be related to service. Go though them slowly, one by one, thinking upon each of them. With each word think about someone that did this service to you and someone that you have done this service to:
The first word is nurturing. Who has nurtured you? How? How did it feel? Who have you nurtured? How did that feel?

Now ask yourself the same questions about these words: protecting, sharing, energising, healing, feeding, listening, helping, supporting.

Service is that which leads to the benefit of the other. And the other might be anyone. It might be your own body, a beloved friend, a total stranger, a community, an animal, a piece of land or the earth as a whole.

Service is love in action.

And this is why it is appropriate that you do service to open your heart. Any service will do, but a small service will allow the flow of a small amount of energy and a big service will allow for the flow of a large amount of energy. The more energy you are permitting to flow, the more your heart is opened. If you find your Great Gift and begin to give it, then you will be permitting an unbounded amount of energy to flow. So that is, obviously, a good idea. If you are seeking to move yourself into this New World then you should obviously discover your Great Gift and give it.

Z: Okay but how? How do I discover my Great Gift?

8: Follow your heart. Constantly listening to your heart and constantly doing what it tells you will lead you forward. And doing that which brings the most Love will move you forward. Your Great Gift is your Heart Song. Singing your Heart Song IS giving your Great Gift. These two things are the same thing. And your Heart Song is what your heart sings to you when it inspires you to find your way back to Oneness.

So... you start by opening your heart. You always start there. And the easiest, quickest and surest way to open your heart is to do an act of pure service. Then see how that feels. That "seeing how it feels" is your opportunity to listen to your heart. It will talk to you in feelings. It will tell you "more of this and less of that". Assuredly not everyone is well-suited to all types of service! Do an act of service and see what you heart has to say about it. What aspect of this doing did you enjoy. What aspect did you not enjoy. Where is there a service that you can do that brings you more joy and less displeasure. Follow your greatest joy to a place where you are giving your greatest gift and are residing only in a state of bliss. Then you will be giving your Greatest Gift. It will seem as if you are doing that which you were MADE to do. It will seem to you that you are uniquely, perfectly suited to this task; as if everything you had ever done up to this point was all just training for this task. It will feel like your truest, greatest purpose. It will give you an amazing feeling of wonderful "rightness" to fulfil this service. And, by doing this task, you will be creating and catalysing Love in the world around you. You will cause a return to Oneness for yourself and inspire it in others around you. And you will be a part of the creation of heaven on earth. You will be making your life sacred and thereby making your world sacred. You will change others around you for the better - not by demanding of them that they must change - no, by changing yourself and by giving your gift.

But it all starts with giving service. Give your Great Gift if you can. If you cannot, then give the greatest service you are able. And if you cannot give great service, then give many small services. Give service.

It is very important, however, that you realise you are not supposed to give all gifts. You are not supposed to be the font of all Love in the whole world. You are not supposed to serve every need that the world presents to you. You are only supposed to give the gift you are best suited to giving. If you give gifts that you are NOT best suited to giving you do two things:

First, you are squandering the energy available to you on lesser expressions. I could put it another way and say you are wasting your time and resources doing something that you are not well suited to doing.

Second, you are doing someone else's job, which is actually doing them a disservice. You see, there is someone out there who is ideally suited to doing this job. Not only are you NOT doing what you are best suited to do, but you are also not allowing this other being to do what they ARE best suited to do.

And this is a very important understanding. You are not alone. You are not the only giver of gifts. You are a vital and irreplaceable part in the infinite dance of Life, and it's not a one-man show! And the flow of energy should also not be a one-way stream! I have called it The Energy Cycle of Love and the word cycle implies a rotation, a giving AND a receiving.

The Ego being believes it is separate and alone. Individual. But the heart-centred creator being realises It is One with all other beings everywhere. The heart-centred creator being realises It exists only with, and through, other beings… only as a part of the great Oneness.

So you cannot give your gift without having others give their gifts to you too. There must be "flow". If there is no flow, then there is no energy cycle. When it is static, it is lifeless. You cannot hoard Love – it must pass though you. So you must give this energy away to others. The more you give, the more you open yourself to receive. But you MUST also be willing to receive! If you do not, you create a blockage. Blockages are the root cause of harm to the psyche, which results in emotional, spiritual and physical illnesses. So be willing to give first, but then be willing to receive in equal measure also.

And when you receive, make sure you honour both the gift and the giver. Be gracious. Say thank you. Give them something back. Keep the energy moving. Keep it alive. Keep it "alove". (he smiles). Let it flow.

And pass it on too! If you have received something that you have found to be of value, then find a way to give that same gift to another. This too keeps it alive. This too opens your heart. This too tells you something about your own Great Gift.

And this is the way the currency of the New Earth will flow: each being will find and express their ever-unfolding Great Gift. And because each being is unique, so too will their Great Gift be unique. There will never be "too much" of that which you will provide, because your expression will be unique. And anything and everything that you need, but are unable to provide for yourself, you will find some other being who desires to offer this as their Great Gift.

And that is the economy. Not a single soul is asking, *"But what is in it for me?"* Not a single soul has need or want. All have abundance. And no one is trying to greedily grab more than they want or need because no one fears not having. There is always abundance because everyone knows they are One.

And as you engage more and more with the energy cycle of Love and less and less with the negative energies, so your tomorrows will become brighter and brighter. And then you will find yourself doing ever greater and greater service. Eventually you will only be creating with the light. You will find no more blockages in your heart. You will realise that you ARE the light.

Z: But what about things like money, 8? You say love is the new currency and that sounds fantastic. But how do I pay for a loaf of bread at the shop with love? If I offer the cashier a big wet kiss, I don't think that'll do. And in the real world people need at least the basic stuff like a roof over their heads, a meal on the table and so on. This takes money. And if I don't have money then I might very soon find myself without a roof over my head or food on my table. So what about that?

8: So you think you need money?

You do not.

Money is, at best, bits of paper with printing on it and, at worst, numbers on a computer somewhere. You can do little with those bits of paper and even less with the computer numbers. These things are, in and of themselves, useless. But because people have agreed to it, they are a means of exchange and so you suddenly think they are important.

But you are once again falling for the illusion that has been presented to you. You believe you need money. But you don't. You want food and shelter and clothing and so forth. And there are many ways to procure these things. Money is one way, yes. It is the way that the system encourages you to use because, when you DO use money, you make others richer. Every time a cent changes hands, some unseen beings get a cut. It is inevitable and unavoidable. You use their system – they get their share!

But there are many, many other ways to do things. And if you are a creator being then you will have no difficulty creating everything that you need. You will always have abundance. So the question really is not about money. It is whether you are a victim or a creator.

Z: (big sigh). 8, I don't know what to say.

I say I am a creator. And I mostly believe I am. I want to believe I am. I think I am moving towards believing I am. But... something like this comes along and it shows me that I am right back at square one and I don't believe I am a creator after all. What to do?

8: (he smiles more kindly) I told you, did I not, that you would have to be patient with yourself? Well here is where the patience comes in. You ARE still looking at your own shadow. You ARE still creating with fear. Your reality shows you this. There is no surprise here and this is exactly the way it should look, given where you are at in your progression. But now it is time for you to take an active hand in changing this. Now it is time to create that you are a creator. Now it is time for you to choose what energy you will be using in your creations.

So lighten up on yourself. Allow that you are still using money and that you still believe you need this external form of energy exchange in your life. Allow that you still fear being without money. That is, quite simply, where you are at right now. It's okay. Let yourself off the hook. Let it be. Do what you think you need to do to make some money. But don't focus all your attention on this. Make sure you focus MORE of your attention on doing service – as I have described above. Give yourself grace and allow yourself to change as fast as you can without causing yourself distress. So, take care of this money business while you think you need it, and then get on with creating yourself anew as a creator being of pure Love.

Can you do that?

Z: Yes. Of course I can. And I will.

8: Good. Because then the energy cycle of Love will begin to flow. And then you will begin to discover the magnificence and beauty of the fact that you are not alone. You are not the only gift giver. There are others around you who are finding their way to their own Great Gift and, as they discover it, so they too are giving it. And, right here in your previous question to me, you have expressed a need. You have said you don't know how to create energy exchange without money. Right? Well what if I told you that there are others who do! There are other planetary realities where beings have created whole civilisations of glorious abundance and they have engaged in energy exchanges of wonderful complexity, without ever even having HEARD of money. If you told them about your money system here on planet earth, they would be mystified that anyone would want to use such a life-negative thing. So the knowledge of how to build these life-positive exchange systems is out there. And not only is it "out there", but it is also available to you right here on planet earth. Just as you are finding your way to your Great Gift through the writing of THE ASCENSION PAPERS, so there are others who are busy giving their Great Gift by working out how to bring those life-positive exchange systems to your planetary consciousness. Usually these would be beings who have had incarnational experiences in these other realms where these life-positive systems of exchange are used. These beings would, by virtue of their past-life experiences and their training and experience in this life, be perfectly suited to working out systems and economies. But they would be beings of Love. They would be seeking to give their gift, just as you are. They would be of unity-consciousness, just as you are. And the systems they will devise will empower and enrich all, not leach and steal from all, as the current system does.

So give your gift. Give it with great abundance. Give it to all who wish it. Give it until you realise that you have a greater gift yet to give. Then give THAT! Move always towards a greater version of yourself giving an ever-greater gift of Love.

Z: So, 8, are you then saying THE ASCENSION PAPERS is my Great Gift?

8: Is this the thing that you can find to do that causes the most Love?

Z: Um… yes, I think it is. I am engaged in a process of transmuting all that was painful and fearful in my own consciousness into something that is beautiful and love-filled. Writing THE ASCENSION PAPERS IS that process. It is the record of my own change, but also the means of that transformation. I guess I am, from my own perspective, retelling the story of What Is in a way that is full of Love, in a way that releases fear. I am retelling the story in a way that is congruent with All being One. Yes, I would say THE ASCENSION PAPERS is the greatest Love story I could conceive of. And this plot mechanism of me being the one who "doesn't know" and asks the questions, and you and J-D being the ones who "do know" and who answer the questions, and the readers being the ones who read the words on the page… well… I slowly begin to realise that this too is just a fabrication, isn't it? We are the same being telling ourselves this story. We are One. We told ourselves many different tales of separation previously and now we are telling ourselves a tale of unity that makes those tales of separation make sense in a new and wondrous way.

(smiles) I guess I got carried away with the answer to your question. The answer is yes, I DO think that this is the thing I can do that causes the most Love.

8: Do you feel, when you are doing this, that this is what you were born to do? That this is the thing you are best suited to be doing? That there is unlikely to be someone else who is better suited to doing this?

Z: Yes I do! I mean there are other people who are better suited to telling the stories they are telling and thank God for them! I wouldn't want to live in a world without all the other wonderful heart-centred, spirit-filled, Love-inspired books that are out there. But this story is uniquely mine to tell. Being the Zingdad who asks the questions and then being the vehicle though which these answers arrive, is my unique gift and privilege. No one else could do exactly this.

8: Well then, you have answered your own question. For so long as this is true, then THE ASCENSION PAPERS is your Great Gift. In due course, you will find a far greater gift to give. But this is it for you, for now.

How do you like it?

Z: I love it! I really do.

8: And how do you find your life has changed as a result of your giving this gift?

Z: (laughs) Oh wow! Radically. Every part of my life has changed. And every single change has been for the better. Miraculously and unbelievably so.

Oh – I begin to see what you are saying! Yes, I see it… following my heart is a process. And the life that I live and the world around me IS changing. But, it is a process.

8: How much Love is there in your life now, compared with, say, a year ago?

Z: I can't even compare. What I had then was deep poverty compared to now. Which is strange because then I was earning a fat income and now I'm not. But my life then was a sad shell of poverty compared to now. My life now is… the only word I can think of is, blessed. Full of light and happiness. Every single thing I do from when I awake in the morning to when I go to bed at night is congruent with my soul and with who I really am. I never feel pushed to do anything that I feel wrong about. The world around me is beautiful. And amazingly I only ever seem to deal with people who are kind and helpful. It's strange, but it's true. Everyone I meet is just wonderful. I hadn't really thought about that until now.

8: There you are. And you have only just begun the journey. And it will be the same for all who engage on such a journey. Open your heart and begin to give your gift, and the world will change for you. It will take time, because you will take time to change. But it WILL unfold for you like a flower that slowly opens. As you open your heart, as you release your blockages, as you allow the Love to flow though you, as you give your gift, so your world will be your mirror. So it will shine Love back at you, so it will give gifts back to you, so it will show its open and abundant heart to you. The world is nothing more and nothing less than a mirror for your soul. You will only ever see shining back at you that which you really are. So shine your light of Love. You will need patience and commitment. But the rewards will amaze you.

Give.

…and…

Receive.

It's like "breathe out" and "breathe in". That's the cycle of breath. This is the cycle of Love.

The gift that you are giving is a wonderful, delightful surprise to many. You know this. Many have expressed to you how they found themselves deeply touched by what you are doing. They find light and joy and truth here. It heals them and transforms them. They find they can tell themselves a new story, for the fact that you are telling yours. You know this. They tell you it is so. So your gift is a good one. Now, can you find in yourself a willingness to receive also? Are you willing to unblock the blockage and receive in like measure to your gift? There are those who have gifts to give that you need to receive. They are perfectly suited to the giving of THEIR gift and it is to the greatest service of Love that they do. It is their Great Gift to give.

Are you willing to receive?

Z: I am, 8. I have had issues with receiving, I know. But now I understand it differently. I am now willing to receive. I am willing to engage directly with the energy cycle of Love.

8: Wonderful, my beloved friend!

In that case, I can move on to the next step. The first step was removing the blockages to love, the second step was engaging in the DOing of Love. The third step is, BEing Love.

3.3 Be Love

I trust that you are now ready to accept that Oneness is your truest state and that Love is your truest expression. I have made it clear to you that it is only as a result of a lot of hard work that you have been able to obtain for yourself this illusion of separation that is the duality experience. And it is only by looking deeply into Love's shadows and creating with what you found there, that you have been able to experience your life as being full of fear, sadness, pain and confusion. And the fact that you can see this to be so is evidence that you are now seeing through that illusion. Seeing through an illusion is the step that comes right before releasing that very illusion. So this is good news.

The path forward involves you first releasing the dark shadow energies, as detailed above in our discussion about energy blockages. Then you should begin to create only with the light energy of Love. More light and less shadow is the process here. In due course, the whole negative-emotion experience will be but a memory. It is within you now, so you shall always have the right to create with these negative emotions if you choose, but I am saying you shall in due course release your belief that you MUST create with them. These illusions that you could be hurt or killed, that someone could take from you what is yours, that you could go without and be left needing and wanting and that you do not get what you create, will become very obvious for what they are… illusions. You will stand up in your own light and own your creations. And none shall be able to take from you without your explicit permission.

And, as you engage with this process, so something else will happen. Service and the giving of your Great Gift is, you see, the DOing of Love. It is therefore an ego function. But it is what I would call right-doing because it is the doing that aligns you with your greatest good. It aligns your ego with your heart. And when you are truly perfectly aligned with your highest nature, then you ARE your highest nature. Then YOU are your Inner-Self, walking here on earth.

Do you follow?

Because this is a very important point.

When you are in every way thinking, acting and being like your God-like Self then you will BE your God-like Self.

You see, it is only through constant hard and painful labour that you are able to maintain your separation from who and what you truly are. If you cease doing all this objectionable work then you will, and must, return to what is true and right – what is natural and normal.

The elasticity of the Infinite Elastic Ball will pull you homewards.

You will feel the movement in your being and it will feel BLISSFUL.

It won't happen all in one go, though. That would be the "direct route" that I spoke of previously. You are not choosing that. You are choosing the slower "scenic route". So for you it will happen in a series of steps. As you cease your "pushing away" a little bit – as the Infinite Elastic Ball pulls you back home a step – you will feel your consciousness change. You will have a transformative, blissful experience and you will suddenly come to new ideas about yourself, your life, your goals, who you are, what you wish to do. And your world will change. In a moment, everything will become more beautiful and life-filled. Everything will become illuminated. Full of light. And the light, of course, will actually be shining out from your own heart. It will be the light of Love that shines from you that will illuminate the world for you!

It will happen. To everyone who chooses to follow their heart, to engage with the cycle of love, to give their gift, to all such beings it is a guaranteed certainty that you will have such a moment when you shall, quite simply, BE Love. And in that moment you will SEE. You will see with your heart what it is that you are moving towards. And because you have free-will always, you will have the right to move towards it faster or to reject it.

None, it must be said, have ever rejected it!

But you will have the choice. And so, if this has happened to you, if you have experienced the light of the divine, then you now know what it was. And if you have not? Then you will know what it is when you do!

Z: Is this what I experienced on the mountain 8?

8: Yes it is. I'd like to discuss that with you now. Why don't you take a moment and write a complete description of what occurred for your readers right now…

Z: Oh, certainly.

My Mountain Experience

To paint the picture properly, I have to tell you about two yuppie city-slickers. This is who my soul-mate, Lisa, and I were. I had my own successful little business providing a large retail corporation with satellite radio services and Lisa was a boardroom warrior for a large multinational biotechnology company. We were living the yuppie life and doing very well at it. I don't want to caricature our lives, so I must say that we were also very involved in our own spiritual pursuits and were somewhat uncomfortable with some parts of the lives we were living. However, this is all just the background context. The important bit came when we were on holiday in April of 2008. As much as we were city-slickers, we always loved nature and spent every holiday we could in an area of my country called The Garden Route. It was mainly the indigenous forests on the slopes of the Outeniqua Mountains (pronounced *Oh-ten-ick-wah*) that drew us there. But for us there had always been a special, indefinable something about the whole area, as if, in our souls, we knew that this has always been our true home here on planet Earth.

On this particular holiday we had an experience that changed us both forever. It occurred while we were on a hike to see an untouched forest of ancient trees. At some point, the trail took us up out of a valley and on a long, tiring, uphill slog. We toiled up the hill, out of the forests and onto a small plateau, overlooking a spectacularly beautiful valley, in the bottom of which a small river wound its way to the sea in the distance. On any given day, this would be the kind of view at which I would stop and marvel. It certainly was beautiful. But on that particular day, standing there looking across the valley at the forested mountains in the distance, something changed. The world around me was suddenly impossibly beautiful. Now, I could try to describe it – I could wax lyrical about the way the sun poured its light down on the earth like golden syrup. I could tell you that each leaf of every single tree looked like a perfect emerald jewel and that the wind through the grass set up a vibration that sang and hummed in my soul. I could tell you that I believed I could see, with absolute and perfect clarity, every single leaf and blade of grass right the way to the distant horizon. I could tell you about the quality of the air – that it had become gelid with the density of pure life essence that surrounded and interpenetrated me and all that was around me. I could tell you how I felt that I was truly ONE with that magnificent landscape and that the earth was my skin and the grass and trees my hair. I could throw pages and pages of such words at you in a vain attempt to share with you the pure, transcendent bliss of that moment, but I would not even be scratching the surface of what that moment was like. Perhaps I could simply say that I believe I actually saw God in the very Life of the land on that day. My heart was opened and a portal was made there, through which I saw the world anew. For the very first time ever, I really SAW. I saw with my heart and my soul instead of just looking with my eyes. And it was beautiful. It was more beautiful than I could imagine anything ever being. This amazing, mystical experience was beyond my ability to even begin to make sense of.

I stood. I stared. I was awed.

I felt.

I knew.

I belonged.

Striving for comprehension, my mind eventually came up with an idea of what to do with this experience. It sent the thought out to the forest saying: "*I see you! I love you! Will you accept us as custodians?*"

And then I gained the presence of mind to wonder what had happened to Lisa. I had no idea how much time had passed since I had last spoken to her, as we huffed and puffed up the steep slope. I turned to look for her. She was a few metres away, down on her knees with her back turned to me. I noticed she was shaking. As I approached her, I realised she was crying, tears shining in her eyes. I got closer and I heard her saying over and over again; "*… yes… yes… yes…*"

In that moment, it felt to me as if Lisa was answering my question on behalf of the forest. Or perhaps the forest had asked her that same question, and she was answering. It felt as if Lisa and the whole of the forest and I were all one being and we were all speaking the same question and answer to ourselves: "*Will you accept us as custodians? Yes… yes… yes.*"

Or perhaps that is just the best way my mind could make sense of an experience that is beyond the mind and beyond describing.

After some time – I have no idea how long – we noticed it was getting late and we had some distance to walk to get back to the car. Reluctantly, but with our hearts full, we walked back to the car in a kind of euphoric, blissful semi-trance. We both knew something life-changing had happened, but had no way to make sense of it.

I am deeply grateful that Lisa experienced this with me. Partly because experiencing it alone would have made it altogether less meaningful, but more so because if I had experienced this alone I would have known that I was now on a journey without her. An experience like this changes you. You are no longer the same person you were before such an event. Everything changes. Certainly your life path and all the things you have previously valued are substantially re-arranged.

It was very clear to me that my Soul had a plan for me and that the forests of the Outeniqua Mountains were a vital part of that plan. I am deeply grateful to The One that Lisa felt exactly the same way.

And here I am now: as I write this I am looking out of a huge picture window at a forest-covered slope on the Outeniqua mountains. Yes, we made it, we moved. We are living here! Right now we are renting a beautiful log home in the Outeniqua forests while we wait for the purchase of our own piece of land to go though. When it does, we'll begin building our home. We have the plans drawn up and we are fast learning everything we need to about creating a self-sustaining, off-the-grid homestead. The sun will provide us with electricity and water heating, the rain and our farm dams will provide us with water. We'll grow our own fruit and vegetables and trade locally for most of the food we need. We'll get almost everything we could want and need right there off our own land. And for the rest, I'll offer my creative outputs to the world and earn what is required. We are SO almost there.

Getting here has taken some doing. I had a business that I couldn't just close up shop and walk away from. I wouldn't have felt right about that at all. So I gave the company to two of my staff members who had showed a great deal of passion and commitment to it. Lisa had just been offered a big step up into the corporate echelons and a salary to match. She turned it down and gave notice instead!. We both spent six months doing a proper and thorough hand-over to those who would take over from us. In that time we put our yuppie house in the leafy suburbs of Cape Town on the market. We sold our zooty city cars. We liquidated our investments and closed all those fear-based financial instruments than no longer made sense to us – all those insurance schemes and the like, which operate from the premise that bad things can happen to me without my first creating them. We gifted a whole mountain of possessions to various thrift shops (why DID we believe we needed all that STUFF?!?) and we lightened the load of our lives, our hearts and our souls. We came to the Outeniqua area looking for the perfect place of our dreams, armed with a sure knowing in our hearts of what it would be when we found it. And then we found it.

And here we are now.

But the physical move in geography is just a very surface symptom. The great move happened in our souls. Once we had SEEN with our hearts, we could never go back to just looking with our eyes ever again. We were transformed.

To give you an idea: before the Mountain Experience I had engaged in writing intuitive conversations on various Internet forums, but there was a different quality to that material. The lens-of-my-own-being filtered things in terms of good versus evil. I myself was very much of a duality mindset and so, naturally the material I received reflected that. I believed that I was on the side of good, working to change the world to make it better. I believed that there were evil forces outside of me that I needed to resist and fight. The Mountain Experience released that from me. I was shown, in the most direct and personal way, that I am ONE with everything around me. I am Life and Life is me and there is no separation anywhere, but that we have the most transient illusion thereof. The other difference between my intuitive conversations then and now was the Victim-mindset that those writings espoused. I was looking for a Rescuer to come and save the world. I could not see that I – or anyone else here on earth – could save us from the mess we have made of everything. And then, towards the end of 2008, the whole Lightship phenomenon happened, or rather didn't happen, depending on your perspective. I'm sure you remember it? It seems that just about every channeller in the world was receiving some variation on a message that a huge Lightship was going to show up in our skies and save us all. I was part of that as I had received some information from a spirit-friend called Adamu (Zingdad Note: See Chapter 1, *"My Life in Lyra"* for more about Adamu) that was incredibly exciting and amazing. And it also didn't happen. Or maybe it did, just not the way we expected. Or… well… exactly what happened there, and what that all means to me, is the subject of a different conversation. I'll be addressing that in greater detail when I begin the Adamu chapters (which will be in a follow-up publication to this one). But for me personally the effect was to shake loose, in quite a dramatic way, my Victim mindset. I decided to be the creator of my own reality. And very shortly after that I began to write The Ascension Papers.

In retrospect I can see that I invited the Mountain Experience. Lisa and I were actively spiritually questing. We had taken a firm, clear, conscious decision to follow our hearts. We were opening ourselves all the time consciously and intentionally to growth and to Love. So, even though the experience took us by surprise, it was still what we wanted and had chosen for ourselves. It was a glorious gift of grace that showed us with absolute clarity what is REALLY important to us. And, seeing that, changed absolutely everything for us. It took time for us to come to terms with this huge change and it took even longer for our outer-world to come to reflect the inner-change as, indeed, it is still in the process of doing.

… and that is the story…

8: Beautifully told. Earlier in this chapter, I said the following to you:

"Love cannot be understood, as it is much greater than the mind that would seek to understand it. Love can only be experienced. And once you have had even a small taste of true limitless, unconditional love, then you will be forever altered. Your life's quest will be to return to that state of Love. In that moment, you will know that there can be nothing even remotely as important to you as existing in that state of union with the divine that IS Love."

And it is so. This is the Saving Grace. If you stop working so hard to be Forget, then you will have a series of awakenings. You will realise that Remember is right there inside your heart. As near as your own heartbeat. And speaking to you all the time. Constantly calling you to wake up. Constantly telling you about who you really are. Ever present… ever loving… gently reminding. All you have to do is to stop trying so hard to be Forget.

Z: And then we will have such a wonderful, amazing blissful experience?

8: The first one, yes. And as you engage with the process and give yourself to Love, so you will have more. Each one is a step-up though the levels of consciousness. With each one, your psyche is moving up though one of the dimensional levels. You are spiritually ascending. And this will happen to you exactly three times as your world will become transformed into heaven on earth.

Z: Three times? Why three times? Why not less? Why not more?

8: To understand that properly, we are going to have to talk about the concept of spiritual densities. The world you are living in right now exists at the third density. In order to be born into that world, you needed to be of 3rd density consciousness. With each Unity-Conscious Moment, you step "up" one density and move closer to being permanently of Unity Consciousness. If you have had one such experience, then you are of 4th density consciousness, even though you still reside in a 3rd density world and inhabit a 3rd density body. When you reach 6th density consciousness, then you attain permanent Unity-Consciousness for the first time. Or let me qualify that: at that level of consciousness you still feel there is value in holding the illusion of separation, but you know absolutely that it IS an illusion. Then you are a Unity-Conscious being living amongst other Unity-Conscious beings in a Unity-Conscious world. That, as far as I am concerned, IS heaven.

But you are just one of many beings who are engaged on this journey home. As you each transform yourselves, so you transform your world. So the planet illuminates. It rises to the light. You are the agents of transformation. You are the saviours of yourselves. You are the ones you have been waiting for.

Z: Whoa, 8! That's a whole lot of amazing in one short paragraph! Can I unpack it slowly?

You are saying that the experience I had on the mountain was a Unity-Conscious Moment?

8: Yes. It was YOUR first Unity-Conscious Moment. The first and the smallest.

It did change your world, didn't it?

The light came into your life and lifted you up, didn't it?

You moved closer to your true nature, didn't you?

You saw your path for the first time with great clarity, didn't you?

Z: Yes. All of that is true.

8: But it did not force or coerce or take your right to choose from you.

Z: No it didn't. But I thought a Unity-Conscious Moment would be...

8: You expected it to be something from "outside of you" that would somehow come and save you from yourself. You thought that the Unity-Conscious Moment would be a light that would shine from outside of your being that would fix everything. This is what you wanted and expected and you were not ready to know that it will never be so. You cannot be saved by an outside agency, without at the same time being a Victim. Without at the same time having your right to choose and create for yourself taken from you. But this cannot happen. No Light-Being or Christ Light or God or angel or whatever you wish to think of, COULD take from you your right to create for yourself, if that being is itself of unity consciousness. What you do to another you do to yourself also, remember? And if some external being declared by its actions that you are broken and in need of Rescuing, then that being would create itself thus also. If that other being removed from you your absolute right to create your own reality as you desire, then it would immediately also take that right from itself and it would cease to be a creator being. It would fall to low consciousness. And then it would no longer be able to save you.

You cannot be saved from outside of yourself.

It is as simple as that.

It cannot happen.

But there is ALWAYS the one great Saving Grace. It is the fact that the light of The One shines always from within you. If you are willing to let it shine, then you suddenly see the grand cosmic joke: you were never lost! You never were anything other than a creator being of magnificent power creating your whole reality. You were always immortal. You were always indestructible. There never was anything to fear.

So yes. That WAS the first of the three Unity-Conscious Moments that you'll experience. Now you know. Now you can go about letting go of the remaining vestiges of separation that you are still creating for yourself and be prepared... the other two will still happen. And each step will make the previous one seem trivial by its magnificence. And then the big one will still occur.

Z: So I am now of 4th density consciousness? What does that mean?

8: For almost all of this book you have repeatedly been promised a chapter dealing with, "Space, Time, Energy Densities and Dimensions". We have touched on some of the salient points, as we have proceeded but now it is time for you to get the whole picture. So that is what we shall do in the next chapter.

Z: Excellent!

And that means this chapter is done?

8: No. This chapter is actually only about to begin. It begins when all these words and ideas and mental constructs about Love stop. It begins when you stop talking about Love and start experiencing it. So take what we have said about Love to heart.

Go now.

Go BE Love.

* * * * *

Essential Truths and Mantras

For your convenience I have extracted the kernel truths that have been shared in this book by Joy-Divine and 8. I find it useful to review these from time to time, as a means of reminding myself of the wisdom that lies behind them. I also like to use some of these as a mantra when, appropriate.

The kernel truths, extracted in order from this book, are:

"There is only one being experiencing the illusion of being many."

"The One is engaged in an experience of Itself as being many."

"Your truth is the tool you use to create yourself."

"If you cannot see the perfection, then you are standing too close to the picture."

"You always get EXACTLY what you create."

"At the level of Oneness, all things always conspire to the greatest good."

"Everything is always perfect."

"I am an infinitely powerful, eternal, immortal creator being"

"The One is"

"You are eternal and immortal"

"Change is the only constant"

"What you put out is what you get back"

"That which you resist persists."

"The mind UNDERSTANDS but the heart KNOWS."

"If there is such a thing as evil, then it is an opportunity to learn about love."

"Evil is any action, which seems to take away a being's right to choose."

"There is not a single thing that is either good or evil but that you feel that way about it."

"You are who YOU say you are."

"Love cannot be understood, as it is much greater than the mind that would seek to understand it. Love can only be experienced. And once you have had even a small taste of true limitless, unconditional Love, then you will be forever altered. Your life's quest will be to return to that state of Love. In that moment, you will know that there can be nothing even remotely as important to you as existing in that state of union with the divine that IS Love."

* * * * *

Author's Note

As you can tell, this book is the first in a series.

In subsequent publications, I hope to gain a deeper understanding about the mechanics of the nature of our reality and how, in specific detail, we might best go about creating our reality consciously, directly and powerfully. 8 has suggested that I will be engaged in the creation of my reality and I expect to be sharing the details of that reality with you, by way of an invitation to you to come and co-create with me. But it must be said that every step of the writing of this book has taken me by surprise in that it has always been more amazing than I could ever have imagined. So I guess I'll have to wait and see where it goes! If you'd like to watch this emergent process with me or, in some way, become a direct part of the creation of THE ASCENSION PAPERS and the new reality that awaits our loving attention, then I'd like to invite you to join me on my website at *http://www.zingdad.com*.

If you wish to make contact with me, you can do so via the contact form on my site.

I also have a blog on my site in which I chat about the things that are going on in my life. If you have enjoyed THE ASCENSION PAPERS then you are very likely to enjoy my blog posts too. You'll find them at *http://www.zingdad.com/blog.*

I'd like to encourage you to enrol for free membership on my website. If you do, then I'll be able to include you on my newsletter and keep you updated as to when new material becomes available. But my main motivation is to build a huge, world-wide family of spirit. I'd like to be able to reach out and contact the members of that family when necessary.

As a member, you'll be able to download some free materials from my site and get others at a discount.

A note about the Guided Journeys

These are recordings that I have created as a means of sharing with you some of the most profound spiritual experiences I have had. THE ASCENSION PAPERS is a great way to share ideas with you, but I wanted to share actual experiences… to take you there and show you first hand.

At the time of writing, I have four Guided Journeys available:

1. Opening your heart and meeting your own divine, God-like-self
2. Visiting your own spiritual Sacred Temple, meeting there with your Spirit-Guides and receiving a message from them
3. Visiting The Halls of Learning to meet the Masters and address any question you have to them
4. Visiting The Healing Room where you are assisted to understand the underlying psycho-spiritual cause of any physical ailment you might have and to release it.

Each of the Guided Journey meditations has an associated blog entry for you to read more about at *http://www.zingdad.com/blog*.

You can find my website at *http://www.zingdad.com*. I look forward to meeting you there.

Wishing you endless Joy
Zingdad

* * * * *

Lightning Source UK Ltd.
Milton Keynes UK
UKOW020612230612

194921UK00004B/3/P